Belonging

Belonging

The Meaning and Future of Canadian Citizenship

EDITED BY

WILLIAM KAPLAN

McGill-Queen's University Press
Montreal & Kingston • London • Buffalo

To the memory of Paul Martin, 1903–1992

© McGill-Queen's University Press 1993

ISBN 0-7735-0985-2 (cloth)
ISBN 0-7735-0987-9 (paper)

Legal deposit first quarter 1993
Bibliothèque nationale du Québec

Printed in Canada on acid-free paper

Canadian Cataloguing in Publication Data

Main entry under title:
Belonging: essays on the meaning and future of
    Canadian citizenship
    Includes bibliographical references.
    ISBN 0-7735-0985-2 (bound) –
    ISBN 0-7735-0987-9 (pbk.)

    1. Citizenship – Canada. I. Kaplan, William,
    1957-

JL187.B35 1993   323.6'0971   C92-090717-2

This book was typeset by Typo Litho composition inc
in 10/12 Baskerville.

Contents

Contributors

DARYL T. BEAN is president of the Public Service Alliance of Canada. He has been active in the union movement for twenty-five years and is also a general vice-president of the Canadian Labour Congress.

DARYL T. BEAN est président de l'Alliance de la fonction publique du Canada. Il milite depuis vingt-cinq ans au sein du mouvement syndical et occupe aussi le poste de vice-président général du Congrès du travail du Canada.

NEIL BISSOONDATH is the author of *Digging up the Mountain, A Casual Brutality*, and *On the Eve of Uncertain Tomorrows*. Born in Trinidad, he has lived in Canada since 1973.

NEIL BISSOONDATH est l'auteur de *Digging up the Mountain, A Casual Brutality* et de *On the Eve of Uncertain Tomorrows*. Né dans l'île de la Trinité, il vit au Canada depuis 1973.

ROBERT BOTHWELL is a historian at the University of Toronto. His many books include a biography of C.D. Howe, histories of AECL and Eldorado, and most recently, with J.L. Granatstein, *Pirouette*, a study of Pierre Trudeau's foreign policy.

ROBERT BOTHWELL est un historien de l'université de Toronto. Il a écrit de nombreux ouvrages dont une biographie de C.D. Howe, des livres sur l'histoire d'Énergie atomique du Canada Ltée et sur l'histoire de l'Eldorado. Il a publié tout récemment, en collaboration avec J.L. Granatstein, *Pirouette*, une étude sur la politique étrangère de Pierre Trudeau.

ALAN C. CAIRNS is a professor of political science at the University of British Columbia. He is the author and editor of numerous articles and books, including *Constitutionalism, Citizenship and Society*.

ALAN C. CAIRNS est professeur de science politique à l'université de Colombie-Britannique. Il a publié et édité un grand nombre d'articles et de livres dont *Constitutionalism, Citizenship and Society*.

MARC COUSINEAU is associate dean at the Faculty of Law of the University of Ottawa. A Franco-Ontarian from Sturgeon Falls, he recently published *Le droit*, a "livre d'introduction au droit pour les étudiantes et étudiants des écoles secondaires francophones de l'Ontario."

MARC COUSINEAU est doyen associé de la Faculté de droit de l'Université d'Ottawa. Franco-ontarien et originaire de Sturgeon Falls, il a publié récemment *Le droit*, un livre d'introduction au droit pour les étudiantes et étudiants des écoles secondaires francophones de l'Ontario.

ROBERT FULFORD is a well-known Canadian journalist and former editor of *Saturday Night*. He recently published a volume of memoirs, *Best Seat in the House*.

ROBERT FULFORD est un journaliste canadien bien connu et un ancien rédacteur de *Saturday Night*. Il vient de publier ses mémoires intitulés *Best Seat in the House*.

J.L. GRANATSTEIN is a well-known Canadian historian and political commentator. He is the author and editor of almost forty books. His current major research projects are a collective biography of Canada's Second World War generals and a history of multiculturalism.

J.L. GRANATSTEIN est un célèbre historien canadien et commentateur. Il a écrit et édité près de quarante livres. Il travaille en ce moment à une biographie des généraux canadiens de la Seconde Guerre mondiale et à une histoire du multiculturalisme.

DARLENE JOHNSTON teaches law at the University of Ottawa. A member of the Chippewas of Nawash band, she has also been admitted to the Saskatchewan Bar and is a member of the Indigenous Bar Association. She is also the author of *The Taking of Indian Lands: Consent or Coercion?*

DARLENE JOHNSTON enseigne le droit à l'Université d'Ottawa. Membre de la bande des Chippewas de Nawash, elle est également membre du Barreau de la Saskatchewan et de la Indigenous Bar Association. Elle est aussi l'auteure de l'ouvrage intitulé *The Taking of Indian Lands: Consent or Coercion?*

WILLIAM KAPLAN teaches law at the University of Ottawa. His books include *Everything That Floats: Pat Sullivan, Hal Banks and the Seamen's Unions of Canada* and *State and Salvation: The Jehovah's Witnesses and Their Fight for Civil Rights.*

WILLIAM KAPLAN enseigne le droit à l'Université d'Ottawa. Il a publié entre autres *Everything That Floats: Pat Sullivan, Hal Banks and the Seamen's Unions of Canada* et *State and Salvation: The Jehovah's Witnesses and Their Fight for Civil Rights.*

PAUL MARTIN is a former member of Parliament, cabinet minister, senator, and high commissioner to the United Kingdom. He was the author of Canada's first Citizenship Act.

PAUL MARTIN a été député, ministre, sénateur et Haut-commissaire du Canada au Royaume-Uni. Il est l'auteur de la première Loi sur la citoyenneté du Canada.

ROSELLA MELANSON is director, Communications and Planning, New Brunswick Advisory Council on the Status of Women, and is also editor-in-chief of *Égalité.*

ROSELLA MELANSON occupe le poste de directrice aux communications et à la planification au Conseil consultatif sur la condition de la femme du Nouveau-Brunswick. Elle est aussi rédactrice en chef d'*Égalité.*

DESMOND MORTON is a past president of the Canadian Historical Association and is also principal of Erindale College. He is the author of many articles and books and is currently writing a history of Canadian prisoners of war in the First World War.

DESMOND MORTON est un ancien président de la Société historique du Canada. Il est directeur du collège Erindale. Il a publié un grand nombre d'articles et de livres. Il écrit en ce moment une histoire des prisonniers de guerre canadiens pendant la Première Guerre mondiale.

PETER NEARY is a historian at the University of Western Ontario. A Newfoundland native, his books include *Newfoundland in the North Atlantic World, 1929–1949.*

PETER NEARY est un historien de l'University of Western Ontario. Originaire de Terre-Neuve, il a publié entre autres *Newfoundland in the North Atlantic World, 1929–1949.*

MAUREEN O'NEIL has had an extensive career in government and recently served as deputy minister of citizenship in the government of Ontario. She is now president of the North-South Institute, an Ottawa-based non-profit public-policy research institute.

MAUREEN O'NEIL a occupé de nombreux postes au gouvernement. Elle a été tout récemment sous-ministre des Affaires civiques du gouvernement de l'Ontario. Elle est maintenant présidente de l'Institut Nord-Sud, institut de recherches sans but lucratif qui est situé à Ottawa et qui s'intéresse aux politiques gouvernementales.

ROBERT J. SHARPE is dean of law at the University of Toronto and is the author of many articles and books. He has also acted as counsel for the Canadian Civil Liberties Association. Between 1988 and 1990, he was executive legal officer of the Supreme Court of Canada.

ROBERT J. SHARPE est doyen de l'université de Toronto et l'auteur d'un grand nombre d'articles et de livres. Il a été aussi conseiller juridique de l'Association canadienne des libertés civiles. De 1988 à 1990, il a occupé le poste d'adjoint exécutif juridique à la Cour suprême du Canada.

MONIQUE SIMARD est une journaliste de Montréal. Ancienne première vice-présidente de la CSN au Québec, elle a été membre récemment de la Commission Bélanger-Campeau.

MONIQUE SIMARD is a Montreal-based journalist. A former First Vice-president of the CSN in Québec, she recently served as a member of the Bélanger-Campeau Commission.

GLENDA P. SIMMS is president of the Canadian Advisory Council on the Status of Women. She began her Canadian teaching career in northern Alberta among the Métis and Cree. She is an acknowledged advocate of women and minority groups.

GLENDA P. SIMMS est présidente du Conseil consultatif canadien sur la situation de la femme. Elle a commencé sa carrière d'enseignante au Canada dans le nord de l'Alberta chez les Métis et les Cris. Elle est reconnue pour défendre la cause des femmes et des minorités.

DANIEL TURP est professeur à la Faculté de droit de l'Université de Montréal et sa spécialisation est le droit international. Il a été consultant pour la Commission Bélanger-Campeau et ses recherches portent en ce moment sur l'autodétermination et la succession d'États.

DANIEL TURP is a professor at the Faculty of Law at Université de Montréal specializing in international law. He was a consultant to the Bélanger-Campeau Commission, and his current research interests include self-determination and succession of states.

MICHAEL A. WALKER is executive director of the Fraser Institute. He also works as an economist, broadcaster, consultant, university lecturer, and public speaker.

MICHAEL A. WALKER est directeur exécutif du Fraser Institute. En plus, il est également économiste, communicateur, consultant, chargé de cours à l'université et conférencier.

Preface

This book, and the Roundtable on Citizenship which preceded it, were made possible only by a generous financial contribution from the Department of Multiculturalism and Citizenship. Eva Kmiecic, registrar of Canadian citizenship, gave this initiative her complete support; Katherine Papanek, a promotion and education officer at Multiculturalism and Citizenship, provided logistical and other assistance.

At the Faculty of Law of the University of Ottawa, Dean Donald McRae rendered wise and valuable counsel. The university provided funding for simultaneous translation at the Roundtable, and Patti Allen, Madeleine Glazer, Barbara Main, and Maureen Martyn ably undertook many of the administrative and secretarial arrangements. Chi Carmody, Julie Pagenais Blackburn, Howard Rosenoff, and Lydia Wakulowsley provided valuable research and other assistance.

I would also like to acknowledge with thanks the contribution of Georgina Pickett and William Young to the Roundtable and to the preparation of this manuscript, as well as Jamie Benidickson, Joe Magnet, and Ruth Sullivan, who commented on this introduction and who made a number of other valuable suggestions.

Philip Cercone at McGill-Queen's University Press heard about the Roundtable in its planning stages and expressed an early interest in the publication of this book. He has supported the project at every stage. Joan McGilvray and John Parry made important editorial contributions. To all of them, my sincere thanks.

William Kaplan
Ottawa
June 1992

WILLIAM KAPLAN

Introduction

Canadian citizenship is not a highly researched field. If anything, the opposite is true, perhaps because many, if not most, Canadians take their citizenship for granted and until recently have given it little, if any thought. Canadians clearly have not turned their citizenship into a source and symbol of national pride. This, of course, is wholly consistent with the Canadian character. English Canadians do not wave flags (except when they are on vacation in Europe), and while some stomp on flags, their numbers are extremely small. Many French-speaking Canadians have a more direct attachment to the flag – not Canada's but Quebec's. Some of our symbols, such as the monarchy, and distinguishing characteristics, such as official bilingualism and multiculturalism, divide rather than unite us, and even those that we all share, including perhaps Canadian citizenship, evoke benign indifference more than anything else.

In many countries citizenship is seen as a great prize and is treasured by those privileged enough to possess it. In Canada this is not the case. Canadian citizenship has never been a source of national unity and strength. Could it be?

Citizenship is a concept with even greater potential than a flag or a national anthem. Unlike our race, our ethnicity, our language, our religion, or any other personal or group characteristic, citizenship is a status that everyone in the community can, in theory, equally enjoy. As such it is a concept with promise and power. With this thought in mind, I invited a group of distinguished people, Canadians by birth or by choice, to write essays on the meaning and future of Canadian citizenship.

These essays were presented in January 1992 at a Roundtable on Citizenship sponsored by the Faculty of Law at the University of Ottawa. In arranging this event, and in the publication of this book, my objective was to stimulate public debate and interest in Canadian citizenship and in that way to place new emphasis on it as a source of national unity and strength. This goal will not be easy to achieve. The essays that follow make it clear that Canadian citizenship means very different things to different people, and the conclusion is inescapable that to some Canadians it means almost nothing at all.

The essays are divided into four broad categories: history; regions; law, constitutionalism, and economics; and individuals and groups. These categories are artificial, for none of these essays can be so narrowly defined and all of them cross over into each of these broadly defined topics. These categories do, however, provide a convenient framework for both reading and discussion, for they reflect the central orientation of each paper considered generally.

HISTORY

The historical origins of Canadian citizenship is the subject of the first essay, by Robert Bothwell. Starting with first principles, and ancient civilizations, Bothwell goes back to Athens and Rome, to discover the intellectual foundations of citizenship as the fundamental expression of the relationship between individual and state. Citizenship is nothing new, it meant something in the ancient world, and it means something in the modern one.

The citizenship of the Roman Empire was not only highly desired, it was also very successful for hundreds of years in holding together a far-flung empire. Romans shared a common heritage, civilization, and citizenship. Roman citizens gave allegiance to the Roman Empire, which in turn extended its protection to its citizens wherever they might be. Over time, the value of Roman citizenship began to decline. Its privileges dwindled and then became burdens. Citizenship was extended, so that more and more people could be taxed, and lost much of its allure; instead of being highly sought, it became something to be avoided.

In the mean time, a competing concept of allegiance emerged: subjectship based on fealty to the crown. Subjectship was also based on allegiance, though differently conceived. It was natural, perpetual, and personal, and it found great favour with the barbarians, continental European kings and British monarchs, for it was a natural relationship if a feudal state. Subjectship quickly took deep root in what was to become the United Kingdom. It did not, however, transplant well in the New World, and its limitations as a common status in an expanding British empire administered from far away soon became apparent.

Naturalization was the early focal point of the brewing conflict between the mother country and the colonies, for the settlement of North America by large numbers of foreign born resulted in a need for new laws that acknowledged that subjectship was not immutable and could in fact change. The conflict came to a head as the American colonies resisted attempts by the British to establish an imperial naturalization scheme and instead passed local laws that varied from one jurisdiction to another. Naturalization in one colony might be accepted in another, but not in the rest. The Parliament at Westminster attempted to create order from chaos, but its legislation was too little too late, and one of its acts, which disallowed two colonial naturalization schemes, was among the factors that led to the Revolutionary War.

In the aftermath of that war, the United States firmly opted for a concept of citizenship that was voluntary, conditional, and institutional, leaving subjectship status to those peoples to the north who remained loyal to the crown. Subjectship in the British North American colonies was also problematic (in part because of Quebec's Civil Code and different history), even after Confederation in 1867. For a long time the fiction of imperial subjectship pervaded Canadian laws, but in the end, Canada had no choice but to abandon common imperial status. As Bothwell notes, "the values of colonial citizenship, the benefits that membership in the political community conferred, were different from those of the mother country even if, in a vast empire, they might still be accommodated." Canada was eventually required to define a citizenship of its own. The only really surprising thing is that it took so long.

J.L. Granatstein offers an explanation. In the context of his account of conscription in Canada during the Second World War, and the efforts of Canadian military authorities to persuade the "zombies" to convert into general service volunteers, Granatstein asks why so many Canadians were unwilling to accept the "hard obligations" of citizenship. Bluntly put, why did large numbers of Canadians refuse to fight and maybe die for their country? The reasons are both historical and complex.

Many French Canadians, with the Conquest vividly in their minds, were unwilling to travel overseas in order to defend the British crown, not to mention its English-Canadian adherents who dominated the country, scorned their language and faith, and discriminated against them in manifold ways. Canada's army was British in composition, outlook, appearance, and training, and when the First World War came along, French Canadians made it clear that they wanted no part. The outbreak of war also led to internment of some foreign born and the disenfranchisement of naturalized "enemy aliens," not to mention discriminatory acts of various kinds. The wartime experience of Ukrainians, Germans, and others reinforced a pre-existing tendency to keep to one's kind.

The lessons of this experience were clear, and they were also ignored. Instead of making every effort in the inter-war period to integrate the disaffected, Canadian politicians played politics with Quebec and did nothing to welcome Canadians of non-British and non-French stock. Quebec had a sense of self, but the rest of the country, where regionalism and particularism flourished, had difficulty articulating shared values and did little to inculcate in society and in schools the values that it could identify. This peacetime failure reaped predictable but unfortunate dividends when Canada next went to war:

The dominion government could not undo its peacetime failure to integrate Québécois and ethnic Canadians into the larger community with clumsy propagandizing crafted under stress of war. Canadians in the Second World War were fighting for democracy and freedom, and the nation's cause ought to have commended itself to all who were fortunate enough to live here. It did not because many Canadians, French-speaking and others, believed incorrectly that their interests, Canadian interests, were not directly threatened by Hitler, Mussolini and Tojo. Others, victims of prejudice and discrimination or economic victimization, believed that they owed scant loyalty to a nation that had failed them. Those who had suffered from the economic collapse of the Depression could not readily have been reached by educational campaigns. But the others might have been. Had Canadian citizenship and distinctively Canadian values been inculcated in the interwar years, the government's wartime task in selling the "hard" obligations of citizenship might well have been easier.

An alternative, though consistent explanation for the failure to create a Canadian identity is offered by Desmond Morton, who writes on divided loyalties and dual allegiance in Canadian history. From the Conquest to Confederation to the present day, Canada and its people have been in search of a national identity, for Canada was, as it remains, a nation of many loyalties.

Morton argues that those who offered Canada as a focus for allegiance had to compete with both smaller provincial and regional identities, which were strongly felt, as well as with membership in the vast and powerful British Empire. The allure of the latter was strong everywhere in Canada except, of course, French-speaking Quebec.

In the end, notions of imperial federation and common subject-ship (which became, with the passage of time, not "common" but riddled with discrimination and prejudices of various kinds) could not withstand war or the twentieth century. The imperial link was, as Morton notes, too costly and of too little value. Allegiance to it fell away, although it would never entirely disappear. However, even in its decline it left an important and continuing legacy, one that reinforced other long-held views, including enduring suspicion among Quebecers, and Canadians of neither British nor French stock, that English Canadians could not be trusted to put Canada first. This mistrust, Morton suggests, in turn legitimized other divided allegiances and created a climate where they continue to flourish to the present day.

Canadian citizenship has not meant much, or at least our politicians and our laws have not treated it as if it did. Nevertheless, Morton concludes, Canadian history proves that, whining and griping aside, our citizenship, broadly considered, is valuable: "We have lived together for a long time. Despite years of teaching that Canada is an instrument of cruel injustice to regions and minorities, after decades of resolute hyphenation, how wonderful it is that the great majority of us, British Columbian, Québécois, Newfoundlander, think Canada is the best place in the world and, despite our different perspectives, we want it to survive. Civis canadensis sum." Unfortunately, Canadian citizenship, as a legal, social, and political concept, has failed to reinforce this reality, for when it was finally introduced, instead of promoting unity, it continued to encourage diversity by retaining British-subject status as an element of Canadian citizenship. Canadian "citizenship" thus became part of the problem instead of part of the solution.

As a criticism of the Citizenship Act of 1947, as it was first passed and as it remains on the statute books, Morton's point is a good one. Moreover, an "easy" citizenship law will be less likely to instill regard for the state than a more difficult one. Some clubs are harder to join than others, and membership should have its privileges. Otherwise, what's the point in belonging?

In passing a citizenship act, however, Canada was taking an important step, and it was the first Commonwealth country to do so. While French Canadians and English-Canadian liberal nationalists supported the initiative, many English-Canadian Tories and imperialists were less than enthralled, and one compromise necessary to secure parliamentary passage was continuation of British-subject status. Nonetheless passage of the act was a significant step, and like the flag and the fight for a Bill of Rights and later a Charter of Rights and Freedoms, it took some measure of political courage.

Credit for the act belongs in large part to Paul Martin, whose essay describes his role in this process. Martin identifies the Second World War as a watershed and as the proximate cause leading to introduction and passage of the legislation. His tale begins with an account of a wartime trip to France:

On a dull and chilly February day, I was driven from Paris to pay my respects to the Essex Scottish and other Canadians in the military cemetery at Dieppe. There were wooden crosses marking some of the graves. The final tombstones had not been erected. The racial origins of the dead were so varied: Anglo-Saxon, French and other backgrounds. It struck me that herein lay the character of Canada, a land of people from diverse national origins ... Nothing has since epitomized the concept of our nation more poignantly for me than that cemetery. Of whatever origin, these men were all Canadians.

On his return home, Martin became convinced of the desirability of creating a separate Canadian citizenship and, with the approval of Prime Minister W.L. Mackenzie King, got to work. His essay provides a detailed account of the steps necessary and difficulties faced. Not all MPs were pleased, and compromises were necessary. It would be a generation before the vestiges of British subjectship were finally eradicated from the statute books. The new act was, however, a start and, to most Canadians, a welcome one at that.

Soon enough the value of our citizenship was put to the test when Newfoundlanders voted to become Canadians. Peter Neary describes this process in his essay, which has more than a little historical resonance, given the 1980 referendum in Quebec and the continuing prospect of a future vote on sovereignty there. Neary describes the political, social, and economic climate in Newfoundland in the twenty years prior to 1948. The situation was bleak in the 1930s and improved in the 1940s only because of spending by Americans who came to Newfoundland as a result of the war. Eventually, the people of the island were given a choice – more of the same, independence, or Confederation with Canada. The battle was fought hard, and it divided Newfoundland society. By referenda, islanders voted for security and provincial status in Canada, rather than for commission government or an independence that would be little more than an empty and impoverished shell. History proves that Newfoundlanders made the right choice, for Confederation gave them a greater measure of economic opportunity and security than they had ever had before. This lesson, Neary notes, as Newfoundland and other provinces adopt decentralist views, is well worth keeping in mind.

For his part, Robert Fulford brings the historical evolution of Canadian citizenship up to date, by considering the reception of citizenship ideals. Fulford acknowledges that public rhetoric and the Charter notwithstanding, all Canadians do not stand equally in their relationship to the state. Nevertheless, this legal fiction, or "wistful hope," is the underlying premise on which Canadian institutions are built, but the symmetry, Fulford argues, is "imaginary."

Fulford's essay is concerned primarily with the state of citizenship in English-speaking Canada. Unlike Québécois, English-speaking Canadians do not identify themselves in any truly meaningful way with their provinces. It is not clear that they identify themselves with anything, but even if they did, Fulford argues that the focus is always changing. They take great pride in equalization and social spending, but both have been around only for a generation or so, and fiscal reality is beginning to take its toll. Other symbols of nation, like the flag, are also relatively new. In Fulford's view, if citizenship is to have meaning, it must be based on a rough Canadian equivalent of what Abraham Lincoln called "the mystic chords of memory," chords that evoke emotions deeper than self-interest and broader than allegiance to race and religion. Unfortunately, the symbols of nationhood, the reasons for English Canada existing, are difficult to identify because they are in an almost constant state of change.

Once upon a time, Fulford observes, the imperial ideal defined Canada; then came English-Canadian nationalism; and there was, of course, the idea of English Canada as a public enterprise state, with national institutions defying geography and uniting what otherwise could not be brought together. These concepts of Canada, and others, have changed over time, perhaps because of the lack of a founding myth, or at least one that has endured. No unifying version of Canadian history has emerged, while words such as "dominion" and symbols such as the crown on post boxes, which in part defined the country, were discarded when they began to look slightly out of date. The intellectual foundations of our citizenship have not, Fulford argues, been properly laid, if they have been laid at all: "Critical theory has given us a term for the process described here: deconstruction. Our habit, over the generations, is constantly to 'call into question,' as deconstructionists say, the basis for our history, to re-assess its symbols and, finding them invalid, eliminate them – and to imply, always, that the generation just before us had everything wrong. Like true deconstructionists we are destined forever to spend our lives rethinking our premises."It is therefore hard to see what, if anything, English Canadians will be able to achieve.

The history of Canadian citizenship is the history of opportunities lost, although there is little agreement about who deserves the blame. By the time the first Canadian Citizenship Act was passed, as Bothwell, Morton, and Granatstein show, it was too late, and in any case that act failed to reverse existing trends toward divided loyalties within an increasingly divided society. The result: tepid Canadianism, erosion of national symbols, and all sorts of prescriptions for reform which are unlikely to attract even modest support. Neither longing nor lament for a common citizenship ideal has any prospect of success. If the history of Canadian citizenship shows anything, especially in English Canada, the prospects of a common future with citizenship as a unifying force are extremely remote.

REGIONS

Acadia. The very name conjures up notions of the expulsion, and of a society and a people that have endured in the face of formidable odds. It also challenges conventional notions of a country consisting of Quebec and "the Rest of Canada," as Rosella Melanson observes in her essay. Most Acadians live in New Brunswick, and in many respects that province is a microcosm of Canada. Acadian culture thrives, and the French language in New Brunswick has been constitutionally entrenched. While few Acadians are satisfied with the status quo, Melanson argues that great gains have been made in the preservation and promotion of linguistic rights and cultural identity. However, more – much more – must be done if the survival of Acadia and Acadians is to be assured:

If Acadie were a person, it would be said to be healthy, except for its cancer. The assimilation rate of close to 8 per cent is a real long-term threat. The inequalities between the Acadian and the anglophone regions are staggering, especially in terms of economic power, transportation networks, unemployment rates, and power in the civil service. Acadians are currently facing more pressure to assimilate than ever before. But they have never had as complete an array of institutions and have never been more actively involved in ensuring their collective future.

What is to be done? First, according to Melanson, there must be recognition that notions of symmetrical provincial status have had their day. Second, the idea of Canada as a bilingual land where individuals share everything except language is, she argues, a romantic myth. It must be jettisoned, and only if and when it is will there be an opportunity for discussion and implementation of the real options for Canada.

What are these options?

The peoples that form Canada – English-speakers, First Nations, Québécois, Acadians, and others – are distinct societies. If the specificity of each is recognized, they will have been treated equally. New Brunswick's specificity lies in the duality of its population, which requires duality in administrative and possibly political structures. Equality that uses the anglophone majority's norm is not true equality. Having control of one's institutions is not special treatment: it is what a people's right to self-determination means. Diversity in equality is supposedly a Canadian contribution to human rights: it can be applied to politics as well.

Melanson is not, of course, the only advocate of extensive accommodation, asymmetry, and establishment of parallel institutions. That is a view shared by Marc Cousineau. He also sees accommodation as the road to be taken, not just to preserve and promote Franco-Ontario, but for Canadian society generally.

Cousineau approaches citizenship as a matter of belonging and suggests that while Franco-Ontarians feel the same sense of historic injustice as do Acadians, a reconciliation of sorts has taken place. Eighty years ago, Cousineau argues, the English majority attempted to destroy Ontario's francophone community by outlawing French schools. The attempt failed, even though for the better part of a century French was not spoken at any institutional level in Ontario.

While Franco-Ontario did not disappear, the consequences of these and other related policies for this community were serious: the level of illiteracy is double that of Anglo-Ontarians, while proportionally twice as many anglophones as francophones proceed to post-secondary education in Ontario. Government policies engendered hatred between French- and English-speaking communities and isolated francophones from meaningful participation in public life.

All of this, Cousineau points out, has begun to change. Ontario now permits and funds French-speaking schools on the same basis as it permits and funds English-speaking schools. Francophones can use French before the courts and in their communications with the provincial government. While Cousineau applauds such changes, he also bemoans persisting bigotry against francophones, and, citing the "English-only" resolutions of some Ontario cities and towns, he points out that had these resolutions stated "white only" the outcry would have been immense. Because they were directed at francophones the response was muted, at best.

Despite incidents of this kind, Franco-Ontarians feel more of a sense of belonging today than at any other time in the recent past. And in the same way that their needs have been recognized, Cousineau argues that the needs of other groups should also be accommodated: "In order to ensure the well-being of the community, we have to accept, for example, that aboriginal peoples may need their own justice system and that some groups such as Jews and Somalis may require their own school systems to feel included in our collectivity."

In Cousineau's view, which is not dissimilar in this respect to those advanced by the authors of other essays in this volume, the time has come to recognize that Canadian society has changed. Canadians do not, in his view, share one set of traditions. That is a myth that needs to be replaced. The experiences of Franco-Ontarians may provide some guidance:

The Franco-Ontario experience suggests that the sense of belonging itself may be an important source of our sense of collectivity. The promise of being valued and allowed to develop fully as an individual without having to abandon a significant element of one's identity is a powerful incentive to work for the preservation and amelioration of the society that holds out this promise.

Canada may be on the verge of destroying itself. One of the main reasons is that anglophones and francophones have never developed the ability to accommodate each other. Had we worked toward making members of both groups sense that they were equal, respected, and valued citizens, we would not be facing the imminent break-up of the country. The lesson is obvious: if we are to thrive as a country and a collectivity, we have to make certain that all Canadian citizens are full participants in our collective project which is Canada.

That "collective project which is Canada" is not, however, wanted by either of the francophone contributors from Quebec. Monique Simard argues in her essay that the time for Quebec independence has arrived, and she leaves no doubt about the fact that she is a Quebecer first and Canadian second: "Cela m'a toujours surprise de me faire poser la question suivante: 'es-tu québecoise en premier et ensuite canadienne ou l'inverse?' Pourquoi surprise? et bien tout simplement parce que pour moi c'est l'évidence même: je suis québecoise et incidemment canadienne."

Simard states that since the 1960s Quebec has evolved to the point where it is now an authentic nation-state with its own institutions, its own social organization, and its own culture and way of life.

While English Canada is in the midst of an existential identity crisis, Quebec knows who it is and what it wants. A new nationalism is alive there, and it is, Simard claims, notable for its rationalism and its serenity. Notwithstanding this strong sense of belonging, Quebec society must still come to grips with the fact that it and the world are changing. The francophones of Quebec must respond to the needs of Quebec women, and in this regard Simard states, harking back to the Meech Lake debate, that women and their organizations in Quebec are perfectly able to look out for their own interests and neither want nor need the interventions of English-Canadian women and their institutions. Quebec must also meet the challenges of the English minority, and it must come to terms with its own tendency toward xenophobia. Having said this, Simard also argues that in this respect Quebec society is neither more nor less tolerant that any other society, impressions in English-speaking Canada notwithstanding.

Quebec must also come to a resolution in its relations with its aboriginal communities. Simard notes that having claimed recognition and the right to self-determination for itself, it cannot ignore the claims of others. Here the challenge will be to integrate this dimension of Quebec reality into the process now under way and to arrive at a mutually agreeable solution despite the complexity of the issues involved. Simard concludes that, in all of this, citizenship is important, but for Québécois it is Quebec citizenship that counts. That being said, Quebec and Canada face many of the same challenges, and she suggests that if they accommodate differences, they can meet these challenges.

Daniel Turp begins his essay with the assumption that Quebec will achieve independence and become a sovereign state. What then, he asks, will become of existing Canadian citizenship? What arrangements can be worked out? And what lessons can we draw from the experience of the European Community? A variety of options exists. Turp suggests that Quebec might choose to grant citizenship to all Canadians domiciled in Quebec at the time of independence or that the two countries could negotiate an agreement providing for the attribution of Quebec citizenship to Canadians living in Quebec and resulting automatically in the loss by those persons of their Canadian citizenship, with certain "option rights" made available in defined circumstances. Another possibility, assuming some form of union, would be creation of joint citizenship which would be superimposed on citizens in both jurisdictions and to which would be attached rights and obligations enumerated in a master treaty governing relations between the two states. This "union" citizenship would help ensure efficient management of the economic relationship and remind citizens in both countries of the historic links that have characterized their relations. Such a citizenship would depend on the arrangements reached between Canada and Quebec. Whether those arrangements are economic or political, or both, Turp argues, a sovereign Quebec will probably seek to facilitate the mobility of its citizens through one form of relationship or another with Canada, and in this regard the experiences of the EC may be of use. Turp's essay is, in short, a calm and reasonable discussion of "what if?" What it does not envisage, however, is that should separation occur there is little reason to believe that English-speaking Canada will adopt that same "calm and reasonable" approach.

To a considerable extent, Melanson, Cousineau, Simard, and Turp agree somewhat; what differences they have may be the result of recognition that Quebec has the numbers, land, and resources to separate but that the francophones of New Brunswick and Ontario do not, and so in those provinces efforts must be directed toward creation of parallel institutions for francophones and for others. This distinction aside, these voices, like many of the others in this volume, accept as a given that, for citizenship to be meaningful, groups must be accorded meaningful equality and accommodated to a very significant degree and in that way encouraged to participate in the community. Whether or not the sum of these parts will bear any resemblance to Canada as it is now known matters little to these authors, for their essays are premised on a "new Canada" in which provincial and regional collectivities dominate and in which group rights, at best, coexist with individual ones and, at worst, dominate them.

LAW, THE CONSTITUTION, AND ECONOMICS

Taking up where Melanson, Cousineau, Simard, and Turp leave off, Alan Cairns considers the fragmentation of Canadian citizenship. His essay begins with the premises that historical and political factors have changed the notion of citizenship as a shared value and that citizenship no longer means the same thing to everyone. While the trend in human affairs has been in the direction of egalitarianism, a counter trend has emerged, and is rapidly gaining ground:

This essay is directed to that counter-trend – to those who argue that uniformity of status is a hegemonic instrument of the numerically or politically strong; to those for whom the claim that Canadians are a single people obfuscates the deeper reality that Canada can survive only as a multinational state; to those for whom differentiated treatment, special status, and affirmative action are variously justified as compensation for past injustice, as necessary to overcome systemic barriers, or as required to produce greater equality of result or condition. To the purveyors of the counter-trend, perhaps the central characteristic of modern society is diversity, a gallery of discordant voices issuing from fundamentally divergent ways of seeing the world. Modernity, or post-modernity, from this perspective, is inescapably plural and should not be compressed into a single mode or manner of expression, thinking, being, and feeling. The Canadian citizenship of the future, accordingly, must seek accommodation with this diversity, both of internal nations and of the multiple identities and cleavages within them.

In this scheme of things, Cairns articulates a "three-nations" view of Canada: Quebec, the rest of Canada, and aboriginal. But even these categories are problematic, for the boundaries of each, not to mention the extent and nature of their membership, are unclear and contested. Cairns directs his essay to a discussion of the relationship among these three groups and concludes that some radical changes are required:

If we survive as one country, we must accommodate diversity without so destroying our interconnectedness that we shall be incapable of undertaking future civic tasks together. Since the latter will be more demanding than yesterday's challenges, we must hope that a citizen body lacking the bond of a standardized citizenship but nevertheless participating in common civic endeavours is not an oxymoron.

The Canadian constitution will, at least, facilitate this task, for, as Robert Sharpe notes in his essay, there is a great gap between citizenship as a metaphor for fundamental rights and privileges and the reality of its limited weight in constitutional law and doctrine. Put another way, Canadian law, which, with few exceptions, provides for everyone to be treated the same, whether citizen or not, also paradoxically provides for different treatment for different groups.

Sharpe argues that for public consumption the term "citizenship" is used as a label for the identification of the most important attributes of being a Canadian. However, the status of being a citizen makes very little difference when it comes to enjoying those attributes or exercising legal rights. This may not have been true in the past, but it is the case now:

The Charter embodies a rich vision of the relationship between the individual and the state, but that vision is not linked to the status of citizenship. The Charter draws a sharp distinction between those few rights accorded exclusively to citizens, which are indicative of full membership in the political community, and most rights which are available to all who are subject to Canadian law. One of the rights available to all, the right to equality, reinforces this distinction by rendering suspect legislative classifications based on citizenship.

Sharpe does not suggest abandoning any attempt at identification of the values, rights, and obligations which bind Canadians together as a political community. However, the constitution "consciously transcends the interests of those who are full members of our political community, and ... one of the fundamental rights we enjoy forbids us from preferring our fellow citizens to the detriment of strangers."

That is certainly not the case almost everywhere else in the world, and in my essay, "Who Belongs?," I consider the law of citizenship generally, and its application in selected countries. A number of points emerge from this review. First, in most countries, citizenship is seen as a great prize and reserved for a relatively select few. In western Europe, for instance, millions of guest workers, including descendants of the original migrants, have no real right of abode and can be sent "home" at any time. In Japan, innumerable Koreans and Filipinos are denied any claim to the citizenship of their birth. In Kuwait, the tenuous toehold of hundreds of thousands of Palestinians is apparent in the aftermath of the Gulf War, while incidents in Africa, Fiji, and Malaysia further illustrate this point. It is hardly surprising, in these circumstances, that citizenship is highly valued.

In contrast, countries such as the United States and Australia welcome outsiders. Similarly, Canada makes citizenship not a privilege but a right. Yet this ease of access may have devalued citizenship. The repressive citizenship laws of other jurisdictions, even though they have resulted in higher status for citizenship, are no model for Canada. Accepted notions of justice and fair play, not to mention the requirements of our constitution, would not permit most of the distinctions that elsewhere are commonplace. However, if citizenship is to mean anything it must mean something, and I suggest that one starting-point is to reconceptualize it as belonging – not in the sense of accommodation of every group interest and creation of parallel institutions and structures on demand, but in the sense of participating in national purposes. Citizenship can serve as a focus of benefits from and obligations to collective projects and shared values and goals transcending one's race, religion, language, ethnicity, and region. Whether or not citizenship can be reconceptualized in this way and still be effective is very questionable, given the almost complete lack of consensus about what our citizenship should or could mean, not to mention what national goals we share.

As an economist, Michael Walker would argue that sovereignty and citizenship are closely connected to the economy and that if a country is bankrupt the capacity to do anything, including making citizenship matter, is in doubt. Walker is concerned with numbers, and his essay is filled with them, along with various charts. His subject is the economic relationship between individual Canadians and the state as considered through the apparatus of government. His essay also examines the costs and benefits of the economic relationship between the provinces and the federal government by looking at the cost and benefits of Confederation.

"Who benefits from existing fiscal arrangements?" is Walker's first question, and he concludes that a majority of citizens benefit from deficit spending. This in turn explains a political process which has consistently failed to come to grips with the huge and growing national debt. As long as the majority of taxpayers receive more economic benefits from the government than they pay in tax, they will lack the incentive to do anything about a deficit that is running out of control. Only in a short-term sense can this economic choice make any sense. In Walker's words, this "creates a political chemistry that has little interest in solving the fiscal problems that beset our country."

This situation may become further aggravated if institutional changes are made to the current constitutional arrangements: "At the moment, the "have-not" provinces are significant net beneficiaries, even though they have together less than a majority of seats in the House of Commons. These seats are of course divided along party lines, in the same way that seats in the "have" provinces are, meaning that there is no clear and unambiguous thrust to enhance net flows into the regions. Clearly, however, an effective Senate with equal representation from each province might well increase distribution of net benefits to the "have-not" provinces." The implications for managing the deficit should the "have-nots" gain increased political power are not encouraging.

While Walker does not say it, the consequences for citizenship are serious if Canadians are required to spend the better part of their tax dollar paying off old debt. Money spent in this way is not available for other things, whether creation of new national institutions and projects or reform and renewal of old ones. As the fiscal crisis deepens, and as the federal government relinquishes its historic role and shifts responsibility for funding social programs to the provinces, notions of national political citizenship will inevitably diminish. When this is combined with an increasingly accommodationist thrust generally, political dismemberment, and the loss of any real shared citizenship, may not be too far off.

INDIVIDUALS AND GROUPS

As is by now abundantly clear, citizenship means very different things for different people and groups. Inherent in many of the essays in this volume is a distinction between individual interests and group rights. This is certainly the case in Daryl Bean's essay; as Bean points out, the union movement is concerned primarily with promotion of collective rights. Individual and collective rights often diverge, but as history in Canada has demonstrated, the union movement is committed to both. It has championed the rights of all citizens, particularly those who have been treated unfairly or discriminated against in the past. Indeed, it can be argued, as Bean does, that individual rights are often enhanced by virtue of strong protection of collective rights. Bean acknowledges that a balance must be reached, in the union movement as in society generally, between the rights of the collectivity and those of the individual. In Bean's view, however, the arbiters of this balance under the Charter have not given appropriate recognition to union collectivities. The Supreme Court of Canada has failed, in his opinion, to acknowledge appropriately the fundamental right of Canadians to bargain collectively and to strike.

Maureen O'Neil considers why meaningful citizenship is illusory for Canadian women. She outlines major changes that have taken place and reviews key events in the struggle for gender equality. Although this activity has resulted in many tangible gains, more, O'Neil argues, needs to be done. Women are underrepresented in politics, in the public service, in the judiciary, and in journalism, to name just a few of the professions where women's voices must be heard if real change is to occur. For gains to be made in these fields, women must be given the resources, time, money, and support at home without which "women in the public sphere must be either without partners or small children – or very rich and with excellent domestic help, like the Queen." As O'Neil observes, most women are not.

Racism, as Glenda Simms shows in her essay, also serves as a barrier to meaningful citizenship. Beginning with the observation that Canadian immigration policy has a history of discrimination, illus-

trated, for example, by the *Komagata Maru* incident, Simms argues
that this legacy is alive and well. The treatment of domestic workers
serves as a case in point. Simms also looks at a number of case
studies, the murder of Helen Betty Osborne and the treatment of
Donald Marshall, Jr., to cite just two, and argues that Canada has
failed to create a climate in which all of its citizens can find justice:
"Why is it necessary to have employment equity programs for
women, the disabled, Native Canadians, and the so-called visible minorities? Does the definition of so many Canadians as visible minorities obscure the real problems of injustice and racism in Canadian
society? Does the targeting of such diverse peoples as one group result in equity, or does it create 'a hierarchy of the oppressed'"?
Simms does not have specific answers to these questions but concludes that it is the responsibility of every citizen to ensure that he or
she is committed to a struggle against racism and that only in this
way will the full fruits of citizenship be achieved.

It is questionable whether achieving "full citizenship" is a generally
accepted goal, as Darlene Johnston notes in her essay. For Canada's
aboriginal people, the experience of citizenship has not been ennobling. The prevailing Canadian mythology portrays a transition
from ally to subject to ward to citizen. This, Johnston asserts, is a lie.
Moreover, this theory of transition constitutes a denial of the inherent self-government rights of the First Nations and is accordingly
characteristic of the practice of Canadian colonialism. In the result,
Canada's aboriginal peoples display resistance and ambivalence to
the notion of Canadian citizenship.

The early respect accorded to the sovereignty of aboriginal persons was quickly replaced by laws such as the Act to Encourage the
Gradual Civilization of the Indian Tribes in this Province (1857) designed to undermine Indian sovereignty. Johnston's essay focuses
on laws and policies of enfranchisement which had as their objective
the diminution in numbers of Indians and of reserve lands. In return for accepting the vote, Canadian Indians would be given property and monetary incentives – money and property that was taken
from their tribe. Moreover, under these statutory schemes, the act of
enfranchisement had the effect of severing a person's Indian status.
This was an offer that many Indians found easy to resist, and only
one Indian was enfranchised under the act.

Confederation did not improve the situation, and the decision to
place "Indians" under dominion jurisdiction was made without consultation or consent. Attempts by dominion authorities to encourage
enfranchisement with terms similar to the previous efforts met with
similar results. No rush to enfranchise materialized:

What did enfranchisement entail for a First Nations individual? At the most basic level, it required self-alienation. The power of the Canadian state to determine one's identity had to be accepted. The Creator's gift of identity as an aboriginal person had to be rejected – cast aside as inferior to that of a British colonial subject. Enfranchisement also involved denial of community autonomy and rejection of the values that community membership represented. It meant standing outside the Circle that contained one's ancestors, language, traditions, and spirituality. For what? To escape the humiliating disabilities that the Canadian state had imposed in the first place. To acquire a separate allotment of land, in contravention of the tradition of communal stewardship of land. To be able to alienate one's allotment, ignoring the needs of future generations. The statistics reveal that the hardships imposed by the Indian Act proved more tolerable than the renunciation of identity that enfranchisement necessitated.

When voluntary enfranchisement failed, compulsory enfranchisement was introduced. As the deputy minister of Indian Affairs explained in 1920: "I want to get rid of the Indian problem." A similar policy re-emerged fifty years later when the Trudeau government's White Paper called on the First Nations to make a choice: either be Canadians, or decide to live as a race apart. As Johnston explains, while the language may have slightly changed, the effects were still the same: "It was still an either/or proposition. Either Indians or Canadians; either outside or inside; either subject to discrimination and coercion or stripped of aboriginality and community." Canada's First Nations have rejected these terms in the past and will continue to reject them in the future: "Before First Nations can be expected to embrace Canadian citizenship, there must be assurances of respect, acceptance, and the right to be different."

Neil Bissoondath does not dispute that all Canadians should have "the right to be different." What he takes issue with in his essay is whether it is in Canada's interest to have an official government policy that not only encourages difference but pays Canadians to be different. Official multiculturalism has simplified and debased culture by reducing it to easily digested stereotypes at events such as Caravan. Culture, under the Multiculturalism Act, becomes an object for display rather than the heart and soul of the individuals formed by it. Whatever multiculturalism does, it does not induce real understanding of others. The effect of all of this, Bissoondath notes, is to encourage divided loyalties, to marginalize Canadians, and to discourage any real love of this country.

If Canada is to survive, and if its citizenship is to become meaningful, then, Bissoondath argues, official multiculturalism must go. It must be replaced by a policy that does not seek to preserve differences but rather has as its objective "melding them into a new vision of Canadianess, pursuing a Canada where inherent differences and inherent similarities blend easily and where no one is alienated with hyphenation. A nation of cultural hybrids – where every individual is unique, every individual distinct. And every individual is Canadian, undiluted and undivided." Whether or not Canada achieves this objective depends, of course, on how one defines one's terms.

CONCLUSION

These essays are, in short, about the failure of our citizenship in the past and its certain failure in the future if we do not change course.

In the aftermath of the Second World War, when Paul Martin introduced the first Citizenship Act, he told the House of Commons: "Citizenship means more than the right to vote; more than the right to hold and transfer property; more than the right to move freely under the protection of the state; citizenship is the right to full partnership in the fortunes and in the future of the nation." Fifty years ago citizenship was about belonging. It is questionable, however, whether there really was a consensus about what belonging meant in the aftermath of the Second World War, or at any other time in Canadian history. Clearly, there is no consensus today.

Apart from those essays that bemoan the failure of our citizenship in the past, the ascendant view of citizenship is that it must mean everything to everyone, and this requires, in the case of Quebec, creation of a separate state or some reasonable decentralized facsimile, and in the case of other disenfranchised groups, recognition of their distinctiveness and creation of institutions to accommodate, preserve, and promote this distinctiveness. The fact that Canadian law reserves few benefits for citizens – most notably, the right to enter and remain in Canada, certain democratic rights, and the right to be considered first for some government jobs – and demands almost nothing from them creates a fertile field for assertion of all sorts of particular and group claims.

Canadians have long recognized that true equality does not necessarily mean treating everyone exactly the same. Accommodation of differences is part of what this country has historically, albeit imperfectly, been about, and one hopes that that will not change. But there may be limits to accommodation. How many distinct societies can coexist in a single state? There is the fiscal question, but there is also the more crucial political question: will distinct societies and parallel institutions further segregate an already divided society, and if so, with what results? Or will accommodations of the kind proposed in this book create a better society? Will they bring meaning to a citizenship that has otherwise been devoid of substance? Or will an emphasis on group claims, just and deserving as many are, divert attention and energy from pressing national issues and some of the other problems that Canada and all its citizens face? More than a few of the essays in this volume raise cause for concern.

Traditional notions of citizenship will probably endure, at least in the short term. But it is clear from these essays that those notions, presupposing as they do shared values and goals, never accurately reflected Canadian reality, except, ironically enough, in Quebec, among many French-speaking Québécois, where active nationalism is subsumed within a vibrant Quebec citizenship. Many English-speaking Quebecers and members of visible minorities in that province have, of course, a much different view. Elsewhere in Canada there is even less likelihood of finding in the future shared meaning than there was in the past. Group rights and group claims are now the distinctive features of Canada. Whatever currency binationalism and biculturalism might have once enjoyed as a unifying ideal is now spent. Accordingly, if citizenship is going to be a nation-building institution, at least in the near future, it will have to be reconceived in many different ways, all of which will enable both individuals and groups, Quebecers, aboriginals, easterners, westerners, northerners, southerners, and racial, religious, and ethnic minorities to belong.

Achievement of a uniform membership ideal expressed through citizenship is impossible, even assuming that it were desirable. The challenge is to find some coherent and principled way in which to define the relationship of both individuals and groups to the state, one that acknowledges the different realities, both individual and group, that comprise Canada, one that recognizes the privileges and burdens of membership in this country, and one that creates attractive opportunities for allegiance on a national scale. The extent to which we redefine citizenship to take into account these factors will determine whether Canada today is a society moving ahead or a nation about to disappear.

PART ONE

History

ROBERT BOTHWELL

Something of Value?
Subjects and Citizens in
Canadian History

A nation, it is commonly accepted, is a community of citizens, a sovereign people. This seems a firm enough definition, but of course in history, especially Canadian history, nothing is straightforward. There are two further problems. From a historical point of view, the design and uses of citizenship are often inconsistent over time. And this being Canadian history, conceptions of a nation, or of membership in a nation, have depended on the actions or ideologies of others: in the first instance, the colonizers of North America, and in the second, the histories and philosophies that they brought with them to this continent. Over the three centuries and a bit that English-language colonists have populated British North America, notions of citizenship have changed considerably. Yet even as one dominant idea succeeds another, vanished sovereignties leave behind a kind of spiritual residue, sometimes potent reminders of paths not taken and roads not followed. This paper, in tracing certain conceptions of citizenship or membership in a national community, will therefore glance from time to time at lost causes and failed alternatives and what they represented.

Let us begin with cultural baggage. The notion of citizenship was familiar to Canada's colonizers from classical studies, from the history of ancient Athens and, later, Rome. It was also well-known from the Bible, which in addition to its religious message filtered through a certain amount of classical political culture. Schoolchildren might be able to quote Cicero, "Civis Romanus sum," or, if they were more inclined to godliness, St Paul, when he boasted, "I am ... a Jew of Tarsus, a city in Cilicia, a citizen of no mean city."[1] Lord Palmerston, the nineteenth-century British statesman and prime minister, and notorious fire-eater, easily parroted Cicero in asserting that a British subject ought to be able anywhere in the world to say "Civis

Romanus sum" and thereby rely on the protection afforded by British justice. Palmerston spoke in language, and used concepts, very familiar to the British (including the colonial British) political class. As for St Paul, his later English readers were meant to know that he was banking on a tradition of citizenship that even in his day stretched back five or six hundred years.

What did that citizenship consist of? Demosthenes in the fourth century BC reminded the Athenians that their citizenship was considered "so worthy and august" that they had strictly limited its bestowal.[2] Though no one knew exactly how Athenian citizenship had originated, during the classical period it existed in a defined territory, descended by inheritance or birth, and was very occasionally conferred on worthy aliens. The grant of Athenian citizenship helped define the concept of citizenship; as its most recent analyst has observed, "Not until something is formed and conceptualized can it be given away; and unless it is something valuable, its gift is not significant."[3]

Citizenship conferred both privileges and obligations. The citizen was "one who shared in the benefits flowing" from the exercise of power, a Platonic idea, according to Sheldon Wolin. To this Aristotle added the idea that a political community was "synonymous with the whole of the citizenry." As for citizens, Aristotle viewed them as political actors and decision-makers. But participation in decisions flowed from the citizen's contributions to the political community.[4]

Political rights were an obvious benefit of citizenship, which was therefore jealously guarded and restricted. In Rome, citizenship and service to the state were closely linked. Although political participation declined, citizenship nevertheless continued to be prized. Roman citizenship, which until the third century AD was sparingly conferred, had a very practical aspect. Possession of it meant that an individual could be extracted from potentially arbitrary local jurisdiction.[5] Extension of citizenship outside the walls of Rome helped confirm "new Romans" in their allegiance; it was a measure of social stability. Yet some contemporaries saw extension of the Roman imperium as destabilizing. "We were [once] all members of one city," the historian Tacitus wrote in the first century AD. In bygone days the restraints and constraints of a smaller society had inhibited irresponsibility and tyranny.[6] Tacitus notoriously expressed a longing for republican simplicity and patriotic virtue in an age of empire. It was a lesson that would not be lost on his readers even in the eighteenth and nineteenth centuries. But at the time Tacitus's lamentations had little effect on an empire – Romania – that was anxious to extend and then defend its boundaries.

In the late republic and the early empire, there were two general classes of inhabitants in the empire – non-citizens, with limited rights, and citizens. As British and British American children were expected to know, St Paul was also a Roman citizen, protected by Roman law. As such, he could appeal to Caesar and extract himself from local courts and customs, exporting himself to Italy from Palestine. Unfortunately for St Paul, the Caesar in question was Nero.

Nero was, of course, the prototypical tyrant. Classical history furnished innumerable examples of the disposition of tyrannical – and hence illegitimate – rulers. Yet under the empire, the prestige of citizenship was such that it continued to be craved; and as one recent authority suggests, its extension in the later empire may have signified a drawing together of the members of the Roman community in the face of extreme external danger, not to mention the presence of alternative societies.7 In the third and fourth centuries, the empire could still protect, and hope to administer justly, its population under Roman law. The law stood in contrast to the caprices of the barbarian kings and the German tribes who were threatening the empire. Roman citizenship, even if universal, was still something to be valued.

The barbarian societies were assumed to be inferior, at least until the fifth century. Only then do we find examples of Romans who happily abandoned a burdensome citizenship, with its legacy of high taxation. Nevertheless, the conception of "Roman-ness" long outlasted Rome itself – in a political sense until 1453, surely the longest-lasting example of effective citizenship in history.

To the eighteenth century, the long-lasting quality of Roman allegiance signified at least as much misplaced loyalty as an admirable, and eternal, conception. The late empire and its Byzantine continuation were, by that token, a mixed legacy. But the eternal aspect of allegiance was something calculated to appeal to monarchs and lawyers, and so it proved in English history and law.

It was the barbarians, not the Romans, who triumphed in the fifth century in western Europe, and the barbarians, or their descendants, such as Lord Palmerston, who established and transmitted the legal forms that eventually took root in Canada. And so in discussing the roots of Canadian citizenship, it is necessary to abandon the word, for the moment. The inhabitants of the British Isles were subjects, not citizens, owing their allegiance to monarchs and not republics or city-states. Though influenced by the classical past and the renaissance present to claim, like Palmerston, a connection between citizens and subjects, or between the Roman empire and the British, the projectors and planters who designed the settlement of North

America emerged from a more passive conception of citizenship – subjectship, really – than had the Romans.

Aliens and subjects were a complicated matter in medieval England. For one thing, it was by no means clear just who was an alien and who a subject. French natives in the lost English provinces in France might, or might not, be proper subjects of the English crown. Irishmen, conquered repeatedly – though for legal purposes, only once – between the twelfth and seventeenth centuries, could not be said to have started out as English subjects. Nor was subjectship merely territorial; in a feudal age it bound subject to monarch in a personal relationship. By the seventeenth century, however, categories of natural-born subject, denizen (landed immigrant, in effect), and alien were firmly established. The latter two were not numerous in an age when large-scale immigration was both difficult and, on the whole, undesired; and it followed that procedures for naturalization were expensive and laborious. And naturalization, as opposed to denization, was a parliamentary, not a royal, prerogative.

As with Roman citizenship, there were advantages to being an English subject, or rather a Protestant English subject, for the Reformation had divided England between the religiously loyal and the religiously and politically suspect. The latter had by no means the same political rights as their Protestant fellows, and their disabilities would last into the nineteenth century. For those who could enjoy them, however, subjectship brought benefits. The most obvious was the unfettered ability to own land, a privilege denied to aliens, even resident aliens, until the nineteenth century. (Aliens could and did own land, but only on the sufferance of the crown; only the crown could challenge their possession.) Aliens might not engage in certain kinds of commerce under the navigation laws.[8] These were advantages that the English were quite territorial about and proved unwilling to share even with the Scots, when under James VI and I the two crowns were personally united. The conflict between personal allegiance and territorial loyalty then assumed an urgent, if not acute form.

The problems engendered by the 1603 succession were such that an artificial case – Calvin's case – was invented so as to clarify what Scots might legally do in England. The jurist Sir Edward Coke pronounced that allegiance was personal and perpetual, similar to that of a parent and child – a conception which he bolstered with appropriate citations from Aristotle.[9] The parent provided protection, and the child owed submission and loyalty. Yet while Scotland and England enjoyed the same monarch, they remained independent – distinct, as it were: a territorial conundrum. Coke solved that by emphasizing the personal element in allegiance, leading to the conclusion that any Scot born after 1603 was, because of James's personal status as monarch of both kingdoms, a naturalized English subject.[10] However, it was not at all clear that someone naturalized in one or another of the king's dominions, especially Ireland, should be accepted as an English subject.[11]

English subjects travelling abroad took their allegiance with them.[12] That happened even when they settled abroad, as they did in North America, even as Coke was elaborating his theories of subjectship. Establishment of English or British colonies along the eastern seaboard of North America presented certain practical difficulties to the authorities at home. It was difficult to make the priorities of abundant settlement coincide with received doctrines or practices of naturalization in an already heavily settled kingdom, and it was in any case inconvenient to exercise day-to-day jurisdiction over colonies separated by thousands of miles and a six weeks' voyage from the seat of government. The colonies needed large numbers of immigrants. Colonial authorities enticed them to come by offers of free land – itself a privilege hitherto associated with subjectship. Once arrived, the immigrants wished to enjoy as far as possible the privileges and immunities of the "old subjects," which included security of tenure in their property.

Precedents existed, especially from the 1680s, when measures were taken to land Huguenot refugees from France as expeditiously and as cheaply as possible, and from the first decade of the eighteenth century, when the same was done for Protestant refugees from the Palatinate. That was a matter of political priority at a time of high religious feeling and patriotic fervour for the wars against Louis XIV of France. But, on the whole, immigrants to the colonies did not attract the attention of the crown or Parliament in London, and the colonial governments therefore made do as best they could. The colonies and their customs received only occasional attention from the British government for the best part of a century, until the wars of the 1750s stimulated the imperial regulations of the 1760s and the revolution of the 1770s.

It is true that in 1740 Parliament enacted a statute providing for easy and inexpensive naturalization of settlers in the American colonies. The act excluded Catholics but included other Protestants than Anglicans, as well as Jews. Those naturalized under it could take their naturalization from colony to colony or to Great Britain itself without regard for local barriers.[13] Nevertheless, most foreigners naturalized in the colonies became subjects through local rather than imperial procedure. Whether such naturalization was purely local in character or was portable throughout the empire was at first very unclear; but colonial authorities had no hesitation in asserting their right to naturalize whomever they chose, and in their own way. That way included residence for a term of years, at a minimum, but immigration, settlement, and naturalization were usually linked closely.[14]

Yet naturalization did not automatically confer all the privileges of native-born subjects. As late as the 1770s it was a matter of lively dispute in Maryland whether a naturalized subject could properly be appointed to an office of trust under the crown – sheriff or delegate to the provincial assembly – or whether such people were forever excluded in favour of the naturally born. In Nova Scotia a prolonged dispute over the rights of Protestant settlers from the Palatinate – their ability to own land – was resolved only by their explicit naturalization in 1758.[15] Catholics, foreign born or native, continued to present even more difficult problems.

There was never any doubt about the subjectship of those brought into the empire by conquest, as Acadia and New France were in the eighteenth century, and as Ireland has been. But in the new province of Quebec, as in Maryland, there was considerable difference of opinion as to the ability of a group of conquered Catholics to take office. The Treaty of Paris of 1763 exempted former French subjects in Quebec from the enforcement of certain onerous acts of the British Parliament; in 1774–5, by the Quebec Act and subsequent instructions to Governor Sir Guy Carleton, Catholics were admitted to the governor's council without any disability. The requirements of the colony and the necessities of government, settlement, and defence took priority, once again, over imperial abstractions and ancient legalities. Those necessities dictated and effectively produced equality of status, security of property, and political participation. And equality, once conceded, itself became a powerful, personal right.[16]

The settlement of the British colonies by large numbers of foreign born had another, somewhat unexpected, effect. Those settlers who had come from the continent of Europe had migrated voluntarily – had chosen British allegiance. Their former subjectship was not immutable; indeed, they had demonstrated the contrary. From that it was a step to arguing that they had voluntarily contracted with their new monarch, trading allegiance for protection. And if the monarch, like Nero, failed in that duty and acted arbitrarily or tyrannically, then he or she violated the basis of the contract.

The political debate that preceded the American Revolution eventually drove the American colonists to argue that their subjectship was different in kind from the rest of George III's constitutional flock. Their experience and their needs were different, as naturalization testified; eventually their political self-definition shifted. By the 1770s Parliament's authority was generally disputed, leaving only a personal link through the monarch.[17] That link was explicitly snapped in the Declaration of Independence of 1776, which declared George III guilty of crimes and aggressions against his erstwhile subjects, who were thereby released from their previous obedience. Instead of subjects they became citizens, harking back to classical times in an age that took seriously the prescriptions of Roman history.

The same declaration that established the basis of American independence also helped to define what came to be the citizenship of what remained of British America. It was not originally clear just who owed allegiance to the newly independent American governments or who might legitimately support the British cause without fear of retaliation. The states were not shy of charging with treason those who remained loyal to George III; yet some American courts conceded that those who physically left a given colony before a formal republican government was established could not be convicted of treasonable acts. Since the relevant government had never extended protection – the subject not being physically present to receive it – the contract of citizenship and consequent membership in a revolutionary community had not been agreed to. But physical presence was all it took. Those who breathed the air of freedom were held to be eternally free, even if by force.

The Treaty of Versailles ending the Revolutionary War attempted to resolve the issue of who was, and who was not, an American citizen or a British subject. Essentially the treaty allowed freedom of choice. Someone who wanted to be an American was. Someone who, on the contrary, wanted to remain British could do so up to 1783. And on both sides of the border, judges and political authorities allowed much more time than that for reflection and repentance before the effluxion of time, the waning of passions, and the grim reaper removed this interesting question from court dockets.[18]

There remained freedom of choice. Historians have tended to emphasize the ideological component of political division in the late eighteenth century. Yet it must be admitted that the events of 1775–83 made it easier for a subject to become a citizen, or vice versa. In fact, the revolution permanently disrupted, both in Canada and in the United States, the seventeenth-century view that allegiance was innate and perpetual. Settlers crossed and recrossed North America's boundaries throughout the nineteenth century, as economic opportunity and/or land grants offered. Those late loyalists who came to Canada through the 1780s and 1790s, and even Americans who came much later, enjoyed considerable public sympathy, as well as a fair amount of official support and reassurance, in establishing themselves. One American revolutionary veteran – on the wrong side – was elected to the Upper Canadian assembly, where he served without protest or challenge.[19]

The Revolutionary War also resolved, for some considerable time, the question whether there could be two varieties of subjectship as between British North America and Great Britain. Though naturalization practices varied on the two shores of the Atlantic, the result was the same: a British subject in Nova Scotia was the same as a British subject in Upper Canada, or in Great Britain itself. And all British North Americans were indisputably British.

The Revolutionary War did not, however, completely resolve whether there could or should be two varieties of subject or citizen within the same colonies. Certain classes of subject continued to labour under forms of discrimination, and as late as the 1830s the "alien question" and religious considerations remained burning issues in colonial politics. Discrimination against aliens was nothing new, and here it was based on a certain doubt whether, in a clash with the United States, immigrants from that country could be relied on. As two recent commentators have argued, "A state which routinely places heavy burdens of responsibility" – such as a war – "on its citizens requires a people with a strong sense of common identity and widely shared perceptions that the state's policies are fair."[20]

The sense of community of Canadians was tried during the War of 1812, and the results were somewhat unexpected. Sir Isaac Brock, commander in Upper Canada, thought his provincial subjects a doubtful lot, prone to American ideas and consequently sedition. The experience of war produced mixed results and, from Brock's point of view, happier ones. The province on the whole remained loyal: some Canadians with impeccably loyal pedigrees supported the American invaders, while some recent arrivals from the republic staunchly supported the British authorities. The question of loyalty – and of the benefits to be derived from it – could be solved only by *omission* and by time.

Since allegiance was not tested in an international context after 1815, the matter did not have to arise in an acute form. William Lyon Mackenzie's rebellion in 1837–38 provoked some questions in international law, but it did not throw into doubt the naturalization of Americans moving to the British colonies. With the abolition of slavery in individual colonies, or in the British empire after 1833, it was also accepted that all persons born on Canadian soil were free, and American courts accepted the doctrine even for the descendants of fugitive slaves from the United States.[21]

There were imperfections in nineteenth-century subjectship, as Mackenzie certainly would have testified. Equality of choice, in deciding to remain or become British, did not necessarily imply equality of status for different parts of the empire. Colonists were not equal in political rights to their fellow-subjects in Great Britain, as long as they resided in the colonies. Moving to Britain could cure that problem, provided one were a native-born Canadian or in other ways, such as term of residence, qualified under British law. Moving to the United States was effectively a safety valve that released a certain amount of political steam early in the century.[22]

There were other forms of discrimination that were not as easily remedied. Women plainly were not equal in political rights, and not merely in Canada. Manhood suffrage remained circumscribed. Lyon Mackenzie testified in 1854, "he had seen how the franchise was exercised by drunkards and the refuse of society in the cities of New York, Albany, Rochester and elsewhere, where universal suffrage prevailed."[23] Yet how could the franchise be restricted when commitment and sacrifice were demanded of all, even drunkards?

Eventually the franchise would become a universal consequence of naturalization. Naturalization, in turn, depended on each colony, as it had before the revolution, or on the application of a British naturalization statute of 1848. Each colony decided, as before, whom it would admit to citizenship. The arrival of self-government in the 1840s entrenched control of immigration and control of naturalization – closely linked issues in colonies of permanent settlement. Naturally, the colonial governments could not prevent the immigration, or limit the political rights, of persons from the British Isles, but where other foreigners were concerned they were happy to lay down their own law.[24] As in the eighteenth century, the question inevitably arose whether citizens of one colony were citizens in another, for, as Sir Wilfrid Laurier observed in 1911, "The certificate [of naturalization] given by a self-governing Dominion was limited to the territory of that Dominion."[25] Laurier, later celebrated as a nationalist by Canadian Liberals, was giving a decidedly broad interpretation to Canadians' sense of community.

The new Dominion of Canada accepted all those previously naturalized in the several colonies of British North America and imposed its own requirements in various immigration acts. The acts defined who might be admitted to Canada and spelled out how citizenship might be acquired and lost. Not surprising, in an entity as varied as

the British empire, there were various ways and means by which immigrants might become naturalized in different areas. Consequently
differences in qualifications between those naturalized in the colonies and those naturalized in Great Britain exercised authorities in
the nineteenth century as in the eighteenth, and the matter was not
fully discussed until the Imperial Conference of 1911. Uniformity of
practice proved difficult to obtain, though all the colonies of settlement discriminated to a greater or lesser degree against nationalities
or races thought to be undesirable or unassimilable. Sir Wilfrid
Laurier lamented that it would have been preferable to accept the
principle that naturalization anywhere in the empire should have
been a good enough principle for all to accept, but his view did not
prevail.[26] The benefits of Canadian citizenship did not include a
perfect licence to be a British subject anywhere in the empire.

The desirability of expanding the benefits of the larger empire
vanished in the 1910s and 1920s along with Laurier's enthusiasm for
portable citizenship. Instead, the twentieth century witnessed the division of the empire and, eventually, even the loss of the notion of a
common subjectship – in Canada, as recently as 1977.

The development of a fully autonomous Canadian citizenship
may seem to be the fruit of late-twentieth-century nationalism. In
many respects that was, of course, the case. But in other ways Canada's practice of citizenship was merely an extension of colonial
practice dating back to the seventeenth century. It was the fruit of
recognition that the requirements, and therefore the self-definition,
of colonial political communities differed radically from that of the
empire as a whole. The values of colonial citizenship, the benefits
that membership in the colonial community conferred, were different from those of the mother country, even if, in a vast empire, they
might still be accommodated. The process of self-definition, of con-
ceiving a separate nationality and a separate citizenship, well illustrates the difficulty of maintaining two standards in a geographically
disparate political entity such as the British empire. But, as generations of politicians, colonial and imperial, might testify, it may also illustrate its inevitability.

NOTES

1   *Verrine orations*, V; Acts 21: 39.
2   Quoted in Philip Brook Manville, *The Origins of Citizenship in Ancient
    Athens* (Princeton, NJ: Princeton University Press, 1990), 3.
3   The first award of citizenship to a foreigner occurred in 476 BC:
    Manville, *Origins of Citizenship*, 209.

4 Sheldon Wolin, *Politics and Vision: Continuity and Innovation in West-ern Political Thought* (Boston, 1960), 57.

5 A.N. Sherwin-White, *The Roman Citizenship*, 2nd ed. (Oxford: Oxford University Press, 1980), 264ff.

6 Quoted in Wolin, *Politics and Vision*, 72.

7 Sherwin-White, *Roman Citizenship*, 468.

8 James H. Kettner, *The Development of American Citizenship* (Chapel Hill, NC: University of North Carolina Press, 1978), 6–7.

9 Ibid., 18–19.

10 Ibid., 22. Hanoverians born between 1714 and 1837 were also considered to be British subjects because of the personal union of the Hanoverian electorship and the British crown: ibid., 146n.

11 Ibid., 40–2.

12 Ibid., 65.

13 Ibid., 75.

14 Ibid., 80, 120–1. Local naturalization was finally banned in 1773.

15 John Garner, *The Franchise and Politics in British North America 1755–1867* (Toronto: University of Toronto Press, 1969), 162.

16 See the discussion in Kettner, *American Citizenship*, 126–8.

17 See Bernard Bailyn, *Ideological Origins of the American Revolution* (Cambridge, MA: Harvard University Press, 1967).

18 See ibid., chap. 7, for an extended discussion of this question. Garner, *Franchise and Politics*, 164, suggests that in the mind of the public the cut-off date of 1783 made little impression.

19 Garner, *Franchise and Politics*, 165.

20 Alan Cairns and Cynthia Williams, "Constitutionalism, Citizenship, and Society in Canada: An Overview," in Cairns and Williams, eds., *Constitutionalism, Citizenship and Society in Canada* (Toronto: University of Toronto Press, 1985), 5.

21 Kettner, *American Citizenship*, 318.

22 Garner, *Franchise and Politics*, 10.

23 Quoted in ibid., 7.

24 William Kaplan, *The Evolution of Citizenship Legislation in Canada* (Ottawa, 1991), 11.

25 Sir Wilfrid Laurier, speaking at the Imperial Conference on 13 June 1911, in M. Ollivier, ed., *The Colonial and Imperial Conferences from 1887 to 1937*, vol. 17 II (Ottawa: Queen's Printer, 1954), 85.

26 Ibid.

J.L. GRANATSTEIN

The "Hard" Obligations of Citizenship: The Second World War in Canada

In the spring of 1944, the Canadian army in Canada was exerting itself to persuade approximately 60,000 home-defence conscripts enrolled under the National Resources Mobilization Act (NRMA) to volunteer for active service overseas. Some of the conscripts, derisively labelled "Zombies" by a harshly critical public in English Canada, had been in the army since 1941, and after years of similar efforts to persuade them, they were by now well-hardened to resist appeals to their patriotism.

The main effort to "convert" Zombies into general service volunteers was taking place at Vernon, BC. No. 13 Brigade had some 5,000 men, almost all of whom, except for the officers and some of the non-commissioned officers, were conscripts, many of them French-speaking. The brigade's commander was W.H.S. Macklin, a permanent force officer of intelligence and ability. In May, Brig. Macklin sent a long report on his efforts at conversion. He and his officers had spoken to the men of all the infantry battalions in groups, and battalion officers had interviewed their men individually. The Protestant and Catholic padres had added their support, the senior Catholic padre telling Macklin that "he had reduced more than one man to tears without succeeding in persuading the man to enlist." Distinguished veterans of the fighting in Italy also spoke to the troops, including Major Paul Triquet, a Victoria Cross winner with the famous "Van Doos."

The results were better than some might have expected, with some 769 men "going active," but there remained a large group of NRMA soldiers who simply could not be persuaded to volunteer for active duty, who "resisted successfully every appeal to their manhood and citizenship." Macklin tried to explain why by noting the differences between general service soldiers and conscripts:

The volunteer feels himself a man quite apart from the N.R.M.A. man. He regards himself as a free man who had the courage to make a decision. He seldom takes the trouble to analyze the manifold reasons put forward by those who won't enlist. He lumps them all together as no more than feeble excuses masking cowardice, selfishness and bad citizenship. In many cases no doubt he is right ... The rift is there all the time ... It can be detected with ease in the attitude of the men. The volunteer is conscious of his position. He is proud of it. He is anxious to work. He salutes his officers and speaks to them with self-confidence. The N.R.M.A. soldier slouches at his work. He tends to become sullen. He nurses his fancied grudge against "the Army" ... He has little self-respect and therefore little respect for his officers.

Many of the French-Canadian conscripts – or so the commanding officer of le Régiment de Hull, Lt.-Col. L.J. St Laurent, said in an appendix to Macklin's report – were willing to serve overseas, but only if the government ordered them to do so: "These men have never been trained from childhood to make important decisions or to think for themselves. They have always been led or advised. They are not yet fully educated for democracy." Others were "passionately and strongly attached to women's apron strings with a childish simplicity. Their mothers, wives or sweethearts have warned them that to sign active ... would break their hearts." Still others did not want to fight for "the English" or "les Anglais," for so they saw the Second World War. History and prejudice, in other words, also played their part.

And what of the English-speaking NRMA soldiers? Macklin was blunt in his assessment of their reasons for refusing to volunteer:

they vary all the way from a large number who have no patriotism at all or national feeling whatever, to a few intelligent men who, I believe, honestly think that by holding out they will force the Government to adopt Conscription [for overseas service] which they feel is the only fair system.

The great majority are of non-British origin – German, Italian, and Slavic nationalities of origin probably predominating.[1] Moreover most of them come from farms. They are of deplorably low education, know almost nothing of Canadian or British history and in fact are typical European peasants, with a passionate attachment for the land. A good many of them speak their native tongues much more fluently than they speak English and amongst them the ancient racial grudges and prejudices of Europe still persist. Here again the process of converting these men into free citizens of a free country willing to volunteer and die for their country will be a matter of education, and I think it will be slow. At present there is negligible national pride or patriotism among them. They are not like Cromwell's "Good Soldier" who "knows what he fights for and loves what he knows." They do not know what they are fighting for and they love nothing but themselves and their land.[2]

Macklin's long assessment had much that was wrong with it. His contrast of the Zombies, slouching and lacking confidence, with the general service soldiers, proud and saluting with zeal, is almost glibly ludicrous, especially when it must have taken some substantial courage and confidence in their position for the conscript soldiers to resist the combined pro-volunteer forces of public, press, army brass, and the GS soldiers around them. Even so, there was much that was correct about the report, most notably its comments that might be lumped together under the heading of "building citizenship." If Macklin could be believed, Canada in the Second World War was paying a price for its troubled history, which had pitted French against English for three centuries, and for its failure to integrate effectively its relatively recent immigrants and to teach them to accept the traditions and values of Canada. The "hard" obligation of citizenship, the willingness to volunteer and die for their country, however crudely that thought was phrased in the brigadier's memorandum, was something that many Canadians of all origins had accepted during the war. That the obligation was far from universally accepted, however, was all too clear, as the experience of 13 Brigade made clear.

Why? Why were so many Canadians apparently unaware of the importance of the issues at stake in the Second World War, as just a war as the world has ever seen and one that brought U-boat sinkings into the Gulf of St Lawrence and to the waters of the west coast?

The reasons are complex, too much so to be easily simplified. For French Canadians, they relate back to the Conquest of 1760, to the sense of having been conquered by an alien race, culture, and religion. How then could Quebec join willingly in defending the British crown when it was that crown – and its English-Canadian adherents – who ruled over them, scorned their language and faith, and discriminated against them in manifold ways? Even after Confederation, the military forces of the new dominion were British in composition, outlook, appearance, and training; efforts to create Quebec regiments that, for example, might wear the Algerian-style uniform of Papal Zouaves foundered on Ottawa's insistence that such garb was un-British – and its unstated concerns that overt military Catholicism was equally so.*

Imperial wars such as the South African War, where the Boers, a small people much like French Canada, were crushed by the full weight of the empire, and the Great War, where English-speaking Canadians demanded that everyone rush to defend Britain's interests, only reinforced the reluctance of Québécois to participate in the military affairs of Canada.[3] Moreover, the shock to the country produced by the conscription crisis of 1917 meant that in the postwar years politicians pledged repeatedly that war would never come again and, even if it did, conscription would never be employed. Quebec's resistance to compulsory military service in 1917 had effectively altered the political debate in Canada.

For those of non-British origin in the rest of Canada, the reaction to war was not dissimilar. For a Ukrainian, a Pole, a German, or an Italian, Britain's wars were not necessarily just, and rhetoric about the need to serve king and country in a scarlet tunic on a parade square in peacetime inevitably rang as hollow as the demand to serve in muddy khaki in a trench in Flanders. The almost automatic firings of foreign-born workers at the outbreak of war in 1914, the internment of citizens of Germany and Austria-Hungary, and the wholesale gerrymander of 1917, when the Wartime Elections Act stripped recently naturalized Canadians of the franchise, all reinforced a natural tendency to keep to one's own kind.[4]

Worse still, the lesson that ought to have emerged from the wartime experience simply failed to do so. Instead of making every effort to integrate the French-speaking, politicians in both major national parties devoted themselves to winning Quebec's support by seeking more independence for Canada, a worthwhile and long-overdue aim but one that implied that the country's national interests would be the major determinant in deciding which, if any, wars to fight. Such interests, of course, were never defined. Conscription became *the* shibboleth phrase, never to be uttered except to frighten voters at election time. And the armed forces were reduced to such

---

* Such attitudes persisted into the Second World War, and Québécois reacted sharply against them. A French-speaking member of the Canadian Women's Army Corps, undergoing language training in Kitchener, Ontario, recalled a skit at course's end where Québécoises sang: "Vous n'aurez pas les petites Canadiennes / Et malgré vous, nous resterons françaises / Vous avez pu angliciser la plaine / Mais notre coeur, vous ne l'aurez jamais." Quoted in Carolyn Gossage, *Greatcoats and Glamour Boots: Canadian Women at War (1939–1945)* (Toronto, 1991), 45–6.

a level of inconsequence that scarcely anyone could conceive of Canada being able to fight successfully any state more powerful than Leichtenstein.[5]

For those of non-British stock, the nation did almost nothing to bind up the wounds of the Great War. There were no attempts worth recounting to integrate those of other than British or French stock into Canada's life and values. The comments of one Ukrainian Canadian growing up in post-war rural Saskatchewan may be taken as typical: "There was no outside world for us. Our own world was very closed – it was the only one we knew. We were so removed! This was the early twenties – our world was Ukrainian. We did what we did in our own way, in the way we felt like doing it. We were all the same, basically one single Ukrainian community, joined together by bonds of national identity and especially by a shared language. We lived Ukrainian ... Everything we did in daily life was permeated with this sense of being Ukrainian, even though we were living in Canada."[6]

Public school education, while compulsory, did little to crack such ethnic exclusiveness. The singing of "God Save the King," "Rule Britannia," and "The Maple Leaf For Ever," and the reciting of patriotic poetry, could do little in and of themselves to teach the values of the wider Canadian community. What was peculiarly and distinctively Canadian about such values as were taught was similarly unclear. British imperial patriotism – the legacy of Nelson, Wellington, and Haig and a map that was heavily painted with red – did little to commend itself automatically to non-British immigrants. And Canada, a country whose nationalism and sense of itself then and later were still largely unformed, had almost nothing else to put in its place other than the much-expressed conviction that the dominion was different from – and better than – the United States. Of course, this situation was less true in Quebec, insulated by language and where the church controlled education and where "la race" was popularly seen to be in danger. If French Canada had its own concept of self, the Canadian tragedy was that there was little sense of shared values as they were understood in the rest of the country; moreover, the anti-immigrant attitudes in Quebec were likely the sharpest in Canada.

The result of these failures was clear. By the 1930s, as fascist leaders in Europe and Asia began their march toward another war, domestic fascism made substantial inroads in Quebec primarily and to a slightly lesser extent in other parts of the country. Anti-semitism and anti-immigration feelings were widespread.[7] At the same time, Nazi and Fascist elements, actively sponsored by the German and Italian consulates, were at work. The consuls distributed propaganda, shaped the educational curricula in schools they sponsored, raised money and volunteers for "patriotic" causes such as the Italian war against Ethiopia, and set up Fasci or Deutscher Bund societies, most especially in Toronto, Montreal, and on some parts of the prairies.[8] The Canadian government did nothing to check such activities which were, after all, largely legal. The Royal Canadian Mounted Police, obsessed with the hunting down of Communists and so understrength that it could provide almost no Italian or German translators to read the foreign-language newspapers, could be of only limited assistance. And until the Germans' seizure of the rump state of Czechoslovakia in March 1939, the Canadian government continued to advertise in Nazi and Fascist newspapers published in Canada.

The chief bureaucrat in Ottawa in charge of formulating a response to what, by spring 1939, was at last recognized as a problem was Norman Robertson of the Department of External Affairs. Shrewd, intelligent, and sympathetic to the difficulties that immigrants to Canada had to face, he made suggestions that were both hard and soft in character. He urged the government to cease its "administrative encouragement" of Nazi and Fascist groups by stopping its advertising and by blocking government employment for "notorious fascists." "The lower middle class attitudes and origins of Fascist and Nazi groups make them particularly susceptible to this sort of social ostracism," he said, adding that Fascists should be "sent to Coventry with the Communists." The government could also employ tax audits as a weapon, refuse immigrant entry to propagandists, and ensure that a close check was made of the records of applicants for naturalization from Germany and Italy, "in the same way that the Police now check the records of persons believed to be of radical or communist sympathies." The government could also consider revoking the naturalization of those whose membership in Nazi or Fascist organizations such as the Bund or the Fasci was "incompatible with the loyal fulfillment of the oath of allegiance they have taken on naturalization."[9]

Robertson was a genuine "small-l" liberal, and, while such suggestions troubled him, he believed that the state had the right and duty to defend itself against those who would destroy it. But he recognized that many of the German and Italian Canadians caught up in the Bundist and Fasci activities were almost literally blameless, so little had Canada done to suggest what was or was not expected of them. In a memorandum written about the same time as his hard-line one,

Robertson had pointed to the steps that might yet be taken to correct the situation. These included English classes "under Canadian auspices – night schools & adult education associations" and the possibility of giving "preferred employment to refugees," something that no government would have lightly contemplated in the Depression. He also wanted social work among immigrant groups, and he lamented that "we've lacked a Jane Addams – no Hull House or Henry Street Settlement – nor any University Settlement work worth mentioning." Other things could be done, too, such as provision of legal aid and medicine for the poor, use of the CBC and National Film Board to instill citizenship, outreach by the political parties, and enlistment of the churches and such organizations as the YMCA into the process of Canadianization. The goal was "a positive affirmation of [the] concept of Canadian Citizenship based on loyalty & domicile [and the] repudiation of 'blood & soil.'"[10]

Even if the government had had the will to act along those lines – and there was no indication that it did – the outbreak of war came too soon, and suspect Germans, German Canadians, Communists, Italians and Italian Canadians, and Japanese and Japanese Canadians were eventually rounded up and interned. The RCMP, often lacking hard information about such elements in the population, proposed broad-brush action, but Robertson largely short-circuited that. Instead, only the leaders and those suspected of treasonous activities were arrested and interned, though not without complaint, then and subsequently, from civil libertarians.[11] In all, 2,423 people were arrested during the course of the war, including 847 Germans, 632 Italians, and 782 Japanese, although only 263 remained in internment at war's end.[12]

How much of a threat those interned amounted to is unclear. Certainly there were no cases of sabotage attributed to German, Italian, or Japanese sympathizers. Robert Keyserlingk's assessment seems largely justified: "The main purpose of moves against German Canadians was less to turn up dangerous agents than to calm the public and make it appear that the government was in control of the nazi threat at home." His conclusion would fit the Italians and Japanese as well.[13]

What impact the government's actions had on the public – and on ethnic Canadians – is less clear than the intent. Barry Broadfoot recounts the story of an Alberta family of German descent that had all four of its sons in the armed forces. "My father, he didn't say much," Broadfoot's interviewee put it, "but my mother said that all the boys, every one, had to go into the war so that this would prove that we were good Canadians."[14] When the government asked Canadians to release it from its pledges against conscription for overseas service in April 1942, those areas in the west with heavy concentrations of German- or Ukrainian-Canadian voters said "no" by large majorities.[15] That support at home, much as Brig. Macklin and his officers would lament years later, must have reinforced the reluctance of home-defence conscripts from those communities to volunteer for overseas service.

So too did the discrimination that ethnic Canadians faced all across Canada. A 1943 report by the Wartime Information Board, the government's propaganda agency, suggested that many immigrant groups were isolated and suffered from low morale: "Letters still appear in the press complaining that 'foreigners' are staying home and taking the jobs of 'real' Canadians who enlist. If this is so, it is not surprising, for numbers of these people, naturalized or not, have suffered years of humiliating discrimination because of their names, accents, or appearance ... [This] cuts its victims off from the only experience which can make them feel like Canadians. And until they feel like Canadians they can have little urge to fight for Canada."[16]

That was self-evidently the case, although the government's propaganda agencies and the Nationalities Branch of the Department of National War Services had been trying for some time, in a clumsy fashion and often with hidden cash subsidies, to reach out to and influence ethnic groups. Prof. Watson Kirkconnell of McMaster University was one of those employed in this campaign. One of his efforts, a pamphlet published in 1940, argued that no European national group could be considered "alien" from the Canadian "way of life," a phrasing that left out entirely the non-white, and he urged his compatriots to "never assume that our fellow Canadians of any origin are *by nature* unworthy of our sympathy, respect and goodwill."

The extent to which such bad sociology succeeded is unclear, and W.R. Young, the leading student of Canadian wartime propaganda, concluded regretfully that "propaganda directed at the ethnic community had a divisive rather than a unifying effect."[17] Certainly that was true in the large Ukrainian community, where Communist and anti-Communist divisions remained sharp even after Ottawa brokered the formation of an umbrella Ukrainian Canadian Committee in 1940, not least because of resentment at the government's refusal to anger the Soviet Union – the ally bearing the brunt of the war against Germany – by endorsing independence for Ukraine.[18]

The dominion government had little more success in Quebec. The propaganda campaign directed at the province from Ottawa simply failed to blunt the widespread sentiment there that Canada ought not exert itself in the war. The fall of France did almost nothing to alter that view, and the new collaborationist government of Marshal Pétain, with its emphasis on "Travail, famille, patrie," was initially much admired.[19] Worse, the political promises that there would be no conscription had been repeated so often between 1919 and the national election of 1940 that they had become an article of faith.

When in April 1942, W.L. Mackenzie King's government asked the entire country to release it from the promises that it had directed at Quebec, the sense of outrage and anger from Montreal to the Gaspé was as sharp as or sharper than it had been in 1917. A massive grass-roots campaign was mounted by la Ligue pour la défense du Canada, a group that included Henri Bourassa, André Laurendeau, and such young leaders as Pierre Elliott Trudeau and Jean Drapeau. The conscription plebiscite produced a huge "non" vote in Quebec – 72.9 per cent, or appreciably close to 90 per cent among French-speaking voters – and from French Canadians elsewhere in Canada.[20] King's government as a consequence was virtually forced to delay implementation of compulsory service until battle losses in northwest Europe and Italy in late 1944 forced its hand.[21] Of course, those delays – and the undoubted additional casualties they produced when infantry battalions went into action short of their needed reinforcements[22] – produced marked outrage in English Canada and worsened relations between French Canadians and their compatriots. That King and the Liberals won re-election in the teeth of the bitterness in the country in June 1945 must be counted a near-miracle – and a testament to the weakness of the opposition Tories and ccfers.

The moral of this tragic story seems clear: the dominion government could not undo its peacetime failure to integrate Québécois and ethnic Canadians into the larger community with clumsy propagandizing crafted under the stress of war. Canadians in the Second World War were fighting for democracy and freedom, and the nation's cause ought to have commended itself to all who were fortunate enough to live here. It did not, because many Canadians, French-speaking and others, believed incorrectly that their interests, Canadian interests, were not directly threatened by Hitler, Mussolini, and Tojo. Others, victims of prejudice and discrimination or economic victimization, believed that they owed scant loyalty to a nation that had failed them. Those who had suffered from the economic collapse of the Depression could not readily have been reached by educational campaigns. But the others might have been. Had Canadian citizenship and distinctively Canadian values been inculcated in the inter-war years, the wartime selling of the "hard" obligations of citizenship might well have been easier.

Has Canada made progress in integrating all its peoples into a common idea of citizenship since the Second World War? To ask the question unfortunately is to answer it. Separatism in Quebec is at historic highs in the opinion polls, and Canada, as it has existed since 1867, may not continue for many more years. In English Canada, moreover, there is increasingly serious opposition to the policy of multiculturalism, enshrined in law for two decades, on the grounds that it has divided Canadians rather than unifying them and alienated minorities from rather than integrating them into the mainstream. Still, the inescapable facts are that there are now almost two million members of "visible minorities" among the 26 million Canadians, and the Canadians whose origins are neither British nor French now number some 38 per cent of the total. That proportion is still rising, and it may well reach 50 per cent within the next decade or so.

What are the implications of this for the "hard" obligations of citizenship? During the Gulf War of early 1991, to cite the most recent example, Canadians of Arab origin were undoubtedly treated badly and identified with the enemy government of Iraq, most often incorrectly. The Canadian Security Intelligence Service and the RCMP mounted a heavy-handed effort to watch, interrogate, and in some cases intimidate the Arab and Muslim communities, and the media focused on those Iraqis and others who expressed support for Saddam Hussein's invasion of Kuwait. This unhappy state of affairs led a Toronto journalist, Zuhair Kashmeri, to write a book, *The Gulf within*, about *Canadian Arabs, Racism and the Gulf War*, and to advance a startling new direction for the foreign policy of an increasingly multicultural Canada.

Canada, Kashmeri said, "did not consider the views of its large Arab and Muslim communities before it decided to join the U.S.-sponsored coalition in the Gulf." He was certainly correct that there was no consultative mechanism in place at the beginning of the Iraqi crisis and correct, too, that the needs of Canadian Arabs and Muslims were simply overridden. For Kashmeri, this was simply unaccepable, and he quotes favourably the views of Rev. Tad Mitsui, a Japanese-born United Church of Canada minister who sees "race involved in judging who is an enemy and who is a friend. For example, Canadians will never think of America as an enemy, and neither can they think of the British or the French as enemies ... But it is so easy for Canadians to think of Arabs as the enemy." Mitsui says, "I think this is not fair. Why can't Pakistan be our friend no matter what? Why can't Iraq, to take the case to its extreme, be our friend? ... And if you expand that logic, if Canada should exist as a multicultural, multiracial country, you cannot take sides with anybody."

For Kashmeri, Mitsui's logic is clear and compelling: "Since multiculturalism advocates celebrating the differences, allowing the traditions and cultures to co-exist, the extension of that policy in foreign policy is a stance of neutrality." Neutrality in the Gulf War would have dampened the backlash suffered by Arabs and Muslims in Canada, and the fear felt by people like Mitsui and Kashmeri "is that today it is Iraqis, tomorrow it could be any of the other nationalities settled here, if Ottawa continues to fall behind Washington in the American quest for a post–Cold War 'New World Order.'"[23]

Whether Canada simply fell in behind Washington in the war with Iraq, as Kashmeri blithely concludes, is debatable. So is whether Canadian national interests can ever be separated on the major international issues from those held in the United States, the superpower with which this country uneasily shares the continent. But the Mitsui-Kashmeri views, which, if they could be extended back to 1939, would have obliged Canada to remain neutral in the war against Hitler lest German Canadians be offended, are simply not debatable in their larger thrust. Canada is not a neutral and pacifist nation, it never has been, and, given its geographical location, it never can be. Canadian Arabs and Muslims unhappily felt discriminated against in early 1991 just as did Canadian Germans in 1914 and 1939. But the significant point surely is that in 1991 there was no indication whatsoever that the German Canadians reacted any differently to the war with Iraq than did the majority of their fellow citizens. In other words, German Canadians over time became Canadians, shaping their political and international attitudes out of the same mix of ideas, received wisdom, and national interests as their compatriots. They had integrated into the mainstream intellectually and, in large measure, physically through intermarriage. Over time, presumably, so will the recently arrived Arabs and Muslims, despite the best efforts of the Department of Multiculturalism.

But to suggest that only a policy of neutrality can preserve social peace in Canada and truly embody the national ideal of multiculturalism is utterly nonsensical. Most Canadians came to believe that Iraq was a dangerous, expansionist power in a vital region, and one that had not hesitated to invade its neighbour, to send missiles against other neighbouring states, and to use ecological terrorism as a war-fighting method. They might well have demanded that a neutral Canada drop its pacifists' cloak and stand up for the principles of collective security which it had pledged to support in the United Nations Charter and other international covenants. The prospects for an even more violent public debate if they had been denied would have been omnipresent.

The implications seem clear. If multiculturalism means toleration of ethnic and religious differences, the great majority of Canadians will support it. If, however, it means putting their political traditions aside and shaping their world-view to conform to a half-baked concept of multicultural neutrality, there is simply no doubt that the policy of multiculturalism will be tossed forcibly into the dustbin. At the end of the 1930s, Norman Robertson called for a positive affirmation of Canadian citizenship based on loyalty and domicile. During the Second World War, Brig. Macklin sought free citizens of a free country, willing to volunteer and die for their country. Old-fashioned as they sound today in the post–Cold War era, those two approaches to the hard obligations of citizenship have much more to recommend them than a policy of multicultural neutrality devoid of substance.

NOTES

1 This was probably incorrect. A study of the 60,000 NRMA soldiers in late 1944 found roughly the national proportions of English-speaking, French-speaking, and non-British or French origin among the conscripts. See J.L. Granatstein and J.M. Hitsman, *Broken Promises: A History of Conscription in Canada* (Toronto, 1985), 207.

2 National Archives of Canada (NA), J.L. Ralston Papers, vol. 50, Mobilization of 13 Bde on an Active Basis, 2 May 1944. There is an abbreviated version of this memorandum printed in C.P. Stacey, *Arms, Men and Governments: The War Policies of Canada 1939–1945* (Ottawa, 1970), 591ff.

3 See, for example, Robert Rutherdale, "'Préparons-nous à la guerre': Francophone Patriotism in Trois-Rivières at the Outbreak of the First World War," a paper presented at the Canadian Historical Association, 1989; D.P. Morton, "French Canada and War, 1868–1917: The Military Background to the Conscription Crisis of 1917," in J.L. Granatstein and R.D. Cuff, eds., *War and Society in North America* (Toronto, 1971), 84ff.

4 See Donald Avery, "Continental European Immigrant Workers in Canada 1896–1919: From Stalwart Peasants to Radical Proletariat," *Canadian Review of Sociology and Anthropology* 12 (1975) 59ff; and John English, *The Decline of Politics: The Conservatives and the Party System 1901–1920* (Toronto, 1977), 153ff. The response of native-born Ca-

nadians to the Great War was surprisingly cool. Of the more than 600,000 members of the Canadian Expeditionary Force who served during the war, almost exactly half were born in Britain, a figure that suggests strongly that the call of home loyalties was directly related to the country of birth.

5 Granatstein and Hitsman, *Broken Promises*, chap. 4.

6 L. Luciuk, ed., *Heroes of their Day: The Reminiscences of Bohdan Panchuk* (Toronto, 1983), 26.

7 See, among others, Lita-Rose Betcherman, *The Swastika and the Maple Leaf: Fascist Movements in Canada in the '30s* (Toronto, 1975); Michael Oliver, *The Passionate Debate: The Social and Political Ideas of Quebec Nationalism 1920–1945* (Montreal, 1991), chap. 7; and C.H. Levitt and W. Shaffir, *The Riot at Christie Pits* (Toronto, 1987).

8 See, for example, John Zucchi, *Italians in Toronto: Development of a National Identity 1875–1935* (Montreal, 1988), chap. 7; L.B. Liberati, "The Internment of Italo-Canadians during World War II," a paper presented at the Canadian Ethnic Studies Conference 1989, 4ff; J.F. Wagner, *Brothers beyond the Sea: National Socialism in Canada* (Waterloo, 1981); and R.H. Keyserlingk, "Breaking the Nazi Plot: Canadian Government Attitudes towards German Canadians 1939–1945," in G.N. Hillmer et al., eds., *On Guard for Thee* (Ottawa, 1988), 55ff.

9 NA, Norman Robertson Papers, vol. 12, file 134, Memorandum, 24 May 1939; NA, Department of External Affairs Records, vol. 822, file 701, O.D. Skelton to Ernest Lapointe, 26 May 1939. See also J.L. Granatstein, *A Man of Influence: Norman A. Robertson and Canadian Statecraft, 1929–1968* (Ottawa, 1981), 82ff.

10 Robertson Papers, vol. 12, file 134, What can be done ..., n.d.; Granatstein, *Man of Influence*, 83.

11 Granatstein, *Man of Influence*, 83ff.

12 Keyserlingk, "Breaking the Nazi Plot," 63–4.

13 Ibid., 61. On the Japanese, see Patricia Roy et al., *Mutual Hostages: Canadians and Japanese during the Second World War* (Toronto, 1990), especially chaps. 2, 4, and 7.

14 Barry Broadfoot, *Six War Years 1939–1945: Memories of Canadians at Home and Abroad* (Toronto, 1974), 15.

15 Granatstein and Hitsman, *Broken Promises*, 171; R.J. MacDonald, "The Silent Column: Civil Security in Saskatchewan during World War II," *Saskatchewan History* (Spring 1986) 56–7.

16 Quoted in W.R. Young, "Chauvinism and Canadianism: Canadian Ethnic Groups and the Failure of Wartime Information," in Hillmer et al., eds, *On Guard for Thee*, 43.

17 Cited in ibid., 35. See also W.R. Young, "Building Citizenship: English

Canada and Propaganda during the Second War," *Journal of Canadian Studies* 16 (Autumn–Winter 1981) 123.

18 B.S. Kordan and L. Luciuk, "A Prescription for Nationbuilding: Ukrainian Canadians and the Canadian State, 1939–1945," in Hillmer et al., eds., *On Guard for Thee* 90ff.

19 W.R. Young, "Working for Unity: The Problems of Public Information in Quebec during the Second World War," Canadian Historical Association paper, 1979, passim.

20 Opinion polling before the plebiscite also found differences in support for conscription between those in upper-income brackets, who favoured it by 72 per cent, and those in lower brackets, whose support was only 54 per cent; urban dwellers (68 per cent) were also more supportive than rural voters (57 per cent). *Public Opinion Quarterly* 6 (Summer-Fall 1942) 312–3, 488–9.

21 Granatstein and Hitsman, *Broken Promises*, chaps. 5–6.

22 See W. Denis Whitaker and Shelagh Whitaker, *Tug of War* (Toronto, 1984), especially chap. 10.

23 Zuhair Kashmeri, *The Gulf Within* (Toronto, 1991), 126ff.

DESMOND MORTON

Divided Loyalties?
Divided Country?

A LEGAL AND EMOTIONAL CONCEPT

Citizenship is both a legal and an emotional concept. It is a means of categorizing individuals and of giving them an identity. Citizenship defines an individual's rights, responsibilities, and opportunities; it also implies loyalty and commitment to a national entity. A citizen can claim the protection of his or her nation and, by the same token, is compelled to contribute to that protection. Because of citizenship's legal and emotional dimensions, its betrayal, or treason, has ranked among the most heinous of crimes and subject to the most ingeniously hideous of punishments.[1] To be a stateless person has been a pitiable condition in our well-regulated age, akin to being stranded on the Kowloon ferry or, more commonly, confined to the canvas, tarpaper, and corrugated iron of a makeshift but permanent refugee camp.

There are clubs, teams, regiments, tribes, and states which, to an inevitably prejudiced eye, are better than others. As a form of membership, citizenship is an attribute to be sought or treasured with an enthusiasm appropriate to the prestige of the group. The pride that Americans take in their citizenship may be mocked and even deplored for its blind chauvinism, but usually with a tinge of jealousy. By dint of a substantial effort, largely begun in the wake of the Civil War, the United States forged from incredibly heterogeneous peoples a remarkably homogeneous sense of civic identity. Among those heterogeneous peoples were former Canadians – the largest single immigrant group in the United States, and the most invisible. To them and to other outsiders, however, the chief attraction of American citizenship may not have been the Declaration of Independence but free access to the world's wealthiest capitalist society. Canadian citizenship has been only slightly less desirable for some of the same reasons: our relative prosperity and freedom and the relative openness of our welcome.

There is an added feature of Canadian citizenship – sometimes an asset and sometimes a liability. It comes with hyphens attached. Canadians, claimed the historian J.M.S. Careless, are a people of "limited identities," open to a variety of allegiances and a recurrent source of frustration to those of his professional colleagues in search of devout and single-minded nation-builders. Canadian citizenship has had to coexist with loyalties to old homelands, newer provinces, or nations within and protected by the federal state, specifically la nation canadienne française.

OLD SUBJECTS AND NEW

The fact of dual allegiances was apparent from the moment of Capitulation in 1760 and more notably from the Royal Proclamation of 1763. The people of New France might be transferred, lands, baggage, and allegiance, from His Most Catholic Majesty to His Britannic Majesty, but would their hearts follow? In 1774, they were granted legal protections for their religion and customs that most of George III's older Catholic subjects would not possess for another half-century – in part because of his own insane fixation on the subject. The Quebec Act made allegiance a matter of negotiation with a distinct French-speaking and Catholic society. In turn, the act aggravated conflict with the king's old subjects in the Thirteen Colonies that, a decade later, unloaded a new, English- and German- speaking "distinct society" on the southern edge of the old Province of Quebec, to say nothing of their refuge-seeking Iroquoian allies. The stew of allegiances grew thicker and could now partially be resolved by new boundaries and arrangements.

Behind the Loyalists, at the behest of Lieutenant-Governor John Graves Simcoe, came the so-called late Loyalists, people whose loyalty was to themselves and their families and whose purpose was the restless search for better land. Though he received few thanks and much ridicule for his beliefs, Simcoe grasped a basic proposition of Canadian citizenship: people acquire it by experience and commitment. People who build farms and businesses and families become citizens, or they move on. Like his successors, Simcoe was desperate to create an economy. As with the Mennonites, Hutterites, and Doukhobors whom later governments would welcome to Canada, it was not private beliefs, however repugnant, that Simcoe cared about, it was skills in clearing and cultivation. In that respect, no one could match the people of the American frontier.

It is easy to ridicule Simcoe's belief that, in a colony governed by the "very image and transcript" of the British constitution, the late Loyalists would infallibly become loyal subjects. Upper Canada was a badly blotted copy of an imperfect government. Yet was Simcoe wholly wrong? Some of his settlers did all that he could have hoped; others joined the American invaders of 1812 and 1813 or prudently left with their baggage. A few late-Loyalist traitors decorated the gibbets on the Burlington Heights. By drawing settlers to Upper Canada at the expense of upstate New York and Ohio, Simcoe gave the province part of the edge that it desperately needed to survive the War of 1812. Taking a chance on divided allegiances paid off. And was there ever to be an alternative to Simcoe's gamble, if Canada were ever to be populated? This was a cold, forbidding country, a second choice to those who did not give special weight to continuing their British allegiance.

The post-1815 immigration brought all the bickering nationalities of the British Isles to Canada, each with impeccable replicas of quarrels that belonged to the Old World, from the schismatic Presbyterianism of the Scots to the savage conflict of Orange and Green among the Irish. The newcomers unconsciously helped provoke the rebellions of 1837 in Upper and Lower Canada and very consciously helped put them down – with support from the king's old allies, the Natives. In virtually their last autonomous and significant political act, the First Nations showed that they understood their likely future at the hands of Reformers and *patriotes*. What they did not anticipate was that the defeats of 1837 and 1838 would be reversed within a generation.

CREATING THE NEW NATION

In the same period in which Americans faced their greatest challenge of divided allegiance, the Civil War, British North Americans were cautiously feeling their way toward union. In the debates between 1864 and 1867, with their contrasting rhetorical styles, George-Étienne Cartier and D'Arcy McGee sought to give meaning to the infant of Confederation – Canada. An assassin's bullet and Bright's disease denied both men the opportunity to give substance to their vision. Among those who attempted the task were the young Canada Firsters – Torontonians in the main, and a lone Nova Scotian. Like others who have attempted to define a Canadian identity, their vantage point seems to have been too low to embrace the curvature of the earth in a country that spans five thousand kilometres. What looked right from Toronto could not encompass Quebec or the Red River or even the two disgruntled Maritime colonies forced into Confederation at Britain's behest.

Confederation coincided with a tremendous outburst of self-conscious nationalism in Europe and the Americas. The word itself must have reminded contemporaries of the southern Confederacy crushed in 1865 and of the German Confederation which, in 1871, would become a new German Empire. French Canadians and a few American Catholics formed the Zouaves pontificaux in 1869 because their allegiance to His Holiness and the Papal States was in conflict with the emerging, if fragile, kingdom of Italy. In the mood of the times, who could be surprised at a new upsurge of nationalism in Ireland or its migrated version among the Irish of the United States and Canada. No wonder Cartier and McGee could believe that their "new nation" would also be borne to greatness on the winds of time. French, English, Scots, and Irish (there were commonly four founding nations in the rhetoric of Confederation, as there are in the shield of the Canadian coat of arms) would merge their respective national talents in a bid to build a country "a mari usque ad mare" – unless the Americans got there first!

A generation later, Ernest Renan gave his majestic definition of nationhood to his audience at the Sorbonne. A nation, he insisted, is not built on speaking a common language or occupying a common territory but on a history of great hopes and achievements: "Avoir des gloires communes dans le passé, une volonté commune dans le présent; avoir fait de grandes choses ensemble; vouloir en faire encore. Voilà les conditions essentielles pour être un peuple ..."

Renan, of course, spoke of France, not Canada, and his thoughts were influenced by the loss of German-speaking Alsace and Lorraine, but his definition applied to the young dominion. Canadians did great things. By 1872 they had created their transcontinental country, and by 1885 they had linked it by rail despite the worst economic depression contemporaries could remember. Had they done it together? Gangs of Irish and Chinese labourers had met in the vast mountainous sea of the Rockies; other gangs of every nationality had somehow bridged the muskeg north of Lake Superior, but many more Canadians remembered their differences. Quebec politicians had exploited the dominion government's desperate need to fund the CPR by extracting cash for their own Quebec–Lac St-Jean railway. In 1885, they mourned Riel, whose theocratic Métis republic would have doomed the transcontinental vision. In 1887, the Nova Scotia legislature voted to secede.

Ontario's Oliver Mowat climaxed fifteen years of battling Ottawa – and winning elections as his province's champion – by summoning provincial premiers to their first conference. Among them was Honoré Mercier, the first post-Confederation premier of Quebec to offer himself as the only authentic and faithful leader of his people. Under Mercier, Quebecers adopted the historically ingenious claim that Confederation was a "compact" of English and French which could be altered only by mutual consent. Canada, by the compact theory, was a country of two allegiances.

MANY ALLEGIANCES

It was, of course, a country of many allegiances – to French Canada, to Ireland, to the British empire, to provinces tricked or forced into Confederation. To speak only of the Irish – they were the largest of the émigré communities from the British Isles, the most divided and the poorest. At Confederation, they had faced the terrible loyalty test of the Fenian Raids, and, in the eyes of most of their neighbours, they had passed. The martyrdom of D'Arcy McGee, Irish nationalist–turned–Canadian patriot and anti-American, helped. Even the Orange Order, if it wanted respectability, had to acknowledge the role of an Irish Catholic in preserving Canada for the empire. Yet Confederation could not end the ugly tradition of Catholic-Protestant sectarianism, and in some respects the Canadian economy and Irish politics helped the problem grow worse in the 1870s and 1880s. From the 1860s to 1919, Fenian alarms served some of the later role of the Communist Party of Canada, providing a popular bogey and justifying enhanced police powers.

From the 1830s, Irish Canadians provided the test-bed for Canada's long tradition of ethnic politics, from pandering to the fears of disdainful or suspicious neighbours to cultivation of leaders and subsidization of ethnic media in return for bloc followings. A Catholic archbishop or an Orange grand master ranked as equals, though their respective influence might be as different as their durability. A typical example of ethnicity in politics was the role of John Costigan, a New Brunswick Conservative MP from 1867 to 1905 and chief spokesman and manager of Irish Catholics. Imagine a Tory party, British to the core, Orange on the rooftops, with John Costigan in the basement demanding official government support for Irish Home Rule and controlling enough votes to beat his own party. You can almost sympathize with the Old Chieftain's binges. In 1882, Macdonald found a quiet moment to slip through the Costigan motion and put him in the cabinet. Ultimately, Costigan, loyal to himself and Ireland, slipped over to the Liberals in time for a comfortable retirement to the Senate.

CIVIS BRITANNICUS SUM

The problem of divided allegiance in Canada is frequently presented as a problem of the French-English relationship. There is another, less familiar but more important perspective. In its formative years, Canadian nationality was confronted by a larger and, to many Canadians, a more captivating rival.

From the first, those who offered Canada as a focus for allegiance had to compete with both smaller provincial identities and membership in that vast and potent entity called the British empire. We misunderstand our history if we forget the tremendous appeal of citizenship in the greatest empire the world had ever seen. English-speaking children were raised with the historical myths of British nationalism, as conveyed by adapted editions of the Irish National Reader and authors as diverse as Macaulay and G.A. Henty. As mid-Victorians, the Fathers of Confederation were conscious of the sweep and majesty of British power. As owners of the world's third-largest merchant marine, Canadians could appreciate the global reach of a British fleet ready to defend the rights, the honour, and sometimes the cupidity of any British subject. If Britain would stand up for an Aegean merchant called Don Pacifico who could claim "Civis Britannicus sum," there was greater security for a Bluenose schooner captain moored in Valparaiso or Aleppo.

What mere Canadian citizenship could compete with the claims of an empire that spanned the known universe? What more powerful civic educator could there be than Mercator's projection of the globe, with its innumerable splashes of pink or red. In its centre, far larger than even its true immensity, lay Canada. What ambitious young Canadian would turn from the privilege of membership in the empire to assert sole allegiance to a country whose population and world stature were comparable – the parallel was commonly stated – to Romania? The empire, if never egalitarian, was also gloriously heterogeneous. Provided that they accepted the racial hierarchies, Canadians could learn from their school readers and their popular fiction how other races revelled in the simple honesty and common sense of a mere handful of white administrators. Within the empire, there was recognition for the achievements of Sir Percy Girouard, builder of Egyptian railways, or Dr. Oronhyatekha, the shrewd Mohawk who organized a fraternal order, the Foresters, into a major insurance company. What greater compliment to the universality of the empire than to hear the effulgent if heavily accented imperial rhetoric of Sir Wilfrid Laurier in that year of jubilee, 1897, or, in 1914, to hear him give Canada's answer to a Great Britain in danger: "Ready, Aye, Ready." The empire took pride in its multiracialism. Conspicuous on the fringes of any oleograph depiction of the "Empire's Defenders," framing the jolly tars and stalwarts of the Brigade of Guards, were men of the North-West Mounted Police or a fur-capped Carabinier Mont-Royal, to say nothing of Sikhs, Hausas, Ghurkas, and members of the Royal Malta Artillery.

Despite those who chafed at English snobbery and bungling or who worried about the poverty and economic decay at the empire's heart, the historian Carl Berger has recorded the grandest vision of their future that any Canadians have ever embraced.[2] At no distant date, strengthened by the natural advantages of their bracing climate, Canadians would take over leadership of the empire. The proconsuls of India, Egypt, and West Africa would be Canadian. The "white man's burden" would be borne by men from Brantford, Glace Bay, and Calgary. Col. Sam Hughes – athlete, editor, and Canada's war minister from 1911 to 1916 – was almost a caricature of the extremes of imperial nationalism. As masthead for his Lindsay paper, he displayed a Canadian red ensign and the verse, "A Union of hearts and a union of hands, / A union none can sever / A union of home and a union of lands, / And the flag, British Union Forever!"[3]

NOT GLORIOUS OR FREE

We know the outcome. After some months in the Homewood asylum, Hughes died in 1921. "Imperial nationalism" did not survive to 1919. Tested in war, imperial federation and imperial citizenship broke down. In a host of ways, practical, legal, and above all emotional, the First World War was Canada's War of Independence. Britain was an ally, not an enemy, but our route to independence was clear from the fall of 1916. Citizenship in the empire was too costly and, as two more generations would discover, of too little value. Kipling's "Recessional" was prophetic. The captains and the kings departed. The world would not forever be splashed with pink; there was no imperial patrimony for a nordic race of Canadians to inherit, and the notion itself had been made despicable by Adolf Hitler and his Nazi followers.

Nor did allegiance to the British Empire, whatever its influence, ever have universal appeal in Canada. Among most French Canadians, loyalties were focused on the desperate struggle for la survivance. Allegiance to the empire depended strictly and explicitly on how the British connection fostered or threatened their collective goal. That Britain must defend the French fact that it had recognized in 1774 was self-evident; that there was any reciprocal duty to defend the one-time conqueror was not. The reluctance of the English-speaking majority to accept Canada as their primary focus of loyalty dismayed such thoughtful Canadiens as Henri Bourassa and ultimately alienated him from Canada itself. Other Canadians, too, had their own loyalties – to their own national heritage and, more commonly, to their own deepening Canadian roots. In 1899 and again in the recruiting years of 1914–16, the older, settled parts of English-speaking Canada – Nova Scotia, New Brunswick, and western Ontario – conspicuously gave up fewer sons and husbands than the cities and the west.

One can exaggerate the tug of imperial patriotism. The rhetoric of empire often flourished in English-speaking Canada largely because it was "glorious and free." In *The Imperialist*, Sara Jeannette Duncan's hero, Lorne Murchison, gets the message from his fellow Canadians in Elgin. The empire is fine stuff for speeches, but not if it costs them money. In 1914 the costs suddenly soared. Between 1914 and 1919, imperial citizenship added almost $2 billion to Canada's national debt, and it cost lives – 60,000 dead and as many more damaged forever in mind or body. Sir Robert Borden, who had taken a relatively united Canada to war, discovered that he and his followers were no longer trusted by Canadians when the war was over. Under W.L. Mackenzie King and his successor, the Liberals would exploit doubts about the true Tory allegiance until the advent of John Diefenbaker.

Between 1939 and 1945, slow learners got another lesson in the cost of sharing the imperial burden. If the cost of the Second World War was smaller – 44,000 dead – and the economic outcome vastly more favourable for Canada, there was a crucial corollary. Even the least perceptive could see that Britain's power had been sacrificed in the two world wars and that the empire was doomed. Canada's future lay beside an assertive neighbour whose citizenship was now more jealously guarded than when Canadians, English- and French-speaking, had poured over the northern frontier on their way to the mill towns and prairie wheat fields.

When Paul Martin and other Canadians embraced the overdue notion of an unhyphenated and proud Canadian in 1945, it was in part because its greatest rival for the allegiance of Canadians – being a British subject – was no longer either glorious or free. Unfortunately, one heritage of that glorious illusion was suspicion among

French Canadians and those of other ethnic origins that British Canadians could not be trusted to put their own North American country first. In turn, that anxiety legitimized other divided allegiances.

CITIZENSHIP, ALLEGIANCE, AND WAR

It sometimes upsets Canadians in the 1990s to find that fellow-citizens, often native-born, retain a loyalty to a long-left homeland such as Estonia, Croatia, or Ukraine that seems to surpass their commitment to Canada. Whether or not it is comforting, it is worth remembering that such loyalties have a very long tradition in Canada.[4] An unhyphenated Canadianism could justify war in 1914 and again in 1939. J.W. Dafoe, editor of Winnipeg's *Free Press*, insisted that these were Canada's wars and that Prussian militarism and Nazism were our enemies too. No one disputed the sentiments, but those were not the arguments that leaped to the headlines of the *Montreal Star*, the *Vancouver Sun*, or even *La Presse*.[5]

If Canada three times went to war because of ancestral loyalties to Britain, these were loyalties that inherently could not be shared across the diverse Canadian population. As one sad result, wartime Canada found itself caught in contests of divided loyalties. Far from uniting the country, Canada's wars heightened ethnic xenophobia. The internment of enemy aliens, begun long after any would-be warriors had left Canada, extended to people who conspicuously posed no threat to anything but their neighbours' wage scales. Chauvinist riots, which began with German-owned shops in 1915, extended by 1919 to Chinese restaurants. After a brief mood of enthusiasm, French Canada largely opted out of the national war effort and bitterly resented the coercion of the Military Service Act of 1917. Under threat of commercial boycott, the town of Berlin became Kitchener. Local bitterness expressed itself in 1917 when a Kitchener audience shouted down the prime minister of Canada.[6]

In the aftermath of the Great War, thoughtful Canadians had time to reflect on what had befallen their country. Some contrasted Canada's experience with that of its neighbour. Americans, too, suffered from divided allegiances that might well have exploded in 1917. After all, German- and Irish-American opinion was a powerful force. President Woodrow Wilson had been re-elected in 1916 on the claim "He Kept Us out of War." The arguments for going to war in April 1917 – unrestricted submarine warfare and the alleged Zimmermann plot – were complex and remote from most Americans' lives. Yet the United States invoked the draft and sustained a major war effort with an astonishing degree of patriotic consensus. Were American concepts of citizenship and patriotism an example for Canada?

In some respects, the power of "Americanism" had gained currency long before 1917. Those who interpret the Manitoba Schools Question of the 1890s solely as part of the struggle for the rights of French and English forget that the Greenway government's "national schools" were less intended to antagonize a Catholic or French-speaking minority than to create a "national" consciousness. Having submerged the Métis and half-breed cultures in their own heedless wave of immigration, English-speaking Manitobans wanted to protect their own institutions and values from the far-greater immigrant wave that approached in the coming century. Whatever deals Sir George Cartier and Bishop Taché may have worked out in 1870, Manitoba needed a unified school system to assimilate newcomers.

In neighbouring Saskatchewan, this was later the preoccupation of Dr J.T.M. Anderson, who won the position of director of education for new Canadians long before he became premier of an ill-fated Depression-era government.[7] Through such apostles of civic acculturation as Robert England, elements of the Saskatchewan experience filtered into the adult education movement and citizenship education programs.

CANADIAN CITIZENSHIP

Though by no means all Canadians agreed at the time, distinctive citizenship was a logical step in the wake of the Second World War. Like other national symbols, it provoked critics on both sides, and the consequent timidity robbed it of some of the positive value that advocates such as Paul Martin had sought for it. Specifically, Canadians would allow no erosion of other loyalties. They insisted on remaining, on the one hand, "British subjects" or, on the other, linked to their own narrower version of Canadian identity, because the country as a whole somehow failed to give full respect to their particular cultural, linguistic, or "national" claim. Indeed, as First Nations spokespersons now claim, some were ignored altogether or inserted *nolens volens* into an unsought "enfranchisement."

By the standards of most European nations, the citizenship that Ottawa created in 1946 and amended in 1976 is easy and undemanding. In peace and even in war, a strong historical prejudice protects Canadians from compulsory military service. For those born in Canada, on a Canadian ship, or, since 1976, in a Canadian aircraft, citizenship comes with a birth certificate. For those who choose to be naturalized, the residence requirement is conveniently brief and occasionally subject to negotiation. The requirement of "adequate" knowledge of Canada has to be modest lest it embarrass the native-born. Is "adequate" knowledge of French or English a serious barrier? The eager and well-advised can shop for a less demanding citizenship judge.

Critics complain that in citizenship, as in shopping, you get what you pay for. The Charter of Rights and Freedoms deliberately left citizens with few advantages over other residents of Canada, beyond the right to vote for politicians or to join that despised species. Citizenship is a prerequisite for some federal appointments, and, when travelling abroad, only citizens can expect Canadian embassies and consulates to take their troubles seriously. At home, only citizens have a right to decide whether their children will be educated in English or French.

Nor is Canadian citizenship bolstered by a plethora of the stirring songs and evocative symbols that enthusiastic citizens of other nations enjoy. Indeed, flaunting symbols might be called embarrassing and therefore un-Canadian. Canada's flag produced controversy when it was unveiled in 1964, and it is unimaginable that there should be a severe penalty for those who burn, tear, or trample it or substitute a marijuana stem for the maple leaf. The new English words of the national anthem displease atheists and feminists, and the original French of Judge Routhier and the music by Calixa Lavallée have failed to placate Québécois. "Avant tout, je suis Canadien" was the marching song of the *patriotes* of 1837, but only grandparents in Quebec call themselves *Canadiens* any more. In a fascinating transformation, a name and a history have been abandoned to "les Anglais" as the price of a new and narrower allegiance.

LEARNING ABOUT CANADA

As a history teacher who has filled a lot of pages, notably at the intermediate school level where few of my colleagues will ever read my work, I would profit enormously from the suggestion that more Canadian history be taught. A great deal is taught now; is it learned? Across Canada, students get three to four years of local and Canadian history and emerge with little more than mental dysentery.

Is that because real history is an adult entertainment, as complex and bewildering as algebra only seems to be. Because it is imposed on 10- and 12-year-olds, its concepts are kept as thin as its vocabulary. Real learning happens when we are mentally ready for it – and for history that characteristically occurs toward the end of high school.

Being Canadian is a matter of experience, not formal learning. In most countries, young people get to know their country through periods of military service. That notion is repugnant to most Canadians, though less so, oddly enough, to Québécois. Some years ago, Ottawa killed a federal program called Katimavik which gave young volunteers a year's work in at least two different parts of Canada, in work that ranged from environmental clean-up to helping out with the elderly. Katimavik was killed for all the usual reasons: it cost money, it had no bureaucratic friends, and, indeed, no one but Jacques Hébert seemed to care much about it. Doubtless it had some problems, but, as someone who kept encountering "Kat-kids" at university and among the disabled, where my wife worked, in all manner of settings, I never saw a program with a better record of shaping citizens of whom I felt proud.

I am Canadian enough to believe that Katimavik worked because it was voluntary. We should not force Canada's values, even down Canadian throats. We learn best about citizenship by living it, and part of that living is the experience of tolerating difference – as most of us, with intermittent grumbling, do. I believe that we shall survive our present discontents – after all, that's what most Canadians, French- and English-speaking, want, and a decent democracy should be able to come up with ways to satisfy them. I even think that Canadians understand what makes them Canadian, although it would never fit in a standard catechism.

However, if we need more help, let us find ways to make Canadian history an adult experience and to help young Canadians get to know their country the way Katimavik did.

CIVIS CANADENSIS SUM

We have a strange Canadian tradition of changing our history with each wave of newcomers. Jacques Cartier, proclaiming North America as the property of His Most Christian Majesty, Francis I, ignored 20,000 years of aboriginal history. The Loyalists promptly assumed that, with their blessed presence, the whole of the province of Quebec would now become British and Protestant. They got Upper Canada instead. The post-1815 immigrants found the Canadas too American and set about making them more British. More recently, Ontario's minister of citizenship added her wisdom by insisting that Cartier and Champlain were racists and, one assumes, unworthy of further study. If a politician, or Ukrainian Canadians, or Black

Canadians, or anyone else want history rewritten to remove their predecessors from the script, they have the advantage of having lots of precedents on their side.

There is, as in law, a price. People who lose their history, as the First Nations know better than anyone, lose their place. They become resentful strangers in a country that neither knows nor respects them. They are victims of robbery without hope of redress. Yet those who rewrite history in their own name gain little but a temporary sense of importance. They are barred from pride in the achievements of those who, within the limitations of their age and generation, made Canada good enough to attract our ancestors or even ourselves. Much as Canadians have ignored the political and technological achievements of our First Nations, presumably politically correct revisionists want us to ignore the incredible feats of travel, settlement, and economic transformation accomplished by Cartier, Champlain, and all who followed in their footsteps.

History is another word for experience. It is neither a weapon nor a user's manual. At best, it encourages patience and a long view.

Canada's traditional bonds of unity may seem more frail than they really are. The third-oldest federal system in the world is no blue baby. We have more in common than our cold-weather custom of mumbling in both official languages. We have lived together for a long time. Despite years of teaching that Canada is an instrument of cruel injustice to regions and minorities, after decades of resolute hyphenation, how wonderful it is that the great majority of us, British Columbian, Québécois, Newfoundlander, think Canada is the best place in the world and, despite our different perspectives, we want it to survive. Civis canadensis sum.

NOTES

1 In Britain, traitors insufficiently privileged by birth to have their heads removed in the Tower of London were to be hanged, drawn, and quartered, with life – and agony – preserved as long as an artful executioner could manage. Even when the British first abolished the death penalty for murder, it remained for treason and for the somewhat more venal sin of setting fire to one of HM's dockyards. In Canada, section 37 of the Criminal Code now offers nothing more awe-inspiring than life imprisonment for high treason and rather less for some forms of mere treason.

2 See Carl Berger, *The Sense of Power: Studies in the Ideas of Canadian Imperialism, 1867–1914* (Toronto: University of Toronto Press: 1970).

3 Cited in Ronald G. Haycock, *Sam Hughes: The Public Career of a Controversial Canadian, 1885–1916* (Waterloo: Wilfrid Laurier University Press, 1986), 25.

4 Did British-Canadians conspire to force their country to get involved in the South African War? The American historian Norman Penlington insisted that the British were responsible through Lord Minto and General Hutton; *Canada and Imperialism, 1896–1899* (Toronto, 1965), 237–60. Using the same evidence and more, Charles Stacey accepted that Canadians themselves were making up their minds, although, he added, "Never since 1899 has the outbreak of war found the national government so deeply and gravely divided." C.P. Stacey, *Canada and the Age of Conflict, 1867–1921* (Toronto: Macmillan, 1977), 61.

5 See Ramsay Cook, *The Politics of John W. Dafoe and the Free Press*, rev. ed. (Toronto: University of Toronto Press, 1971), 66–7. In 1937–38 proportionately more Canadians than people from any other country but France volunteered for the Republican side in the Spanish Civil War. Whatever the role of ideology in their choice, ethnic ties to Spain are almost invisible in the lengthy lists of names in Victor Hoar, *The Mackenzie-Papineau Battalion* (Toronto: Copp Clark, 1969), 239–49, and William C. Beeching, *Canadian Volunteers, Spain, 1936–1939* (Regina: Canadian Plains Research Centre, 1989), x–xxix. The case of Canadians who involved themselves in the first Arab-Israeli War is more complex, since Jews and non-Jews were involved. See David Bercuson, *The Secret Army* (Toronto: Lester & Orpen, Dennys, 1983).

6 A valuable account of one part of Canada in wartime is Barbara M. Wilson's *Ontario and the First World War, 1914–1918: A Collection of Documents* (Toronto: Champlain Society, 1977).

7 See Anderson's *The Education of the New Canadian* (Ne York, 1918).

PAUL MARTIN

Citizenship and the People's World

No one who lived through the Second World War escaped its impact. As a back-bench member of the House of Commons through most of the war, my experience is understandably coloured by that perspective. One of the most memorable moments for me remains the solemn hush of the members when Prime Minister Mackenzie King told us on 6 June 1944 that Allied troops had begun to land on the northern coast of France. Canadian forces were taking part in the long-awaited Normandy landings which we all hoped would be the beginning of the end in the war against Germany. On that day, Parliament and Canada were as one. The lack of enthusiasm of some Quebec members for Canada's war policies momentarily evaporated as Maurice Lalonde led the House in paying tribute to France's hour of liberation, launching into "God Save the King" and "La Marseillaise." A ragtag parliamentary chorus struggled its way through both anthems. At this point, the end of the war had become more than an unachievable dream.[1]

While D-day constituted a major step toward realizing the post-war world for which we all longed, consideration of a better life after the war had begun for me long before. The fact that most of our energies had to be focused on the war did not mean that the government should not prepare for the post-war period. In my judgment, the objectives of the war and the subsequent peace were two sides of the same coin, and it was unfortunate that many Canadians did not see the connection between the kind of peacetime world we wanted to live in and the ideals for which we were fighting. The country, I contended, was not in the struggle just to preserve the imperfections of past decades but was striving to achieve a more equitable and decent society. I expected that social and economic research, such as that of Sir William Beveridge and Leonard Marsh, in Britain and

Canada would result in realistic and precise proposals for a richer and more secure life for all when peace came.[2]

It was my opinion that Canadians would not countenance a return to the economic injustices of the pre-war years. Reconstruction, therefore, meant examining proposals covering the spectrum of Canada's political, economic, and social life. The Atlantic Charter of August 1941, which reaffirmed aims that looked to the world's eventual liberation from fascist tyranny, linked the principles for battle to the objectives of a post-war world. The Charter, though little more than an exercise in exhortation, accepted an important principle: war is tolerable only when it is associated with reforms.

I had the opportunity to state my views when I became a member of the House of Commons special committee on reconstruction and re-establishment in March 1942. Its thirty-four members carried out their own analysis of what was needed. We listened to the social scientists working on the advisory committee on reconstruction headed by F. Cyril James, principal of McGill University. And yet I was aware of the limitations of handing creation of the post-war world to the social scientists. I remained mindful of E.H. Carr's comments in *Conditions of Peace* that the war "has also provided ... a moral purpose which has revived the national will ... [But] there is no guarantee that out of it will grow a more permanent purpose to create in time of peace a new world ... The crisis cannot be explained – and much less solved – in constitutional, or even in economic terms. The fundamental issue is moral."[3]   My speeches and ideas on reconstruction were not restricted to Canada. Canadians had to consider the kind of world, as well as the kind of country, in which they wanted to live. In my view, the only guarantee of true reconstruction in Canada was successful international political and economic collaboration.[4] At the International Labour Office (ILO) conference in Philadelphia in 1944, I supported the policy of helping other nations to achieve the social security desired in Canada itself. I got another chance to put my ideas forward at another ILO meeting in London, England, in January 1945. We discussed the way in which the ILO's plans, programs, and objectives could be meshed with the new international organization that would become known as the United Nations.

While I was on my trip, most of my free time was spent visiting Canadian servicemen. Seeing the effect that the struggle was having on their lives depressed me quite a bit and reaffirmed my determination to do whatever I possibly could to prevent wars like this from ever happening again. Also, I was permitted to visit the troops in France and the Netherlands, and nothing could have deterred me from visiting the graves of those who had fallen at Dieppe. The effect of the seaborne raid on occupied France on 19 August 1942 was indelibly engraved on my mind. Canadians had composed the bulk of the Allied forces, and one of the chief regiments was the Essex Scottish, recruited mainly in my home area, which had suffered terrible casualties. Very few officers returned to Britain, and close to one hundred men in the regiment died on the beach at Dieppe.[5]

On a dull and chilly February day, I was driven from Paris to pay my respects to the Essex Scottish and other Canadians in the military cemetery at Dieppe. There were wooden crosses marking some of the graves. The final tombstones had not been erected. The racial origins of the dead were so varied: Anglo-Saxon, French, and many other backgrounds. It struck me that herein lay the character of Canada, a land of people of diverse national origins. I walked among the graves, noting the names, so many of which I had known back home. I saw the grave of one young fellow whose father was violently against Canadian participation in the war. This had not stopped the young man who gave his life on the Dieppe beach. Nothing has since epitomized the concept of our nation more poignantly for me than that cemetery. Of whatever origin, these men were all Canadians.

The few months after my return on 10 February 1945 provided me with a satisfying mixture of high-flown idealism and practical politics. My European visit had given me ample grist for promoting a new post-war international order and for championing the exploits of the Canadian forces at the front. The visit confirmed for me the need for international co-operation to avoid such dreadful waste in the future. This was the message that I brought home. The job that Canada's armed forces were doing, I told the press, dwarfed to insignificance all petty domestic squabbles. The men serving overseas exemplified a unity of purpose and action that those of us at home should try to emulate. What the army could do overseas, we could and must do at home.[6]

A little less than two months later, I held a position from which to make some of this happen. On 18 April, Mackenzie King selected me to become secretary of state. Later that day, I met with Norman McLarty, the outgoing minister, and Dr. E.H. Coleman, the undersecretary. We spoke generally about the department, but even this short chat made me realize that I did not know much about its working. I would have to wait to find out more because Canada was in the middle of a campaign for a general election which the prime minister had called for 11 June.

The Liberals won the election, and I retained my seat and my place in cabinet. For my part, the election campaign was fought on the need, both nationally and locally, to keep the ball rolling in the area of social and economic reform. I argued that recent advances resulted from the fact that those who wished to see changes had gained a say in government. The best examples of this were measures such as the family allowance legislation that gave a monthly sum to the mothers of all Canadian children. I also pointed out that there was a great danger not in a CCF victory but in the election results splitting the progressive elements and allowing reactionary Toryism to take control. I reminded my audiences that "The Progressive Conservatives are progressive before an election and Conservative after one."[7]

During the election campaign, I set the wheels in motion on a project that had come to mind when I was visiting the military cemetery at Dieppe. There, pondering the status of those who had served their country and had died overseas, I realized the desirability of establishing a separate Canadian citizenship. During the war, I had mentioned the need for such legislation,[8] but my visit to Normandy had turned this thought into a crusade. Mackenzie King had demonstrated considerable enthusiasm for a citizenship act when I first mentioned it to him during the election campaign. I could see that I had struck a sympathetic chord as I talked to him about my experiences at Dieppe and my conviction that it was essential to incorporate into law a definition of what constituted a Canadian.

In my own mind, and I am certain in the prime minister's, this piece of legislation would help to complete Laurier's vision of a separate Canadian nation. At the end of the war, the best sort of nationalist feeling pressed us forward. King forthrightly referred to citizenship in a speech from Winnipeg, and I brought the subject up again shortly after the votes had been counted.

As secretary of state, I could help prepare a citizenship act that could be my own contribution to post-war reconstruction in Canada. There was no such thing in law as a Canadian citizen; the terms then most frequently in use were "Canadian national" and "British subject." For some time, ambiguities in the three acts that dealt with citizenship had caused trouble. The Naturalization Act of 1914 sought to provide for application of extraterritorial powers in order to give naturalized British subjects in Canada the right to be designated Canadians abroad as well as at home. It followed earlier acts that had existed since shortly after 1867. In 1921, C.J. Doherty, the secretary of state, introduced the Canadian Nationals Act which met Canada's commitments to the League of Nations in order to make this county eligible for election to the International Court of Justice – an admirable but very limited purpose. Furthermore, this act defined Canadian citizenship only by reference. There was an unrelated but existing definition in the Immigration Act of 1910 which set out who was permitted to enter and to live in Canada. Few countries established citizenship by immigration legislation; even the definition in this act was circumscribed and determined citizenship only for immigration purposes. The complications of the three statutes left some individuals who lived in Canada without any nationality or with a nationality in one part of the Commonwealth, but not according to Canadian law. This should have been remedied years before.

Following the general election, the prime minister reiterated his approval, and I became enmeshed in preparing the first piece of legislation that I would introduce as a minister – a citizenship act. This experience taught me a lot about the way that government works.[9] For example, my deputy, Dr. E.H. Coleman, belonged to the old school of empire and was opposed in principle to such a measure. Although he helped me as best as he could, I went elsewhere to find the support and knowledge that I needed. One of the most helpful individuals to new ministers was Arnold Heeney, the clerk of the privy council. Often, I would go to him if I were making a submission to cabinet and discuss the best means of bringing it forward.

I discovered that while he had been at Oxford, Gordon Robertson of the prime minister's office – later an outstanding clerk of the privy council and secretary to the cabinet – had studied the whole range of nationality laws in and outside the Commonwealth and Empire. I had already talked to him and found his knowledge of the greatest value in helping me develop my plan. In spite of King's offer to help me, he replied to my request for Robertson's services by expostulating, "Robertson! He won't be able to help you." This, I knew, was a device to discourage my temporary use of one of the most intelligent men on King's staff. In the end, however, the prime minister consented and Gordon was grudgingly lent to me. Thus it was that Robertson and David Mundell of the Department of Justice, as well as representatives from External Affairs, the Department of Immigration, and the Privy Council Office, set up a committee to study the question of citizenship throughout the summer of 1945.

Those people who were interested in citizenship education, as well as nationalists who wanted to remove the vestiges of the colonial past, provided public backing for my proposal. Throughout the war, the adult education movement in Canada had sponsored programs to make Canadians aware of their distinctive identity. These courses had been devised mainly for immigrants, but there was great general interest in "citizenship education," not just for those who had moved to Canada but also for the millions who had been born here. The wartime Bureau of Public Information had established the Canadian Council on Education for Citizenship and encouraged formation of the Nationalities Branch of the Department of National War Services.

Late in August 1945, T.S. Ewart, a lawyer, supported the case for action in an impassioned letter published in the *Ottawa Citizen*. He deplored the fact that Canadians lived under statutes that provided for the designation "British" on registration of births, marriages, and deaths and were described as "British subjects" on their passports. "These stupid regulations," Ewart fulminated, "are caused by the inability to recognize the change in status of our country from that of a colony ... [to an independent nation]." I agreed and was determined that there should no longer be any question of divided allegiance.

On 4 September 1945, cabinet considered draft legislation to repeal the Canadian Nationals Act and certain provisions of the Immigration Act under a new bill that would also redefine the status of Canadian citizens, British subjects in Canada, and aliens. One provision would give a married woman the same right to choose her nationality as her husband, and, when adopted, this made Canada the first nation in the Commonwealth to recognize the separate and independent status of women.[10]

After I had made my presentation to my colleagues, the prime minister remarked that an act based on these proposals would remove any apparent lack of equal status that Canada might have had when compared to other independent nations. While I agreed with King's desire, I could not support his conclusion at all: in my view it was juridically incorrect. After all, Britain and the other sovereign Commonwealth states, with the exception of Eire, had no separate citizenship. Canadians were, and under the bill would continue to be, British subjects. Citizenship, as I saw it, would give all Canadians a common status.

The cabinet accepted my report, and later that day I drafted a paragraph for inclusion in the forthcoming speech from the throne that would proclaim the government's intention to proceed with the bill. Four days after the opening of Parliament on 6 September, I gave the legislation advance publicity in my speech on the address. Symbols, I told the House, were important to a nation, and the government's decision to clarify and regularize the status of Canadian citizenship constituted a major feat. Our membership in the family of nations had been recognized; we had won our certificate of nationhood; it now remained to designate ourselves citizens of our country, not only in fact but in legal enactment.[11]

For a time in early October, it looked as though introduction of the bill might be delayed; cabinet decided on 10 October to defer placing the proposed legislation on the order paper.[12] It was obvious that most of my colleagues had other priorities. As in my very first years in Parliament, those from prairie constituencies were preoccupied with wheat sales and price stability. I, too, was so caught up with other things – especially a strike of Ford workers in Windsor – that I was not as forceful in promoting the measure as I could have been.

However, the same day that cabinet decided to defer the bill, the CCF's G.H. Castleden prodded the government by moving that the House of Commons should express its favourable view of measures to enact citizenship legislation. Nevertheless, he indicated that he would not proceed with his motion if I gave an assurance that my proposals would be put before the House. When I gave this undertaking, Castleden dropped his motion, and a week later cabinet approved the bill for introduction.

I unveiled my most important initiative as secretary of state on 22 October when I moved for leave to present Bill 20 respecting citizenship, naturalization, and the status of aliens. The purpose of the bill, I told the House, was to remove the anomalies and confusions that had surrounded the old legislation and to create a new status of Canadian citizen that would neither take away from any one who now had it nor eliminate, for persons born or naturalized in the future, the status of British subject. It was "of the utmost importance that all of us, new Canadians or old, have a consciousness of a common purpose and common interests as Canadians."[13]

To my disappointment, the bill was allowed to die on the order paper at the end of the session and had to be introduced in 1946. There were several reasons for this. The opposition reasonably requested time to digest the complicated provisions affecting Canada's relations with the Commonwealth. The whole government's legislative program had bogged down, and the House was very far behind in discussing government business. Also, Mackenzie King was in Britain at the prime ministers' conference, and I wanted him to be in the House when the bill was debated.

The bill's postponement gave me time to speak extensively on the subject and to promote it through newspaper articles. Grant Dexter of the *Winnipeg Free Press* published a series of five articles outlining the benefits of the legislation and generally educated the public about its scope and intent. "The old order," wrote Dexter, "has been allowed to drag along until the present time."[14]

I hoped that this support and my determination would prevent the citizenship act from suffering the same fate that befell efforts to decide on a new Canadian flag to replace the Union Jack. The announcement in the 1945 speech from the throne that the government wished to pursue the issue had opened the floodgates. The country had divided so emphatically over this issue that the prime minister referred the flag question to a joint committee of the Senate and of the House of Commons for recommendation. We all knew that the question had become so controversial that the real task of the joint committee was to allow the situation to cool down. Privately, I recognized that there was little chance of success is selecting a Canadian flag this time around. Little did I foresee that it would be two decades before the debate would be over – and that it would be conducted in almost as acrimonious a manner as in 1945.

I still felt very strongly that promotion of a new flag and the citizenship legislation were not expressions of a narrow nationalism but were understandable demonstrations of pride in Canada and its growing autonomy. Nationalism as an expression of communal bonds I did not feel was a danger, but I did fear the exaggeration of that consciousness. The recent memory of Nazism was a great corrective to chauvinism. In Canada, however, it was my belief that there had been too little, and not too much, national pride. By working to strengthen it further, we were not weakening our ties with the Commonwealth or with Britain. In fact, compared to the pre-war years, Canada, I thought, was becoming more outward-looking and would be better fitted to play its full part in the world if Canadians had a sense of community expressed by appropriate symbols.

The parliamentary session that opened in mid-March 1946 provided an opportunity to expand upon the importance of citizenship as an expression of the Canadian ideal for which Laurier had striven. Using this theme in moving second reading of the citizenship bill, reintroduced early in the session, I told the House of Commons that the measure demonstrated the maturing of Canada as a nation. In two world wars, we had borne our full and serious responsibility; our fighting men had brought honour to their country. For the unity of the country and for the fulfilment of its potential, it was of the utmost importance that Canada should give its people the right to designate themselves Canadian citizens in law as well as in fact. Previous efforts had not succeeded – notably, the citizenship bill introduced in 1931 by C.H. Cahan, the secretary of state in R.B.

Bennett's government. I was determined to rectify that failure. It was not to our credit that Canadians could not address one another with the full sanction of the law as citizens of our country.

The citizenship act would eliminate difficult personal situations where the wife of a Canadian citizen or a person born out of Canada whose father was a national at the time of birth had trouble entering the country. There was also the problem of the prohibited immigrant to Canada – a person who could not enter Canada under the Immigration Act yet was entitled to a Canadian passport. It would remove the vagueness and, in some instances, the lack of a legal basis for determining nationality. The proposed act would get rid of difficulties encountered by External Affairs arising out of the need for diplomatic protection for Canadians abroad.

One of the bill's major aims was to provide for "a more effective and impressive ceremony of admission into the Canadian family." Our citizens, I reminded the House, were made up not only of those who were familiar with British institutions but also of those who had arrived from all over the world. An appropriate ceremony would make the adoption of citizenship more than an ordinary administrative procedure.

The proposed act had seven sections. The first dealt with those who were born in Canada, on Canadian ships, or to Canadian parents domiciled abroad; it defined them as Canadian citizens by right of birth. The second section concerned those who were not born Canadian but who acquired citizenship at a later date; it provided that people who had been naturalized in Canada, non-Canadian British subjects who had lived in Canada for five years or more, and non-Canadian women who had married citizens and come to live in Canada would become citizens forthwith. It also set out the qualifications for those who would acquire citizenship in the future under conditions that resembled those in the Naturalization Act, except that non-nationals who served abroad in the armed forces would require only one year of residence in the country, instead of five. Those who wanted citizenship would have to file a declaration of intention not less than one year, and not more than five years, before naturalization. The bill also substituted twenty years of residence for a knowledge of English or French (this would allow many long-time residents, from eastern Europe, for example, to gain citizenship). British subjects, who hitherto had been able to become Canadian citizens simply after five years' residence, would still have that privilege but would have to take out papers to prove it. (This was a change more in procedure than in substance, since non-Canadian British subjects had no right of entry under the old act until they had been domiciled in Canada for five years). Married women would have the right to choose their own citizenship.

The rest of the bill dealt with various other issues, such as loss of citizenship, that might occur after acquisition of a foreign nationality. Canadian citizens would retain their status as British subjects. Under the new act, those who were British subjects in other parts of the Commonwealth would be recognized as British subjects in Canada. The act, in short, was designed to guarantee that no one would lose any rights or status that he or she already possessed.

I pointed out in summary that "for a young nation, Canada has done great things and Canadians have derived a growing national pride from what Canada has accomplished. We feel that we can afford to hold our heads high and be proud of the fact that we are Canadians." If there was

one thing from which we in Canada have suffered to the detriment of this magnificent country, it is from a feeling of divisiveness – lack of that fervent and urgent unity that can make a people work together as a great community with conviction that the welfare of all is the goal of their effort. It is not good enough to be a good "bluenose" or a good Ontarian or a good Albertan. Sectional differences and sectional interests must be overcome if we are to do our best for Canada. The only way this can be done is through encouragement of a feeling of legitimate Canadianism ...

Citizenship means more than the right to vote; more than the right to hold and transfer property; more than the right to move freely under the protection of the state; citizenship is the right to full partnership in the fortunes and in the future of the nation.[15]

John Diefenbaker, the first speaker for the Conservative party, agreed with what I had said, particularly with my claim that the bill symbolized our aspirations as a nation. He added that it had achieved a lifelong dream of his. However, he proposed that a citizenship act should be followed by a bill of rights. Diefenbaker criticized the section requiring a British subject from a Commonwealth country to file a notice of intention with the citizenship court in the same way as others before becoming a citizen. Would, he asked, this provision not strike at the unity of British citizenship? I said that it would not.

The House divided on the bill much as I had expected. A substantial number of members worried that Commonwealth relationships would deteriorate in the wake of the act. Diefenbaker's unjustified objection that it would split the Commonwealth was taken even further by his colleagues such as Tommy Church, an old-style imperialist, who took a determined stand against it. Liguori Lacombe, MP for Laval-Deux-Montagnes, expressed the French nationalist position that urged the elimination of Canadians' status as British subjects in order to eradicate all evidence of inferiority.

The reaction of these two extremes proved beyond a doubt that the bill was a careful balance of opinion expressed in terms that accommodated the general wish for a separate Canadian citizenship. For my part, I would have preferred to leave out the section of the bill that stated that Canadians remained British subjects – it left Canada with a mark of inferiority.[16]

However, I recognized that if Canadians' status as British subjects had been done away with in my bill, it would not have passed. The compromise was a wise one and ensured passage of a measure that could not, and did not, seek to placate the extremists.

We thrashed out this compromise in cabinet because my colleagues themselves were of two minds about including the provision regarding British subjects. Finally, it was left for Mackenzie King and me to decide. The prime minister agreed with my political instincts when I said that if we omitted mention of the question of British subjects entirely, and just created Canadian citizenship, we would not avoid the issue. Someone, I argued, would be bound to ask about the legislation's effect on Canadians' status as British subjects. An offhand response to this question, saying that the bill left us British subjects by default, would not satisfy anyone. We could, I thought, take the wind out of the Tories' sails by including a bold statement in the bill itself. And this is what we did.

The *Globe and Mail* still complained that it was unreasonable to force a British subject to live in Canada for five years before taking out citizenship. I had already bowed to the opposition and removed the bill's provision that, like everyone else, British subjects had to be examined before a citizenship court. Instead, they were allowed to apply to the secretary of state for a certificate after fulfilling their residence requirement. Almost without exception, French-language newspapers supported the bill and severely castigated the Tories' carping attitude. My compromise, however, gave me the general support of Conservative papers such as the *Globe and Mail*.[17] There was, I realized, little to be done about the hidebound opposition from true-blue imperialists who objected to classing "Britons" with "Slavs" and who railed against the bill as another example of French Canada's forcing its will on the rest of the country.[18] Equally adamant, *Le Devoir* claimed that "la double allégeance que ça soit envers le Canada et l'Empire ... c'est la négation même de la citoyenneté canadienne et encore plus du patriotisme canadien."[19]

During the debate on second reading, John Diefenbaker re-opened the question of a bill of rights and offered an amendment to the effect that a certificate of citizenship should be deemed to include certain rights (freedom of religion, freedom of speech, and the right to peaceable assembly; no suspension of habeas corpus except by Parliament; and no compulsion to give evidence before any tribunal in the absence of counsel or other safeguards). This amendment, I argued, was unacceptable, since already the law of the land included these rights in the common law, the Magna Carta, and the legal system. No act of one Parliament could limit the freedom of action of its successors, and rights could be infringed pursuant to the authority of any Parliament. Therefore, the only means of providing greater guarantees than currently existed would be to enact an organic law that could not be changed by the Canadian Parliament; but at the time, this type of law did not exist in the British system of government. In the American constitution, there is a declaration of rights that arose as the testament of revolution, but a bill of rights for Canadians must differ widely in concept and implementation. The British system, as Tennyson said, was that for "A land of settled government, / A land of just and old renown, / Where freedom slowly broadens down / From precedent to precedent." A fundamental constitutional departure, I contended, should not be taken in a section of an act that prescribed conditions for the issuance of citizenship certificates; it should be, if anywhere, in a bill by itself. Diefenbaker's argument, however, gained considerable public support. The *Globe and Mail* claimed that "parliament has permitted, without any serious protests, the steady infringement of the rights which belong to all Canadians."[20]

On 14 May, when this historic bill was reported back to the House from the committee of the whole, I thanked the members for their contributions and co-operation. The CCF leader, M.J. Coldwell, spoke appreciatively of my handling of a difficult measure. I also thanked Mackenzie King for the assistance of Gordon Robertson, who had continued as my chief assistant during the bill's passage through the House. It became an act by royal assent on 27 June and was proclaimed by the governor general on 1 July 1946.

Despite the new ground broken for the Commonwealth countries by the Canadian Citizenship Act, those who believed that the act conferred little benefit reacted adversely. Some argued that my French-Canadian outlook had provoked me into introducing a bill that would divide Canada completely from Britain. This argument even made its way into New Zealand's Parliament, where the attorney general, H.R.G. Mason, concluded that the act was an indication of a spirit of separateness by the French-speaking Canadian population that could not be controlled. He and others who felt this way totally misinterpreted my motives.

With great pride, I took part in the ceremonies in the august chambers of the Supreme Court of Canada to mark the new status of Canadians. These took place during Citizenship Week on the night of 3 January 1947, two days after the new act had come into force. Under the solemn eyes of the chief justice and his brother judges, resplendent in their ermine-trimmed robes, people from various parts of Canada received the first citizenship certificates. After my opening remarks about the significance of the act as a symbol of the achievement of nationhood, Prime Minister Mackenzie King received the very first certificate. It pleased him greatly when the audience applauded as he began, "I speak as a citizen of Canada."[21] Wasyl Elnyiak, one of the first Ukrainians to farm in western Canada, received his certificate immediately after the prime minister. Elnyiak was a very old man and came to the ceremony only after a great deal of arm-twisting. We had discovered him after a long search through the immigration department's records. Only once during the ceremony did the applause equal that given to the prime minister. The audience was acknowledging Mrs. Stanley Mynarski of Winnipeg who went forward with the Victoria Cross of her son pinned to her dress. King stood up and bowed to her as she passed near his chair. The presence of the recipients of the certificates brought home the symbolism of the ceremony to those in the room, as well as to those listening in on the national radio broadcast of the proceedings.

Another major ceremony took place in the large rotunda of Montreal's Hôtel de Ville on 8 January 1947. Mayor Camilien Houde had gone out of his way to co-operate, and what he organized was impressive. Over a thousand citizens assembled to witness the chief justice of the Quebec Superior Court present certificates to the mayor and to others who represented the City of Montreal and the Province of Quebec. My speech tried to answer those who did not like the provision that Canadians would remain British subjects, and I spoke positively about national pride while deprecating fanatical racism and nationalism.

Two days later, I received my own certificate of citizenship from Judge Albert Gordon at a gathering in Patterson Collegiate in Windsor. I recalled in my remarks that during my visit to the cemetery at Dieppe, I had formulated a desire to recognize the common sacrifice of those who lay there. The lads from the Essex Scottish who rest in the cemetery at Dieppe and the tens of thousands of others in military cemeteries on several continents symbolize the contribution of all Canadians, and this legislation, which affirms our common national condition, was enacted to honour their memory.

NOTES

1 House of Commons, *Debates*, 6 June 1944, p. 3564.
2 For an example of one of my early speeches on reconstruction see Paul Martin, "War Aims and Peace Aims," *Canadian Spokesman* (April 1941) 14–17.
3 House of Commons, *Debates*, 24 March 1942, p. 1573. The committee was established on a motion of Ian Mackenzie. Its chair was J.G. Turgeon, member for Cariboo. E.H. Carr, *Conditions of Peace* (London: Macmillan, 1942), 124–5.
4 House of Commons, *Debates*, 20 June 1944, pp. 4010ff.
5 Thirty-two officers and 521 other ranks embarked from England, and five officers and forty-nine other ranks returned. The rest either died or were non-fatal casualties who spent the rest of the war in prisoner-of-war camps. See C.P. Stacey, *Official History of the Canadian Army in the Second World War*, vol. I, *Six Years of War: The Army in Canada, Britain and the Pacific* (Ottawa: Queen's Printer, 1966), 389.
6 *Windsor Daily Star*, 19 and 20 Feb. 1945.
7 Ibid., 2 June 1945.
8 On 4 May 1942, I had told the committee on the defence of Canada regulations that Canada's naturalization laws were in a deplorable state.
9 Because of the range of its activities, the department was a good place to learn. At that time, the secretary of state held responsibility for the Civil Service Commission, the Custodian of Enemy Property, and the Registrar of Bankruptcy. The minister was not the Civil Service Commission's administrative chief but its channel for reporting to cabinet and to Parliament. The King's Printer and the Public Archives reported to the secretary of state, as did the branch that looked after incorporation of companies under federal charter. In addition to this, at the end of the war, the department acquired the Naturalization Branch of the Department of National War Services.
10 Cabinet conclusions, 5 April 1945, King Papers (J4 series, vol. 419), National Archives of Canada.
11 House of Commons, *Debates*, 10 Sept. 1945, pp. 59–64.
12 Cabinet conclusions, 10 Oct. 1945, King Papers (J4 series, vol. 419).
13 House of Commons, *Debates*, 22 oct. 1945, pp. 1335–7.
14 *Winnipeg Free Press*, 22–23 and 25–27 March 1946.
15 House of Commons, *Debates*, 20 March 1946, p. 131, for introduction of the bill for first reading. The motion for second reading was made on 2 April (ibid., pp. 502–17), and the House went into com-

mittee to study the bill on 29 April (ibid., pp. 1015–39; 2 May,
pp. 1114–64; and 14 May, pp. 1499–1509). The motion for third
reading was introduced on 15–16 May (ibid., pp. 1575–91).

16 In subsequent legislation, this was corrected when the status "British subjects" was removed from the act.
17 *Globe and Mail*, 5 April 1946.
18 *Toronto Telegram*, 6 April 1946.
19 *Le Devoir*, 7 Dec. 1945.
20 *Globe and Mail*, 10 May 1946. The *Winnipeg Free Press*, 20 May 1946,
supported this argument.
21 J.W. Pickersgill and D.F. Forster, *The Mackenzie King Record*, vol. IV,
1947–1948 (Toronto: University of Toronto Press, 1970), 5–6. The
other recipients were Giuseppe Agostini, a conductor for the CBC; Kjeld
Beichman, a Danish-born potter from New Brunswick; Maurice
Labrosse of Ottawa and his Aberdeenshire bride; Yousuf Karsh, the
famous photographer; Mrs. R.P. Steeves of Vancouver; Gerhard
Ens of Rosthern, Saskatchewan; and Andrew B. MacRae, a descendant
of one of the oldest families in Prince Edward Island.

PETER NEARY

Ebb and Flow: Citizenship in Newfoundland, 1929–1949

Citizenship implies costs and benefits, duties and obligations, as well as rights and advantages. During the 1930s, for an alarmingly high proportion of the people of Newfoundland the costs of citizenship were high and the benefits remarkably few. In truth, during that tumultuous decade, the value of citizenship was diminished shockingly as the Depression undermined both private and public life. The clear evidence of this devaluation was suspension of elected self-government in 1934 in favour of government by a commission appointed by the United Kingdom. In a famous phrase, the Canadian historian A.R.M. Lower characterized the development of Canada as a progress from "colony to nation."[1] Self-government lay at the heart of the British imperial tradition, and the emergence first of dominion status and then of a commonwealth of co-operating nations under one crown was the finest expression of the constitutional and political genius of the English-speaking people. In the 1930s this pattern was broken in Newfoundland, as it took a step away from the road onward and upward that Lower discerned in Canada's history. The suspension of self-government forced on Newfoundland was a humiliation not found in the history of any other present-day Canadian provincial jurisdiction.

How and why did such an unprecedented event occur? The answer is to be found in a unique combination of political, social, economic, and financial circumstances. In 1921 – more than four centuries after its rediscovery by Europeans in the fifteenth century – Newfoundland (including Labrador) had a population of only 263,000. This population, moreover, was widely scattered, and, although a railway had been completed across the island of Newfoundland in 1897, communication to many parts of the country was difficult. In 1927 the territory administered from St John's was greatly enlarged when the Judicial Committee of the Privy Council fixed the boundary between Newfoundland and Canada in Labrador and so gave the former a domain on the mainland of North America of some 292, 218 km². This decision was later described by one of R.B. Bennett's Quebec correspondents as akin to a defeat on a battlefield, and the 1927 decision still rankles in Quebec, where territorial and constitutional questions are inevitably intertwined.

Considering its small population, Newfoundland enjoyed in the 1920s an exalted constitutional status. The country had sent a regiment overseas in the Great War and had representation in the British Empire delegation at the Paris peace conference. Newfoundland was not a member of the League of Nations, but its premiers attended imperial conferences and the country was covered by the Balfour Declaration of 1926 and by the Statute of Westminster of 1931. Newfoundland called itself and was in fact a dominion, albeit a less assertive and self-conscious one than Canada. As befitted its status, Newfoundland had its own high commissioner in the United Kingdom.

All of this was at variance with a remarkably vulnerable economy. Newfoundland was a society of European settlement which had been built on the production and sale of dried salt cod, one of the great foods of history, and in the 1920s a large proportion of the labour force was still engaged in this activity. In 1869 Newfoundlanders had rejected Confederation with Canada, and in the 1890s another attempt at union also failed. In its fishing economy Newfoundland looked away from the North American continent to markets in the Mediterranean, Caribbean, and South America, areas with warm climates where saltfish was a prized commodity before the advent of refrigeration. Accordingly, in the nineteenth century an economic basis for union with Canada did not exist.

Nevertheless it was realized in Newfoundland from the 1860s onward that the country was dangerously dependent on one product and that economic diversification was a compelling necessity. This thinking led to the building of the Newfoundland railway, designed to open up the country to development. In 1895 an important iron-mining venture began at Bell Island in Conception Bay to meet the needs of the blast furnaces of Cape Breton, and in 1905 and 1923, respectively, the foundations were laid for pulp and paper operations at Grand Falls and Corner Brook. By the 1920s, therefore, Newfoundland had a more diverse economy than ever before, but its three main industries – fishing, forestry and mining – were all dependent on exports and so highly sensitive to shifts in demand and price in the international marketplace.

Individually, Newfoundlanders had a notable ability to survive, but collectively they had little control over their economic destiny. Added to this was something else. Like the governments of the Dominion of Canada and of the Canadian provinces, the government of Newfoundland had over the years built up a public debt. The two biggest causes of this debt were borrowing to pay for the construction and operation of the Newfoundland railway and to pay the heavy cost of participation in the Great War, which had also taken a heavy toll in human life. Interest payments to Newfoundland's creditors were due in the middle and at the end of each calendar year. They were made from revenues that still came mainly from customs receipts. Income tax had been introduced in 1918, but it eventually ran into stiff resistance from those who could afford to pay it, and it was abolished in 1925, only to be restored in 1929.

Newfoundland's creditors received their interest payments through the Bank of Montreal, the country's banker. The bank's role in the country was revealing. Thus, even though Newfoundland had not joined Canada, its own financial institutions had gone the way of many of those of the Maritime provinces within Confederation – that is to say, they had been supplanted by the bigger and stronger financial institutions of central Canada. In 1895 the last two commercial banks in St John's failed, and Canadian banks then established themselves in the country, and in the 1920s only a small government-owned savings bank was left in local hands.

Against this background, Newfoundland's economic vulnerability can be simply explained. Its ability to make interest payments, which were fixed by contract, depended mainly on revenues from customs receipts, and these in turn depended on trade. In an emergency, which could obviously develop quickly, Newfoundland had no automatic source of assistance. Unlike a Canadian province, its risks were not spread over a larger economy and population. If a province got into trouble, it could look to Ottawa, which, while it could be parsimonious and mean-spirited, could not disown all responsibility for the affected population. Newfoundland, by contrast, could depend only on something much more nebulous, namely, membership in the British Empire. This link Richard Squires, premier from 1928 to 1932, once described as "that thin red cord of sentiment and of blood."

The economic and financial crisis for which Newfoundland was ripe manifested itself with shocking suddenness after the Wall Street crash of October 1929. The Newfoundland government was quickly brought to the rawest of Depression dilemmas: should it honour in every detail its contracts with its bondholders, or should it give priority to meeting the needs of the growing army of the poor? At the bottom of the Depression, about one-third of the Newfoundland people depended on relief, but in 1932–33 fully 63.2 per cent of the government's meagre revenue went to making interest payments.

As the crisis unfolded after 1929, the Squires government turned to a series of increasingly desperate expedients. Initially, it was able to borrow money from a syndicate of the Canadian banks operating in the country, led by the Bank of Montreal. But the banks soon came to regret their involvement. In 1932 Newfoundland floated a bond issue, the "Prosperity Loan," but it was sold with great difficulty, and it became clear that this particular well had now also run dry. Newfoundland also tried to sell Labrador to Canada for $110 million, an amount that would liquidate its debt, but this offer was not taken up by Ottawa, which was beset by massive financial and economic problems of its own. In the end, Newfoundland could keep up payments only with help from the British and Canadian governments. In return, Newfoundland passed into a form of receivership and had its finances supervised by an official sent out by the British Treasury.

In June 1932, just under three months after a mob had ransacked the Colonial Building, the seat of the Newfoundland legislature, the government of the country changed hands. The new premier was Frederick Alderdice, a businessman, an ardent imperialist, and a social and economic conservative. Alderdice personified orthodoxy, but so desperate was the situation facing the country that even he contemplated a radical act. This was to reschedule unilaterally Newfoundland's interest payments. The country's financial obligations would not be repudiated, but creditors would have to accept that they could no longer enjoy the luxury of certain and fixed payments in a world in which so much else had gone wrong. Alderdice's approach is today the conventional one of some developing countries for dealing with their huge debts, but in the 1930s the proposal was heretical. London came down hard on him: no British country could break its contracts, and if Newfoundland were to do so, it would never be able to borrow again.

Against this background and with Newfoundland still careening from one six-month payment to the next, the British, at the end of 1932, made a new condition in return for continued support. This was that St John's agree to appointment of a royal commission "to examine into the future of Newfoundland and in particular to report on the financial situation and prospects therein."[2] The commission would be appointed by London, but the United Kingdom, Canada, and Newfoundland would each nominate one member.

The Alderdice government agreed to this, and the royal commission, chaired by Lord Amulree, a Scot, held its first session in St John's on 16 March 1934. British policy at this stage was to keep Newfoundland afloat but to do so in co-operation with Canada. Canadian participation was important to the British for two reasons. One was to share the cost. The other was to keep alive the prospect of Newfoundland joining Confederation, an old British objective. But as the Amulree commission went about its business, this policy gradually unravelled. In May, E.N. Rhodes, the Canadian minister of finance and a Nova Scotian, told Amulree that he was against Confederation because Newfoundlanders "would really in effect become another Ireland – not in the racial sense, but a nuisance and always grumbling and wanting something." Labrador, he added, was "not worth possessing."[3]

Then, in the summer of 1933, Canada refused to help with Newfoundland's mid-year interest payment. In effect Canada abandoned Newfoundland and the British were left to carry on alone. How they were willing to do so was spelled out in the report of the Amulree commission. The United Kingdom would guarantee Newfoundland's debt and provide an annual grant-in-aid to balance the country's budget, but Newfoundland in return would have to agree to suspension of self-government. Instead there would be administration by a commission of government appointed by the United Kingdom. This would consist of the governor and six commissioners, three drawn from Newfoundland and three from the United Kingdom. This was strong medicine, but it was quickly swallowed by the Newfoundland legislature. The plan was then embodied in an act of the British Parliament, and the commission of government was inaugurated in St John's on 16 February 1934.

The commission of government did not represent the complete denial of democracy because it was accountable to the Parliament of the United Kingdom through the Dominions Office. It was, however, a body that Newfoundlanders had no part in electing. Henceforth they were denied a direct voice in their own affairs, and the value of their citizenship was thereby debased. Not until they had become Canadians would Newfoundlanders again vote in a general election for a legislature. Such was the political and constitutional cost of the economic and financial collapse that had overtaken them.

Given the place of responsible government and of the "colony to nation" tradition in the British empire, how was such an astonishing reversal in constitutional practice justified? The answer is to be found in the report of the Amulree commission. This was mainly the work

of the commission's secretary, P.A. Clutterbuck of the Dominions
Office, a mandarin's mandarin and a dreamer of high Tory dreams.
The report documented the impact of the Depression on Newfoundland's trade and finances. This was difficult to deny. But it
went on to argue that the root cause of the malaise was not the
worldwide economic catastrophe but the dissipation of resources
and an imprudent administration at home. In an analysis that reflected a widespread suspicion in the 1930s that party politics and
economic efficiency were incompatible, the report advanced the
view that Newfoundland had spent wildly and foolishly and that its
politicians had bribed the people of the country with their own
money. It was their evil machinations that lay at the heart of the crisis that had devastated the country.

Though he was not named in the report, the villain of the piece
was clearly Richard Squires. What Newfoundland needed to coun-
teract so much wrongdoing was "a rest from politics"[4] and administration that was pure and principled – the antithesis of the
self-serving approach of the party man. This is what commission of
government would provide. In time, when the poison had been removed from the system and the evil deeds of the past corrected, a re-
deemed Newfoundland could recover self-government. According
to the act of the British Parliament establishing the commission, this
would be done "on request" of the people and when the country was
"self-supporting" again.[5] This was a vague commitment which, as
time would show, left the initiative very much in British hands.

Empires, it has been said, are sentimental at the periphery and cal-
culating at the centre. Newfoundland in the 1930s was a case in
point. Alderdice welcomed the proposal as exemplifying the best of
the British empire; the mother country was coming to the rescue of
a daughter dominion in distress. He did not dwell on the fine print
of the change in constitutional status, but in the Dominions Office in
London things were very different. There close attention was given
to every detail and to every contingency, so as to secure the British
position. This would have important long-term consequences.

The two opposition members of the Newfoundland legislature,
Gordon Bradley and Roland Starkes, tried to have the proposal
modified so as to give Newfoundlanders some direct say in their own
affairs. They did not, however, oppose commission government as
such; it had strong backing from local businesses and was endorsed
by a variety of community groups, including the powerful Great
War Veterans' Association. Whatever opposition there was did not
manifest itself in serious organized protest, and once the changeover

was made, the British, except perhaps in the late 1930s, never felt insecure in their hold on Newfoundland.

For Newfoundland's political life the consequences of the events of 1933–34 were profound. Having the vote in a democracy is a fundamental right. Only in St John's did Newfoundlanders now cast ballots, and there only for the city council, which the commission of government so disliked that it would cheerfully have abolished it but for the possibility of adverse public reaction over the removal of the last vestige of democracy. But there was something else beyond the right to vote. The analysis by the Amulree commission had made politicans into pariahs, and this characterization lingered long after the 1930s. Government by commission not only ended elections but also smashed the party system and therefore left the people of the country without popular leaders and a principal means to mobilize opinion for political action. Politicians are often excoriated, but they are indispensable to democracy, and they reflect in their actions the societies that produce them. In 1934 Newfoundlanders lost not only their legislature but also much of the apparatus of democratic politics, which was said to be the cancer that had eaten away their substance and laid their country to waste. With this, citizenship reached a low ebb: after 1934, as a people, Newfoundlanders could not vote, could not run for office, and had no electoral means to call their government to account.

A sizeable part of the population, moreover, was and remained miserably poor. Early in the life of the commission, the English artist Rhoda Dawson came to Newfoundland to teach school and resume work for the industrial department of the medical mission that Sir Wilfred Grenfell had established with headquarters at St Anthony. Her Newfoundland work includes a cartoon, depicting row by row the social structure of Newfoundland. At the apex are the governor and his lady. In the next row are lawyers, accountants, and other professionals. The next level features clergy and academics, the latter no doubt from Memorial University College. Below them are the yeomanry – the small proprietor fishers, loggers, and miners. Next down, confined in a dark tunnel, are the people of relief, and below them, in a cave and encumbered with balls and chains, are the members of the commission of government. The depiction is remarkably insightful and neatly captures the social situation facing the commission.

The British commissioners who arrived in 1934 were shocked and dismayed that things could be so bad. What they thought can be followed through the family correspondence of Sir John and Lady Hope Simpson, a rich source for understanding the period. Sir John was the first commissioner for natural resources in the new government, and both he and his wife, Quita, were trenchant observers. Their letters mix extended description with blunt opinion. Soon after they arrived in St John's, Lady Hope Simpson wrote that the city was nothing more than "a dirty foul-smelling slum."[6] The Hope Simpsons were appalled by the evidences of greed and maladministration. "The island," Quita wrote, "seems to be like a farm that has been ruined & left ... The bad farmer impoverishes his land – the good farmer enriches it. The merchants here have put nothing they could help back into the island: they have taken their fortunes abroad – spent their money in England. Can you blame them? ... Who would invest their money in an island where government was so corrupt! So the island is reaping the harvest that the merchants have sown. The faith of the people in the English Commissioners is pathetic."[7] In the same vein, Sir John wrote that "all the assets of the country, the forests and the water powers and the mineral areas" had "been given away with both hands" and were now "largely held by speculators waiting to sell them to financiers."[8] Newfoundland was "the Congo over again."[9]

The Hope Simpsons were also stunned by the low relief payments in effect but could see no easy way out. The distinction between relief and wages had to be maintained, and those on relief had to be kept "less eligible" for society's benefits than those who were still working. Otherwise pauperization would only spread further. However, the government could not itself afford to provide work for the unemployed. The conundrum of relief and work was summarized by Lady Hope Simpson in a 1934 letter:

The trouble is ... that the dole is utterly insufficient – $1.50 a month for a man, 60 cents for a child! ... It is terrible. Daddy [Sir John] has to decide whether to tell the British Government that we must have additional money for a dole that will support life until the country can get onto its legs again. It has to be a case of this must be done or I go. The dole is bad, we know – it is abused we know. But how can you supervise the administration of the dole on an island like this with ⅓ of the population on the dole & that population – a population equal to about the population of Leicester – scattered in tiny settlements round 6000 miles of coast – settlements that are inaccessible except by boat & quite inaccessible except in calm weather & seldom accessible at all as there are so few boats. It is a fearful problem ... Everyone says that the dole is the ruin of men: but what can you do? You can't let them starve when there is no work to give them. For work you could not pay them less than $20 a month & the British Gov[ernment] would not stand for the amount needed for that. Living is so much dearer here than in England. The problems here are terrible.[10]

In the spring of 1936, the Hope Simpsons toured part of the south coast of the island and saw one of the hardest-hit parts of the country. In Grey River, Sir John made these notes: "A nightmare settlement. Clothing appalling. Saw girl in school in cotton nightshirt & bare legs. Houses delapidated. Everyone short of trawls and nets but all have dories ... No potato seed. Very little work done in gardens. People not fit to work. About 30 families. 23 children in the school. Lots of wood, but lethargy prevents any repairs."[11] Lady Hope Simpson's most vivid memory of the place was of "a girl child of about six with straight fair hair & delicate features standing on the edge of a wharf seeing us off ... – bare legged & bare footed in a grimy white nightgown, snow on the hill side behind her."[12] "I wanted to go back," she wrote, "& wrap her in my coat & carry her into her house." At Grey River and a good many other communities, survival was the first priority in 1935, and where keeping body and soul together is uppermost, citizenship is an empty shell.

The Hope Simpsons took the position that the root problem of Newfoundland was morale. Quita wrote in April 1934:

I think the mass of people are so accustomed to having everything done for them that they rather take for granted that the mother country should shoulder the difficulties the Newfoundlanders have created for themselves ... The morale of the people has been undermined by all the conditions of their lives – the low standard of living – the starvation food, really – the isolation of the little outports with lack of interests & incentives – I think the character of the people is going to be the greatest problem here. What is the good of putting things right if, as soon as the Commission's work is done, the people slip back into their old ways. It is a reformation that is needed – a moving of the spirit – the in pouring of new waters of life.[13]

In August 1934, after visiting Glenwood in central Newfoundland, Sir John wrote that "the energy and morale" had been "sapped out" of many dole recipients.[14] "There are scarcely any gardens," he reported, "the reason being that should any energetic people run a garden, the loafers steal all the produce! That is pretty awful, and it shows how the people have degenerated. Truly, our problem is largely a morale problem." The most important task facing the com-

mission was "the re-establishment of public morality and private morale."[15] The "next generation" was the hope of Newfoundland, and
the key to its improvement was "a better system of education."[16]

How did the commission of government attempt to cope with such
adversity? It sought reform in a number of directions but always, of
course, with an eye to keeping the grant-in-aid within bounds that
the Treasury in London would tolerate. Relief was marginally improved, a cottage hospital system was started, and a force, the Newfoundland Rangers, was formed to give the government a better link
with the rural population. In education, the government attempted
to reform the existing denominational system, but with limited success. To get people back to work and to revive the economy, the
commission first favoured a program of land settlement, a familiar
1930s panacea, but this met many obstacles and produced only small
gains. In 1936 the government adopted a long-term plan of reconstruction which played down resettling people in favour of building
on existing strengths.

One of the big surprises in the history of the commission is the extent to which it crossed local businessmen, who had been all for the
suspension of self-government. Hope Simpson believed that the
local business community had antediluvian attitudes and blocked
progress. He did not hesitate to confront this issue, and after attending one memorable dinner party in St John's he wrote as follows:

The merchants are incorrigible. On Monday we dined with the Charles Har-
veys. They are fish merchants and at the table were Sir Edgar Bowring
(millionnaire) also interested in fish and Herbert Outerbridge – fish merchant. Then there was my colleague [Frederick] Alderdice [now commissioner for home affairs and education] & myself. I raised the question of the
fisherman & his woes. All four fell upon me. "He is used to it. He has never
had anything better. After all he is happy, he can eat blueberries and gets his
firewood free, and can catch rabbits in the winter." And Alderdice warned
me that the u.k. Commissioners w[oul]d. be unwise to encourage the people
to demand any higher standard of comfort. And all of those men are living
in luxury & driving motor cars, because the fisherman is starving & has no
decent clothes. "Starving" is an exaggeration, but the standard of life is
lower than anything you can find in Europe. It makes you realize how the
love of money is the root of evil.[17]

Unfortunately for the commission, its plans for development ran up
against the major recession that hit the North American economy in

the late 1930s. The result was more adversity, so much so that in May 1939 the population on relief was larger than it had been in May 1934. In these straightened circumstances the best defence that P.A. Clutterbuck could make for the commission in an internal British government memorandum was that things would have been worse if it had not been there. This, however, belied the rhetoric of 1934. So too did a discussion in the Dominions Office in April 1939 about relief administration in Newfoundland. The "dole rations," the representatives of the commission of government present reported, provided "a bare subsistence" for those dependent on them. People on the dole and without other resources "could manage to keep going without impairment to their health, provided they did not undertake any hard work or expose themselves to severe winter conditions."[18] Clearly, if citizenship had been devalued in Newfoundland in 1934, it had not appreciated very much five years later.

The coming of war in September 1939 changed all this by producing a stunning reversal in Newfoundland's economic fortunes. Because of its constitutional relationship with the United Kingdom, Newfoundland, unlike Canada, was automatically at war when the British entered the conflict. At first the commission of government thought that the costs of war would require retrenchment in other areas, but the country was soon enjoying unprecedented prosperity and the government unheard-of revenues. By 1942, unemployment had been wiped out, grants-in-aid were a thing of the past, and the country was making interest-free loans in Canadian dollars to the now hard-pressed British. The source of this economic deliverance was to be found in the strategic position that Newfoundland occupied in the North Atlantic, given the imperatives of air and submarine warfare.

Canada quickly discovered that it could defend its territory only by ensuring the defence of Newfoundland. Conversely, the United Kingdom soon had to acknowledge that it did not have the means to defend vital installations in Newfoundland, and so, at the urging of the commission of government, Canada was asked to do the job for the duration of the war. Canadian troops first arrived to defend the air bases at Botwood and Gander, but in time Canada built air bases at Torbay and Goose Bay and, on behalf of the Admiralty, operated a big naval base in St John's.

The Americans were not far behind, and they were drawn to Newfoundland for the same reasons of continental defence that brought Canadians there. In September 1940 the British agreed to give the United States, for ninety-nine years, base sites in a number of their transatlantic territories in return for fifty used destroyers. Base sites were promised the United States in Newfoundland "freely and without consideration."[19] The Americans chose sites at St John's, on the Argentia Peninsula, and at Stephenville. The terms of their tenure were spelled out in the Anglo-American leased bases agreement of 27 March 1941, which made the areas in question de facto extensions of the American homeland. By the time this agreement was signed, American contractors were already at work in Newfoundland and money was flowing there as only the United States military knew how to make it flow.

Meanwhile, Newfoundlanders had been enlisting in sizeable numbers in the armed forces of the United Kingdom, in a forestry unit recruited by the commission of government at British request, and in a home defence force. Newfoundlanders also volunteered for the merchant marine and for tug rescue work. The Canadian armed forces also attracted Newfoundland recruits, and beginning in 1942 Canada was allowed to recruit directly in the country for various military purposes. Over time more than 12,000 Newfoundlanders left their country to serve. Base construction on the island and in Labrador and recruitment for service at home and abroad put Newfoundland on the economic high road. War made service the hallmark of citizenship, and service implied both rights and rewards. If Newfoundland's economy was transformed by the Second World War, its citizenship was also redefined.

Looking back in 1949, the novelist Margaret Duley wrote that "the Newfoundland civilian was stunned" by the arrival of the first outside military forces.[20] Suddenly the whole way of life of the Newfoundlander seemed in jeopardy: "He had always had his country and his roads to himself. He could dawdle, and enjoy both in the spirit of undisturbed ownership. Now he felt dispossessed, crowded on his own streets, mowed down by the ever-increasing numbers of dun-coloured, army-vehicles. The strangers were strutting, becoming the 'big-shots.' They looked down their noses at the natives. They were disdainful of a hard old heritage. They began to call the townsfolk 'the Newfies' and like Queen Victoria, the Newfoundlanders were not amused."[21]

"Announcement of the bases agreement with the United States was "like a blow beneath the belt, the absolute change, a possible change of sovereignty that stuck in the local throat."[22] The Americans were coming for ninety-nine years, and not even the "greatest optimist of longevity" could "hope to live long enough to get his country back to himself." This was "unbelievable": "Newfoundland was shaken to the core of her old rugged heart; and the first reactions were tempestuous. An ancient privacy was being violated, an independent country was being invaded, and it was useless to insist that a people had been consulted. So *that* was what Newfoundland was worth to Britain. Sold, up the river, for fifty destroyers."[23]

In a recently published family memoir, Eileen Hunt Houlihan of Freshwater, Placentia Bay, recalls her family's eviction from its house in the autumn of 1941 to make way for the base at Argentia.[24] She was living with her widowed mother. They had to move with the compensation for their property yet to be decided. Moreover, because labour was now in such demand in the area, they were unable to have another house built. They stored their belongings in a hastily constructed shed and went to live with a relative. Eileen, her mother, and her brother Frank, on leave from the Canadian forces to assist with the move, had to cover the final part of the journey there on foot and at night. She records that as they climbed a landscape feature known locally as the "Devil's Bit," because of its steepness, her brother joked that they were like the Polish refugees who had so recently fled before Hitler's army.

Hunt Houlihan's memoirs, however, also give evidence that in the long run the relationship between Newfoundlanders and the local American military was highly successful. Once they had recovered from their initial shock, Margaret Duley noted, and had begun to examine the terms of the bases agreement "more craftily,"[25] Newfoundlanders could see its advantages. The Americans were "rich" and "paid the highest wages for the shortest hours." They promised a "reign of prosperity" in which the "bread and butter" of Newfoundland fishers "would no longer be subject to the caprice of the seasons, or to the foreign markets." Once this was understood, the outlook of Newfoundlanders was: "Let the Yanks come!"

The legacy of this transformation was that later, when ordinary Newfoundlanders who were affected by these events remembered the rough side of the dislocation of 1940–41, they usually blamed the commission of government. They held it responsible for anything and everything that went wrong and believed that it sold out Newfoundlanders individually and collectively. Ultimately, attitudes toward the Americans were shaped by the employment that they provided and by intermarriage. These positive aspects pushed into the background the memory of the hard bargain that Washington had driven in the first place.

That they and the Canadians were promoting a social revolution in Newfoundland was well understood by American officials. It was as though the Americans had found a lost tribe in the Atlantic. The natives were backward and downtrodden, but improvement and betterment were possible. Yankee ingenuity and example would lead the way. In June 1941, George Hopper, just appointed US consul general in St John's, reported that the number of US citizens in Newfoundland would soon reach 10,000. The visiting Americans and Canadians were spending an estimated three million dollars per month, and the total annual foreign trade of the country had increased by more than 50 per cent overnight. Stores were "unable to fill orders," in part because the demands of the "new population" were "different from normal or native tastes."[26] Merchants were not used to handling goods of the quality to which Americans were accustomed. Accommodation was also in short supply, and competition for many categories of labour was keen.

The many changes in progress, Hopper ventured, were shaking Newfoundland to its foundations:

As to social effects it may be said that opinions are rather mixed. To the old conservative English element, many of them more old-fashioned than in England itself, this influx of the energetic hustling Westerners from the United States and Canada is regarded with doubt and foreboding. It is feared that their pleasant easy way of living on their traditions may never return, while some of them actually feel discomfitted and "put out" because the stores and streets are crowded with busy people, army trucks and noisy lorries puffing up the hills with their heavy loads of construction material. However, these dear old Tories do not hesitate to cut up their commodious homes into flats to be rented out to newcomers at unheard of prices, and content themselves with small quarters while the rent money rolls in. The younger generation, including especially the sons and daughters who have travelled to the American continent for business or for their educations, are naturally more modern in their outlook and are willing to let the old way of life die its natural death. However, the elder statesmen have been able so far to retain the left side of the road for driving their American cars which are not built for that purpose. In time even this jolly old custom will disappear, and Newfoundland will justify its name.[27]

Hopper was prescient. In 1948 Newfoundland drivers did move over to the right side of the road, in a change that signified just how much their country had moved in a North American direction.

Social revolutions inevitably have political consequences, and the British understood that the one under way in Newfoundland was no exception. In the short term they could maintain the constitutional status quo with the argument that politics must be set aside in the interest of winning the war. But in the longer term, mounting pressure for constitutional change could be expected, and this would probably be irresistible.

In August 1941, Winston Churchill and Franklin Roosevelt met in Placentia Bay in a celebrated encounter which has been called "the first summit."[28] From their talks came the Atlantic Charter, a statement of eight "common principles" on which they based "their hopes for a better future for the world."[29] The third principle proclaimed respect for "the right of all peoples to choose the form of government under which they will live." Now that Newfoundland was prosperous again, it was hard to square this principle and the more general democratic rhetoric of the war with the maintenance of commission of government, and the British knew it. Accordingly, behind the scenes they began to plan for change.

In 1942, Clement Attlee, Britain's deputy prime minister and leader of the Labour party, visited Newfoundland and wrote a penetrating assessment of its current political situation.[30] He found "some experienced commissioners" of the opinion "that the corruption stressed by the Amulree report had been exaggerated." Attlee doubted if Newfoundland's political leaders had been any worse "than those of Canada or Australia." The problem was that they had had "a narrower margin to work on." Unfortunately, government in Newfoundland had been regarded historically "as a thing out of which the citizen got something, not as something to which he contributed service." This attitude had been reinforced by the dependence of the government on indirect taxation. The commission had been "set up under Treasury influence at a time when retrenchment was all the rage and when the world was slowly emerging from a great slump." Newfoundlanders had expected that under the commission "large sums would be available for development." Their expectations had been "unreasonable," but their disappointment was understandable. The commission was aloof and preoccupied with the "administrative machine." Regrettably, it had "not prepared the people for the restoration of self government."

"For the last nine years," Attlee wrote, "the population, except in the municipality of St. John's, has had no practice in democratic self government. None of the younger members of the community have ever taken part in elections. This absence of the practice of democracy has not been in any way balanced by any teaching of its theory as far as I could ascertain." "I sum up the attitude of most Newfoundlanders," he concluded, "as that of a man who having had a spell of drunkenness has taken the pledge ... is tired of it and would like to be a moderate drinker but does not quite trust himself."

As a first step, the British dispatched a parliamentary "goodwill" mission to Newfoundland in 1943.[31] Members were to gather information with a view to forming "some idea both of the potentialities of the country and of the capacity of Newfoundlanders to take charge of their own affairs." With the mission's work in hand, the British government announced in December 1943 that soon after the end of the war in Europe it would provide Newfoundlanders with machinery to decide their own constitutional future. This helped to keep down the political temperature in Newfoundland, but at a price: it left the last word to Newfoundlanders themselves. Henceforth, the British would have to work within this framework.

Nevertheless, as events would show, they had left themselves considerable leeway. As late as 1944 some official circles in London imagined that Newfoundland might revert to self-government, provided that a development program was instituted beforehand and that an independent Newfoundland did not interfere with it and was under other financial controls. The development scheme would cost the United Kingdom $100 million. By 1945 the British had abandoned this approach because of their own financial situation and had concluded that Newfoundland should join Canada. In 1945, P.A. Clutterbuck went to Ottawa to explain the British position and got agreement that the United Kingdom and Canada would work together to steer Newfoundland toward Confederation. Canadian interest in and knowledge of Newfoundland had blossomed through the war, but the US presence there gave London a lever in its dealings with Ottawa that it had lacked in the crisis of the 1930s. Given the history and sensibilities of Newfoundlanders, the British and the Canadians agreed that Confederation would best be promoted behind the scenes, as opportunities arose. London and Ottawa knew what they wanted but, given the promise that the British had made in 1943, they could get it only through the free choice of Newfoundlanders. The stage was thus set for a decisive political round in Newfoundland which would once more redefine the nature of the country's governance.

In 1945, the British announced how constitutional decision-making in Newfoundland would proceed. A national convention would be elected on a constituency basis. This body would advise London on the constitutional choices that would be put to the people in a referendum. The key word here was "advise." The British kept to themselves the last word as to what would be on the ballot, and in the end this proved crucial. The national convention began its deliberations on 11 September 1946 and eventually sent delegations to London and Ottawa. After the return to St John's of the Ottawa delegation, the Canadian government submitted draft terms of union to the convention through the governor of Newfoundland. At the end, however, the convention recommended to the British that the choices on the ballot be "Responsible Government as it existed prior to 1934" and "Commission of Government." A proposal to add Confederation to this list had been defeated by twenty-nine votes to sixteen.

The British therefore exercised the power that they had so skilfully kept in reserve and specified three choices on the ballot: "1. COMMISSION OF GOVERNMENT for a period of five years"; "2. CONFEDERATION WITH CANADA"; "3. RESPONSIBLE GOVERNMENT as it existed in 1933." Whitehall now also ruled that because the choice to be made was decisive, it would have to command majority support. A second referendum would therefore have to be held if the first did not produce such a result. For a second vote, the option with the least support in the first would be dropped from the ballot.

A second vote was indeed required. The first referendum, on 3 June 1948, produced 69,400 votes for responsible government, 64,066 for Confederation and 22,311 for commission of government. The second, on 22 July 1948, gave Confederation 78,323 votes to 71,334 for responsible government. Final terms of union were then negotiated by the two countries. These were signed in Ottawa on 11 December 1948, and in accordance with them Newfoundland became a province of Canada on 31 March 1949.

Through a complex series of events, Newfoundlanders had become the first and only people to enter Confederation by popular vote. At the ceremony in St John's marking the occasion, a collective certificate of Canadian citizenship was presented to Sir Albert Walsh, the first lieutenant-governor of the new province. Walsh had served in the Newfoundland legislature, had been a prominent member of the commission of government in its last years, and had led to Ottawa the delegation that negotiated the final terms of union. The certificate covered "every Newfoundland British subject ... coming within the relevant provisions of the Canadian citizenship Act."[32] Henceforth the persons so described would be "entitled to all rights, powers and privileges and subject to all obligations, duties and liabilities to which a natural-born Canadian citizen ... [was] entitled or subject."

Needless to say, the referenda campaigns were hard fought. The principal proponent of Confederation in the national convention was Joey Smallwood, an outsider in Newfoundland society who stirred up in the local gentry the same paranoid hatred of the party man which had led their class so strongly to favour commission of government in the 1930s. Smallwood had run for the Liberal party of Richard Squires, and to many he was the tainted heir of that controversial leader. Smallwood opened his campaign for Confederation with a series of eleven articles in the St John's *Daily News*. He stressed the advantages that would come from Canada's welfare-state programs – unemployment insurance, family allowances, and old age pensions. Newfoundlanders had a gallant history, but as a country they could not go it alone. Confederation offered them the chance to be themselves while having opportunity and security. It was the answer to the hard lesson that the country had learned in the 1930s. There was no organized campaign for the continuation of government by commission, but this option nevertheless achieved a substantial vote in a number of constituencies and some 14.32 per cent overall in the first referendum.

The campaign in favour of responsible government was complex, and, in the absence of polling data, it is hard to be precise about the motives of the many who favoured this option. Some Newfoundlanders wanted to go back to independence, plain and simple. But an argument was also made that the time to negotiate with other countries was after Newfoundland had got back its own elected government. Such an administration would make a better deal for the country than the commission of government could. The British, moreover, had promised Newfoundland that self-government would be restored, and this promise should be kept.

This argument had considerable appeal, but it is hard to say where advocacy for responsible government as a first step ended and anti-Confederation sentiment began. Certainly, the *Independent*, the newspaper of the Responsible Government League, portrayed Confederation most negatively. "How will it affect our way of life?," this paper asked in one issue. It gave this answer:

An interesting question that last one – have you ever thought about it? You go to bed one night a Newfoundlander, you wake up the next morning and find you are a Canadian, and instantly you will begin to wonder. The night before you felt a certain security for as a Newfoundlander you knew what to expect. Now everything is changed, you are a Canadian, and your feeling of security has disappeared. You don't know what is going to happen to you. You are governed no longer from St. John's but from Ottawa. You are no longer in the hands of your own people but strangers who do not know you, do not know your wants, are unfamiliar with your way of living, never hear of the places in which you live and don't talk your language. And these strangers will not try to understand your way of doing things, they will immediately begin to make you conform to their ways. And they will bring their own ideas with regard to taxation – they will brings taxes you never heard of and they will expect you to pay directly out of your own pockets for services that previously your own government paid for.[33]

On family allowances, one of the biggest carrots being offered by the "Confederates," the *Independent* warned that people should not be deceived into thinking that they could spend as they liked the money that might come to them. They would have to spend it "under government control"; it was "not for free spending by the parents."[34] "You cannot do as you like with it," the *Independent* pronounced, you "can't even buy a loaf of bread for yourself out of it."

Such sentiments were hardly calculated to provide the basis for future negotiations by an independent Newfoundland government for union with Canada. It must also be remembered that even though Canada, after the events of the war, wanted Newfoundland in Confederation, Ottawa moved cautiously. W.L. Mackenzie King's government always had to negotiate with an eye to dominion-provincial relations and had to be careful not to give Newfoundland any advantage that might arouse the jealously of existing provinces, especially in the Maritimes. How an independent Newfoundland would have fared in negotiations with Canada can only be speculated upon, but the nervousness of Ottawa and the prior rejection of Confederation in the referendums hardly suggest easy dealings between the two countries.

Yet another complicating factor was the emergence of a party, led by St John's businessman Chesley Crosbie, in favour of economic union with the United States. Attempts were made in the national convention to send a delegation to Washington, and there was widespread feeling in the convention and elsewhere that the country was owed a quid pro quo for the bases given to the Americans in the emergency of 1940. The commission of government had vetoed any approach to Washington, and in truth the Americans were pleased with the prospect of Confederation. They had no reason to go against the wishes of the United Kingdom and Canada in relation to Newfoundland. Furthermore, their own best interest would be served by what these countries favoured. The Americans had what they wanted in Newfoundland and did not want to have their essential rights there jeopardized. If the United Kingdom could no longer guarantee these rights, it was better to have responsibility pass to Ottawa, a known quantity, than to an independent government in St John's obsessed with righting old wrongs.

Crosbie received no encouragement from the US government, and he did not succeed. He also faced the problem that what he wanted was not on the referendum ballot. To pursue Crosbie's objective,

Newfoundlanders would have had first to opt for responsible government as it existed in 1933, next get a government committed to economic union with the United States, and then persuade the Americans to negotiate. This was all highly speculative, whereas the offer from Canada to the national convention was real.

Given the closeness of the second referendum and the hard-fought battle, there were some bitter feelings on the losing side. It is one thing to be beaten in a general election; it is another thing altogether to lose in a referendum that closed one chapter of history and opened another. Many budding political careers were nipped in 1948, and Joey Smallwood bore the brunt of much of the resultant frustration. To some supporters of responsible government, Smallwood was nothing but a usurper who had sold his country out. He was subsequently premier of Newfoundland from 1949 to 1972, but his opposition always had an implacable Joey-hating edge that probably owed something to the bitter winner-take-all struggle of 1946–49.

The Responsible Government League got up a big petition to the British House of Commons after the second referendum. This called again for restoration of self-government in accordance with the promise that the British were said to have made in the 1930s and condemned any negotiations with Canada "other than by representatives of a duly elected Government of the people of Newfoundland."[35] The league also attempted to block Confederation through the courts, but neither of its initiatives succeeded. Confederation had behind it the force of majority vote in a free and fair election, and in a democracy that is hard to deny.

In his wonderfully evocative *The Danger Tree*, David Macfarlane writes that when his Newfoundland maternal grandfather, Josiah Goodyear, heard the news of the "Confederate" victory over the radio in Grand Falls, he got up from his armchair and said, "Oh my poor country."[36] "Nothing he saw of confederation," his grandson continues, "ever changed his opinion."

For her part, Margaret Duley felt mixed emotions as the hour of Confederation approached. She probably typified a good many Newfoundlanders. At the beginning of 1949 she was busy writing a history of the Caribou Hut, a hostel for allied servicemen that had been operated in St John's during the war by the St. John's War Services' Association. Duley saw in its record of hospitality, service, and care an image of the best that Newfoundland embodied. As they awaited their change of status, Newfoundlanders, she wrote, were taking stock of their "salty past" while "experiencing the apprehension of the waiting-room."[37] There was much to reflect on. The fight of Newfoundlanders with the elements through their long history had been "an unnegotiated thing," but there was strength as well as hardship in that.[38] An "old island" had given "her children salt on their lips, rock in their souls, and sea-sounds in their ears."[39] Newfoundland's past was "never trivial" because "nature could not permit it."[40] What then was there to say "to every Newfoundlander now moving off from an old heritage?" "Only this," Duley answered, "that we will remember all that is good in the past, but we will anticipate the good in the future too ... Old Newfoundland – Hail and Farewell."[41] These are memorable words, an epitaph of sorts. They are a reminder, too, of just how much the events of 1946–49 in Newfoundland pitted sentiment against security, "a hard old heritage" against greater economic certainty. Security justifiably won out, but the sentiment was real and the adjustment that followed therefore not without its rough side.

The blessings of the Canadian welfare state certainly eased the transition, as Joey Smallwood, himself no mean publicist for Newfoundland's "salty past," understood they would. The general prosperity of Canada in the 1950s, a prosperity in which Newfoundlanders shared, did so as well. Another plus was the willingness of some prominent supporters of responsible government to lay down arms and mend political fences with Joey Smallwood's triumphant Liberal party, the successor to the Newfoundland Confederate Association. Prominent among the realists were Chesley Crosbie and Don Jamieson. In the final analysis they were too clever to fight history and a government with a big future. Others on the responsible government side had the option of rewriting their personal histories and consoling themselves with the thought that it was not Confederation as such that they had opposed but the process by which it had been brought about. Whether or not this was the case was now conveniently irrelevant.

With this message the defeated were able to find a place for themselves in the Progressive Conservative party. Under the leadership of George Drew, Canada's Conservatives had called on the King government to consult the existing provinces before admitting Newfoundland to Confederation. King had taken the position that a cabinet that was representative of all the provinces could act with the consent of Parliament to admit Newfoundland. After this was done, Drew linked his party in the new province with former supporters of responsible government as it existed in 1933. Predictably, his party did not get very far in Newfoundland for a good many years. Smallwood and the Liberals cashed in on their identification with the manifest success of union until a new generation arrived that knew the 1930s and 1940s only as history.

So smooth was the transition that a decade after union it would have been difficult to stir up any opposition to Confederation as such, and no one tried. Newfoundlanders had settled down to their new citizenship and, along with other Canadians, were busily building the consumer society and expanding the welfare state. This was politically a hard combination to fight.

In 1949, the same year that Newfoundland joined Canada, the British sociologist T.H. Marshall gave lectures at Cambridge University on the subject of "citizenship and social class," a major post-war preoccupation in the Western democracies. Marshall discerned three stages in the evolution of citizenship – "civil, political and social."[42] The first concerned the achievement of "individual freedom – liberty of the person, freedom of speech, thought and faith, the right to own property and to conclude valid contracts and the right to justice."[43] The "political element" meant "the right to participate in the exercise of political power, as a member of a body invested with political authority or as an elector of the members of such a body."[44] The "social element" involved "the whole range from the right to a modicum of economic welfare and security to the right to share to the full in the social heritage and to live the life of a civilized being according to the standards prevailing in the society."[45]

With the suspension of self-government in 1934, Newfoundland may be said to have deviated sharply from this normal evolution of society and citizenship. Confederation put its people back on track by restoring the political aspect of citizenship, albeit within a federal framework, while giving them more economic opportunity and security than they had ever had. In sum, it made them participants at last in the full citizenship of which Marshall spoke.

That is worth remembering in a period of renewed constitutional debate in Canada. So too is something else about the pivotal 1930s and 1940s. The events of the Depression and the war cast a long shadow across the writing of Canadian history. Interest in these two decades remains high not only because of their intrinsic importance but because abundant documentary evidence is available for their study. They are now very fashionable decades indeed. Many anglophone historians in this country, liberal and centralist in views, are stern critics of the performance of the Bennett and King governments in the 1930s. By their reckoning, the Canadian government's response to the Depression was both conservative and inappropriate. The 1930s were a low, dishonest decade at home as well as abroad. Power was inappropriately distributed in the country and was too decentralized.

National problems required national solutions that were not forthcoming. The Depression was like the war that followed in that it required Ottawa to take the lead. Unhappily, this did not occur: King and Bennett, for all their partisan differences, were very much alike. They both feared bringing down the financial house of cards; they both believed in balanced budgets; and they both adhered to the poor law principles of less eligibility and local responsibility as indispensable to keeping the work ethic alive. Provincial and municipal governments had responsibilities for relief and unemployment which they were not able to bear. Yet Ottawa failed to shoulder the burden.

Not surprisingly, this analysis produces anxiety about the present enthusiasm to decentralize. Decentralization, a good many of our historians would observe, was not always the Canadian way. In the 1930s the pressure was on to get Ottawa to assume duties, not the other way around, but Ottawa lacked the will to do so. Worse still, in relation to some vital matters it could not do so because of difficulties posed by the constitution. The history of the long and difficult process by which Ottawa obtained the power to legislate in relation to unemployment insurance – something achieved only in wartime conditions – has been a special concern of anglophone historians.

Perforce, this episode encourages a questioning approach to present trends in Canadian federalism. If it was so difficult to move necessary power to Ottawa in the past, is it wise now to move it away from there with what seems like indecent haste? This is not, of course, to argue that there is a specific constitutional prescription to be derived from the study of history. Nevertheless, for a good many of its English-speaking practitioners at least, the study of the Canadian past breeds a great deal of caution in constitutional matters and emphasizes complexity and interdependence.

The history of Newfoundland in the 1930s and 1940s is part of that cautionary tale. That history indeed affords an unusual insight into the ebb and flow of power and citizenship. What Newfoundland needed in the 1930s was a guarantor and to get off the narrow margin on which it lived, something that it eventually achieved through Confederation. In a time of decentralizing pressure in Canada – not least from Newfoundland – it is worth remembering that power once flowed profitably and constructively in the opposite direction. As the generation of Newfoundlanders who experienced the social shocks of the 1930s and 1940s might well testify, in Canadian history small has not always been beautiful. For them, independence without substance only diminished citizenship.

NOTES

1 This was the title that he gave to his celebrated history of Canada, the first edition of which was published in 1946.
2 United Kingdom, Parliamentary Papers, Cmd. 4480, *Newfoundland Royal Commission 1933: Report*, ii.
3 See Peter Neary, *Newfoundland in the North Atlantic World, 1929–1940* (Kingston and Montreal, 1988), 20.
4 *Newfoundland Royal Commission 1933: Report*, 195.
5 United Kingdom, *The Public General Acts*, 1933–34, 10.
6 Balliol College, Oxford, Hope Simpson Papers, Newfoundland correspondence, Quita Hope Simpson to Ian (son) and Sheila (daughter-in-law), 26 April 1934; quoted by permission of Jacynth Hope Simpson, literary executor of J.B. Hope Simpson. The Hope Simpson Papers deposited at Balliol College are copyright the Hope Simpson family.
7 Ibid., Quita Hope Simpson to Ian and Sheila, 19 April 1934.
8 Ibid., John Hope Simpson to Greta (daughter), 1 April 1934.
9 Ibid., John Hope Simpson to Sheila and Ian, 21 March 1934.
10 Ibid., Quita Hope Simpson to Ian and Sheila, 19 April 1934.
11 Ibid., John Hope Simpson to Greta, 25 May 1935.
12 Ibid., Quita Hope Simpson to Ian, 25 May 1935.
13 Ibid., Quita Hope Simpson to Greta, 5 April 1934.
14 Ibid., John Hope Simpson to Ian and Sheila, 3 Aug. 1934.
15 Ibid., John Hope Simpson to Greta, 13 May 1934.
16 Ibid., John Hope Simpson to Ian and Sheila, 3 Aug. 1934.
17 Ibid., John Hope Simpson to Maisie (daughter), 26 Sept. 1935.
18 Quoted in Neary, *Newfoundland in the North Atlantic World*, 55.
19 United Kingdom, Parliamentary Papers, Cmd. 6224, 1940, *Exchange of Notes regarding United States Destroyers and Naval and Air Facilities for the United States in British Transatlantic Territories*, Lothian to Hull, 2 Sept. 1940.
20 Margaret Duley, *The Caribou Hut: The Story of a Newfoundland Hostel* (Toronto, 1949), 11.
21 Ibid.
22 Ibid., 11–12.
23 Ibid., 13.
24 Eileen (Hunt) Houlihan, "Eileen (Hunt) Houlihan's Family Memoirs," introduction by Peter Neary, *Newfoundland Studies* 7 no. 1 (Spring 1991) 48–64.

25 Duley, *The Caribou Hut*, 13.
26 National Archives and Records Administration, Washington, DC, RG 165, box 2639, 4020, enclosure in Military Intelligence Division, "Regional File," 1922–44, Memorandum for Assistant Chief of Staff, G-2, from Clayton Bissell, 7 Oct. 1941.
27 Ibid.
28 Theodore A. Wilson, *The First Summit: Roosevelt and Churchill at Placentia Bay 1941* (Boston, 1969).
29 H.V. Morton, *Atlantic Meeting* (London, 1943), 149.
30 For this, see Peter Neary, "Clement Attlee's Visit to Newfoundland, September 1942," in *Acadiensis* 13 no. 2 (Spring 1984) 101–9.
31 See Neary, *Newfoundland in the North Atlantic World*, 216.
32 See Peter Neary and Patrick O'Flaherty, *Part of the Main: An Illustrated History of Newfoundland and Labrador* (St John's, 1983), 170.
33 Quoted in Peter Neary, ed., *The Political Economy of Newfoundland, 1929–1972* (Toronto, 1973), 148.
34 Ibid., 149.
35 Neary, *Newfoundland in the North Atlantic World*, 334.
36 David Macfarlane, *The Danger Tree* (Toronto, 1991), 23.
37 Duley, *The Caribou Hut*, 81.
38 Ibid.
39 Ibid., 82.
40 Ibid.
41 Ibid.
42 T.H. Marshall, *Class, Citizenship and Social Development* (New York, 1964), 78.
43 Ibid.
44 Ibid.
45 Ibid.

ROBERT FULFORD

A Post-Modern Dominion: The Changing Nature of Canadian Citizenship

People look for a common idea of citizenship ...
They think that, whatever differences we have, we've
got to share with everybody else a common idea of
what it is to be a Canadian – or an American or a
Briton. In Canada we can't really have that, because
we have these very different kinds of societies where
the idea of what it is to belong is very different.
– Charles Taylor [1]

As much as it is a legal fact created by legislation, citizenship is a metaphor: for most people, in most countries, it stands for a tangle of human connections, past and future, at the same time that it defines entitlements and reponsibilities. In every country the metaphor is complicated by local feeling and frequently called into question by the unfolding surprises of history – such as, in northern Europe, the recent arrival of a generation of new human beings, the children of guest workers, who may or may not be allowed to live permanently in the countries of their birth. The issue can be made more difficult still if a society refuses to recognize and articulate the meanings that citizenship holds for its citizens. This is one oblique description of our own current problem, which in 1987 found its fatally succinct expression in the phrase "distinct society."

In Canada, traditional public rhetoric implies that in matters of citizenship one Canadian is precisely the same as another. Even the Charter of Rights and Freedoms, because it applies equally to all of us, seems to suggest that every citizen stands in the same relationship to the state as every other citizen. If that were true, it would make the metaphor neater and the country easier to govern; but (as Charles Taylor is not the first philosopher to note) it is not true and can never be. The majority of Canadians, Taylor acknowledges, belong to Canada as individuals – their relationship with the federal government, and with the idea of Canada, is one to one. But many Quebecers and many aboriginals maintain a quite different relationship. Their citizenship, on the metaphorical though not yet the legal level, is layered. It reaches the federal level by passing through a layer of emotion and entitlement that is closer to them. They belong first of all either to Quebec or to an aboriginal society; only then, as members of these collectivities, do they acknowledge their status as Canadians. This is why, as Taylor puts it, "a single model of citizenship" is not a possibility in this country. Yet a great many Canadians (most famously the current premier of Newfoundland) yearn for the day when all residents of all provinces will declare themselves Canadians first and loyalists of their regions or races second.

On the basis of this wistful hope, our major national institutions structure themselves according to a wholly imaginary symmetry. In public we live by a kind of fiction. At federal-provincial conferences, ten premiers stand side by side, pretending to express parallel realities, when in fact one of them leads not a provincial legislature but a "national assembly." He represents, in other words, something that may be called a province in federal law but definitely is not *only* a province, certainly not one like the others. Many people who grow up in English-speaking Canada experience great difficulty understanding this central fact of Canadian life: that the provincial government is an incomparably greater force in Quebec than in any other province. No resident of Ontario would dream of suggesting that Queen's Park carries the burden of maintaining the province's culture and way of life; yet this has been precisely the central function of successive Quebec governments, especially since the decline of the Roman Catholic church in the early 1960s.

For the most part, Quebec's governments have performed the task superbly, accepting federal help graciously in nearly all their activities while jealously guarding and slowly expanding Quebec's sense of national destiny and duty. They have never for a moment allowed Quebecers to forget the Quebec layer of their citizenship. Elsewhere in Canada, even among aboriginals, collective identity comes and goes; in Quebec it is seldom absent. As a result, French Canada at this moment seems, as a polity, unstoppable. Its politicians may fall into the rhetoric of fear and paranoia when discussing the failure of the Meech Lake round (paranoia can be a strategy, too), and its demographers may from time to time prophesy the withering away of the francophone community; but it seems inevitable that – whatever constitutional arrangements are made – French Canada will stride confidently into the twenty-first century with its sense of citizenship intensely complicated but clearly robust.

English-speaking Canada, the main subject of this paper, is another matter. While French Canada's mission – survival of a unique society in a difficult and often hostile milieu – has been clear for centuries, the purpose of English-speaking Canada has traditionally been unclear, controversial, contradictory, and, above all, changeable. The spiritual or emotional basis for citizenship in it was shaky at the beginning and has not grown noticeably stronger on the road from colony to nation, despite our earnest efforts to create a firm, clear identity. In the most practical terms, Canadian citizenship is a prize, and those who receive it on the day they first open their eyes are among the luckiest humans; our inheritance is exceptional freedom, unlimited opportunity, and only minimal obligations. (It is forty-seven years since the last Canadian was drafted for military service – two generations, including my own, have miraculously escaped what much of the world has traditionally accepted as the routine duty of male citizens). But, of course, we are not satisfied with these practical benefits – and we are right not to be. We would be less than human if we did not imagine, or hope for, a powerful element of transcendence in our collective experience.

For many individuals, Canadian citizenship carries symbolic and cultural power. Most people I know, most people whose work I read, and most people whose lives are reflected in public-opinion polls have little trouble making an emotional connection with Canada for themselves. What they cannot manage is to articulate this connection in a way that permanently attracts a rough consensus among their fellow citizens. We all have our own Canadas, which many of us clearly find satisfying, and in which many of us take great pride, but making these multifarious personal Canadas cohere into a collectivity appears so far to be beyond our intellectual range. Where can we find an all-encompassing, binding element? In our history? In the arts? In our relationship with the land, particularly the north? In the federal government's role as provider of social programs and equalizer of opportunities?

The last of these, curiously, has been mentioned in recent years as a unique accomplishment – "unique" not in its standard dictionary meaning but in a special Canadian definition, "different from the United States." The point of special pride seems to be that we provide fairly good medical care for everyone and the United States does not. This is an unlikely basis for anyone's sense of citizenship and seems unlikelier still when we reflect that the United States may eventually adopt a medical system much like ours, a number of polls having indicated that this is the desire of many Americans. For the moment, however, medicare is occasionally cited as proof that Canadians are more compassionate than others – though, again, the "others" almost always turn out to be not New Zealanders or Chileans but, of course, Americans. "We are frequently told," writes the historian Michael Marrus, "that Canadian society is less competitive, less cruel, less rapacious than other societies. True or not, this is certainly our image of ourselves, a flattering self-definition."[2] Comparative studies of gifts to charities in the United States and Canada made it clear long ago that individual Canadians are in fact far more miserly than Americans; but Canadians can reply that they make their gifts to the less fortunate through their taxes, acting as citizens rather than patrons. Those who need help receive it not in the form of charity but as one of the entitlements of the citizen, a method that is likely to be more fair and certain to be more dignified than charity.

In this process, transfer payments from Ottawa and the word "equalization" play a crucial role, symbolic as well as practical; the entire rhetorical framework of compassion collapses if government help is not provided equally across the country. But recent changes in fiscal policy, the result of a federal deficit created by the same social policies, have made the future of federal involvement look dubious. The Economic Council of Canada touched on the problem of citizenship when it discussed these changes in its 1991 annual report: "The government's decision to alter its commitments to the existing fiscal arrangements with the provinces unleashed pressures for de-centralization, because the main source of legitimacy for its involvement in areas of formal provincial jurisdiction was the fact that it paid some of the bills. Thus the fiscal crisis has undermined the federal role as guardian of some key values of Canadian citizenship."[3] If the responsibilities for social programs shift to the provinces, then citizenship is doubly diminished: the taxpayer loses the right to pay as a Canadian, and the client loses the entitlement to services as a Canadian.

For this reason it seems dangerous as well as fatuous to ground the meaning of citizenship in social programs, particularly those (such as medicare) that have been established for only a generation or so. If citizenship has any meaning beyond the purely practical, it must find roots that go deeper than the social legislation, however commendable, of the Pearson era. There must be, somewhere, a rough Canadian equivalent of what Abraham Lincoln called "the mystic chords of memory," chords that evoke emotions deeper than self-interest and broader than allegiance to race or region.

In Ottawa this has been recognized as a problem for generations, and official responses have ranged from successful (the establishment of a Canadian flag by the Pearson government) through contentious (forcing the Canada Council to put the Canada wordmark on its cheques, to remind clients where the money comes from) to risible. In this last category we can put both the falsely enthusiastic Canada Day demonstrations created by the government in the 1970s (one year the slogan was "Canada, I Want to Shake Your Hand!") and the symbolism invested by at least some federal officials in government-promoted lottery gambling. That particular aspect of participatory federalism came to an end in 1979, when the Clark government turned over to the provinces the right to run lotteries – a change still bitterly resented by Jean Chrétien, as he said recently when recalling happier times for Canadian federalism in the 1970s: "Every month there was a big [Lotto Canada] show on national TV with singers from Quebec and British Columbia and Newfoundland together, and millions of Canadians were watching, full of Canadian pride ... There was an important symbol at every kiosk – people bought a ticket with a Canadian flag. They [the Conservatives] give it away to the provinces. Not only did they lose the $300-million [annual revenue], but they didn't even get a thank you."[4]

This image – millions of people realizing their citizenship more profoundly as they sat before their TV screens, listening to a mixture of French and English while holding betting tickets in their hands – at least begins to suggest the desperation that federalists experienced as they confronted the victory of the Parti Québécois in 1976 and the weakness of the ties binding citizens to the federal government. In that same period, and apparently out of the same feelings, they made a small and so far permanent change in both our official languages, inserting the word "Canadians" where previously they might have said "the people" or "citizens" or "taxpayers." It started, according to my memory, with several members of the Trudeau cabinet, who began saying, over and over again, that such-and-such a law would benefit "all Canadians" rather than all the people. Quickly this usage leapt the floor of the House of Commons and became part of standard Opposition rhetoric ("Will the minister assure Canadians that ...?") and then spread across the country, to the editorial pages as well as the provincial legislatures. It is now a national linguistic reflex, rarely noticed in this country. A stranger might imagine that all these people insist on repetitiously using the word "Canadians" out of an irrational fear that their listeners would otherwise imagine they were speaking about the welfare (or hopes, or dreams, or grievances, or whatever) of Algerians or Tasmanians. The real reason, of

course, is the now unconscious (though at first quite conscious) belief
that if a word is repeated often enough it will develop a meaning.

Nevertheless, the meaning remains obscure. Most attempts at
definition either dissolve in vagueness or resort to the purely negative: a Canadian citizen is someone who is not a citizen of another
country. Long ago, Northrop Frye defined English-speaking Canadians as Americans who reject the Revolution, but that description
holds little meaning in a time when many Canadians are unaware
that the United Empire Loyalists existed and when even those once
called "UEL stock" have ceased to make a point of their ancestry.
More recently, Daniel Latouche has said that the coast-to-coast existence of anti-Americanism, or at least a determined un-
Americanism, is proof in itself that English Canada is a nation –
"there must be a nation somewhere in the back to support such a
widely held feeling of 'us–them'."[5]

But if the nation is there, then it must have a history, a set of symbols
expressing nationhood, and a reason for existing. These items are,
after all, standard equipment for nations. In English-speaking Canada, unfortunately, the history is simultaneously obscure and dangerous, and the symbols have an odd way of vanishing from sight.
The national raison d'être is even more difficult to establish, since it
changes with what seems to be, in the context of national purpose,
blinding speed. English Canadians are often called exceptionally
conservative, but in dealing with the most fundamental of all national questions – why is there a Canada? – we are astonishingly
changeable, even feckless.

Imagine that in 1892 a social scientist asked representative sam-
ples of Japanese, French, and American citizens to define the purpose of their nation-states, and imagine that in each country an
equivalent sample was asked the same question in 1992. The Japanese, French, and American citizens of 1992 could be expected to
answer roughly as their forbears did; certainly we would find strong
similarities in each of the two sets of responses, particularly in termi-
nology. But if the same experiment were performed in English-
speaking Canada, we would obtain two sets of answers so different
as to be unrecognizable. Those from 1892 would inevitably refer to
the crown, the empire, British traditions, and so on – all elements
that would be present only in minute traces, if at all, in the 1992 sam-
pling. And if both samplings represented not the whole population
but the elites, political and intellectual, then the differences might be
even more striking. English-speaking Canadians, and in particular
the articulate elites, are engaged more or less permanently in rein-

venting their own idea of Canada, simultaneously discarding out-
dated concepts and inventing new ones to fit current circumstances.

How many have been invented, how many discarded? An exhaustive survey would produce a dozen at least. In the late nineteenth century one seemed especially attractive, the imperial idea, a
notion so distant now that young people brought up in the last quarter of the twentieth century find it (in my experience) not only out-
landish but literally incredible. The leading intellectual of the day,
Rev. George Monro Grant (1835–1902), the principal of Queen's
University, expressed it with such eloquence and power that at
times, before certain audiences, he made it seem almost inevitable.
In his view, Canada would rise not against but within the British Empire, taking an ever more prominent place in the empire's affairs,
until eventually (he implied) it would be as great as England, or
greater. Our most intelligent course, he preached, was "to seek, in
the consolidation of the Empire, a common Imperial citizenship,
with common responsibilities, and a common inheritance." The empire was not an alien force, temporarily holding sway over Canada,
but a permanent and valuable part of Canadian life; in fact, it was as
much Canada's empire as it was England's. For Grant, the next act
in the unfolding of Canadian history was imperial federation, "a
union between Mother Country and Canada that would give to Canada not only the present full management of its own affairs, but a
fair share in the management and responsibilities of common affairs."[6] Canadians would be peers and not dependants of their fellow citizens in Britain. The more patriotic Canadians became,
therefore, the more devoted they would be to the empire in which
Canada's destiny was to be found. If the obvious question were
asked – what about French Canada, which lacked the "common inheritance"? – the imperialists were ready with an answer. French
Canada could best be protected under the crown. Certainly it would
flourish far better within an imperial Canada than in the United
States.

Grant's approach took hold, and it remained a part of the English-
Canadian spirit long after Grant himself, and his fellow intellectual
imperialists, were gone; it lingered even after Canadian membership in the empire (or the Commonwealth) lost its political value.
Through the two world wars, and after, loyalty to Canada and loyalty to Britain were complementary, and equally essential, aspects of
patriotism. As a child in British Toronto during the Second World
War, I sang "There'll Always Be an England" at least as often as
"The Maple Leaf Forever." In the early 1960s, Arthur Lower told
me that after he made a public statement favouring a Canadian flag

he received telephone calls accusing him of treason. "Could that happen in any other country?" he asked.

The imperial idea attracted little support in French Canada, and our elites eventually came to believe that "imperial citizenship" was not our likely future. For generations, all Canadians remained British subjects in law; but whether this constituted a "real" as opposed to legal citizenship was a matter of personal taste and unresolved dispute, particularly at the time of the First World War. Our central problem, then as now, was that there was no clear historical referent, no higher symbolic court (of race, religion, language, culture) to which we could appeal the decisions of government. An Italian could argue that there were Italians before there was a country called Italy; but where could we find a pre-political and pre-legal Canadian citizenship? Certainly not in our history. The key event in our past, the battle on the Plains of Abraham, was not a subject to be explored mythically, because there was and is no pan-Canadian way of calling it either a victory or a defeat; to this minute it remains a sensitive issue, perhaps the only eighteenth-century battle, anywhere, that cannot be discussed without anxiety.

Divisiveness, many Canadians decided long ago, is not to be tolerated, and if possible not even mentioned. The year 1759 cannot be permitted to echo in our "mystic chords of memory." We fear our past rather than embracing it. W.L. Mackenzie King, a great reader of history, created a certain idea of Canadian citizenship by carefully sanding away the edges of national dispute. He understood that our belief in Canadian (as opposed to British or Quebec) citizenship was shallow, and – unlike the politicians of the 1980s and 1990s – he had no desire whatever to test it or define it. He was satisfied, for the moment (a long moment, as it turned out), with a kind of minimalist citizenship, ill-defined and therefore unthreatening. He let statesmen elsewhere become famous for articulating national beliefs; he was a success because he did *not* articulate what he and Canada were doing. F.R. Scott wrote about his influence on the citizens:

We had no shape
Because he never took sides
And no sides
Because he never allowed them to take shape.

He skillfully avoided what was wrong
Without saying what was right,
And never let his on the one hand
Know what his on the other hand was doing.[7]

King drove intellectuals like Scott to distraction; they wanted clear definitions, which were just what he hated, feared, and scrupulously avoided. He had something in mind, of course. He was gently guiding Canada out of the British and into the American empire, an inevitable transition that could best be managed, as he saw it, more or less in silence. Naturally, he was unwilling to discuss this change in any way that could be understood by the public. In King's era, and for a few years after, the job of describing the purposes of English Canada, which had earlier seemed so natural to a public-spirited Presbyterian clergyman such as Grant, fell to a new priestly caste – academic historians. For at least two generations, Canadian elites (and through them the public as a whole) drew their ideas about the purpose of Canada from a remarkable group of historians: Donald Creighton, Harold Innis, Arthur Lower, W.L. Morton, Frank H. Underhill, and a few more. Their observations and theories spread out from the universities to the mass media and the schools. Lacking a clear, vibrant constitution, and lacking visionary political leaders, we listened with uncommon attention to the historians, giving their profession a place in our political culture that it has achieved in only a few other countries.

But historians, while more thoughtful than politicians, were, as a class, equally changeable in their views. Those who read their work, or studied with them, were led through a series of distinct and often mutually exclusive assumptions about the essential role and purpose of Canadian federalism. In the 1960s, Ramsay Cook described this process with remarkable clarity:

As the fiftieth anniversary of Confederation approached, in 1917, a Canadian historian faced with the task of explaining the meaning of Confederation might have concluded that his country's founders intended to build a nation capable of assisting Great Britain and her allies in their magnificent effort to make the world safe for democracy. Ten years later, the historian ... might well have replied that the objective of Confederation was to lay the foundations of a nation capable of winning full autonomy within the British Commonwealth. Another historian, in the midst of the Great Depression, would probably have insisted that the intention of the founders was to establish a nation with a central government strong enough to guarantee all Canadians a reasonable standard of living and social welfare. At the end of the Second World War, yet another practitioner of this sensitive craft might have claimed that the far-seeing statesmen of 1867 had intended to build a nation capable of interpreting Europe to America, and vice versa. A decade ago [i.e. in the mid-1950s] the answer would certainly have been that the great object of Confederation was to build a nation in the northern half of the North American continent strong enough to resist annexation to the United States.[8]

What Cook describes is a series of academic improvisations, theories thrown together to satisfy the needs of the moment and then more or less abandoned (though without the embarrassment of public recantation) when the moment passed. In the Vietnam War period, roughly 1965–75, the last item on Cook's list became even more popular. Canadians, including some who had previously shown little interest in the problems of the Canadian state, now realized anew that its greatest virtue was in fact negative: it was not America. The empire was gone, but the spirit of the United Empire Loyalist walked the land again, embodied in nationalists such as the philosopher George Grant. The republic to the south was now, once more, highly suspect. This coincided roughly with the rise of Quebec separatism, the first serious challenge to Confederation in generations.

The enthusiasm in English Canada for Pierre Trudeau in 1968 was not only a response to the threat of national dissolution but also an expression of faith – for some, newfound faith – in the future of Canada as distinct from the United States. Citizenship had been reborn in English Canada as a by-product of the Vietnam War – and thousands of the young Americans who moved to Canada to avoid the war turned out to be among our most enthusiastic citizens, some of them taking positions (particularly in cultural politics) that their Canadian-born equivalents found either bracingly or terrifying radical. This new expression of citizenship – "the new nationalism" was a term used frequently – affected certain cultural institutions, especially in book publishing and the theatre, but it failed to take a firm grip on the popular imagination. One reason was that it found no noticeable echo in post-1968 Ottawa. To Ottawa, the new nationalism looked elitist, Toronto-centric, and irrelevant both to the French-English division and to the needs of poorer regions. It evoked similar views elsewhere. In the early 1970s, when I lectured on some of these issues at the Nova Scotia College of Art and Design, one student said that what I was describing was "Ontario politics" – a not entirely unfair comment.

More important, nationalism in English Canada remained quite separate from nationalism in French Canada, though strenuous attempts to find a common ground were made. What kept them apart was the same force that inadvertently encouraged English-Canadian nationalism – the United States. In theory, at least, the two nationalisms should have come together on this, since the leading advocates of both favoured some form of democratic socialism. But where this

produced in English Canada an aversion to American capitalism, it
appeared to produce in Quebec only an aversion to Toronto capitalism. Certainly Quebec nationalists have never shared the anti-
Americanism of their equivalents elsewhere in Canada.

In the 1980s, as these divisions became clear, another part of the
foundation of citizenship in English-speaking Canada was under
pressure, as it remains today. For generations we had believed that
Canadian public enterprise, from railroads through electricity to
broadcasting, both set us apart from the Americans and provided
better solutions to our problems than market capitalism could offer.
That idea is by no means dead, but neither can it be called flourish-
ing. Consider how significant it seemed in 1961 to James Eayrs, one
of the most thoughtful political scientists of that era, who was attempting to describe the differences between the United States and
Canada:

The Canadian attitude towards public enterprise has been more pragmatic.
People being fewer, capital scarcer, climate harsher, distances and other
natural barriers even more formidable, the impulse here to state action has
been stronger. It has been reinforced by the political motive of building and
sustaining a Canadian nation. These together explain the wide range of government activity ... The state has become an entrepreneur, producing
power, marketing wheat, running railways and airlines. It is even in the entertainment business, furnishing, through the Canadian Broadcasting Corporation, amusement and uplift ...

Capitalism itself seems less secure. Canadian investors prefer bonds to eq-
uities, and life insurance to either. A strongly Puritan streak runs through
our national life, and what has stamped us is the early Puritanism, with its
hostility to conspicuous acquisition, rather than the later variety in which en-
trepreneurial success becomes the hallmark of virtue. In French Canada the
influence of Catholic social theory has worked against the spread of the capitalist ethos, and even today few French-speaking Canadians are in positions
of business power. Our staple-producing economy has been more vulnerable to catastrophic depression. Deep scars and bitter memories survive the
1930s. Capitalism, even the greatly improved capitalism arisen from the
ashes, is still on trial. There persists a small but influential party of democratic socialism, unique in North America, devoted to the creation of a Canadian society in which private enterprise would find no place on the
commanding heights of big industry, big transport, and big communications.[9]

Today, a writer such as Eayrs would have to modify almost every
word in that passage. He would have to note, for instance, that pub-

lic power utilities, once thought to be unarguably successful (Ontario Hydro, for instance) are now regarded with deep misgivings by large sections of the population, sections not easily describable as either conservative or liberal. He would have to acknowledge that both English-Canadian and French-Canadian aversion to conspicuous acquisition has apparently disappeared, and he might perhaps even point out that in the 1980s one of the world's most feverishly and disastrously acquisitive capitalists was a French Canadian nurtured in English Canada, Robert Campeau. He would certainly have to note that the CBC has been on the defensive for at least two decades and now, in the multi-channel era, seems to be in more or less constant danger of sinking in an ocean of commercialism. And, of course, he would have to note that, while the New Democrats now hold power in three provinces, they long ago ceased even to talk about controlling the "commanding heights" of the economy. In general, he would have to conclude that the public sector which we once regarded as essential to the Canadian style is now everywhere in retreat; in the present context of international business, the very idea of Canadians operating any differently from people elsewhere is itself under question. There may be no logical reason to accept the idea that global economics imposes the same global standards on everyone; yet that idea seems to be attracting widespread support. If it in fact proves to be the operating principle of the future, then we can hardly imagine that we will be able to look to our economic institutions for a sense of distinctness.

There are those who imagine that ideology can define nationality and citizenship, and certainly the various ideologies of the past (such as imperialism) have been called on, from time to time, to play this role. In the debate over the Free Trade Agreement, in the late 1980s, there was more than a suggestion that those supporting the government were, as the Liberal leader put it, selling out the country; counterconceptually, those who opposed the FTA could be seen as patriots, adherents of a pro-Canada ideology and therefore perhaps more acceptable as citizens. There ran through that debate a strong undercurrent of what would in other circumstances be called bigotry. There was a sense that those supporting the FTA were somehow un-Canadian because they failed to express what was regarded in some circles as the orthodox Canadian view. This emerged most clearly in comments by the writer Farley Mowat, who opposed the FTA, about another writer, Mordecai Richler, who supported it. As Mowat said: "This guy is a non-Canadian. Mordecai Richler has his own sense of identity. It's his Jewish identity and it's his little neighbourhood identity. He has no sense of Canadian identity at all. I am proud of being a chauvinist nationalist. This is my country. I may not love it but, by God, I'll defend it. And I don't like people who make their livelihood here, who then treat it lightly, pass it off and, in effect, betray the trust of the rest of the population."[10]

Mowat was not by any means alone in holding those views (the poet Al Purdy, for instance, supported him publicly), and there has always been a stream of thought holding that certain views can be equated with pro-Canadian or un-Canadian feelings or activities. Nor was Mowat the first or last to link such views to ethnicity. Indeed, there was a time when views such as his prospered in English-speaking Canada and might well have provided an ideology – noxious, of course – for the English side of the Canadian state. Fortunately for decency, and for the rest of us, views like Mowat's were made politically as well as inherently invalid by the immigration waves that began with Mediterranean immigrants during the St. Laurent and Diefenbaker periods in the 1950s and broadened in the 1960s and 1970s to include representatives of just about all types of humanity. Today it would be hard to imagine the residents of Canada coming together on any exclusionary definition of patriotism, much less one that was linked to race.

Those relative newcomers who arrived in Canada in the last thirty or so years would have found it very odd indeed if we had tried to enlist them as ideological foot-soldiers in either a war against American culture or a revival of British influence. However, we have done neither them nor ourselves (I write as an Old Canadian, born in Ottawa in 1932) any great favour by slowly obliterating the country's symbolic landscape. We have, for the most part, written off our history as unimportant – so far as public discourse is concerned, Canadian history is little more than a series of picturesque and unconnected anecdotes. Newcomers to Canada find themselves in a curiously pastless country, where the oldest writers anyone quotes were living ten years ago and the political parties seem rarely even to mention traditions that stretch back farther than the 1960s. (In the case of the parties, history was made especially problematic in the 1980s by the 180-degree reversal of course by both Liberals and Conservatives on the most important issue in foreign affairs, our relations with the United States.)

Our history as a country of warriors has become even vaguer, to the point where many young citizens have lost any sense of an independent Canadian contribution to the two world wars. Robert Martin, a law professor at the University of Western Ontario, has suggested that this is because we have, almost unconsciously, become a nation of pacifists who believe that warriors in our history are best ignored. And so, he argues: "We are actively involved in Canada today in abolishing our own history. A person can graduate from high school in Ontario without having done a course in Canadian ... history. We are forgetting that we have a past. Or where it is acknowledged that we do have a history, we are being taught to be ashamed of it."

If we now ignore such matters as our military history, we also do whatever we can to strip away the symbols of our British past (in one generation we abolished titles, in the next we took the crown off the mailboxes) and even our own peculiarly Canadian past. My favourite example is the word "dominion." I grew up in a country of which my own children have seldom heard, a place nobody speaks about now, "the Dominion of Canada." The Government at Ottawa was "the dominion government," and when the prime minister and the premiers met it was a "dominion-provincial conference." All parliamentary documents and schoolbooks used "dominion." Then, at some point in the 1950s, it vanished, and today only an antiquarian kook would use it. Where did the word go, and why?

Erasing "dominion" from our language could be seen in this context as an act of vandalism, like cutting down a forest or bombing a cathedral. Good words are not much easier to create than forests or cathedrals, and this one was a prize – the only word that Canada ever contributed to international politics. As a political term, it was invented by Sir Leonard Tilley, a Father of Confederation from New Brunswick, who borrowed it from Psalm 72 (God "shall have dominion from sea to sea"), partly because many believed that Americans would find the phrase "Kingdom of Canada" an offence to republican sentiment. Everyone agreed that it sounded good. British colonies ascending later toward independence, such as Australia and New Zealand, decided that they, too, would be "dominions." Perhaps that's where the trouble started: people spoke of her majesty's "overseas dominions." Rudyard Kipling, in "Recessional," wrote of Britain holding "Dominion over palm and pine" – we obviously were the pine, and some Canadians didn't like the sound of it.

So gradually this Canadian usage began to seem like a term of colonial oppression, though in fact the opposite was true. When the move to abolish it appeared, in the 1950s, those who wanted to keep it were made to look like old fogies or colonialists. Those who wanted to drop "dominion" were obviously modern, independent, and anglophobic in a healthy way. They stood tall, and they won – at least partly because Prime Minister Louis St. Laurent was on their side and (as his chief lieutenant, Jack Pickersgill, later wrote) dominion "could not be translated into French" – a statement that was neither disputed nor tested. Donald Creighton, bitterly lamenting the death of the word, wrote in one of his last books that it was buried without proclamation or ceremony, being replaced by an American-sounding word, "federal." The late Eugene Forsey died an unrepentant "dominion" man, however. In the second edition of *The Canadian Encyclopedia* (1988), he noted, without even conceding that it was anachronistic, that in the Constitution Act, 1982, "Dominion" remained Canada's official title. By then, of course, it was a mere legality, another historical artifact discarded when it began to look slightly out of date.

Critical theory has given us a term for the process described here: deconstruction. Our habit, over the generations, is constantly to "call into question," as deconstructionists say, the basis for our history, to reassess its symbols, and, finding them invalid, eliminate them – and to imply, always, that the generation just before us had everything wrong. Like true deconstructionists, we are destined forever to spend our lives rethinking our premises.

Deconstruction, of course, is an essential ingredient in post-modern thought, and perhaps it is as a post-modern state that Canada can best be understood. If a casual student of post-modernism studies Canadian history, post-modernist terms spring frequently to mind. The events of the last three decades, for instance, have "de-centred" Canada, making it unsure what is the core and what is the periphery, a condition that post-modernism regards as highly desirable. As a post-modern state we recognize the "indeterminacy" (another key term) of our history and utterly reject, as all good post-modernists do, one agreed-upon "master narrative" that would enslave all of us to a single vision. We prove conclusively (in everything from "dominion" to "distinct") that language is a matter of treacherous, shifting meanings, always freighted with irony. The key to post-modernism is its "questioning of any notion of coherent, stable, autonomous identity (be it individual or national)"[11] – and what could be more Canadian than that? Finally, if we shift the metaphor to architecture, post-modernism is the design condition to which Canadian constitution-writers, and for that matter most Canadians, yearningly aspire – a modern, functional building, pleasingly and nostalgically decorated with neo-classical forms. Call it a post-modern dominion.

NOTES

1 Charles Taylor's remarks were made in the course of an interview with Peter Gzowski on "Morningside," CBC Radio, 8 Nov. 1991.

2 From Michael R. Marrus, *Mr. Sam: The Life and Times of Samuel Bronfman* (Toronto, 1991), 14.

3 Quoted by Jeffrey Simpson in the *Globe and Mail*, 13 Nov. 1991.

4 Chrétien was quoted in a front-page article in ibid., 22 Nov. 1991.

5 From Daniel Latouche, "Canada: The New Country from the Old Dominion," *Queen's Quarterly* (Summer 1991).

6 Quoted in Carl Berger, *The Sense of Power: Studies in the Ideas of Canadian Imperialism, 1867–1914* (Toronto, 1970), 66 and 121.

7 In F.R. Scott and A.J.M. Smith, eds., *The Blasted Pine* (Toronto, 1957), 36.

8 In Ramsay Cook, *Canada and the French-Canadian Question* (Toronto, 1966), 168.

9 James Eayrs, *Northern Approaches* (Toronto, 1961), 5.

10 Mowat was quoted in Toronto *Metropolis*, 18 Jan. 1990, and in the *Globe and Mail*, 29 Jan. 1990.

11 Linda Hutcheon, critical theorist, in "As Canadian as ... Possible ... under the Circumstances," in Gerald Lynch and David Rampton, eds., *The Canadian Essay* (Toronto, 1991), 339.

PART TWO

Regions

ROSELLA MELANSON

Citizenship and Acadie: The Art of the Possible

> There are epics that haunt history searching for the
> nations that placed them in our memory.
>
> Michel Roy[1]

If asked to name a jurisdiction that is officially bilingual, whose population is two-thirds English-speaking and one-third French-
speaking, whose head of government must be bilingual to be elected,
where the French-speaking community wants more control over its
affairs and some of them call for separation, most people would say
Canada. It would also be correct to say New Brunswick.

The significant Acadian presence within New Brunswick makes it
an excellent microcosm of Canada and Canadian tensions. Micro-
cosms being miniature representations, the options available to Quebec, for example, are only dreamt of in Acadie. Acadie is the other
variation on the Canadian theme. It challenges the notion of Canada
as Quebec and ROC (the rest of Canada).

Acadians, of course, are not only found in New Brunswick, but
85 per cent of Acadians in the Maritimes, or 250,000, are concentrated in that province, and modern Acadie is situated there. New
Brunswick is the only province where a francophone minority ex-
ceeds 6 per cent of the population and where the renewal rate of the
French-mother-tongue population is almost adequate to maintain itself, despite losses to assimilation. The great majority of New Brunswick's Acadians live in areas where francophones predominate,
along the northern and eastern shores. The Acadians' history established their claim of being a people, and the current vigour of their
culture leaves no doubt.

Few Acadians would propose New Brunswick as a model for the
Canadian situation, mostly because their gains fall far short of what

is needed to live in French, but also because they know how much the situation of francophone communities varies across Canada and that each does what is possible in its own context. Some Canadians do point to New Brunswick as a model of "bonne entente." Moncton's Acadians protesting the lack of French in that city remember being told by city hall that there was in fact one city street with a French name, Bonaccord Street. That kind of "bon accord" is for outside consumption.

However, the level of discontent in Acadie is nowhere near that in Quebec. This is because Acadians are proud of the phenomenal changes that they have brought about in the last twenty-five years; but it is also because Acadians have hardly begun to develop the political dimensions of Acadie. As for francophones elsewhere in Canada, linguistic rights and cultural identity were the first preoccupations of Acadians. New Brunswick's Acadians may be awakening to the need to "Acadianize power."

The current constitutional crisis has potentially serious consequences for Acadie. If Quebec negotiates a separate relationship, what is left of Canada will be 95 per cent English-speaking and 5 per cent French-speaking. Acadians in New Brunswick would still have the same presence in that province, but the political support for official-language communities would be diminished, nationally and provincially. Francophones outside Quebec might become nostalgic for the attention that they had as hostages of the Ottawa-Quebec struggle. Some Acadians, however, would be relieved that one form of colonialism – that from Quebec – would be reduced and that control of the francophone identity in Canada would be shared.

Survival of the Acadians, the first permanent European settlers north of Florida, is not assured. Whether the current Canadian crisis is of Yugoslavian proportions, as some have suggested, or a "crisette," as others propose (or even if, as this author suspects, it is simply a rare convergence of mediocre leaders, soulless politics, dysfunctional institutions, unsettled differences, and a recession economy), it illustrates the fragility and lack of protection of the Acadians as a national community.

Hearing so many Canadians – politicians, columnists, Quebecers even – refer to "Quebec and English Canada" has been a sobering experience for francophone minorities and Acadians. The impression is clear that what little they have acquired was obtained on someone else's coat-tail. Or as the Federation of Francophone and Acadian Communities of Canada has said, they seem to be medals that are worn when it is useful and stored away when no longer necessary.

Acadians in New Brunswick are, of all the francophone minorities, closest to obtaining "droit de cité" as a people. The New Brunswick Official Languages Act of 1969 gave individual language rights of Acadians symbolic status on the same footing as the English language. The Act Recognizing the Equality of the Two Official Linguistic Communities in New Brunswick (1981) provided Acadians a collective right to participate in government and to distinct institutions. New Brunswick's law recognizes two majorities coexisting within the boundaries of the province. One majority has 67 per cent of the vote, and the other, 33 per cent, and Acadians' rights and privileges are still exercised mostly in the context of political and economic institutions defined and controlled by the anglophone community. Acadians base their hopes of gaining effective droit de cité on increased duality and creation of Acadian administrative regions within New Brunswick.

ACADIE 1604 TO TODAY

> My God, can it be true that you're not making any more land for Acadians?
>
> Jean-Baptiste Cyr,
> Acadian, born 1710 in Beaubassin, Acadie[2]

Acadian settlers from 1604 to the Deportation in 1755 paid little attention to either French or British authorities, establishing a separate identity – possibly the first modern Canadian identity. Founded earlier than Quebec by French immigrants from a different part of France than Quebecers, Acadie can claim to have always had a distinct identity from Quebec. Acadians had a unique, mostly self-sufficient life-style in the New World, based on dike-building.

They traded with New England in the seventeenth century even though this commerce had been banned. They seemed to prefer a quiet, apolitical existence on their lands, having come from the Poitou-Charente region of France, torn by war for generations, and settling in a land that soon became a strategic "suburb" of both New France and New England. Because they reclaimed land with their dikes, they had not settled on the aboriginal peoples' hunting or fishing grounds and had friendly relations with them, a fact that would play a role in some of the British and French decisions about what to do with the Acadians. For almost 150 years, a French-speaking society flourished in the Maritimes. In 1671, when the first census was taken, 500 Acadians were counted. Seventy-five years later, close to 15,000 were living in the Maritimes.

Acadie would change hands seven times in its first 100 years. Survival became the first order for Acadians. When the British ruled, the Acadians were known as the "neutral French" because they refused to swear allegiance to the British crown unless Acadian neutrality in case of war was recognized. They wanted it clear that they would not fight with either the British or the French. These qualified oaths were accepted by some British governors, formally establishing a distinct Acadian reality. Governors who tried to force them to take an unqualified oath were sometimes threatened with mass emigration by the Acadians, who knew that their trade and labour were needed, as well as their relations with the aboriginal peoples.

When the French ruled, the French authorities were critical of the Acadians for their independence and obstinacy. In 1713, when the Treaty of Utrecht gave Acadie (then Nova Scotia) to England while France kept Cape Breton and Prince Edward Island, the Acadians were given one year to take the oath or leave Acadie. They were initially encouraged by France and England to move to Cape Breton and Prince Edward Island, which were still French possessions, but few did. They lived in peace in British Acadie until mid-century. There were few British settlers, and Nova Scotia remained essentially Acadian until 1749. No assembly of delegates was organized in Nova Scotia, as was done elsewhere, because it would have been dominated by Acadians.

The Acadians were reaching a significant population base, but their position in a conquered land became precarious once more when war erupted again between France and England and Nova Scotia became a prized strategic location. By 1755, the die was cast with the appointment of a new lieutenant-governor who saw the Acadian presence and neutrality strictly as a military defence problem; neutrality was no longer an option. He organized their deportation to British possessions, since he did not want Acadians to reinforce the French presence elsewhere. He acted "in such a way as may best answer our design in preventing their reunion." Although such enforced exile was not unheard of at the time (even the French in 1746 had ordered that any Acadian not loyal to the French crown be expelled), it was unusual because the Acadians were not sent back to their country of origin and because it occurred over forty years after the Conquest. The Acadian deportation was essentially a dispersal which almost became genocide.

Between 1755 and 1763, about 75 per cent of Acadian population, close to 10,000 persons, were deported to American colonies or to England. About half died of disease and deprivation on the ships or in the holding areas set up for them. Families were often separated.

Many families hid in the woods and, with the help of aboriginal peoples, made it to New Brunswick or Quebec.

In 1763, peace returned with the surrender of all of New France to England. As an Environment Canada publication puts it, "By the time the Anglo-French struggle for North America was finally resolved, the Acadians were among its most visible and most tragic victims."[3] There were only about 4,000 left in the Maritimes. Many of those who were exiled to the American colonies began their quest to return to Nova Scotia. Most who made it back actually moved into unsettled, isolated regions of New Brunswick, having lost their former fertile lands to the arriving Loyalist and British settlers. In that sense, Acadians did not totally disperse as had been intended and as happened in the case of many other exiled peoples, such as the Scottish Highlanders. The Acadian deportation was, ultimately, a displacement.

In 1761, Acadians represented 17 per cent of New Brunswick's population. One hundred years later, they were 36 per cent, and in 1971, 37 per cent. Until the second half of the nineteenth century, the population was still atomized and had no college, no newspaper, no professional elite, and no forum for discussion. In the 1850s the Acadian epic became famous through H.W. Longfellow's poem "Evangeline." Acadie was in fashion. Some have suggested that the mythology of Evangeline and the exaltation of Acadians' suffering served to inhibit their awakening to their inferior status and revolt against their treatment. For the Acadian elite of the time and the Catholic church, deportation and return were useful as romantic myths that kept people docile. In any case, a certain renaissance of awareness began in the 1880s, and by the end of the decade some of the symbols of a nation were in place: a flag, a national holiday, a hymn. Acadian colleges and hospitals were being established.

It is significant that Acadians rejected Canadian federation in 1865–66. Whereas Quebec saw in Confederation a means to free itself somewhat from Upper Canadian power, Acadians did not believe that their collective project of Acadie would be advanced by it. The French presence in the Maritimes was in fact ignored by the constitution of 1867.

Until the 1960s, Acadian society, like New Brunswick in general, was very closed and rural. The docile nature of Acadians during those years was encouraged by the Catholic clergy. The survival of the Acadians up to the 1960s can be attributed to isolation, neglect, and underdevelopment as much as to collective will and "critical mass." After the deportation, the Acadians were bent on avoiding confrontation with the English, and they lived unobtrusively. Their national holiday, 15 August, traditionally features a "tintamarre," where as much noise as possible is made; as legend has it, this is a way of "coming out of hiding and saying, 'we are still here'."

The 1960s represented for Acadians, as for everyone else, massive change and urbanization. An Acadian, Louis-J. Robichaud, was elected premier of New Brunswick in 1960. He brought about extensive reform through his Equal Opportunities Program. Equalization of the tax structure and centralized administration of education, health, and social services brought Acadian regions into the modern age. The Schools Act of 1967 was actually the first provincial legislation to recognize the presence of francophones. What education had been available in French before then was either outside the public system or unofficially tolerated by the Education Department. The Robichaud decade ended with adoption of New Brunswick's Official Languages Act in 1969 (even preceding the federal act, although the provincial legislation was implemented over several years). The act applies only to the provincial government and not to municipalities, hospitals, or the private sector. Premier Richard Hatfield continued the reform and support for the Acadians from 1970 to 1987. New Brunswick soon became a member of la Francophonie, a world commonwealth of francophone nations, mostly as a result of Ottawa's desire to dilute the political impact of Quebec's ascension to member status.

Université de Moncton had been founded in 1963, and within five years it saw momentous student demonstrations against both English oppression and the Acadian "establishment." Head-on conflict with the English supremacist mayor of Moncton in the late 1960s ended with the mayor as the apparent winner, but the bare-faced hostility would give impetus to the new Acadian nationalism. The need to take control of the economic reins of Acadie was recognized, and in regions where Acadians were a majority, some inroads were made with regional socioeconomic intervention.

The Parti Acadien was created in 1972 and would eventually propose a separate province. It contributed to the development of nationalist alternatives and got 12 per cent of Acadian votes before it disappeared in the early 1980s.

The New Brunswick Society of Acadians was created in 1972, from the National Society of Acadians, to promote collective consciousness and apply political pressure to move Acadians from a linguistic community to a "distinct society."

The struggle for unilingual schools and separate school districts in the 1960s and 1970s saw massive popular participation. When, after years of conflict, unilingual school districts were created and the school boards could return to debating education instead of language, the benefits of duality were made evident to the Acadians. Duality was implemented in the Department of Education from the deputy ministers down. Community colleges were also based on the principle of duality. Teachers' associations, school trustees, and home and school associations soon also separated.

The cleavage between the "official" preference of English-speaking New Brunswickers for bilingual associations and Acadians' desire for dual, or parallel groups would be repeated in many organizations. Associations of municipalities, sports organizations, Women's Institutes, and arts groups all separated along linguistic lines at the initiative of their Acadian members during the 1970s and 1980s. English-speaking New Brunswickers were sometimes left behind before they became aware of Acadian discontent. Acadians saw no need and no benefit to continuing in a bilingual setting.

Whereas in a common, even bilingual structure, Acadians often still had to speak English, obtain majority support for their projects, and depend on translations, an Acadian-controlled structure gave them power. Bilingualism would never allow Acadians to attain equal status with anglophones. Meanwhile, many anglophones thought that bilingual organizations were a liberal solution that fitted the ideal of "bonne entente" and Canadian nationalism and that they were being established for the benefit of Acadians. But Acadians knew that little real bilingualism was being implemented and that bilingual services were at best an attempt to provide for individual, not collective, rights. In any case, Acadians reacted to the artificial nature of bilingual organizations and realized that if they themselves were the ones to have to accommodate bilingualism, then the official languages were not really equal.

The traditional political parties, although they support duality, have not joined the move to parallel structures.

Among anglophones, lack of awareness of the Acadian reality and aspirations remains total. "Acadie" to most anglophones is that which existed before the British conquest. The teaching of the French language in English schools in New Brunswick has always been extremely weak: apart from being taught often by unilingual English teachers, it made no reference to the living cultural context and geographical situation. The anglophone population is barely cognizant that Acadians have their own institutions, media, artists, and international relations. Only a fraction of what English and French media deal with is common to both. English media coverage of Acadian issues concerns linguistic conflict exclusively. The provincial English newspaper made reference to Maurice Chevalier and Gallic joie de vivre when it attempted to characterize a prominent Acadian singer. The provincial French newspaper hardly recognizes news that does not have a francophone-anglophone angle. Exposure to bilingual settings is rare for anglophones, as is seen whenever translation service is provided at public meetings. Anglophones will not initially request translation devices, having never realized that these are provided for them – the unilingual group. Many anglophones think that institutional bilingualism has actually been implemented; outside the Acadian peninsula in northeastern New Brunswick, few Acadians can obtain service in French, beyond reception areas.

In 1979, a provincial Convention of Acadians was held after a year of local meetings on the political options of the Acadian community. Out of about 1,000 participants, who were at least somewhat representative of Acadie, fully 53 per cent chose a separate Acadian province in Canada as their ideal solution and fully 48 per cent thought that this was feasible. The New Brunswick Society of Acadians was mandated to act on the convention's resolutions. The society, convulsed by the autonomist outcome of its convention, was forced to replace its executive and renege on the convention mandate. Continued federal support for the society was a factor, but so were the provincial government's promises of action on collective rights made after the convention.

Like Canada following the 1980 Quebec referendum, New Brunswick's government acted to calm the new nationalism. In 1981, the political parties unanimously adopted Bill 88, An Act Recognizing the Equality of the Two Official Linguistic Communities in New Brunswick, which a government spokesperson said was half-way between the status quo and an Acadian province. The provincial government also obtained entrenchment in the Canadian constitution in 1981 of the principles of its Official Languages Act, making the province constitutionally bilingual.

Bill 88 states that the government acknowledges the existence of two official linguistic communities and wishes to recognize their equality and enhance their capacity to enjoy and safeguard their heritage. It also wishes to enshrine in its laws principles that provide a framework for action on the part of public institutions and an example to private institutions. The bill then says:

Acknowledging the unique character of New Brunswick, the English linguistic community and the French linguistic community are officially recognized within the context of one province for all purposes to which the authority of the Legislature of New Brunswick extends, and the equality of status and the equal rights and privileges of these two communities are affirmed.

The Government of New Brunswick shall ensure protection of the equality of status and the equal rights and privileges of the official linguistic communities and in particular their right to distinct institutions within which cultural, educational and social activities may be carried on.

The Government of New Brunswick shall, in its proposed laws, in the allocation of public resources and in its policies and programs, take positive action to promote the cultural, economic, educational and social development of the official linguistic communities.

While the Official Languages Act aimed for language equality and recognized individuals' right to use their own language in contact with the government, Bill 88 sought equality of the two linguistic communities and recognized the Acadians as a people, or at least as a community. There was no longer a majority and a minority in New Brunswick. Acadians could develop their collective project within the framework of Bill 88. The act is an example of the second generation of language rights, promoting development of official-language communities rather than bilingual services.

Bill 88, however, provided no mechanisms for creating true equality and is an empty framework that has yet to be completed with political and economic rights. But it will be the legal and political basis of future Acadian claims. The current government has promised to entrench in the Canadian constitution the principles of Bill 88 but has not yet done so. It did propose a constitutional amendment to that effect in 1990 to accompany the Meech Lake Accord. When that accord died, the provincial and federal governments let the Acadian amendment die also. A bilateral amendment could be made at any time, under section 43 of the constitution.

Acadian organizations are urging both levels of government to entrench not just the principles but the four goals of the legislation: equality of the two linguistic communities in terms of rights, privileges, and status; government commitment to protect and promote this equality; guarantee of the right of both communities to their own educational, social, and cultural institutions; and protection of the provisions of Bill 88 so that future amendments that diminish them must meet certain strict criteria. The third goal is the most unlikely to be entrenched, because it would give constitutional leverage to the case for dual institutions. While that principle is already currently contained in the provincial legislation, its entrenchment in the constitution might create an obligation to act.

So important is Bill 88 to the Acadian community's view of itself that its constitutional entrenchment was identified as the trade-off for Acadians' endorsement of the Meech Lake Accord. That document gave little space to francophone minorities and none at all to francophone peoples outside Quebec, such as the Acadians. The New Brunswick Society of Acadians came out in support of the Meech Lake Accord "so that Quebec with its demographic importance and political strength as the only Francophone government in North America could once again be part of the discussion around the constitutional negotiating table." The society also called for entrenchment of Bill 88 through a Canada–New Brunswick process. It termed this proposal the Acadian solution and defended it "on the basis of our conviction that it has the two-fold advantage of correcting the Meech Lake Accord's imperfect description of Acadian aspirations without, however, requiring that it be re-opened."

The 1991 federal constitutional proposals did not show any more awareness of the gains of the Acadians. They recognized francophones outside Quebec only as individuals who speak French, while Acadians have already been recognized by legislation and by themselves as more than that. The government of Quebec has similarly proposed a "code of minorities"; the cynicism and indifference that it displays toward francophones outside Quebec is such that the president of the New Brunswick Society of Acadians has said that Acadians have understood that they must fight their own battles.

The constitutional protection of Bill 88 would ensure that Acadians could develop the homogeneous institutional infrastructure needed to live in French, to exercise the rights and freedoms of free citizens. Just like Quebec and the First Nations, New Brunswick's Acadians want "cultural sovereignty" and believe that constitutional protection of Bill 88 will launch the process, especially since it states that the government of New Brunswick shall promote the cultural, economic, educational, and social development of the official linguistic communities when it adopts laws, allocates public resources, and develops policies and programs. Acadians hope to gain the same decision-making powers and dual institutions in the judicial, cultural, economic, and other areas that they have obtained in education.

Entrenchment of all of Bill 88 has become a strong rallying point for Acadian leaders and groups. The constitutional instability following the Meech Lake Accord and the growing interest in a union of the Atlantic provinces are urgent new reasons for its entrenchment. The election of the anti-French Confederation of Regions (COR) party as the official opposition in New Brunswick in September 1991, with 21 per cent of the popular vote, is another. COR filled a void created by the eradication of the Progressive Conservative party after Richard Hatfield overstayed his welcome. Many COR candidates and partisans are disaffected PCs. As the official opposition, at least until 1996, COR's eight MLAs (of fifty-eight) will force the assembly to deal more openly with the anti-French element that has always been present. That element now has a direct voice and is no longer limited to influencing the traditional parties from the inside. The party's lack of enthusiasm for any other issue but blaming francophones, be they Acadians, Quebecers, or French, points out its lightweight status. The fanaticism and hatred displayed by COR members and partisans may attract more of the same, especially in a slow economy, but it may also have a Leonard Jones effect: the 1960s mayor of Moncton spurred Acadian pride and action and awakened moderate anglophones, even while seemingly slowing progress toward linguistic equality.

BEYOND BILINGUALISM

Good fences make good neighbors.

Robert Frost

At the height of the current constitutional crisis, the New Brunswick government felt compelled to take some initiative that would reaffirm a commitment to bilingual nationalism. It introduced an exchange program between anglophone and Acadian municipalities, to complement an existing program for students. Such is the irrelevance of institutional bilingualism: while the majority group gets a warm glow from endorsing official bilingualism and having cultural exchanges, the minority group is left wondering who asked for these. Was the objective to allow the Acadians to develop as a people, or was it to make Acadians more acceptable to the majority? Exchanges with other francophone communities would be of greater interest to Acadians. The two official languages remain unequal if Acadians must bear the cost of making bilingualism work.

Acadians are not separatist; they still identify with New Brunswick as their province and even hope to see the capital city of Fredericton some day reflect the provincial duality. They participate enthusiastically in provincial politics; about one-third of MLAs are Acadians. But the glow of official bilingualism has long since faded for Acadians. In 1982, a task force on the impact of ten years of official bilingualism reported:

In almost all cases, the working language of the departments is English. French is used very rarely, even in the Department of Fisheries which has 72% bilingual personnel ... The only exceptions are internal communication in particular sectors, notably in the north of the province.

The provincial Act is no more effective than the federal Act, mainly because of the much more timid measures taken in New Brunswick to ensure linguistic competency of civil servants in both official languages and the increased presence of Francophones in the civil service ... It is difficult to realize equality of the language in a context where civil servants are content to react to individual requests, without any obligation to provide their services directly in both official languages, and where it is possible to respect the letter of the law by providing a low quality of service. The dependence of the system on translation and interpretation, its singular use of intermediaries in the form of bilingual receptionists and secretaries, have caused important delays and an often unacceptable quality of information received for those requiring a service in French.

The most frequent problem raised when people spoke to us about bilingualism in New Brunswick is, without dispute, that of the quality of service provided. The cynicism of the Francophones with respect to the Official Languages Act has come to a high level and, from now on, they refuse to be forced to beg for so-called special services which are in fact inferior. Equality of status signifies above all services of the same quality without delay; it means the right of Francophones to a system of distribution of services that reflects their values and in which they share fully. For all practical purposes, the equality of status means the establishment of a system of duality more so than an Anglophone system with certain linguistic capabilities in the "other" official language.[4]

Following that 1982 report, administrative duality emerged as a goal for Acadians. Duality seemed the approach best suited to the needs of New Brunswick. Under duality, certain branches of government would be divided into English and French sections. Technical services would be shared, and policies would be co-ordinated. Duality seems the only way to allow realization of all four objectives of bilingualism as set down in the report:

1. All government services should be offered directly in the language of the client and be of equal quality, whether provided in English or French;
2. All citizens should have reasonable access to a career in the public service and the possibility of working in the official language of one's choice;
3. Both language groups should be equitably represented in the public service;
4. The local identity of linguistic groups should be recognized and government administration should reflect the geographic distribution of the population.

The report also studied the impact of the official-languages policy on the boundaries of administrative regions. The concept of Acadian regions was emerging, but existing administrative regions did not take into account linguistic and cultural factors, creating obstacles to implementation of the policy. Thirty-one maps were found for fourteen different government departments, all oblivious to the distribution of linguistic communities. This negation of geographical positioning continues to the present.

In recognition of the regional identity of Acadians, the report proposed adoption of restructured administrative maps compatible with the linguistic characteristics of the population. Francophone regions would be created where the government would have a primarily francophone profile, in the public service, road signs and toponomy, and so on. Relocation of certain provincial agencies to francophone regions was also proposed, in order to give Acadians "the essential feeling of belonging."

These changes toward duality and regionalism have not yet been implemented. Through Bill 88 and the principles of duality and regionalism, Acadians hope to take back the right of all free citizens to administer their own affairs. As an Acadian lawyer, activist, and now government MLA stated in 1985, "Despite all the obstacles before us, of which our own indifference is not the least, we believe that we already have all the tools necessary to spur our collective development."[5]

In the absence of a territorial Acadie, Acadians seek a mental map of Acadie, with the infrastructure and agents to make it a real place to live.

CONCLUSION

If Acadie were a person, it would be said to be healthy except for its cancer. The assimilation rate of close to 8 per cent is a real long-term threat. Inequalities between the Acadian and the anglophone regions in New Brunswick are staggering, especially in terms of economic power, transportation networks, unemployment rates, and power in the civil service. Acadians are currently facing more pressure to assimilate than ever before. But they have never had as complete an array of institutions and have never been more actively involved in ensuring their collective future. They have worked through the complexities of their relationship with Quebec. They have begun to understand that regaining majority status is the only option that respects their culture.

The solutions that Acadie can consider are half-way between two extremes: the status quo and a separate province. They are choosing to exercise their right to self-determination by superimposing a mental map of Acadie on the territory that it shares. Other international examples can be found.

What does the Acadian model suggest to the Canadian idea of citizenship? The notion of symmetrical provincial status is at best no longer useful and at worst a form of systemic discrimination. The idea of a bilingual land where individuals share everything except the language is a romantic myth. The peoples that form Canada – English speakers, First Nations, Québécois, Acadians, and others – are distinct societies. If the specificity of each is recognized, they will have been treated equally. New Brunswick's specificity lies in the duality of its population, which requires duality in administrative and possibly political structures.

Equality which uses the anglophone majority's norm is not true equality. Having control of one's institutions is not special treatment: it is what a people's right to self-determination means. Diversity in equality is supposedly a Canadian contribution to human rights; it can be applied to politics as well.

NOTES

These sources, in addition to the ones cited in numbered notes below, were helpful in the preparation of this essay: Michel Bastarache, "Dualité canadienne, spécificité du Québec: contradiction ou complémentarité?" *Égalité*, Moncton, no. 22 (Fall 1987–Winter 1988); Michel Bastarache and Michel Saint-Louis, "De l'égalité formelle à l'égalité réelle entre les deux communautés linguistiques du Nouveau-Brunswick," *Égalité* no. 7 (Fall 1982); Jean-Guy Finn, "L'aménagement linguistique au Nouveau-Brunswick," *Égalité* no. 19 (Fall 1986); Diane Lamoureux, *Citoyennes? Femmes, droit de vote et démocratie* (Montreal: Éditions remue-ménage, 1989); Jean-William Lapierre and Muriel Roy, *Les Acadiens, que sais-je?* (Paris: Presses universitaires de France, 1983); Bernard Richard, "La revendication linguistique ne suffit pas," *Égalité* no. 6 (Summer 1982); Société des Acadiens du Nouveau-Brunswick, *Pour un nouveau contrat social – Plan d'action 1984–1989* (1984); Société des Acadiens et des Acadiennes du Nouveau-Brunswick, "Langues officielles: Pour une égalité réelle," *Égalité* no. 29 (Spring 1991); and Léon Thériault, *La question du pouvoir en Acadie* (Moncton: Éditions d'Acadie, 1989).

1 Michel Roy, *L'Acadie des origines à nos jours* (Quebec: Éditions Québec/Amérique, 1981), 299.

2 Thomas Albert, *Histoire du Madawaska* (n.p.: Imprimerie franciscaine, 1920), 85.

3 Environment Canada, *La déportation des Acadiens – The Deportation of the Acadians* (1986).

4 *Toward Equality of Official Languages in New Brunswick – Report of the Task Force on Official Languages* (Fredericton: Government of New Brunswick, 1982), 161, 136, 413.

5 Bernard Richard, "Le mythe de l'égalité," *Égalité* no. 15 (Spring–Summer 1985) 110.

MARC COUSINEAU

Belonging: An Essential Element of Citizenship — A Franco-Ontarian Perspective

Our concept of citizenship is founded on political structures the foundations of which are quickly becoming irrelevant. For example, the countries of the European Community are in the process of redefining the notion of the nation-state, the basic unit of international law and politics. This transformation is possible only because the underlying reasons for the creation and maintenance of the nation-state have themselves largely been rendered obsolete by the economic and political realities of the late twentieth century. As the foundation of the concept undergoes these radical changes, so by necessity must the derivative idea of citizenship.

In its strictly legal sense, citizenship is intrinsically linked to the concept of the nation-state. One is always a citizen of a state. My status as citizen of Canada entitles me to certain rights of citizenship — for example, to carry a Canadian passport, to enter the country at will, and to vote in Canadian elections. I did not earn these rights; they are simply a by-product of an accident of birth. I do not have to like my country or admire its policies and practices to be its citizen. In fact, I can devote my life to living off the state or to dismantling its fundamental political structures and values without losing my citizenship or any of its associated rights and privileges.

Canadian citizens who emigrated to Canada or sought political refugee status here simply changed their membership in a nation-state. They did not earn their Canadian citizenship in the sense that one earns an honour or an accolade. They may have been victims of persecution in their country of origin and in need of refuge, but that is not equivalent to having earned membership in our collectivity. As well, their Canadian citizenship is unconditional. Immigrants and refugees are not obliged to contribute to our collectivity in order to obtain or retain their citizenship. For immigrants and refugees, the status of citizen of Canada is independent of any prior or subsequent contribution to our nation-state.

Even stateless persons derive their status from the concept of the state. It is because they are not citizens of any state that they are stateless and therefore need the protection offered by organizations such as the United Nations.

A state may modify the rights and obligations that it attaches to citizenship; the citizens will nonetheless remain citizens of that state. A state may, for example, abolish the right to vote or the right to leave the country at will. It may require national service or extract from its citizens a significant portion of their income solely for the administration of programs reserved for a small elite portion of the population. The citizens of the state in question are no less citizens than they were prior to these enactments. In other words, it is very difficult to attach to the legal idea of citizenship any right or obligation that defines the concept.

The legal sense of citizenship may thus be devoid of any substantive meaning other than the simple fact of being a member of a particular nation-state, but identification with one's nation-state was for generations of citizens a significant, if not primary, element in their self-definition. Particularly in Europe, people proudly assumed the mantle of citizen of their nation. French, German, Italian, or English citizens had no qualms about being, above all, French, German, Italian, or English.

For a number of years, Canadians, or at least a majority of them, probably felt the same identification with their country as did Europeans. However, for historical reasons, their attachment to Canada has never been as secure as that of Europeans to their nation-states. I doubt whether all aboriginal Canadians have been moved by their allegiance to this nation-state. Similarly, the conscription crisis during the First World War indicates that many French-speaking Canadians did not feel the same sense of identification with the country as did their anglophone counterparts. The current constitutional difficulties suggest that, in 1992, Canadians have varying degrees of attachment to the country.

At the other extreme, the disintegration of the Soviet Union demonstrates that citizenship in a nation-state does not translate into an overriding love for one's nation. Ukrainians, Latvians, Estonians, and Lithuanians jumped at the opportunity to rid themselves of their citizenship in the Soviet Union.

Recent events in eastern Europe, western Europe, and Canada confirm that citizenship in a particular nation-state does not in itself imply any real loyalty to the nation-state in question. Without a sense of loyalty and adhesion on the part of the members of the community, collective action becomes progressively more difficult. The three examples of differing levels of attachment to the nation-state suggest that there must be other elements, beyond simply being a citizen of a country, that give meaning and substance to the relationship between the citizen and the state. An alternative basis for loyalty to the nation-state is needed to ensure willing participation in collective projects as well as the very survival of the political entity in question.

A new foundation for collective action is especially needed at the present, when the concept of the nation-state is rapidly becoming less and less relevant. Canadians inherited their concept of the nation-state from Europe. European states were successors to the various kingdoms that dominated the continent in medieval times. At a time when land was the primary source of wealth, it was reasonable and understandable that those in power sought to consolidate their power and wealth over defined geographical areas. Lines of defence were naturally drawn around domains controlled by those who could extract wealth and influence from the protected areas. Other concerns, such as wars and religious beliefs, influenced the political map of Europe. Holland is a good example of the importance of religion in the formation of some European states. Nevertheless, with few exceptions, the nation-states of Europe derive their origins from the medieval kingdoms that preceded them.

Over time, other factors, such as a shared history and unitary language and culture, solidified the nation-state. There was no need to question the desirability of the nation-state as long as it proved itself capable of protecting the physical and economic security of its rulers and citizens. A nation could not guarantee to win every war or economic struggle, but all wars and economic struggles were issues that belonged to nations to win or resolve.

In the second half of the twentieth century, neither defence nor the economy belongs to nations. Both have transcended the boundaries of the nation-state. Long gone are the days when we could feel secure that the Canadian state could protect us from invasion or from the impact of economic decisions made in Japan, Europe, or the United States. The move toward international free trade is a necessary institutional response to the realities of the world economy.

Similarly, any identification with a uniform language and culture in such states as the United Kingdom, Italy, France, and Germany is quickly being rendered obsolete by modern migrations, primarily from poorer to wealthier countries. This migration will intensify as population growth and ecological pressures in some poorer countries make survival there more and more difficult. It is no longer possible to think of Britain, for example, as homogeneously white, Anglo-Saxon, and Protestant. Racism and bigotry in England, Germany, and France are, in part, the result of the refusal by a portion of the population to admit that their countries have changed irrevocably.

The same phenomenon is occurring in Canada. The majority of English and French Canadians shared a common language and culture with the other members of their community. In Ontario, for example, for two hundred years, nearly everyone accepted and shared in the dominant white Anglo-Saxon culture. Aboriginals, Mennonites, Franco-Ontarians, and others who did not embrace the dominant culture were excluded and marginalized, both socially and economically. Their numbers, however, remained small and did not pose a threat to the hegemony of the dominant culture. They simply did not exist. As in Europe, immigration has drastically altered the profile of the province's population. As well, for a variety of historical reasons, the previously excluded groups no longer accept their role as second-class citizens. Women, who shared in the dominant language and culture but who were excluded from the political and economic spheres, are also rejecting the traditional presumptions which gave to Canadian society its façade of cohesion through a common language and culture.

Though the traditional sources of identification with one's country may be rapidly disappearing, the need for attachment remains. As stated earlier, a person has little choice but to be a citizen of a state, and for most Canadians, there is little choice but to be a citizen of Canada. In spite of what is happening in Europe, for the foreseeable future at least, the nation-state will remain the political unit through which collective projects and identity will be possible. However, because the traditional reasons for adhesion to the nation-state are less and less relevant, we can no longer assume that being a Canadian will in itself suffice to assure attachment to the country. Unless we ground our membership and pride in the Canadian collectivity on solid principles which can attract and secure proud attachment to our collectivity, the division and discord we are currently experiencing threaten to become a permanent fixture of Canadian life.

"Belonging" must be an essential component of any meaningful concept of citizenship. It is impossible to contemplate a citizen's willing participation in a collective project of the state unless that citizen feels that he or she belongs to the collectivity. Furthermore, without that sense of belonging, the citizen is likely to feel alienation and hatred toward the state, and his or her actions will reflect this antipathy

toward the collectivity. In other words, it is in society's interest to include all of its citizens in its activities. To exclude any of its members
is at best a waste of the energies of the excluded members and likely
to be counter to the interests of the collectivity.

Citizens know whether they are welcomed members of the collectivity. Their sense of belonging or not-belonging is derived from the
actions of the state or the citizens around them. When Franco-
Ontarians learned that Sault-Ste-Marie had declared itself English
only, they knew that they did not belong. It had been made abundantly clear to them that they were not welcome there. When a Sikh
is told that he cannot wear his turban in a legion hall, he knows with
painful certainty that he does not belong. When people feel that
they belong or do not belong in a group, it is because the group has
done something to engender the sentiment. Consequently, the sense
of belonging needed in the Canadian collectivity will be fostered
only when Canadians adopt attitudes and policies aimed at assuring
that all citizens feel included.

My experiences as a francophone born, raised, educated, and now
working in Ontario serve as a good illustration of the importance of
the sense of belonging to the relationship between an individual and
his or her collectivity. The relationship between Franco-Ontarians
and the larger Ontarian community has undergone a fundamental
transformation in the last twenty years. Where we were once an oppressed minority without any recognized rights, we have since been
made to feel an integral and, at least at the institutional level, a valued component of the province. Predictably, the attitude of the
Franco-Ontarian community toward the anglophone majority surrounding it has also radically changed in response to the majority's
recognition of our right to exist as a thriving community within the
larger whole.

In order to understand the transformation in the relationship between the francophone community and the province of Ontario,
one must first know and appreciate the historical and social context
in which these changes occurred. The francophone community in
Ontario antedates the arrival of General Wolfe on the Plains of
Abraham.[1] In short, we were the first Europeans to settle in the
province and the second people to inhabit the territory.

The first European communities in Ontario were francophone. In
the seventeenth century, the French administrators of the colony established forts and trading posts throughout the province in order
to exploit the fur trade. They added forts along the southern rivers
and lakes of the territory to protect their interests in the fur trade
from the British who were established in British North America.

Later, villages developed around some of these forts. For example, the first elementary school founded in Ontario was in 1786 in the region of L'Assomption (Windsor), where approximately 100 francophone families had settled. Similarly, the Georgian Bay and Sault-Ste-Marie regions were first colonized by francophones. The irony with respect to the settlement of Sault-Ste-Marie is too obvious to merit further comment.

Later generations of francophones emigrated to Ontario from Quebec, attracted by the work created by the development of the province's resources. In the nineteenth century, the lumber industry brought thousands of francophones to the Ottawa region. Francophones still make up approximately 20 per cent of the people of eastern Ontario. In the Hawkesbury area, francophones represent 85 per cent of the population.

Francophones were quick to follow the railroads as they opened up northern Ontario in the late nineteenth and early twentieth centuries. They worked in forestry, mines, agriculture, and pulp and paper. Today, their descendants form approximately 30 per cent of the population of the north. In many communities, their numbers exceed this percentage. For example, in Timmins, francophones account for 45 per cent of the population, and in Sturgeon Falls, my hometown, we comprise between 75 per cent and 80 per cent of the town's residents.

Anglophones mistakenly assume that Franco-Ontarians are Québécois who somehow drifted a bit too far west. Though some may indeed be recent arrivals, the vast majority are descendants of several generations of citizens who played a vital role in the growth of the province. According to the 1986 census, there are 543,835 francophones in Ontario, representing 6.0 per cent of the province's population. In three of the province's six regions, francophones are an important minority: in northeastern Ontario, they make up 30 per cent of the population; in north-central Ontario, 23 per cent; and in eastern Ontario, 18 per cent. These numbers are not insignificant.

For several generations, the two linguistic communities appeared to coexist in relative calm. There were some conflicts, such as those between Irish and francophone lumber workers in the Ottawa region in the mid-nineteenth century. However, at the institutional level, the two groups generally tolerated and respected each other. Throughout most of the nineteenth century, for example, francophone schools, primarily under the control of the Catholic church, had the same status and enjoyed the same privileges as the English-language schools in the province.

Peaceful coexistence came to an abrupt end late in the nineteeth century. The Riel Rebellions, first in Manitoba, but more important in the later Saskatchewan confrontation in 1885, galvanized Canada along linguistic lines. Most of English Canada saw Riel and the Métis as traitors who needed to be destroyed. English Ontario lined up behind the expedition sent west to crush the uprising. In general, French Canada supported Riel. Québécois and Franco-Canadians perceived the hanging of Riel in 1885 as a crime perpetrated by the state against French Canadians.

In addition, religious conflict between Protestants and Catholics was imported from Ireland. In 1860, there were over 100,000 Orangemen in Ontario devoted to the destruction of Catholic influence in the province. Since nearly all francophones in Canada at that time were devout Catholics, they were an obvious target of anti-Catholic sentiments. In the provincial election of 1894, the Protestant Protective Association, formed solely to combat the purported evils of Catholicism, got some of its members elected, as well as some Conservatives who had openly endorsed its policies.

Throughout this period, Ontario newspapers fomented hatred against francophones. In the 1880s, editorials described French Canadians as backward, ignorant "habitants" doomed to remain mired in intellectual inferiority. The blame was put on the quality of education in francophone schools. The Ontario government reacted. In 1890, the legislature passed a bill making English the sole language in schools, including all communications between teachers and students. Francophones ignored the law.

The conflict reached its climax in 1912, when the Conservative party used its vast majority to implement an English-only policy for Ontario schools. "Le Règlement 17" is infamous among Franco-Ontarians. It represents a deliberate attempt to destroy our language and our culture. Prompted mainly by Irish Catholic clergy, and in particular by the bishop of London, Monsignor Fallon, Ontario promulgated a regulation limiting French to one hour per day in any of the province's schools, irrespective of the language of the pupils or the community.

The francophone community refused to obey the regulation. The Ottawa Separate School Board officially adopted a resolution to the effect that it would not abide by it. The government reacted by cutting all subsidies to the board. When francophone members tried to find alternative funds, anglophones on the board obtained an injunction which blocked the attempt and ordered the board to dismiss teachers who refused to obey the regulation. Without funds, the board had little choice but to close its schools. The government opened schools under its direct control. Anglophone Catholics attended, but francophones stayed away. For two years, francophone students obtained their education outside the jurisdiction of the board or the province. The dismissed teachers taught them without pay in whatever accommodations they could find. Some francophone trustees went to prison for ignoring the regulation.

The regulation was finally amended in 1927 and repealed in 1944. The effects, however, were felt for most of this century. The battle over "le Règlement 17" had two significant consequences for my community. First, it made us aware of our minority status. It made us realize that we were at the mercy of the whims of the anglophone majority. We could no longer simply coexist; anglophones would not permit it. Francophones would have to fight for every right and privilege grudgingly bestowed. Francophones learned that they would have to mobilize and mount whatever campaign was necessary to preserve their language and culture.

Second, and more important, it made us hate the English majority in the province. As a child growing up in the 1950s, I felt the impact of "Le Règlement 17" daily. The English were very much "les maudits Anglais" – our enemy. Across the road from my primary school was an English primary school. The only contact between the two was fighting. We communicated through rocks thrown across the road. Though I could speak English, I did not know or even meet any anglophones until I was well into my secondary school education. I did not want to, and I presume that anglophones in my village had very little interest in meeting me. In any case, mutual distrust and even loathing assured little contact.

Ontario's continued refusal to allow French-language public schools badly hurt the francophone community in the province. Prior to 1988, Ontario did not fund Catholic education beyond primary school. For most Franco-Ontarians, this meant that publicly funded education in French ended at grade eight. Pupils who had received their primary education in French Catholic schools were forced to enrol in English secondary schools and compete with students whose mother tongue was the language of instruction. Inevitably, many bright young francophones quickly fell by the wayside. There are, for example, several small unilingual francophone communities around Sturgeon Falls. Children received primary education there in French. On graduation, they had to attend secondary school in Sturgeon Falls Secondary School, which operated almost exclusively in English. Understandably, the attrition rate was extremely high.

My community continues to feel the effects of years of being denied secondary education in our language. Our functional illiteracy rate is double that of the anglophone community. Among a sizeable portion of our population, the rate is above 35 per cent. Only half as many Franco-Ontarians attend post-secondary institutions as do their anglophone counterparts.[2] Not only is this a terrible waste of a community's and a nation's potential, it also condemns a significant proportion of a generation to poverty, low self-esteem, and strong alienation toward society and toward those who have received the full benefits of membership in our country.

Education represents the future of a community. Francophones knew that schools were the key to their future, and they concentrated on extending their rights in this field. Before 1969, when francophone secondary schools were first permitted in the province, my community did not have a future. We could assimilate, but if we wished our children to retain their language and culture, we had little choice but to emigrate to Quebec, as did many of my childhood friends.

Other institutions in the province also had little regard for francophones. Prior to 1968, for example, MLAs could not address the legislature in French. Before 1984, French could not be used in the province's courts. The state did not want us to participate in its structures.

The message was made painfully clear to me when I was a journalist in Sturgeon Falls in the mid-1970s. One of my tasks was to report on the magistrate's court which sat once a month in the Legion Hall. A bilingual judge would travel from Sudbury to hear the cases. The proceedings were in English only. Sturgeon Falls is 75 per cent to 80 per cent francophone. During one of the trials, a francophone witness was having some difficulty answering in English. I was asked to act as translator. The judge was perfectly bilingual, as was the person acting as crown attorney; both the accused and the defence lawyer were francophones. In other words, every key member of the court understood French perfectly well.

I stood beside the witness stand as the defence lawyer and later the crown attorney asked a question in English. I would translate, but before the witness could answer, the lawyers and the judge would discuss, in French, the accuracy of my rendering. When agreement was reached, the witness would answer in French and I would translate, and again discussion ensued. This farce continued until the end of the witness's testimony. Experiences like this made it very clear that the state was willing to go to absurd lengths to ensure that

French remained a marginal, unrecognized, and valueless language. As a francophone, I found it equally clear that the state considered me a marginal, unrecognized, and valueless citizen.

In the late 1960s, Ontario's attitude started to change. Prompted primarily by the changes in Quebec and at the national level, Ontario recognized that it could not ignore the linguistic reality of the country and treat francophones as second-class citizens. Gradually, it augmented our rights. Conscious, however, of significant anti-francophone sentiment, it felt that it could not accord francophones many rights and privileges all at once.

We were first granted the right to secondary education in French. Later, in 1984, the Courts of Justice Act was amended to enable francophones to use their language within the judicial system; section 135 declares French to be an official language of the province's courts. Further amendments in 1989 removed all remaining obstacles to full access to the courts in French. In 1986, the French Language Services Act guaranteed for most francophones services from their government in French. As well, French-language school boards were created in Toronto and Ottawa-Carleton. A third has been announced for the Prescott-Russell region. Finally, Cité Collégiale, the province's first French post-secondary institution, was opened in Ottawa two years ago.

Institutional changes are crucial. First, the institutional level is representative of the attitude of the state. By opening its institutions to minorities, the state is sending a clear message to its citizens that the old exclusions are no longer tolerated. Second, the state works best at the institutional level. It has often been said that the state cannot legislate love or tolerance. Though the state cannot directly alter people's attitudes and prejudices, it can, through its institutions, create the climate that will foster desired attitudes. At this, the state can be quite effective. Recent campaigns against smoking and drunk driving have produced radical attitudinal changes. State activity, however, cannot be limited to advertising. The publicity campaign to eradicate drunk driving was accompanied by changes to the Criminal Code and stricter enforcement practices. It is primarily, through modifications to its institutions that the state can effect desired changes in its citizens.

Finally, the beneficiaries of the new policies and the corresponding institutional changes receive the message that they are now accepted as equal and valued participants in the collectivity's projects. For francophones, the institutional changes described earlier have meant that for the first time in nearly one hundred years, we can lead our lives as Ontarians without having to relinquish our language, our culture, and a significant part of our identity.

Predictably, this fundamental transformation of our place in the province has dramatically changed the collective spirit of my community. Twenty, and even ten years ago, francophones had an extremely negative impression of "les Anglais" and of their own fate in the province. This sentiment was well-founded. A great deal of time and effort was devoted to complaining about the treatment that we received at the hands of the majority. Quite frequently, it drifted into maudlin self-pity.

Last summer, I had the pleasure of attending "le Sommet de la Francophonie," a gathering of approximately 400 people representing all the major francophone associations of the province as well as all segments of our population. The purpose of the convocation was to develop the community's priorities and strategies during the current constitutional negotiations and for the next few years. The mood of the assembly was remarkable. Gone were the whining and the endless bemoaning of our fate. It had been replaced by cheerful optimism. The concerns of the group have also moved beyond the plight of francophones in the province. Because we have finally been permitted to take our place as a major component of a larger whole, we can afford to direct our attention to the problems of the whole itself. This new vision is certainly healthier and more beneficial to both the francophone community and the province than was the historical antagonism between the English and French communities.

Although the relationship between the two groups has improved immensely in the last few years, much remains to be done before the province can claim that its francophone minority is being treated equitably. Francophones are aware that no other group is the object of as much scorn. When Sault-Ste-Marie, Thunder Bay, and fifty other communities declared themselves English-only two years ago, we were effectively told that we were unwelcome in much of the province. The justification offered for such action was the existence of the French Language Services Act. The municipalities knew that the excuse was spurious. Section 1 of the act specifically excluded municipalities from the application of the act. When told of the exclusion, the municipalities' reply was that the province could, perhaps, possibly, maybe one day amend the act to include municipalities. The reply makes it clear that the gesture was intended to show Canada's francophones that Ontario is English-speaking and that French was not going to be permitted. To my knowledge, none of the municipalities has repealed its English-only resolution.

The anglophone community in the province has tolerated this act of bigotry against my community. There was no spontaneous universal declaration of revulsion by anglophones against this intentional act of bigotry. Had the municipal resolutions declared themselves white only or had specifically excluded the Jewish or native communities, the outcry would have been deafening. However, because it is aimed at the francophone population, the majority remains noticeably silent.

In New Brunswick, the Confederation of Regions Party received 20 per cent of the popular vote during the last provincial election. Its electoral platform consisted of one policy: "no bilingualism here." For the francophone minority, that message translates into "no French here." The Reform party, which has a similar anti-bilingualism, anti-francophone policy, has between 12 per cent and 17 per cent support in all the latest polls. Still the vast majority of the anglophones in power remain quiescent. When Sheila Copps recently attacked the inherent bigotry in Reform's policies, she was accused of being hysterical. The message to francophones is clear: in this society, bigotry directed at you is more acceptable than bigotry or racism directed at other minorities.

Responsibility for inclusion of the minorities within the collective whole belongs with the majority. By majority, one does not simply mean numerical majority. For example, women in our society are clearly in a minority position in spite of being slightly superior in numbers to men. Those in the majority position are those with power over society's important institutions.

Members of the various minorities who wish to take their rightful place in these institutions depend on the good-will of the majority. Francophones, for example, cannot simply insist on a francophone university in Ontario in order to receive what they demand. Since power rests with others, it is those others who must grant the minority's request. Ultimately, the decision to share power and institutions with members of minorities belongs to the majority.

The francophone experience in Ontario demonstrates that it is to the benefit of both the minority and the majority to include as many groups and individuals as possible in the larger collectivity. A refusal by the majority to include those with less power dooms the minority to its inferior status. The minority will concentrate its efforts on fighting the majority, and the majority will not only lose the potential contribution of the minority to its projects, but it will expend a great deal of its own energy in order to prevent the minority from assuming its rightful place in the collectivity.

Finally, morally, we no longer accept that groups remain excluded simply because they do not share all the attributes of the majority.

The majority has an obligation to accommodate the minority, and it must respect this duty, for both moral and practical reasons. A society cannot ignore or oppress any of its communities. Group identification can be based on a variety of factors, such as race, religion, language, gender, region, and physical handicap. Most individuals belong to more than one group. We can be in a majority with respect to one or more criteria but be in the minority with respect to others. For example, I am a white male with no significant physical handicap. In spite of having received the benefits of being a member of these majorities, I feel my strongest loyalty to the group which has been denied full access and participation in society's institutions. Although I have not been denied much in our society, I still identify with those of my community who, because of their language, have fared less well than I. My experience is not uncommon; the pain of injustice is overpowering. Accordingly, any exclusion is likely to be felt by all of those excluded. The members of that group will resent the majority as strongly as francophones did until very recently. Like francophones, they will also dissipate much of their energy in changing their fate rather than contributing to the larger collective's projects.

All societies seek to maximize their potential. This can be achieved only when a significant proportion of members participate willingly in its undertakings. No one will want to assist in a project unless he or she feels that the project is of personal benefit. In other words, it is an essential condition of any well-functioning collectivity that its members identify with it. They must sense that they belong.

It is up to society to ensure that its members have this sense of belonging. Members of minorities no longer accept that their only choice is between exclusion and assimilation. They insist on being permitted to participate as equal members in a society which enables them to belong as themselves. Society must be willing to adjust its institutions to facilitate the full participation of as many of its members as possible. It is because Ontario was prepared to change its institutions that Franco-Ontarians sense that they fully belong in the province.

Perhaps Ontario and Canada will have to repeat this approach with respect to other groups. In order to ensure the well-being of the community, we have to accept, for example, that aboriginal peoples may need their own justice system or that some groups such as Jews and Somalians may require their own school system in order to feel included in our collectivity. Similarly, if women feel excluded by sexist and gender-biased language, we should be prepared to amend our speech, and if our laws discriminate against same-sex couples, we should move to alter them. I do not want to imply that these and other changes would always be easy to implement. On the contrary, they would necessitate major attitudinal, institutional, and financial modifications. However, as a community, we should be prepared to do what we can to ensure that our institutions encourage the sentiment of being a valued member of the collectivity.

Our society must also trust the groups that desire institutional changes. It is not up to the majority to tell the excluded when it is proper to feel excluded. First, this attitude is both insulting and patronizing. Second, only a member of a minority can appreciate his or her experience and know what is needed to correct the situation. If as a francophone I feel threatened, hurt, and angry that the Association for the Preservation of English in Canada sold videos in which we were told that we were needed in Canada like a person needs AIDS, it is not up to the majority to say that I am mistaken. Similarly, if I sense that the only way in which my community can thrive in Ontario is through our own schools, it is not up to anglophones to say I am wrong. I accept that negotiations and compromise will frequently be needed. However, these must start from the premise that society is obliged to accommodate minorities that have well-founded sentiments of exclusion and oppression.

The argument that such accommodation risks destroying the traditions that hold the country together is not persuasive. First, it is a myth that we all share the same set of traditions. Millions of Canadians do not have a sense of attachment to the traditions of the majority. Second, because a majority of Canadians have a tradition, it does not make that tradition more valuable or valued than that of the minority. Finally, our so-called traditions are constantly being adapted to our changing society. For example, Christmas is no longer primarily a Christian holiday. We have modified Christmas to fit our secular society. All we need to do in order to realize that different traditions do not threaten the fabric of Canada is to acknowledge the fact that, in reality, our traditions consist of several sets of constantly evolving traditions.

We have very little choice but to recognize that we have to change our perception of our collectivity. Historically, citizenship was often sufficient to coalesce the majority of the population around the nation's projects. Those who did not fit into the mould were simply ignored, or, worse, oppressed. Today, for a variety of historical and sociological reasons, simple citizenship no longer suffices. We need to replace the foundation for our sense of belonging to the Canadian community in order to ensure full participation in our collective endeavours.

The Franco-Ontarian experience suggests that the sense of belonging itself may be an important source of our sense of collectivity.
The promise of being valued and allowed to develop fully as an individual without having to abandon a significant element of one's
identity is a powerful incentive to work for the preservation and
amelioration of the society that holds out this promise.

Canada may be on the verge of destroying itself. One of the main
reasons is that anglophones and francophones have never developed the ability to accommodate each other. Had we worked toward
making both groups sense that they were equal, respected, and valued citizens, we would not be facing the imminent break-up of the
country. The lesson is obvious: if we are to thrive as a country and
a collectivity, we have to make certain that all Canadian citizens are
full participants in our collective project which is Canada.

NOTES

1 Most of the historical data cited in this essay are taken from Robert
Choquette, *L'Ontario français, historique* (Montreal: Éditions Études
Vivantes, 1980).

2 *Les francophones tels qu'ils sont. Regard sur le monde du travail franco-ontarien*
(Ottawa: Association canadienne-française de l'Ontario, 1985).

MONIQUE SIMARD

La citoyenneté et le Québec

> Mon identité nationale en ce qui me différencie ...
> C'est en assumant mes racines québécoises, mes origines que je n'ai pas choisies ... que je peux m'ouvrir au monde, à l'autre; c'est en assumant ma spécificité québécoise que je suis citoyen du monde, être humain.
>
> Jean-Marc Piotte[1]

Si la citoyenneté se définit comme étant l'état d'être un citoyen: "membre d'un État considéré du point de vue de ses devoirs et de ses droits civils et politiques"[2] d'entrée de jeu, il m'apparaît que pour les Québécois cette appartenance est premièrement à l'État québécois et secondairement à l'État canadien.

Ceci peut sembler peu nuancé à titre d'introduction mais, à mon avis, il est important de dissiper une fois pour toute cette ambiguïté qui contribue à alimenter depuis trente ans la confusion et inévitablement l'absence de compréhension de ce que ultimement "Québec wants?" Au risque de paraître redondante, il n'en demeure pas moins utile de rappeler combien le fossé de l'ignorance et de l'incompréhension est grand entre les deux peuples fondateurs de la Confédération et encore davantage chez les nouveaux arrivants, qui dans bien des cas "y perdent leur latin", quant à nos identifications respectives.

Cela m'a toujours surprise de me faire poser la question suivante : "es-tu québécoise en premier et ensuite canadienne ou l'inverse?" Pourquoi surprise? et bien tout simplement parce que pour moi c'est l'évidence même : je suis québécoise et incidemment canadienne. Pas même canadienne-française mais québécoise puisque ma référence quant à mon identification propre, étant une enfant de la Révolution tranquille, au-delà de ma langue et de ma culture, aux plans civil, politique et économique, a été avant tout le Québec.

C'est peut-être surprenant pour ceux qui ont été témoins depuis le milieu des années soixante de l'implantation du bilinguisme et du bi-culturalisme officiels, voyant là la dissipation de la nécessité d'une identification forte au Québec pour maintenir sa langue et sa culture. Mais c'est au cours de cette même période que s'est bâti et consolidé à jamais le cadre dans lequel s'exprime désormais la citoyenneté québécoise, à savoir la construction d'un authentique État-nation pour "... une société globale qui a ses propres institutions, sa propre organisation sociale, sa culture et un genre de vie spécifique."[3]

Le Québec est devenu plus un pays qu'une province, ce qui a eu pour conséquence de le rendre bien davantage une société civile qu'un groupe ethnique. Ce faisant, la population composant cette société a mise de côté l'appellation canadienne-française pour prendre celle de québécoise et a encore beaucoup de difficulté à comprendre qu'on lui refuse la reconnaissance de son caractère distinct puisque à la face même ses distinctions ont toujours existé et elles se sont à bien des égards renforcées.

La Révolution tranquille a été considérée, à tort, comme étant seulement la modernisation aux plans économique, social et idéologique du Québec, plongé dans les grandes noirceurs du Duplessisme pendant trop longtemps. Mais fondamentalement la Révolution tranquille a été le remplacement du Canada par le Québec, et le remplacement de la religion, longtemps omniprésente et dominante, par le nationalisme. "Le Grand bond en avant" du Québec des années '60 et '70 l'a doté de ce qu'il a aujourd'hui pour être un pays. Nationalisation de l'électricité, création de la caisse de dépôt et de placement, réforme du Code civil, adoption de la charte des droits et libertés, réformes diverses (aide-juridique, assurance-automobile, etc.).

Tout est en place, structures politiques et économiques, cadres et balises à la protection de sa langue et de sa culture, multiples symboles d'identification et de fierté nationales : au Québec on est citoyen ... du Québec.

LE DÉCALAGE POLITIQUE

Le sociologue Simon Langlois parle de décalage politique[4] entre le Canada et le Québec et on ne pourrait trouver expression plus juste pour décrire la relation entre ces deux entités. En effet, depuis plus de trente ans maintenant, le Canada bouge en réaction aux demandes du Québec mais toujours un peu trop tard, ce qui le maintient dans une perpétuelle situation de décalage, de retard, quant aux réalités et aux exigences du Québec. S'il est vrai que les structures, les règles et les lois évoluent et s'adaptent aux réalités sociales changeantes (par exemple à la condition des femmes, à la présence de minorités culturelles, etc.), il est aussi vrai d'affirmer qu'elles le font généralement avec toujours un peu de retard sur la réalité. Frustrant ainsi ceux qui la vivent.

Ainsi, il a fallu près d'un demi-siècle de réclamations et de lutte pour que le fait français soit reconnu dans les institutions du Canada. Quand cela fut enfin accepté, il était déjà trop tard, l'État du Québec s'étant déjà constitué comme principal appareil politique des francophones de ce pays. La même chose s'est produite au sujet du bilinguisme. Longtemps les Canadiens français se sont battus pour l'obtenir, lorsque celui-ci fut enfin reconnu, le Québec avait déjà opté pour la promotion du français seul (loi 22, loi 101, etc.). En ce qui concerne les symboles d'affirmation nationale, on observe le même phénomène : drapeau, hymne national, le Canada a toujours eu du retard sur le Québec, ayant pour conséquence que le Québec s'est affirmé comme pays sur certains aspects plus vite que le Canada. Et, d'une certaine façon, le rapport à la citoyenneté s'y est exprimé aussi plus rapidement.

C'est ce décalage politique, découlant sans nul doute d'une mutuelle incompréhension, qui marque notre histoire politique. Comment s'adapter et s'ajuster si on ne comprend pas les différences et les spécificités propres à chacun et encore moins les accepter? Comment évoluer au même rythme?

Peut-être voit-on poindre aujourd'hui une réelle bonne volonté de vouloir comprendre et d'accepter ces différences. Mais n'est-il pas trop tard? La distance qui s'est créée, consolidée et accentuée entre les deux sociétés est indéniable. Le terrain à parcourir est grand. Trop grand peut-être.

Dans son numéro de janvier 1992, la revue *Actualité* (publication de Maclean Hunter) publie un sondage sur les différences entre les Québécois et les autres Canadiens. On y apprend que la société distincte, au-delà de la différence linguistique, se manifeste dans ses habitudes de vie, au restaurant, dans la façon de se vêtir, dans ses croyances et ses valeurs et même ... au lit! Le sondage nous révèle des distinctions marquantes qui témoignent de l'épanouissement incroyable des Québécois aux niveaux de l'expression, du mode et des habitudes de vie et des valeurs. Une des questions les plus révélatrices du sondage de la revue *Actualité* était la suivante : "Est-ce que vous préférez les gens qui font leur devoir ou qui recherchent leur bonheur?" 51% des francophones québécois ont répondu le bonheur, 42% le devoir alors que 25% des Canadiens ont répondu le bonheur et 63% le devoir ... est-il nécessaire d'en dire plus long?

Le résultat d'une telle démarche et d'un tel progrès était inévitable : le Québec, s'engageant résolument dans la voie de son affirmation à tous les niveaux, alimentait les aspirations souverainistes. Pour plusieurs, la survie du Québec en tant que nation en est dépendante et le nationalisme grandissant des Québécois n'est à toute fin pratique que l'expression de leur volonté d'exister.

En continuant de traiter les Canadiens français en minorité, le Canada anglais s'est encore une fois décalé puisqu'au Québec cela fait longtemps qu'ils se comportent et assument leur majorité. Le remarquable processus d'affirmation nationale du Québec a été en fait sa seule façon d'imposer sa survie, puisque la crainte et la peur de disparaître l'habitent perpétuellement.

LE CANADA ANGLAIS

Le sentiment et la crainte de disparaître comme "société distincte" sont désormais ressentis au Canada anglais notamment depuis l'introduction du traité de libre-échange avec les États-Unis. L'angoisse, bien connue des Canadiens français, de se voir un jour perdus dans une Amérique du Nord "modèle US" habitent les nationalistes du Canada anglais. Et l'appellation "Canada anglais" est de toute façon de moins en moins appropriée puisque sa composition change plus que celle du Québec. Ces changements ont pour effet de briser son homogénéité, rendant ainsi sa situation plus complexe et encore plus éloignée de celle du Québec. En effet, lorsque le Canada anglais était majoritairement composé de descendants anglo-saxons, donc d'un des deux "peuples fondateurs", les parallèles avec le Québec pouvaient se faire plus aisément. L'identification à une culture, à une mère patrie et à des symboles s'y rattachant s'effectuaient sans problème. On a qu'à voir, encore à ce jour, le culte qu'entretiennent les "Anglais" à la famille royale britannique pour s'en convaincre. Mais, comme il y a de moins en moins d'Anglais "de souche", le groupe linguistique anglophone est désormais composé majoritairement de personnes dont la langue maternelle est autre que l'anglais. Il en résulte donc une difficulté de compréhension à l'égard de ce qui tient la société québécoise, société extrêmement homogène en comparaison. En effet, les Canadiens d'origine ukrainienne, chinoise ou encore grecque, à titre d'exemple, ont beaucoup de difficulté à comprendre pourquoi les Québécois francophones d'une part ne se plient pas à la règle de la majorité anglophone, comme ils le font, et d'autre part constitueraient une société distincte de la leur. Si c'était le cas, pourquoi ne pas avoir une société distincte des Canadiens d'origine italienne, d'origine égyptienne, etc. Bref, en quoi le Canada n'est pas lui aussi un "melting pot" à l'américaine? Quant aux Anglais "de souche", il est normal qu'ils se cherchent à travers le tout. Ne possédant plus la soudure sociale propre à une identification forte, ils ont de la difficulté à se définir un pays.

La crainte de ne plus exister, de disparaître s'est particulièrement manifestée au cours du débat entourant le libre-échange avec les États-Unis. Les perceptions et les peurs du Canada à l'égard de l'ALE ont démontré plus que jamais la fragilité de ce pays. Le Québec, par contre, et à tort bien souvent, n'a jamais ressenti aussi fortement cette crainte, trouvant chez lui les éléments nécessaires à sa cohésion et à son existence face aux États-Unis. L'évaluation différente qui a été faite de l'ALE illustre à quel point les perspectives sont différentes entre le Canada et le Québec.

Pour le Canada anglais l'ALE constituait : 1 – une menace économique, particulièrement à l'Ontario, qui bénéficiait depuis plus d'un siècle des stratégies économiques et industrielles du Canada; 2 – une menace politique, notamment à la social-démocratie canadienne qui s'est exprimée dans des choix sociaux différents de ceux des Américains (système de santé national, secteur public fort, etc.); 3 – une menace au plan culturel notamment en se rendant plus vulnérable à l'invasion de productions culturelles américaines (livres, T.V., disques, etc.); 4 – une menace à la souveraineté nationale, en ce sens que l'ALE accentuerait la dépendance économique du Canada par rapport aux États-Unis à un tel degré qu'il lui serait à peu près impossible de prendre ses propres orientations notamment en matière environnementale, énergétique tout comme au plan de la défense.

L'ALE constituait le projet néo-conservateur des grandes corporations nord-américaines visant à servir leurs intérêts et ceux des États-Unis.[5] Dans toutes les provinces du Canada, y compris à Ottawa, s'est développée une vive opposition à l'ALE. Les grands partis politiques, le NPD et le PLC, les syndicats, les groupes populaires, les agriculteurs et le monde culturel et intellectuel se sont mobilisés pour tenter de faire échec au projet et du même coup renverser le gouvernement Mulroney. Ce dernier étant perçu, depuis son élection en 1984, comme étant d'une part à la solde des grandes corporations et des Américains parce qu'il avait été, entre autres, président de l'Iron Ore du Canada et d'autre part mandaté d'affaiblir le Canada et son pouvoir central fort pour mieux appliquer des politiques économiques et sociales néo-conservatrices. Et qu'il se servait du nationalisme québécois, de ses revendications et exigences pour réintégrer la confédération canadienne, comme prétexte à la décentralisation du pays.

Au Québec, l'opposition à l'ALE était moins forte. Composée surtout des syndicats, des producteurs agricoles et des groupes popu-

laires, elle ne bénéficiait pas d'une opposition politique, ce qui l'a
affaiblie considérablement aux yeux de la population. En effet, le
PLQ et le PQ appuyaient sans réserve le libre-échange avec les États-
Unis et aucune opposition sérieuse n'est venue du monde de la culture, ce dernier se sentant probablement à l'abri des États-Unis à
cause de la langue.

Il en a résulté une perception, largement répandue au Canada,
que la bataille du libre-échange a été perdue à cause du Québec[6]
parce que premièrement l'opposition au libre-échange y était beaucoup moins vigoureuse et que deuxièmement c'est le vote québécois
en 1984 et en 1988 qui a été déterminant pour faire élire le gouvernement Mulroney. L'élection de 1988 a permis la ratification de
l'ALE et, y voyant une attaque sérieuse au Canada, à sa spécificité
face aux États-Unis, à son modèle de société d'État central fort, les
forces d'opposition se sont concentrées sur un autre projet qui leur
apparaissait tout aussi menaçant : l'accord du lac Meech.[7]

À mon avis, l'échec de l'accord du lac Meech est en partie lié à la
défaite des opposants à l'ALE et, dans la mesure où celui-ci aurait été
écarté, il est plausible de croire que les discussions au plan constitutionnel auraient pris une autre allure. L'accord du lac Meech,
objet de critiques de plus en plus virulentes au fil des mois de consultation pour sa ratification et ultimement rejeté, avait néanmoins re-
cueilli l'assentiment des onze premiers ministres et des trois grands
partis fédéraux, et ce, malgré les dissensions causées. Ce qui constituait une réalisation de taille au plan politique. L'ardeur à vouloir
démolir cet accord par la suite est, à mon avis, issue de la grande
amertume des Canadiens d'avoir échoué dans leur bataille contre
l'ALE. Quoique la forme et le fond fissent défaut, il n'en demeure pas
moins que pendant une certaine période de temps on a assisté à un
rare "unanimisme" politique quant à la volonté de faire accepter l'accord du lac Meech. Les libéraux et les néo-démocrates ont travaillé
fort à dissoudre leurs oppositions politiques internes, et les nationalistes québécois, quoique très critiques au départ, ont été habilement
orientés à donner leur assentiment en cours de route.

L'ALE est en vigueur, aucune et aucune formule constitutionnelle
agréée, le Canada "anglais" cherche à se définir par rapport aux
États-Unis, par rapport au Québec et par rapport à sa propre composition. Cette angoisse, si fortement ressentie, se transforme par-
fois en colère à l'égard du Québec lorsqu'il réalise qu'elle n'est ni
ressentie ni partagée par celui-ci. Au contraire même, puisque para-
doxalement le Québec, qui en principe tenait le plus à l'accord du lac
Meech, a célébré son échec.

Le Québec veut détruire le Canada. Plusieurs le croient et le craignent, voyant dans les demandes et les exigences du Québec les éléments de la destruction du Canada et par conséquent de son identité nationale.

Les célébrations de nationalisme qui ont suivi l'échec de l'accord du lac Meech en ont choqué plus d'un, qui y ont vu la preuve que le Québec ne voulait pas du Canada. Alors qu'en fait il y a tenu pendant un certain temps, mais s'en est distancé au fur et à mesure que s'étirait le débat sur Meech et la société distincte. Les Québécois, au fond, ne voulaient peut-être pas de l'accord du lac Meech, mais je crois qu'ils y ont cru à une certaine époque, voulant en finir avec les questions constitutionnelles une fois pour toutes. Mais la virulence de l'opposition manifestée à l'égard de la reconnaissance de la société distincte a provoqué au Québec une réaction majeure qui, au-delà du contenu comme tel de l'accord, a enclenché un cheminement politique pendant la période de discussions visant à sa ratification. Peu à peu, avec certains événements l'alimentant (jugement de la Cour suprême sur la loi 101, le piétinement du drapeau québécois, Sault-Ste-Marie se déclarant unilingue, etc.), le Québec a dépassé Meech et il est devenu évident au fil des mois que les compromis de la fin (rapport Charest) ne pouvaient plus suffire et qu'au contraire ils sont venus catalyser un nationalisme grandissant qui a explosé au lendemain de l'échec de l'accord.

Cette nouvelle vague de nationalisme, car il s'agit bien d'une nouvelle vague puisque, après la perte du référendum en 1980, pour plusieurs la flamme s'était éteinte, a des caractéristiques bien distinctes qui font en sorte que ni Meech ni aucune autre proposition y ressemblant ne lui sont désormais satisfaisantes. Encore une fois, il s'est opéré un décalage politique qu'on ne peut que constater aujourd'hui. Il est peu probable qu'autre chose que la souveraineté ne satisfasse désormais une majorité de Québécois. Et c'est d'ailleurs, à l'étonnement de plusieurs, une des conclusions de la commission Bélanger-Campeau.

L'APRÈS MEECH

Cette commission mise sur pied par le Premier Ministre Bourassa afin d'échapper aux pressions pour la tenue de consultations démocratiques plus directes (ex : référendum, assemblée consultative) dans ses conclusions a renforcé toute la vigueur dont témoigne la nouvelle vague de nationalisme québécois. L'exemple le plus probant étant la proposition, le cas échéant, de tenir au plus tard en octobre 1992 un référendum sur la souveraineté. Le Premier Ministre Bourassa a dû se résoudre à adopter une loi (loi 150) qui prévoit cette éventualité et à la mettre en oeuvre si les autres avenues ne se débloquent pas.

Les conclusions de la commission Bélanger-Campeau ne pouvaient pas être autres. Pour ceux et celles qui ont suivi les audiences publiques, d'ailleurs télédiffusées in extenso en direct, il aurait été difficile de conclure autrement. Jour après jour des groupes, des individus et des experts sont venus témoigner de leur lassitude à faire comprendre au "reste du Canada" ce qui pour eux était élémentaire, à savoir premièrement qu'ils appartenaient à une société, non pas meilleure mais différente, deuxièmement qu'ils avaient une culture propre, "singulière" et troisièmement qu'elle était très difficile à protéger et à conserver dans un contexte nord-américain. Qu'ils avaient donc raison de craindre l'assimilation – chiffres à l'appui – et qu'ils possédaient les éléments d'un projet de société propre à leur épanouissement et qu'ils avaient besoin d'outils, s'ajoutant à ceux dont ils s'étaient déjà dotés, pour poursuivre la construction et la consolidation de leur ... pays. Voilà l'essentiel du message transmis. Il était donc difficile d'arriver à d'autres conclusions que celles retenues. Certes il y a eu des témoignages d'experts qui se sont enfoncés dans des subtilités obscures de droit constitutionnel, mais ils ne sont pas parvenus à détourner l'attention du message principal. Des intellectuels de renom, réputés pour avoir toujours donné une dernière chance au fédéralisme, sont venus témoigner de leur dégoût face à la tournure des événements, voyant dans le rejet de la reconnaissance de la société distincte l'ultime preuve de l'impossibilité de s'entendre.[8]

Grand exercice de démocratie, la commission Bélanger-Campeau a peut-être dépassé le résultat attendu par le Premier Ministre Bourassa lorsqu'il en proposait la formation en juillet 1990, un mois à peine après l'échec de Meech. Lui-même a dû naviguer très habilement au sein de son propre parti pour apaiser le courant souverainiste montant. Tentant de gagner du temps et recherchant les conclusions les moins compromettantes possibles, ce qui d'ailleurs caractérisera à vie Robert Bourassa, il a hérité du Rapport Allaire qui en soi va beaucoup plus loin que Meech. Un autre décalage s'est opéré. Le rapport Allaire, qui revendique 22 compétences exclusives pour le Québec et en laisse 5 à Ottawa, illustre combien effectivement le Québec a dépassé le contenu de l'accord du lac Meech.

Le nationalisme post-Meech se distingue des autres vagues par son caractère "rationnel", une certaine forme de sérénité et par l'appui qu'il recueille chez une majorité de Québécois. Le raisonnement développé par plusieurs est le suivant : ce n'est pas le Québec qui a rejeté le Canada, mais bien ce dernier qui nous a rejetés en refusant de reconnaître notre caractère distinct, deuxièmement le Québec a accepté de prendre le "beau risque"⁹ et cela ne nous a rien rapporté, troisièmement il y a un risque que le Canada tente d'en enlever davantage au Québec (voir les propositions constitutionnelles de septembre 1991) et enfin que le Québec a trop à perdre de ces sempiternelles discussions constitutionnelles et que sa survie et son dynamisme vont davantage être servis par son accession à la souveraineté et par la négociation d'une autre forme d'association avec le Canada.

Et, pendant que les Québécois s'appliquent ce raisonnement et cette logique, dans le reste du Canada il semble qu'on en soit encore à se chercher, à se définir, à se poser la question si le Canada peut exister sans le Québec, comment et sur quelles bases.

En fait la société québécoise, même en perpétuel danger de disparition, ne vit pas de crise existentielle. Elle existe, elle sait sur quelles bases repose cette existence, elle veut continuer d'exister et est prête à se battre pour ce faire. Par contre, du côté du Canada, les signes de crise existentielle sont apparents. C'est en écoutant avec attention les Canadiens exprimer leurs angoisses quant à la définition du type de société, par conséquent aussi de l'État, auquel ils aspirent, à leur confusion quant au bilinguisme et au biculturalisme que j'en arrive à cette constatation.

Le Québec, comme société, a dû combattre pour survivre et il possède donc les réflexes de survivance lorsqu'il se sent menacé. Quoique objectivement plus vulnérable à son environnement nord-américain, par sa taille et sa langue, la société québécoise possède les soudures solides pour se démarquer, se distinguer et de fait exister. La peur de disparaître qui nous anime depuis si longtemps nous a maintenus dans un état d'alerte et de lutte.

Dans certains cas nous avons réussi à nous maintenir; dans d'autres non, pensons notamment à la communauté francophone du Manitoba, jadis si nombreuse et dynamique qui, faute d'écoles pendant plus de soixante ans, s'est assimilée dans une très grande proportion. Au Québec, par contre, la partie est presque gagnée, puisque devant le danger de se faire mettre en minorité sur notre propre territoire, nous avons pris les moyens pour proclamer et assumer notre caractère majoritaire. Il est malheureux cependant de dire, et encore plus de constater, que pour les francophones hors Québec la partie est probablement perdue, à l'exception peut-être des Acadiens du Nouveau-Brunswick. Ce n'est pourtant pas l'acharnement et la détermination qui ont manqué pour se maintenir mais, malgré quelques gains obtenus de haute lutte, tout est venu trop tard. Le processus d'assimilation était trop engagé pour s'arrêter malgré l'adoption de la loi sur les langues officielles.

Depuis trente ans, tout a été mis en oeuvre pour développer l'État québécois, auquel se réfère aujourd'hui une majorité de Québécois. Pour celle-ci, le gouvernement se trouve à Québec, l'identification politique se fait à Québec et la citoyenneté, au plan de la quotidienneté, s'exprime à la "québécoise." La fierté des Québécois, par exemple, à l'égard de leur système d'assurance-maladie ou encore de la réforme de l'éducation, quoique cette dernière se soit un peu éteinte, réfère à des réalisations québécoises et non canadiennes, même si c'est dans le cadre de programmes canadiens qu'a pu être réalisée la réforme de la santé. Il en va de même pour les progrès et réformes réalisés au cours des années '70, tels que l'adoption de la charte des droits de la personne, la réforme de l'assurance automobile et l'établissement d'un programme d'aide juridique.

Tout renvoie à Québec et presque rien à Ottawa qui, qui plus est, est perçu, dans bien des cas, comme un frein au développement du Québec. En effet, comme il se doit en politique, on s'octroie les réalisations et on rejette le blâme des non-réalisations sur le dos des autres. La perception largement répandue au Québec est que le Québec s'est réalisé malgré le Canada. Cela a eu pour conséquence d'accentuer l'identification au Québec, puisque c'est par le biais du gouvernement du Québec que se réalisent et sont obtenus les services de l'État, à quelques exceptions près.

Partage des pouvoirs, champs de compétence exclusifs : ces revendications concrétisent, au-delà des déclarations de principe, la véritable différence entre le Québec et les autres provinces. Le Québec, armé de compétences exclusives dans une majorité de secteurs, pourrait façonner son État et son appareil gouvernemental, ses programmes, ses priorités et, par conséquent, renforcer ses rapports avec ses citoyens.

Le rapport Allaire est un nouvel exemple du décalage politique qui s'est opéré entre le Québec et le reste du Canada dans la foulée de l'échec du Lac Meech. Alors que le partage des pouvoirs occupait peu de place dans l'accord de Meech, il est devenu primordial suite à la tenue de la commission Bélanger-Campeau et du congrès du PLQ en mars 1991.

LE QUÉBEC EN MUTATION

Entre les souverainistes, les indépendantistes et les néo-fédéralistes, il y a un consensus pour rejeter le statu quo et octroyer plus de pouvoirs au Québec. Dans tous les cas, il y aura une transformation importante du Québec, ce qui aura pour conséquence, fort probablement, d'accentuer l'identification des Québécois à l'État québécois.

Immigration, culture, communication, formation de la main-d'oeuvre, pour ne nommer que ces domaines, deviendront, peut-être, de compétence québécoise. S'ajoutant à la santé, à l'éducation et aux outils économiques, dont le Québec s'est doté depuis quelques années, le contrôle québécois de ces secteurs, qui occupent beaucoup de place dans la vie des citoyens, renforcera, ce faisant, leur rapport avec l'État.

L'État a joué un rôle central dans le développement du Québec, de sa société distincte et de son épanouissement. Et, dans la perspective de changements politiques importants à venir, l'État québécois continuera de jouer un rôle majeur.

Le Québec, souverain ou pas, aura, au même titre que d'autres sociétés, à relever des défis liés à la nature même de sa composition, de plus en plus hétérogène, et à faire face aux corrections historiques exigées par les peuples autochtones. Tout comme il aura à composer avec les revendications de différents groupes qui aspirent à transformer en profondeur les valeurs et le fonctionnement de la société. Les défis qui se posent aux Québécois ne sont pas plus grands ou plus petits que ceux qui se posent aux autres. Ce qu'il y a de particulier, cependant, c'est la possibilité réelle pour les Québécois de les relever dans un nouveau cadre politique. Un nouveau cadre politique qui pourra susciter l'énergie, l'enthousiasme et le dynamisme nécessaires pour transformer en profondeur et faire les virages marquants de toute une société.

Pour une majorité de Québécois, cette transformation ne peut pas se réaliser dans le cadre du Canada. Les deux "peuples fondateurs" ont évolué historiquement de façon telle qu'aujourd'hui ils se perçoivent, à tort ou à raison, comme étant le frein de leurs épanouissements respectifs. Ils ne s'identifient pas l'un à l'autre. Or, ne faut-il pas une identification commune comme condition essentielle pour se sentir et se percevoir citoyens d'un même pays?

NOTES

1 Jean-Marc Piotte, *Conjonctures* no 10-11 (automne 1988).
2 *Petit Larousse* (1990).
3 Simon Langlois, "Une société distincte à reconnaître," *Action nationale* (avril 1991).
4 Ibid.
5 Bruce Campbell, "In the Image of the Eagle: Remaking Canada under Free Trade," *Canadian Dimension* (mars 1990).
6 Philip Resnick, "Free Trade, Meech Lake, and the Two Nationalisms," *Queen's Quarterly* 97 no 2 (été 1990).

7 Daniel Latouche, "Quebec and Canada : The Last Rejoinder,"
   Queen's Quarterly 97 no. 7 (hiver).
8 Voir le rapport de la commission Bélanger-Campeau, "L'avenir politique et constitutionnel du Québec" (mars 1991); Alain G. Gagnon
   et Daniel Latouche, *Allaire, Bélanger, Campeau et les autres* (Québec :
   Québec-Amérique, 1991).
9 Formule utilisée par Brian Mulroney auprès des Québécois pour
   "donner une dernière chance" au Canada en 1984.

DANIEL TURP

Citoyenneté québécoise, citoyenneté canadienne et citoyenneté commune selon le modèle de l'Union européenne

Si l'avenir se traduit par la mutation du Québec en État souverain, et ce scénario d'avenir est plausible si l'on examine les tendances de l'opinion au Québec et au Canada, de même que les errements et écueils de l'actuel processus de réforme constitutionnelle, il n'est pas inutile d'aborder dès maintenant la question de la citoyenneté en regard de l'hypothèse de l'accession du Québec à la souveraineté. Cette question n'a pu échapper aux politiciens, comme en font foi les échanges entre la secrétaire d'État aux Affaires extérieures du Canada et le chef du Parti québécois[1] et a d'ailleurs fait l'objet d'analyses de l'une des commissions parlementaires spéciales instituées par la *Loi sur le processus de détermination de l'avenir politique et constitutionnel du Québec.*[2]

En n'occultant pas cette réalité possible de l'accession à la souveraineté du Québec, le professeur Kaplan me donne ainsi l'occasion de vous livrer des réflexions sur les futures citoyenneté canadienne et citoyenneté québécoise, et des aménagements dont elles pourront faire l'objet, tout en m'invitant, avec discernement, à tirer, pour l'avenir des relations entre les citoyens du Canada et du Québec, des leçons de l'expérience européenne.

Bien qu'un tel exposé puisse déranger, choquer même celles et ceux qui ont fait ici l'éloge de la citoyenneté canadienne et de son unicité et militent en faveur d'une identité canadienne renforcée,[3] je voudrai dès lors consacrer sa première partie à l'examen des rapports que pourraient entretenir la citoyenneté canadienne avec une future citoyenneté québécoise et étudier dans une deuxième partie l'hypothèse de l'adoption d'une citoyenneté commune selon le modèle de la citoyenneté de l'Union européenne.

LA CITOYENNETÉ QUÉBÉCOISE ET SON AMÉNAGEMENT AVEC LA CITOYENNETÉ CANADIENNE

En application des règles de droit international général relatives à la succession d'États, l'accession du Québec à la souveraineté entraînera l'émergence d'une nouvelle citoyenneté et amènera à la fois le Québec et le Canada à poser un certain nombre d'actes juridiques en la matière. La position du droit international sur cette question a été fort judicieusement résumée ainsi :

It is the municipal law of the predecessor State which is to determine which persons have lost their nationality as a result of the change; it is that of the successor State which is to determine which persons have acquired its nationality. The function of international law is at the most to delimit the competence of the former to retain certain persons as its nationals, and of the latter to claim them as its own ... The predecessor State would seem to lose its competence in international law to claim the inhabitants of absorbed territory as its nationals when the bond uniting it with them is dissolved.[4]

Ainsi, l'attribution de la citoyenneté québécoise relèvera-t-elle de la compétence discrétionnaire du nouvel État souverain québécois et il appartiendra à celui-ci de déterminer les titulaires de cette nouvelle citoyenneté. Il importera également que le Québec se penche sur le sort à réserver à la citoyenneté canadienne que détiendront encore de très nombreux habitants du nouvel État québécois au moment de l'accession à la souveraineté.

La citoyenneté québécoise

Que ce soit dans une éventuelle déclaration de souveraineté, dans une *Loi sur la citoyenneté canadienne*[5] adoptée à titre provisoire ou dans un nouveau *Code de la citoyenneté québécoise*,[6] l'un des premiers actes que devra poser l'État souverain québécois est l'établissement des critères d'acquisition de la citoyenneté québécoise.[7]

En ce qui concerne les personnes qui se trouvent sur le territoire du Québec au moment de l'accession du Québec à la souveraineté, plusieurs possibilités s'offriront au Québec. Ainsi, le Québec pourra vouloir conférer sa nouvelle citoyenneté à tous les citoyens canadiens, domiciliés au Québec ou y résidant au moment de l'accession à la souveraineté ou depuis une période déterminée avant la date d'accession à la souveraineté. S'inspirant du *Code de la nationalité*

française, il pourrait toutefois ne pas tenir compte de cette citoyenneté et prévoir que tous les individus domiciliés sur le territoire du
Québec à la date d'accession à la souveraineté acquièrent la citoyenneté québécoise, à moins que ces individus puissent effectivement
établir leur domicile en dehors de ce territoire.[8] Le Québec pourrait
préférer réserver sa nationalité aux personnes nées sur son territoire ou dont les parents ou grands-parents sont nés sur le territoire,
ce qui permettrait d'ailleurs à un certain nombre de personnes résidant à l'extérieur du Québec d'acquérir la nouvelle citoyenneté québécoise. Sans doute, une combinaison de ces divers critères serait
retenue par le Québec de façon à ce que les personnes désireuses
d'acquérir la nouvelle citoyenneté québécoise ne soient pas privées
de cette possibilité.

En ce qui concerne les nouveaux arrivants, le Québec pourra faire
siennes les thèses du *jus soli* et du *jus sanguinis* et prévoir ainsi que
toutes les personnes nées au Québec après l'accession à la souveraineté ou nées à l'étranger de parents ayant la nouvelle citoyenneté
québécoise deviendront citoyens québécois. La naturalisation pourrait également conduire à l'obtention de la nouvelle citoyenneté québécoise de même qu'il est à prévoir que, pendant une période
transitoire, le Québec se donne la possibilité d'accorder sa citoyenneté à titre exceptionnel.[9]

Cette attribution de la citoyenneté québécoise ne signifierait pas
pour autant la perte de la citoyenneté canadienne pour les nouveaux
citoyens québécois et il faut s'interroger dès lors sur l'aménagement
de ces deux citoyennetés.

La citoyenneté canadienne des citoyens québécois

L'attribution de la citoyenneté québécoise aux citoyens canadiens
aurait comme conséquence de conférer une citoyenneté additionnelle à ceux-ci et d'engendrer des conditions de double citoyenneté.
Cette situation pourrait être évitée si le Québec n'autorisait pas ses
nouveaux citoyens à détenir une double citoyenneté ou exigeait
d'eux qu'ils renoncent à la citoyenneté candienne pour obtenir la citoyenneté québécoise. Elle pourrait également ne pas se produire si
le Canada décidait que l'acquisition d'une citoyenneté québécoise
faisait perdre la citoyenneté canadienne.[10]

Il n'est pas dans l'intérêt du Québec de refuser aux Québécois le
droit de conserver leur citoyenneté canadienne et les autres citoyennetés qu'ils pourraient détenir, si une telle possibilité leur est confé-
rée. Comme l'a très bien compris le chef du Parti québécois, le
Québec n'a qu'à laisser le Canada décider du sort à réserver à la ci-

toyenneté canadienne des personnes à qui le Québec aura conféré la citoyenneté québécoise. Si le Canada devait retirer la citoyenneté canadienne à ceux et celles qui sont devenus citoyens québécois, ou qui doivent déménager dans une autre province pour la maintenir comme l'a d'ailleurs laissé entendre la secrétaire d'État aux Affaires extérieures,[11] il risquerait de porter seul l'odieux d'un tel retrait et d'appliquer aux citoyens québécois une règle qu'ils n'appliquent d'ailleurs pas aux personnes détenant la nationalité d'un autre État souverain.

Pour éviter que le Canada n'ait à porter seul l'odieux d'un tel retrait et s'il entendait limiter les cas de double citoyenneté, le Canada et le Québec pourraient conclure un accord prévoyant des aménagements en la matière. Cet accord pourrait notamment stipuler que l'attribution de la citoyenneté québécoise aux citoyens canadiens, domiciliés ou résidant au Québec, entraîne la perte de la citoyenneté canadienne. Il devrait toutefois inclure, comme le stipule la *Convention des Nations Unies sur la réduction des cas d'apatridie*[12] à laquelle le Canada est partie,[13] des dispositions visant à assurer qu'aucun cas d'apatridie ne résulter de l'accession du Québec à la souveraineté.[14]

Cet accord, comme certains autres accords de dévolution,[15] pourrait prévoir également un droit d'option pour une certaine catégorie de citoyens canadiens et québécois. D'aucuns argueront qu'il pourrait ne pas être dans l'intérêt du Québec ou du Canada de favoriser le droit d'option de l'ensemble des citoyens canadiens du Québec, puisque son exercice entraînerait l'existence d'une importante population canadienne dans un autre État souverain. Pour éviter un tel problème, s'il en est, seuls les citoyens canadiens qui ne sont pas nés au Québec ainsi que les citoyens canadiens nés au Québec, mais qui n'y sont pas domiciliés ou n'y résidant pas au moment de l'accession à la souveraineté, pourraient se voir conférer le droit d'opter pour la citoyenneté canadienne ou la citoyenneté québécoise. Ces personnes pourraient disposer d'un délai pour procéder à une telle option et les accords relatifs au droit d'option ont en règle générale prévu un délai de deux ans pour les fins de l'exercice de l'option.[16]

Mais la perte de la citoyenneté canadienne et l'option pour une citoyenneté québécoise ou canadienne s'imposent-elles vraiment? Les rapports historiques qu'auront entretenus les citoyens canadiens et les nouveaux citoyens québécois avant l'accession du Québec à la souveraineté ne justifieraient-ils pas que les citoyens québécois et canadiens puissent détenir à la fois les citoyennetés canadienne et québécoise? Cette hypothèse d'une double nationalité généralisée ne serait pourtant pas unique, puisque l'expérience hispano-américaine révèle l'existence de régimes intégrationnistes en matière de nationalité. Ainsi, plusieurs traités hispano-américains ont institué la double nationalité conventionnelle en faveur des nationaux espagnols et de ceux de plusieurs pays d'Amérique latine, dont les nationalités coexistent.[17] Ces traités permettent ainsi aux titulaires d'exercer leurs droits et d'assumer les devoirs à titre de citoyens dans les États parties à ces traités.

Si cette expérience veut être écartée au motif que la désintégration d'une fédération justifie le refus de maintenir la citoyenneté antérieure de ceux qui ont contribué à la rupture de l'État[18] ou en raison de fait que l'accession à la souveraineté ne justifie pas la rétention de cette citoyenneté antérieure,[19] l'expérience luso-brésilienne pourrait davantage inspirer le Canada et le Québec et heurter moins les susceptibilités des nouveaux dirigeants. Cette expérience amènerait ceux-ci à conférer à leurs nationaux, domiciliés sur le territoire de l'autre État, "le pouvoir d'exercer des droits inhérents à la qualité de citoyen, c'est-à-dire les droits politiques, sans préjudice de la préservation et de l'unicité de son statut national primitif."[20] Dans ce cas, la double nationalité ne serait pas généralisée, mais les citoyens de l'un et l'autre des États seraient assimilés pour les fins d'exercice de leurs droits et devoirs sur le territoire des deux États souverains.[21]

Mais le Canada et le Québec pourraient plutôt vouloir créer une citoyenneté additionnelle, commune à leurs citoyens respectifs pour favoriser le maintien d'une union économique et la circulation plus libre des personnes sur les territoires du Canada et du Québec. C'est ici que les expériences relatives aux citoyennetés communes, et notamment la récente expérience européenne, peuvent devenir utiles et inspirer les solutions que pourraient vouloir retenir les États canadien et québécois.

LA CITOYENNETÉ COMMUNE SELON LE MODÈLE DE L'UNION EUROPÉENNE

Si le processus d'accession à la souveraineté est accompagné d'une négociation destinée à maintenir des liens entre le Québec et le Canada, les deux États pourraient envisager d'instituer une citoyenneté commune, que certains qualifient d'intercitoyenneté ou de citoyenneté supranationale.[22] La notion d'une citoyenneté commune, se superposant aux citoyennetés existantes, n'est pas nouvelle puisqu'elle a déjà existé dans le cadre de la Communauté française[23] et qu'elle déploie encore ses effets dans le Commonwealth.[24]

Dans l'hypothèse probable où le Québec demeurerait au sein du Commonwealth, les citoyens canadiens résidant au Québec et les citoyens québécois résidant au Canada pourraient également être considérés comme citoyens du Commonwealth.[25] Cette citoyenneté commune aurait d'ailleurs comme conséquence de ne pas faire des Canadiens et Québécois des étrangers dans leurs pays respectifs, de consacrer un statut personnel particulier sur le territoire de l'autre partie et de conférer à ceux-ci certains droits qui dérivent d'un tel statut.[26] Cette citoyenneté serait toutefois commune à l'ensemble des pays du Commonwealth et dépasserait dès lors le cadre des relations canado-québécoises.

Si le Canada et le Québec envisageaient la création d'une citoyenneté commune additionnelle, sans doute l'expérience communautaire européenne s'avérerait-elle pertinente, tout en étant la plus contemporaine. Certes, il n'est pas nécessaire de créer une telle citoyenneté additionnelle pour permettre une circulation plus libre des personnes sur les territoires du Canada et du Québec, comme le démontre l'expérience européenne elle-même. Ainsi, le droit de circulation et de séjour a été garanti, dans les limites prévues au Traité de Rome, sans qu'il n'ait été nécessaire d'instituer une citoyenneté commune. Ces droits se sont traduits par des mesures d'ouverture des emplois publics, la reconnaissance mutuelle des diplômes et des mesures de protection du consommateur, étroitement liées aux activités des agents économiques des ressortissants communautaires.[27]

Mais, les Européens ont paru vouloir consolider ces droits de circulation et de séjour, tout en garantissant certains droits politiques. Ils ont voulu créer à cette fin une citoyenneté dont les attributs sont définis dans le Traité d'Union européenne qui pourrait inspirer les promoteurs d'une citoyenneté commune aux Canadiens et Québécois.

La citoyenneté de l'Union européenne

Donnant suite au projet de la présidence luxembourgeoise[28] et à l'idée d'une Europe des citoyens,[29] le Traité sur l'Union européenne[30] énonce parmi ses objectifs de renforcer la protection des droits et intérêts des ressortissants de ses États membres par l'instauration d'une citoyenneté de l'Union[31] et institue une telle citoyenneté.[32] Toute personne ayant la nationalité d'un État membre est titulaire de cette citoyenneté[33] et les citoyens de l'Union jouissent des droits et sont soumis aux devoirs prévus par le Traité de Rome.[34]

Le droit de circuler et de séjourner librement sur le territoire des États membres, dans les conditions prévues par le Traité de Rome et par les dispositions prises pour son application,[35] est reconnu au citoyen de l'Union et pourrait élargir la portée du droit tel qu'il est actuellement reconnu aux ressortissants communautaires.[36]

Le Traité d'Union élargit également l'étendue des droits électoraux[37] et confère d'abord le droit de vote et d'éligibilité aux élections municipales dans l'État membre où il réside, dans les mêmes conditions que les ressortissants de cet État.[38] Il confirme ensuite le droit de vote et d'éligibilité d'un citoyen de l'Union aux élections du Parlement européen dans l'État membre où il réside dans les mêmes conditions que les ressortissants de cet État.[39] D'autres droits politiques, tels que le droit de pétition au Parlement européen[40] et le droit de s'adresser à un médiateur, sont également reconnus au citoyen de l'Union.[41]

Le Traité d'Union européenne innove par ailleurs en conférant au citoyen de l'Union européenne le droit à la protection diplomatique et consulaire de tout État membre dans un pays tiers où l'État membre dont il est ressortissant n'est pas représenté. Ce droit doit s'exercer dans les mêmes conditions que les nationaux de cet État et est assujetti à l'établissement par les États entre eux des règles nécessaires et aux négociations internationales requises en vue d'assurer la protection diplomatique.[42]

Ces droits, qui sont susceptibles d'être complétés par d'autres droits,[43] donnent un contenu concret à la citoyenneté commune aux nationaux des États membres de la Communauté européenne. Cette citoyenneté nouvelle correspond bien à la finalité économique de l'expérience d'intégration européenne, mais dépasse cette finalité en lui donnant un contenu politique destiné à rendre l'union sans cesse plus étroite.[44]

Sans doute, cette expérience contient-elle de riches enseignements dont le Canada et le Québec pourraient tirer des leçons s'ils décidaient d'établir une citoyenneté commune, qui se superposerait, tout comme la citoyenneté de l'Union européenne s'ajoute aux nationalités des douze États de cette Union, aux citoyennetés canadienne et québécoise.

La citoyenneté commune des citoyens canadiens et québécois

L'étendue des droits découlant d'une citoyenneté commune des Canadiens et des Québécois dépendrait à bien des égards de la finalité de l'union que voudrait édifier le Canada et le Québec.

Si cette finalité devait être économique, le modèle communautaire serait dès lors d'une pertinence indéniable et il y aurait lieu d'examiner attentivement les dispositions du Traité d'Union européenne sur le droit de circulation et de séjour ainsi que l'ensemble des actes communautaires aménageant l'exercice des droits du citoyen de l'Union européenne en la matière. L'expérience communautaire européenne pourrait offrir des enseignements utiles pour déterminer les avantages tangibles dans la vie quotidienne des citoyens d'une éventuelle union du Canada et du Québec. Le Québec et le Canada pourraient dès lors envisager la création d'une citoyenneté de l'Union pour assurer une gestion efficace de l'union économique et rappeler aux citoyens canadiens et québécois les liens historiques qui ont caractérisé leurs rapports et les liens économiques qui perpétuent ces rapports.

Sans doute, les gouvernements d'un État québécois et d'un État canadien souverains envisageraient-ils aussi de faciliter l'exercice du droit de séjour et de circulation des citoyens de leur union à l'intérieur du territoire par la création d'un passeport de nature similaire au passeport européen.[45] Ce passeport, dont l'existence remonte au 1er janvier 1985, est encore délivré par les autorités nationales et comporte deux mentions distinctes, celui de la Communauté européenne et celui du pays d'émission. L'expérience européenne pourrait ici encore inspirer les négociateurs d'une union entre le Canada et le Québec et sans doute cette mesure pourrait-elle être acceptable pour les interlocuteurs québécois qui ont même déjà évoqué l'idée d'un passeport nord-américain.[46]

Si l'union entre le Canada et le Québec devait avoir une finalité politique similaire à celle de l'Union européenne, comme le souhaite l'actuel premier ministre du Québec,[47] il ne serait pas surprenant que l'on veuille aussi proposer la création d'un Parlement élu et que des droits de vote et de pétition soient reconnus aux citoyens d'une telle union, voire même des droits de vote et d'éligibilité aux élections locales. La reconnaissance d'un droit de protection diplomatique comme celui que contient le Traité d'Union européenne dépendrait à bien des égards de la capacité d'un Québec souverain d'assumer une telle représentation aux lendemains de l'indépendance et il n'est pas impossible qu'ici encore le Traité d'Union européenne puisse servir de modèle au Canada et au Québec.

Il en irait sans doute autrement de l'union qui serait négociée par un gouvernement du Parti québécois, avec la collaboration du Bloc québécois, et dont la finalité serait essentiellement économique. Dans ces conditions, l'expérience communautaire pourrait être d'une valeur limitée puisque le citoyen d'une telle union, qui ne compterait pas parmi ses institutions un Parlement élu, ne pourrait ni voter pour un tel Parlement ni lui adresser de pétition. Privée de finalité politique, il est par ailleurs douteux que l'on veuille conférer un droit de vote dans le cadre d'élections locales, comme cela est en voie de se produire dans l'Union européenne. Seuls des droits économiques et sociaux paraîtraient utiles pour atteindre les fins de l'union et seraient susceptibles d'être conférés au citoyen d'une union économique négociée par des partis souverainistes.

L'expérience communautaire en matière de citoyenneté, aussi jeune soit-elle, pourrait néanmoins être utile dans le contexte d'une négociation d'un Traité instituant une Union canado-québécoise.[48] Si les Québécois paraissent disposer dès maintenant à envisager cette hypothèse, que la Commission d'étude sur les questions afférentes à l'accession du Québec à la souveraineté s'est déjà intéressée aux modes d'association économique d'un Québec souverain avec le Canada[49] et qu'elle peut recevoir et analyser une offre de partenariat économique,[50] il est moins clair que les Canadiens, et leurs représentants, dont l'hésitation devant un scénario d'accession du Québec à la souveraineté est manifeste, veuillent constituer une telle union avec le Québec.

Si, d'aventure, certains voulaient commencer à y réfléchir, et il est grand temps à mon avis que cela se produise au Canada, l'expérience de la nouvelle Union européenne devrait être considérée pertinente et guider la réflexion des Canadiens et des Québécois, dont il est espéré qu'elle soit empreinte de bonne foi, de courtoisie et de respect mutuel.

NOTES

1 Voir "McDougall in Passport Warning," Montreal Gazette, 11 décembre 1991, A-7, et P. Poirier, "Minister Wrong on Citizenship, Parizeau Says," Globe and Mail, 12 décembre 1992, A-3. Voir aussi une déclaration antérieure de Jacques Parizeau sur la question reprise dans G. Normand, "Parizeau : après l'indépendance, les Québécois pourront rester ... canadiens," La Presse, 31 octobre 1991, A-1 et 2.

2 LQ 1991, c. 34. La Commission d'étude des questions afférentes à l'accession du Québec à la souveraineté a produit un document intitulé Succession d'États : la nationalité, 14 janvier 1992, et fait réaliser une étude par le professeur Claude Emanuelli de l'Université d'Ottawa sur L'accession du Québec à la souveraineté et la nationalité, janvier 1992.

3 Sur cette identité canadienne, il est instructif de lire le document préparé par le gouvernement fédéral au soutien des plus récentes propositions constitutionnelles intitulé L'identité canadienne : des valeurs communes (Ottawa : Ministère des Approvisionnements et services, 1991).

4 D.P. O'Connell, *State Succession in Municipal and International Law*, vol. 1 (Cambridge : Cambridge University Press, 1967), 501–2.

5 LRC, c. C-29.

6 Après avoir fait régir la question de la nationalité par des dispositions du Code civil français, la France s'est dotée d'un *Code sur la nationalité*, Loi no 73-42 du 9 janvier 1973, qui, comme la *Loi sur la citoyenneté canadienne*, regroupe l'ensemble des dispositions relatives à la citoyenneté.

7 Sur les critères d'attribution de la nationalité, voir J.F. Rezek, "Le droit international de la nationalité," *RCADI* 198 (1986) 337.

8 Code de la nationalité française, art. 122.

9 Voir à ce sujet les développements que le professeur Emanuelli consacre à l'élaboration d'un futur régime de la nationalité québécoise dans son étude, *L'accession*, 27–64.

10 Le Parlement du Canada devrait à cette fin amender la *Loi sur la citoyenneté*, LRC 1985, c. C-29, et prévoir dans la partie II que l'acquisition de la citoyenneté québécoise constitue un cas de perte de la citoyenneté canadienne. Si un tel changement législatif n'était pas effectué, les personnes remplissant les conditions mentionnées à l'article 3 de la *Loi sur la citoyenneté* continueraient de jouir d'un droit à la citoyenneté canadienne et d'avoir la qualité de citoyen canadien. Cette position est confirmée par les commentaires faits par l'avocat Mendel Green, rapportés dans Poirier, "Minister Wrong," qui n'hésitait pas à affirmer que "Ms McDougall has made an error in law. She's wrong." Voir aussi les commentaires d'une éditorialiste confirmant que "the present law would allow that, but there would be pressure to change it" : D. Francis, "Quebec's Separatists Raise a Storm," *Financial Post*, 14 décembre 1992, 10.

11 Poirier, "Minister Wrong."

12 RTNU 989 (1975) 175. Cette Convention a été adoptée le 30 août 1961 et est entrée en vigueur le 13 décembre 1975.

13 [1978] RT Can. no. 32. Le Canada a adhéré à cette convention le 17 juillet 1978 et elle est entrée en vigueur à son égard le 15 octobre 1978.

14 Voir art. 10.

15 Pour un examen sommaire de tels accords, voir Emanuelli, *L'accession*, 19–22.

16 Voir à ce sujet les développements consacrés au droit d'option par J. Brossard, *L'accession à la souveraineté et le cas du Québec* (Montréal : Presses de l'Université de Montréal, 1976), 526–30. Voir aussi Emanuelli, qui fait notamment un examen de la pratique conventionnelle en la matière : *L'accession*, 19–22.

17 Voir à ce sujet les développements de l'auteur Rezek, "Le droit international," 380–2.

18 Voir à ce sujet les propos du premier ministre Brian Mulroney, selon lequel "You're either in or you're out. You're either Canadian or
   you're not, you don't get the benefits – you don't get any benefits
   – of citizenship of Canada because these benefits we are going to keep
   for the citizens of Canada ... This is one country. When you're a
   citizen of Canada you get the benefits and the responsibilities of Canada
   and we don't share those with anybody" : M. Trickey, "Canada Is
   not a Buffet, PM Warns," *Vancouver Sun*, 30 novembre 1991, A-8.

19 Cette position paraît être exprimée dans la proposition du Gouvernement du Québec, *La nouvelle entente Québec-Canada : proposition du gouvernement du Québec pour une entente d'égal à égal : la
   souveraineté-association* (Québec : Éditeur officiel du Québec, 1980),
   60–1.

20 Voir Rezek, "Le droit international," 382–4.

21 Un tel statut était souhaité par le gouvernement du Québec, dans
   sa Proposition de 1980, dans laquelle est affirmée que "les citoyens canadiens pourront jouir des mêmes droits au Québec que les citoyens
   québécois au Canada" : Québec, *La nouvelle entente*, 61. Voir aussi J.-P.
   Charbonneau et G. Paquette, *L'option* (Montréal : Les Éditions de
   l'Homme, 1978), 423.

22 Voir F. de Castro, "La nationalité, la double nationalité et la supra-
   nationalité," *RCADI* 102 (1961) 631.

23 Ibid., 604–7.

24 Emanuelli, *L'accession.*

25 Ainsi le *Code civil du Québec* ou le *Code de la citoyenneté québécoise* pourraient contenir une disposition analogue à l'article 32(1) de la *Loi sur
   la citoyenneté canadienne* qui stipule que "les personnes qui, dans un
   autre pays du Commonwealth, jouissent du statut légal de citoyen ou
   ressortissant de ce pays ont, au Canada, les statuts de citoyen du
   Commonwealth."

26 Les auteurs Charbonneau et Paquette font par ailleurs remarquer
   à cet égard que "les citoyens du Commonwealth ne jouissent pas d'un
   statut bien différent de celui des étrangers, si ce n'est que la citoyenneté des autres pays du Commonwealth peut s'acquérir avec plus de
   facilité" : *L'option*, 424. Sur cette question, voir aussi de Castro,
   "La nationalité," 602–4.

27 Pour l'étendue actuelle du droit de circulation et de séjour dans
   la Communauté économique européenne, voir E. Gaillard, D. Carreau,
   et W.L. Lee, *Le marché unique européen* (Paris : Pédone, 1989), 57–74.
   Voir aussi M.-F. Labouz, *Le système communautaire européen* (Paris :
   Berger-Levrault, 1988), 2e éd., 62–3. Les actes communautaires relatifs à ce droit de circulation et de séjour sont reproduits dans J.-C.
   Séché, *Libre circulation des personnes dans la Communauté : entrée et sé-*

jour (Bruxelles : Commission des Communautés européennes, Bruxelles Office des publications officielles des Communautés européennes, 1988).

28 Le texte du Projet est reproduit dans *Europe Documents*, no 1722/1723, 5 juillet 1991. Pour un commentaire de ce projet et des dispositions relatives à la citoyenneté de l'Union européenne, voir D. Vignes, "Le Projet de la présidence luxembourgeoise d'un Traité sur l'Union," *Revue du Marché commun*, 1991, 504, en particulier aux 508–9.

29 Comme le font remarquer E. Gaillard, D. Carreau et W.L. Lee, *Le marché*, 55, la formule générique "Europe des citoyens," apparue dès 1975, est d'un usage courant depuis le Conseil européen de Fontainebleau de juin 1984 et tout en étant "frappante par son pouvoir évocateur, elle demeure fort imprécise dans sa portée." Voir aussi à ce sujet les rapports du Comité ad hoc "Europe des citoyens," adressés au Conseil européen de Bruxelles, reproduits dans *Bulletin C.E.* nos 2 et 17 (7/1985) ainsi que l'étude de A.C. Evans, "European Citizenship : A Novel Concept in EEC Law," *American Journal of Comparative Law*, 32 (1984) 678.

30 Ce traité a été signé le 2 février 1992 à Maastricht et a été publié par l'Office des publications officielles des Communautés européennes (ISBN 92-24-0960-0) (ci-après dénommé le Traité d'Union).

31 Traité d'Union, art. B.

32 L'article G-C du Traité d'Union, insère une deuxième partie, intitulée "La Citoyenneté de l'Union" au *Traité instituant la Communauté européenne*, ainsi qu'il est réintitulée (ci-après dénommé Traité CE). Cette partie contient les nouveaux articles 8 à 8E du Traité CE. La citoyenneté de l'Union est instituée par l'article 8 §1, al. 1.

33 Traité CE, art. 8 §1, al. 2.

34 Ibid., art. 8 §2. Il est intéressant de constater que les citoyens de l'Union ne se voient pas conférer directement les droits civils et politiques contenus dans la Convention européenne des droits de l'Homme et ses protocoles additionnels. Le Traité d'Union contient toutefois en son article F §2 une disposition qui stipule que "l'Union respecte les droits fondamentaux, tels qu'ils sont garantis par la Convention européenne de sauvegarde des droits de l'Homme et des libertés fondamentales, signée à Rome le 4 novembre 1950, et tels qu'ils résultent des traditions constitutionnelles communes aux États membres, en tant que principes généraux du droit communautaire." Sur la question des droits de la personne dans le contexte communautaire européen, voir *L'Europe, société humaine* (Bruxelles : Commission des Communautés européennes, Office des publications officielles des Communautés européennes, 1990).

35 Ibid., art. 8A §1. Le §2 précise quant à lui que le "Conseil peut arrêter des dispositions visant à faciliter l'exercice des droits visés au paragraphe 1; sauf si le présent traité en dispose autrement, il statue à l'unanimité sur proposition de la Commission et après avis conforme du Parlement européen."

36 V.E. Gaillard, D. Carreau et W.L. Lee, *Le marché*. Voir aussi F. Burrows, *Free Movement in European Community Law* (Oxford : Clarendon Press, 1987), 117–213.

37 Sur les débats entourant la reconnaissance de droits électoraux, lire Evans, "European Citizenship," 705–10.

38 Traité CE, art. 8B §1. Cet article précise par ailleurs que ce droit sera exercé sous réserve des modalités à arrêter avant le 31 décembre 1994 par le Conseil, statuant à l'unanimité sur proposition de la Commission et après consultation du Parlement européen; ces modalités peuvent prévoir des dispositions dérogatoires lorsque des problèmes spécifiques à un État membre le justifient.

39 Ibid., art. 8B §2. La même clause de réserve et de dérogation suit la reconnaissance de ce droit de vote et d'éligibilité, si ce n'est que les modalités d'exercice du droit devront être arrêtées avant le 31 décembre 1993.

40 Ibid., art. 8D §1, qui renvoie au nouvel article 138D du Traité CE.

41 Ibid., art. 8D §2, qui renvoie au nouvel article 138E du Traité CE.

42 Ibid., art. 8C.

43 L'article 8E stipule en effet que le "Conseil, statuant à l'unanimité sur proposition de la Commission et après consultation du Parlement européen, peut arrêter des dispositions tendant à compléter les droits prévus à la présente partie, dispositions dont il recommandera l'adoption par les États membres conformément à leurs règles constitutionnelles respectives."

44 Cette notion d'union sans cesse plus étroite se retrouve dans le préambule du Traité CE et est d'ailleurs réitérée dans une terminologie sensiblement différente dans le Traité d'Union. Ainsi, l'article A §2 affirme que "le présent traité marque une nouvelle étape dans le processus créant une union sans cesse plus étroite entre les peuples de l'Europe, dans laquelle les décisions sont prises le plus près possible des citoyens."

45 Pour les textes prescrivant l'institution d'un passeport uniforme, voir les résolutions du Conseil européen publiées dans *JOCE* : no C.214, du 19 septembre 1981, et no C.179, du 16 juillet 1982.

46 Voir à ce sujet "Lucien Bouchard croit au passeport québécois advenant l'indépendance," *Le Devoir*, 5 novembre 1991, 1 et 4.

47 Ce souhait est évident à la lumière du projet de question référendaire formulée par Robert Bourassa à l'occasion d'une visite officielle aux Communautés européennes à Bruxelles. Cette question était ainsi for-

mulée : "Voulez-vous remplacer l'ordre constitutionnel existant par
l'existence de deux États souverains associés dans une union économique, responsables à un parlement élu au suffrage universel?" :
voir à ce sujet F. Tremblay, "États souverains associés? Bourassa soulève
un coin du voile de la question référendaire," *Le Devoir*,
7 février 1992, 1 et 4.

La formulation de cette question est quelque peu différente de
la formulation qui paraît remonter à 1979 et qui avait été présentée
par Robert Bourassa à l'occasion d'une entrevue qui n'avait jamais
fait l'objet d'une publication : "Voulez-vous remplacer l'ordre constitutionnel existant par deux États souverains associés dans une union
économique, *laquelle serait responsable* à un parlement élu au suffrage
universel?" : voir "Bourassa : l'entrevue oubliée," *L'Actualité*, 15 septembre 1990, 11–12.

La position du Parti libéral du Québec est moins claire sur cette
question puisque dans le Rapport du Comité constitutionnel du Parti
libéral du Québec du 28 janvier 1991, mieux connu comme le Rapport Allaire, il est affirmé que "dans la mesure où la proposition avancée
ne déboucherait pas sur un accord avec le reste du Canada dans
des délais raisonnables, le Parti libéral du Québec recommande que la
population soit invitée par voie référendaire à se prononcer en faveur de la souveraineté du Québec, avec un effort pour conclure après
une association économique" : voir Parti libéral du Québec, *Un Québec libre de ses choix*, 28 janvier 1991, 57. Le projet de résolution stipule
quant à lui que "dans le cas où il n'y aurait pas entente sur la réforme proposée par le Québec, que le gouvernement du Parti libéral
du Québec propose l'accès du Québec au statut d'État souverain;
que dans cette deuxième hypothèse, le Québec offre, au reste du Canada, l'aménagement d'une union économique gérée par des institutions de nature confédérale."

48 Pour le texte d'un tel projet de Traité, voir D. Turp, "Exposé-
réponse," Commission sur l'avenir politique et constitutionnel du Québec, *Les avis des spécialistes invités à répondre aux huit questions posées
par la Commission*, Document de travail no 4 (ISBN 2-550-21733-0),
annexe 3, 1083–1115.

49 La Commission d'étude des questions afférentes à l'accession du Québec
à la souveraineté a produit un document intitulé *Partenariats économiques : Les relations commerciales d'un Québec souverain*, 16 janvier 1992,
où la question des liens économiques avec le Canada est évoquée
(pp. 10–11) et a fait réaliser une étude par le professeur Ivan Bernier
de l'Université Laval sur *La dimension juridique des relations commerciales d'un Québec souverain*, janvier 1992.

50 Voir la *Loi sur le processus de détermination de l'avenir politique et
constitutionnel du Québec*, LQ 1991, c. 34, art. 3.

PART THREE

Law, the Constitution, and Economics

ALAN C. CAIRNS

The Fragmentation of Canadian Citizenship

The theory and practice of Canadian citizenship, in the broadest political sense, have been not eternal, unchanging verities, but rather
materials for an unending debate. The pre–First World War debates
between the imperialist British Canadians and the rival liberal nationalists were, although the word may not have been used, about
citizenship, about whether the boundaries of political community
and civic allegiance were restricted to Canada or also, through ties of
kinship and political tradition, encompassed the mother country.
The debates surrounding the conscription crises of both world wars
were citizenship controversies about the extent and nature of civic
obligation.

Citizenship has always been central to the debates about who Canadians were and what they should become. Nevertheless, in spite of
its centrality, it has been an underexamined constitutional category.
This essay provides an interpretive commentary on some of the tensions of contemporary Canadian citizenship, especially as reflected
in constitutional politics. While this may seem a limited vantage
point, constitutional politics is the supreme vehicle by which we define ourselves as a people, decide which of our present identities we
should foster and which ignore, and rearrange the rights and duties
of citizen membership. This essay considers citizenship from a historical, political, and sociological, rather than a legal perspective.

The two major portions of this essay, following several brief introductory sections, discuss "A Three-Nations View of Canada" and
"The New Diversity and Citizenship." A short conclusion brings the
threads of the argument together. The pressures of time, and the
essay format, along with the fundamental indeterminacy of where
Canadians are and where we might be heading, have engendered
more speculation and conjectures in the following pages than is cus-

tomary in academic analyses. Many of the unqualified statements that follow are 'iffy,' or are drawn from imagined futures that may never happen, or rest on implicit social theories that may well be wrong. I agree with Casey Stengel – or was it Yogi Berra? – that prediction is always difficult, especially when it deals with the future. Prediction, however, is not therefore to be avoided, but is to be taken with a grain of salt.

INTRODUCTION

The New Salience of Citizenship

A few preliminary comments on the enhanced visibility and prominence of citizenship will set the stage.

(1) The gradual weaning of (especially British) Canadians from the British connection – the historic progression from colony to nation, culminating in the 1982 Constitution Act – confronts Canadians with basic questions of sovereignty, identity, and their place in the world, answers to which must address our citizenship.

(2) Globalization presents people with an unending stream of products, ideas, values, and new identities that threatens to destabilize links between citizen and state unless they are constrained by the positive identification with the polity that an enriched practice of citizenship can generate.

(3) The threatened breakup of Canada – a crisis of citizenship and community – raises the fundamental question: to what community or communities do Canadians wish to give their allegiance?

(4) Citizens are made as well as born. Immigration-induced change in our ethnic demography makes citizenship a crucial instrument for bridging cleavages between old and new Canadians who decreasingly come from the traditional 'supply' sources of our country's first century.

(5) The behaviour that the modern state requires of its citizens cannot be achieved by coercion, an increasingly inefficient instrument for securing compliance in a complex contemporary democratic society. Meeting economic competition, responding to environmental threats, and sustaining the civic empathy that a multiracial society needs require autonomous civic behaviour that alienated subjects will only grudgingly provide.

(6) The constitutional recognition vigorously demanded by aboriginal peoples will require unique citizenship status.

(7) The Charter of Rights and Freedoms of 1982 has profound effects on citizenship. Pierre Trudeau saw it as an instrument to

transfer sovereignty to the people. Although the simultaneous introduction of an amending formula designed as an instrument of governments frustrated that goal, the Meech Lake fiasco suggests that governmental control of the amending process is illusory. That an amendment package with the noble intent of returning Quebec to the constitutional family with honour and enthusiasm foundered on widespread public opposition indicates that the ultimate authority over constitutional change is slipping away from the governing elites of executive federalism to the citizenry. Significantly, Charter supporters in the "rest of Canada" (ROC) were key players in the defeat of Meech Lake, and the Charter's possible erosion by the "distinct society" clause was their leading concern.

(8) The constitutional crisis has undermined the authority of elites and of executive federalism. In a democratic era, citizens cannot be treated as chattels whose fate can be determined behind closed doors and announced as a fait accompli to a deferential and grateful public. A mandate obtained through a referendum was an essential requirement for legitimation of the extensive constitutional change of sovereignty-association that the Parti québécois government sought in 1980. That same pressure to give citizens the last say lies behind the proposed Quebec referendum on sovereignty or renewed federalism in 1992. In general, the attention devoted to referenda and constituent assemblies in the past few years, more than in the entire previous century,[1] suggests a profound change in Canadian constitutional culture. The deference formerly accorded governing elites has been replaced by suspicion and distrust.[2] While agreement is lacking on the amending process appropriate to the new constitutional people that Canadians are becoming, the starting point is recognition that citizens are now constitutional actors to a degree that our predecessors in the first century after Confederation could not have predicted.

These challenges can be met only by changes in the very conception of citizenship – changes of citizens' behaviour, identity, and values that can be implemented not from above, but only by a cooperative enterprise of citizens and governments.

While comprehensive analysis of the above catalogue of pressures playing on citizenship would require a monograph, a more limited focus on the fragmentation of citizenship by multiple nationalisms and by the politicized diversity of modernity will capture much of the tension surrounding citizenship in Canada. It is our fate to have to think through the possibility and acceptability of a citizenship that is not the same for everybody at a time when the burdens of citizenship are increasing.

The Fragmentation of Citizenship

The tendency to think of citizenship as a single, uniform status is not surprising. Citizenship is the legally defined status of official membership in the political community, one that by its nature we would expect to be unvarying.

The angry use of such phrases as "second-class citizens" and "second-class provinces" as indicators of injustice reveals the powerful hold of equality, defined as sameness, on our constitutional imagination. Indeed, from one perspective, Canadian history is a record of positive responses to the tight linkage of the powerful norm of equality with that of universalism; hence the steady move to a universal franchise as former restrictions were dropped and the move toward a colour-blind immigration law, which suggests the triumph of the equal-treatment norm applied to the pool of potential citizens. More recently, the Charter, though not without special categories that speak to some but not all of us, clearly had levelling implications. In particular, it was explicitly hostile to diversities in the availability of rights based on province of residence.[3] Finally, the attempt of Trudeau's Liberal government to end special status for Indians, though unsuccessful, was based both on a principled aversion to categorizing people by race and the belief that special status was a millstone that held those very people back.

These examples all suggest the historical potency of the egalitarian impulse in opposition to special status and differentiated treatment of the core components of citizenship. Inequalities were increasingly put on the defensive in areas where citizenship symbolism was involved. In each of the above cases, the challenged inequality was viewed as detrimental or demeaning to those subjected to it. Hence, its removal was considered as liberating, as rejection of inferior treatment – although status Indians obviously disagreed. While in the long sweep of history, an egalitarianism tending to uniform treatment may be the dominant trend, a powerful counter-trend is now gathering momentum in Canadian and other Western societies.

This essay is directed to that counter-trend – to those who argue that uniformity of status is a hegemonic instrument of the numerically or politically strong; to those for whom the claim that Canadians are a single people obfuscates the deeper reality that Canada can survive only as a multinational state; to those for whom differentiated treatment, special status, and affirmative action are variously justified as compensation for past injustice, as necessary to overcome systemic barriers, or as required to produce greater equality of result or condition. To the purveyors of the counter-trend, perhaps the central characteristic of modern society is diversity, a gallery of

discordant voices issuing from fundamentally divergent ways of seeing the world. Modernity, or post-modernity, from this perspective,
is inescapably plural and should not be compressed into a single
mode or manner of expression, thinking, being, and feeling. The
Canadian citizenship of the future, accordingly, must seek accommodation with this diversity, both of internal nations and of the multiple identities and cleavages within them.

Historically, and even now in the 1990s, the major diversities
whose successful accommodation was the supreme task of Canadian
statecraft have been the territorial particularisms of federalism. Indeed, for our first century, students of the constitution strayed little
beyond federalism. Canadian commentators eulogized or vilified the
Judicial Committee of the Privy Council of Westminster in terms of
its impact of federalism. The institutional management of the permanent French-English dualism of Canadian life was seen largely as
a problem of federalism, with Quebec's provincial autonomy as the
central response. Federalism was the key institutional variable facil-
itating expansion from four provinces to ten provinces and two territories. Would Newfoundland have joined Canada in 1949 had
provincehood not existed to allow significant powers of self-rule
to accompany extension of federal jurisdiction to these new
Canadians?

Thus the claim that Canadians are a federal people is profoundly
true. However, federal and provincial memberships do not exhaust
Canadians' salient civic identities. In this essay I shall give the well-
known features of federalism less than their proportionate due in
order to focus on newer phenomena, where our understanding is
limited and where conventional wisdom has not yet emerged from
the competitive political-intellectual struggle to define who we are.
Although Canadians are still deeply influenced by their federal and
parliamentary past, viewed either as a heavy burden or as a rich heritage, their civic identities and patterns of community affiliation are
changing rapidly. Even the basic challenge posed by Quebec to our
constitutional continuity is much more than a standard provincial
challenge to federalism. At a deeper level, it fits into a three-nations
version of Canada (Quebec, aboriginal, and rest-of-Canada) that
now vies with the more conventional ten-provinces, two-territories
federal version that we have inherited.

A THREE-NATIONS VIEW OF CANADA[4]

From a non-federal perspective, Canada is the home for three sociological nations – Quebec, the rest of Canada (ROC), and aborigi-

nal. Their boundaries are unclear or contested; the extent and nature of their political organization vary; their members belong to and identify with the pan-Canadian community with differing degrees of enthusiasm. Their nationalisms are dissimilar and generate distinctive constitutional ambitions. That of Quebec is the contemporary expression of a historical community, the francophone majority that has long nourished a national identity, though previously less attached to the state than now, when it has a powerful government at its disposal. That of the aboriginal peoples is relatively new, although experiences of dispossession, subordinate status, and unjust treatment are of long standing.

The modern roots of aboriginal nationalism lie in the status-Indian nationalism born of reaction to the assimilating proposals of the 1969 federal White Paper[5] and its subsequent, contagious diffusion to Inuit and Métis. It is powerfully expressed by aboriginal political organizations. Both aboriginal and Québécois nationalisms are ascending, nation-preserving, or nation-creating. Their adherents sense that history is on their side, and they are the vanguard of stronger, liberating nationalist governments of the future. Their political elites employ the language of nationalism both as an automatic ritual incantation and as an aggressive challenge to what they view as an assimilating pan-Canadian nationalism.

For ROC, nationalist self-identification is more potential than actual, more reluctant than striving, for the majority's preference would be to leave things as they are. ROC nationalism is defensive and unorganized. Essentially, it is Canadian nationalism in retreat, besieged by rival Québécois and aboriginal nationalisms. The acronyms that describe it – ROC (rest of Canada) and CWOQ (Canada without Quebec) – clearly indicate its residual, salvaging character and ambitions.

Ambiguities and imprecisions abound in a three-nations view of Canada, as the politics and sociology of community are at variance. The rough nationalist equation of Quebec with its francophone majority is an injustice to anglophone and allophone Quebecers and reduces one million francophones outside Quebec, primarily in Ontario and New Brunswick, to an irrelevant diaspora; the casual identification of ROC with anglophone Canada or, worse, English Canada leaves Quebec's anglophones outside the community with which they strongly identify, overlooks non-Quebec francophones, and chills the Acadian heart by its non-recognition of New Brunswick's distinctive and proportionately large French-speaking community. It also suggests a homogeneity in anglophone Canada that in reality is now multicultural and multiracial, albeit with English as the unifying language.

Federalism fits only crudely and imperfectly with the three-nations reality of Canada. It confines nearly two million anglophone and francophone Canadians to the provincial territories of the other majority. And, with the exception of Northwest Territories, it is more an unsympathetic container for than sensitive expression of aboriginal realities. "Unfortunately for cultural nationalists, and fortunately for supporters of cultural diversity and pluralism," states Peter G. White, "there is no part of Canadian territory, except for aboriginal reserves, that is the exclusive preserve of any one cultural group."[6] Further, the aboriginal "nation," as noted below, is in fact a diversified array of communities and identities, not a cohesive or coherent, united single nation. While the lack of congruity between political and ethno-national boundaries poses major challenges to future constitution-makers, it inhibits expression of, rather than denies the reality of, the contemporary existence of the three national communities of identity and sentiment, coexisting with a challenged pan-Canadian political nationalism. To put it differently, the exceedingly difficult constitutional challenge is to adapt the constitutional structures of federalism, which are appropriately sensitive to provincial territorial pluralism, to the untidy three-nations reality briefly described above. That adaptation will almost certainly require an entrenched third order of aboriginal government.

While non-aboriginal Canada has long been seen through a dualist lens, as two founding peoples, as *The [French and English] Race Question in Canada*,[7] or as René Lévesque's two scorpions in a bottle,[8] the contemporary two-nations view has moved on. Its accommodation within a reconstituted Canada is problematic. A succession of commissions, task forces, attempted constitutional settlements, and inquiries – the Royal Commission on Bilingualism and Biculturalism, the Pepin-Robarts Task Force on Canadian Unity, the Meech Lake Accord, the Bélanger-Campeau Commission – has documented the escalating intensity of Quebec's demands. The no-longer junior Quebec partner, expressing a francophone nationalist political consciousness that has retreated from French Canada to Quebec, appears ready to translate its nationhood into independent statehood if necessary. As Quebec's goals appear less and less capable of federal accommodation, a parallel, incipient political identity of the "other" slowly crystallizes, now conceived as ROC, a revealing new designation, rather than English Canada. The citizenry of ROC is induced, initially reluctantly, to see that the comfortable Canadianism natural to the majority, in which it had merged itself, indeed lost itself, is eroding under the impact of Quebec nationalism. Accordingly, ROC begins to see itself as a potentially distinct political entity.

For Quebec's nationalists, a two-nations view is an aggressive posture, a vehicle for making claims for equality of national status within a reconstituted Canada or outside it. It suggests the terms on which Quebec will stay. For ROC, however, Quebec's dualist demands suggest terms that may be impossible to meet within Canada. For Québécois, dualism is an attempt to make the country conform to their historical vision of a binational partnership, hitherto imperfectly realized. For ROC, Quebec's challenge is a jolting reminder that its empathy for the French fact was always subordinated to its more passionate allegiance to Canada as a whole. Contemporary Quebec's attachment to Canada is clearly conditional. ROC's allegiance to a Canada in which Quebec is a province rather than a nation now verges on the anachronistic. However, ROC's potential support for a two-nations–inspired transformation of the Canadian constitutional order is problematical at a time when standard provincehood no longer appears acceptable to Québécois.

The search for a constitutional agreement between Quebec and ROC is complicated immensely by the emergence of a set of aboriginal national players to constitutional prominence. The aboriginal First Nations "embraced the death of the [Meech Lake] Accord ... wholeheartedly and joyously ... [as] the rejection of a constitutional lie – the lie of only two founding nations in Canada."9 As a result, the arrangement that Canadians seek has to encompass three, not two nations.

In fact, of course, it makes no sense to regard the aboriginal peoples as a single nation. Not only are there the three basic categories of aboriginal peoples identified in the Constitution Act of 1982 – Indian, Inuit, and Métis – but the word "Indian" itself is a legal fiction, behind which there are numerous distinct aboriginal nations with their own histories and separate community identities.10

Aboriginal nationality is a label for an indeterminate number of nations divided by tribe, treaty status, location, presence or absence of a land base, and by a history of separate administration for status Indians that Inuit and Métis lacked. Given the absence of a land base for Métis and non-status Indians, except for a few isolated cases, their nationalist ambitions for self-government are more limited and difficult to achieve than are those of their more fortunate, landed indigenous kin.

Aboriginal nationalism, therefore, is the aggregate reaction of many indigenous peoples to their shared experience of historical subordination. That experience receives contemporary expression in the constitutional category "aboriginal" in the Constitution Act, 1982, which brings the national organizations of Indian, Inuit, and

Métis peoples to the constitutional bargaining table under one constitutional rubric. This elite interaction, however, and overlapping aboriginal objectives generate no vision of a single pan-aboriginal political community with its own government. In that sense, aboriginal peoples are unlike many Third World peoples who, faced with analogous divisions, had the prize of a single government left by the departing imperial power as an incentive to overcome historical tribal and other invitations to fission.

The high aboriginal profile today is the legacy of the defeat of the assimilationist policy of the 1969 White Paper aimed at status Indians, the subsequent dawning recognition that some form of Indian special status is here to stay, the over-spill of that recognition to the Inuit and Métis, the deployment of the new constitutional label "aboriginal peoples" in the Constitution Act, the holding of four aboriginal constitutional conferences (1983–87) to define aboriginal rights, and the crystallization of aboriginal demands around the concept of aboriginal self-government. Given the momentum behind the last named, the aboriginal drive for self-government is unlikely to be checked. The prospective third order of government to accommodate it will express aboriginal values and will reinforce aboriginal identities.

Contemporary pressure for aboriginal special status is extensive. The Supreme Court's *Sparrow* decision of 1990 makes it clear that the federal government has a responsibility "to act in a fiduciary capacity" for aboriginal peoples: "The relationship between the Government and aboriginals is trust-like, rather than adversarial, and contemporary recognition and affirmation of aboriginal rights must be defined in light of this historic relationship."[11]

Demands for self-government are accompanied by parallel support for an aboriginal justice system.[12] The federal government has proposed separate aboriginal representation in the Senate.[13] A prestigious aboriginal task force reporting to the Royal Commission on Electoral Reform has advocated separate aboriginal representation in the House of Commons.[14] A degree of aboriginal exemption from the Charter is already provided for in section 25. Further exemptions will be sought as aboriginal self-government develops, although federal support may not be forthcoming. A de facto if not de jure Inuit quasi-province is likely to appear reasonably soon in the eastern half of NWT. A royal commission with a daunting mandate on aboriginal affairs is now under way. The new president of the Native Council of Canada has bluntly asserted his desire to gain the same perquisites now enjoyed by on-reserve status Indians for non-status and off-reserve Indians, so as to end what he called the government-imposed apartheid system among aboriginal people.[15]

Historical revisionism now reaches into the highest ranks of government, with the minister responsible for constitutional affairs, Joe Clark, reminding Canadians of the many aboriginal contributions to Canadian history, including "the fact that Louis Riel is a Canadian hero."[16] The federal minister of justice has indicated that limited versions of self-government for aboriginal "groups" without a land base are possible.[17] In sum, there is a massive, broadly based battery of developments taking place – all heading in the same direction, to different degrees of positive, permanent, unique constitutional treatment for about one million aboriginal Canadians.[18]

The more overtly political and institutional proposals noted above are given momentum by a supportive intellectual and moral climate. Recent task forces and royal commissions have documented prejudice, discrimination, and a depressing litany of indicators of social disorganization and anomie in many aboriginal communities that give legitimacy to extraordinary measures. Sympathetic scholarship on aboriginal issues, aboriginal political organizations, special university programs, reinterpretations of history, and the development of aboriginal nationalist doctrine[19] all contribute to an encouraging climate for aboriginal nationalism. Additional sustenance comes from the vigorously exploited access to international forums and the skilful manipulation of international support, from the Pope to the United Nations.[20]

The differences between aboriginal and francophone Québécois nationalism are profound – most crucially between a numerically decisive provincial majority, with a cohesive sense of historic collective identity, in control of a large and powerful province, and the differently constituted, heterogeneous assemblage of Indian, Inuit, and Métis, each capable of further subdivisions, and with a dispersed and scattered existence across a continent. They also, however, share many similarities. The assimilating objective of the White Paper of 1969 replicated Durham's very similar attitudes to French Canadians more than a century earlier, and his similar recommendation. Both assimilationist policies were resisted by their intended beneficiaries and are retrospectively defined as misguided attempts to achieve unrealizeable goals.

Under the label "founding people" or "First Nations," both link their right to distinctive survival to historical priority. Both groups have coined new labels – Québécois, First Nations, Inuit, Déné – that symbolize their nationhood. Both aboriginal peoples and francophone Québécois are national minorities worried about cultural and linguistic assimilation. Each resists submergence in an undifferentiated Canadianism. Each stands outside multiculturalism and denies its application to themselves. Both groups envisage a special status for themselves; both seek government power appropriate to their situation; they see government as a vehicle not only for self-expression but for ensuring an ongoing distinctive existence.

The three-nations view of Canada is implicit in the constitutional process now under way. The Quebec government's official posture is to bargain only one on one, nation to nation, with the federal government. The unique aboriginal status in the constitutional process is evident in the four parallel aboriginal constitutional task forces that are consulting their separate indigenous constituencies on their preferred constitutional futures. Aboriginal specificity is equally evident in the understanding that aboriginal leaders will participate in a first ministers' conference on the constitution, a status accorded to no other non-governmental group.

The aboriginal position, based on joint proposals in 1990 from the Assembly of First Nations, the Native Council of Canada, and the Inuit Tapirisat, demanded "a full, ongoing role in future constitutional discussions as of right and on the same footing as the provinces. This submission also made it clear that the national aboriginal organizations view all constitutional amendments as important to aboriginal people, not only amendments that mention aboriginal people."[21] Thus Ovide Mercredi informed Constitutional Affairs Minister Joe Clark "that natives are not just a special-interest group in this constitutional round; that they will be dealing government-to-government in these national-unity discussions."[22] Recognition that aboriginal peoples are not simply another ethnic group in multicultural Canada or just another interest group – labels they resolutely resist – is also evident in the federal constitutional proposals – *Shaping Canada's Future Together: Proposals* – where the section "Shared Citizenship and Diversity" devotes more space to "Canada's First Peoples" than to "Recognizing Quebec's Distinctiveness."[23]

Significant, and revealing, in the present constitutional round both Quebec and aboriginal peoples prepare separately and self-interestedly for their constitutional futures. In Quebec, the Allaire and Bélanger-Campeau inquiries saw constitutional change almost exclusively from the perspective of Quebec. In fact, the indifference toward Canada (or ROC) in these reports was monumental. The Allaire Report, in particular, was a self-indulgent exercise in narcissism. While Bélanger-Campeau was a more serious enterprise, a reader would find in it little internal evidence that its writers were Canadians as well as Québécois, for the latter identity had vanquished the former. Aboriginal peoples were (as of January 1992) conducting their own constitutional inquiries, separated from the main federal parliamentary committee on a renewed Canada. The latter committee, by default, duplicating the experience of the Spicer Commission, gravitated toward becoming an outlet for the voice of non-aboriginal ROC.

The nation-to-nation bargaining strategies of Quebec and the aboriginal peoples are acts of powerful symbolism. Their behaviour as nations in the bargaining process is an anticipatory assertion of the status that they seek to have recognized in the outcome. In each case, the strategy is designed to weaken the legitimacy of or redefine the Canadian bargainer across the table. Quebec nationalist strategy in the post-Meech round is the contemporary version of the strategy that successfully trivialized the support of Trudeau and the federal Quebec Liberal caucus for the 1982 Constitution Act by contrasting it with the claimed true voice of Quebec in the national assembly that decisively opposed the 1982 package.

Quebec's position, with conscious inaccuracy, treats the federal government as a surrogate for anglophone Canada, or ROC, implicitly discounting Quebec's numerically strong caucus representation in the governing Conservative party. The clear purpose is to eliminate or weaken Ottawa's capacity to represent and speak for the federalist component of Québécois identity. That component has been provincialized, controlled by Quebec's provincial politicians who deploy their conditional, profitable federalism in battle with the indépendantistes at home, while proffering it to ROC as an arrangement that can continue only if the latter's offers are sufficiently attractive. The federal government's role, from the Quebec nationalist perspective, is to act on behalf of ROC and thus to deny its constitutional obligation to speak for all of Canada, acting on the advice of all MPs and cabinet ministers, including those from Quebec.

An analogous assumption is implicit in aboriginal strategies which have their leaders attend first ministers' conferences in a nation-to-nation role. According to the Native Council of Canada, by 1980 aboriginal leaders decided to get involved because "it was very clear that we could not trust others to protect Aboriginal interests," and it was "our right" to be at the table, because the future of "our people and land is at stake."[24]

Both Québécois and aboriginal nationalists act as if their people did not have dual identities and loyalties, one of which is Canadian and is legitimately represented by the federal government. Instead, they implicitly deny, or at least downgrade, the "other" identity of Québécois and aboriginal peoples as Canadians. They treat the Canadian identity as that of the other, of the external party that sits on the other side of the table and therefore speaks as an outsider, through Quebec and aboriginal leaders, to Québécois and aboriginal peoples. In 1987 the Assembly of First Nations asserted that the "federal government's relationship is to First Nations as collectivities, not to our citizens as individuals." As Cassidy and Bish note, "from this perspective, Indian people are, first and foremost, citizens in their First Nations. Their primary relationship with the federal government, with Canada, is as part of these First Nations."[25] This approach by status Indians is clearly a legacy of the Department of Indian Affairs' historic policy of viewing citizenship, specifically the franchise, and retention of Indian status as incompatible. Until 1960, enfranchisement meant relinquishment of Indian status. Contemporary Indian attitudes to the franchise, and to the parliamentary representation to which it leads, are still shaped by the recollection of its former use as a coercive instrument of assimilation.

Since the federal government acts on behalf of an older order that still survives, and is based on the coast-to-coast representation of all Canadians as individuals in Parliament, the theory and practice of representation are in disarray. The question of who speaks for whom, and in what capacity, no longer has an accepted answer for Québécois and aboriginal peoples. Their nationalism has eroded the capacity of the federal Parliament and cabinet to speak for and effectively represent them, and the Canadian component of their civic identity is accordingly diminished and on the defensive. Changes in the relative status of the Canadian and Québécois, or aboriginal, components of individual civic identity mirror the larger struggle by competing elites to dominate the "voice" of their people.

These realities are sensed but seldom articulated in public. They belong to the category of tacit constitutional silences, the discreet acceptance of contradiction and ambiguity that surfaces in transitional eras. Formally, Parliament based on universal suffrage (for the Commons) and cabinet still occupy the stage, capable in theory of speaking for all Canadians. In reality, the federal Parliament and the community conceptions on which it is based are on trial. Quebec's nationalist elites no longer view theirs as an ordinary province, no longer fully accept Ottawa's role of speaking for all Canadians, including Québécois, and implicitly attribute to that government an identity and a capacity that it lacks – spokesperson for and government of ROC.

Politically, of course, emasculation of the federal role in Quebec extends the political reach and bargaining power of the provincial government and places Quebec's federal MPs in limbo. Similarly, aboriginal leaders act on the premise that their peoples are not conventional citizens. The leaders are the vanguard of a new order of government that will diminish the authority of the traditional federal and provincial governments over their peoples. The roles they now assume are anticipatory, not reflective of offices and statuses that now exist. Aboriginal leaders seek to monopolize the voice of their peoples and minimize the capacity of the elected elites of federalism to speak for them.

The cumulative and composite message of Québécois and aboriginal weakening of Ottawa's capacity to speak authoritatively for either group is to underline a three-nations definition of Canada and to press for redefinition of the federal government as the government of the rest-of-Canada minus its aboriginal population. Simultaneously, of course, aboriginal nationalism denies the capacity of the government of Quebec to treat the aboriginal nations in its midst as minorities that can be compelled to participate in a Quebec independence which they categorically reject. Hence the conflict between Québécois and aboriginal nationalism is unusually intense, for they may confront each other in a "when the chips are down" scenario.[26]

Implicit recognition of the three national communities emerged from the 1990–91 hearings of the Spicer committee. The Spicer Report noted that the commissioners had made only limited and ineffectual contact with francophones in Quebec and more generally with aboriginal peoples across the country.[27] Consequently, the document became an ROC report, excluding aboriginal peoples. The commissioners, reflecting their own hearings, noted a developing self-consciousness in ROC, clearly a by-product of the disappearing evidence of Quebec's positive allegiance to Canada,[28] coupled with the recognition that some "special place"[29] for aboriginal peoples lies ahead.

ROC nationalism has special characteristics. It has a clear territorial location – Canada outside Quebec. Psychologically, it is an imitative reaction to the Quebec government's attribution of nationhood to its people and, to a lesser extent, to aboriginal nationalism. Prospectively, it is an anticipatory nationalism getting ready for a future it may reluctantly inherit. Retrospectively, it is a residual nationalism, a second choice that emerges because the Quebec partner no longer appears willing to adhere to the pan-Canadian nationalism that ROC would prefer to retain. ROC's inchoate nationalism is thus based on a hesitant retreat from a faltering pan-Canadian vision, to whose survival a mix of serious effort, lingering hopes, and nostalgia is still directed. It is a nationalism by default, created on the rebound.

However, whether or not Quebec departs, ROC nationalism is here to stay. If Quebec cannot be accommodated within a revised federalism, ROC will also emerge as one or more independent countries, at which time it will either sport the institutional and constitutional clothing it has inherited or devise arrangements appropriate to its new circumstances.

If Quebec remains, ROC will still have a distinctive sense of itself, as a counterpart to whatever explicit status Quebec has achieved. The constitutional history of recent decades has driven home the fragility of the bonds between Quebec and ROC. For the foreseeable future, their cohabitation within the same polity will be perceived as precarious. The presence of a Quebec that remains with unique status will be a daily message that the surviving, formal Canadian unity is calculated, conditional, and reasoned, rather than emotional. Such a Quebec will be a clear reminder that ROC too is a nation in waiting.

The national status and identity of ROC, however, at least until it inherits a post-secession Canada without Quebec, is ambiguous and uncertain, for ROC has no corporate existence. It is headless and officially voiceless. The federal government cannot and will not now speak for it, not because the leaders of the two major Canadian parties have leaders from Quebec[30] but because Ottawa's mandate is to govern for all of Canada and to transmit the peoples and territories that it has inherited intact to future generations. The provincial governments cannot speak for ROC because their mandate is provincial, and each of them speaks only for a territorially delimited segment of the Canadian population. Even an aggregation of nine provincialisms and two territories does not constitute ROC.

One of the crucial, overlooked tensions in the present situation, therefore, is the inchoate nature of ROC. As a future without Quebec is a distinct possibility, ROC has the same need for self-expression, self-education, and socialization for independence as Quebec for its possible future outside Canada. Quebec builds on a long history of introspection. ROC does not. The Francophone Québécois identity has been strengthened by the enduring and ever-renewed self-consciousness of a minority. ROC identity is shapeless, ambiguous, and devoid of historical roots. Québécois now have a government that reminds them of who they are, and thus of what they might become. ROC now has no government that addresses it as such. Quebec openly juggles two futures – renewed federalism and independence – through national assembly committees examining their relative strengths and weaknesses. ROC, as part of Canada, prepares seriously for only one of the two main futures – renewed federalism – that await it. ROC is gravely weakened by its majority control of all governments outside Quebec, NWT excepted, and its majority share of federal government representation. Structurally, ROC is weakened, not strengthened, by its control of so many governments.

If Quebec remains in Canada, ROC, made conscious of its existence by the constitutional perils through which it has lived, will experience a certain lack of identity, ambiguity in its self-perception, and frustration of its political selfhood, for it will have no single lever exclusively available to promote, shape, and then preserve an identity kept indistinct by the absence of supportive cues to give it definition. Unless the accommodation of Quebec is based on a decisive asymmetry, with Quebec wielding powers possessed by no other province, and in which the federal government in most policy areas becomes the instrument of ROC, the latter people will be frustrated by its elemental inability to act collectively, by the absence of the routine daily reminders that it exists. This absence will be poignantly underlined for ROC by the high profile of a Quebec government fashioning its people, of aboriginal governments giving sustenance to aboriginality, and of the province-building activities of the provincial governments in ROC's midst, and by the memory of a not-too-distant past when it was the governing majority in coast-to-coast Canada.

In the Canadian past, it was Quebec or French Canada that argued for enhanced recognition of dualism in order to strengthen its own status and power against a majoritarian pan-Canadianism at the service of English Canada. For English Canada, in the past, dualism was not a natural inclination born of a need for self-expression but was rather, when recognized, a concession by the numerically strong. At least until the 1960s, however, dualism did not detract from the reality that English Canada could view the central government as an instrument for its national purposes, which were thought of as Canadian purposes. If Quebec remains, at the cost of a gravely weakened centre, dualism in the form of ROC nationalism is likely to become the rhetoric of the numerically strong but institutionally incomplete. Dualism may well become the ideology of the ROC majority seeking equality. ROC, frustrated by the discrepancy between its numbers and its enfeebled capacity for collective self-expression through government, may not readily adapt to its condition in a constitutional order whose flexibility has been deployed in accommodating Québécois and aboriginal nationalism.

If the Canada of the future is to be made up of three national communities, Canadians will have to learn to live with fundamentally divergent notions of citizenship. In Charles Taylor's terms, both Quebec's francophone majority and the aboriginal peoples are bearers of or possessors of "deep" diversity that goes beyond the shallow "first-level" diversities of multicultural/multiracial Canada.[31] Whether their deep diversity is in fact qualitatively more profound and more integral to their identity than Sikh identity is to Canadian Sikhs is both doubtful and irrelevant. They have more history on their side than later arrivals. They are not newcomers on whom the primary burden of adapting to the host society is placed. More important, their employment of the language of nationalism is considered legitimate, as is their search for enhanced governing powers for their advancement and protection as national minorities in an unsympathetic environment. They are not minorities like the others, which come to a country that is an ongoing concern and which sets the terms for those who are not "first" or "founding" peoples.

It is already evident that the uniform application of the Charter to Quebec and to aboriginal peoples is challenged,[32] although there is some evidence of support for the Charter among aboriginal women,[33] and "Inuit are willing to consider the application of the Charter ... to self-government arrangements."[34] What has become a symbolic signifier of citizenship for many ROC Canadians may come to apply fully to only a limited, albeit the largest component of a reconstituted Canada sensitive to the three national communities in its midst.

A positive response to a three-nation definition of Canada is also likely to challenge the norm of equality of the provinces which has become practically an icon, especially in western Canada. Although de jure equality may be preserved in formal obeisance to the principle, de facto inequality is likely to emerge with Quebec assuming more responsibilities than other provincial governments. The dynamism of Quebec's differentiation will be driven by the continuing presence of a strongly nationalist or indépendantiste party in an adversarial political system, with parties alternating in office. No other provincial system will have these characteristics.

Although we are only in the early stages of our understanding, it is probable that the self-governing status of aboriginal peoples will create a third order of government. Tony Hall correctly observes: "It is no longer sufficient to envisage federal-provincial relations as the sole axis of governmental authority in Canadian federalism. Aboriginal-federal relations constitute the hidden axis of our federal system."[35] According to the Penner Report, "Self-government would mean that virtually the entire range of law-making, policy, program delivery, law enforcement and adjudication powers would be available to an Indian First Nation government within its territory."[36] Aboriginal governing powers will almost certainly be constitutionally entrenched, unlike those of municipalities which are delegated from the provincial governments. Following on the recommendations of the Penner Report directed to status Indians,[37] self-governing aboriginal peoples will wield a unique mix of jurisdictions, employing some powers that are otherwise federal and others that are otherwise provincial. There will be marked diversity in the powers wielded by individual aboriginal peoples, varying from near-provincehood in a Nunavut that will emerge when NWT is geographically split up, to off-reserve aboriginal agencies administering limited services to aboriginal peoples scattered across a metropolitan region.

Thus the third order of aboriginal governments will be unlike the second provincial order in two ways. The powers that such governments wield will transgress the federal-provincial division of powers, and unlike the rough equality of the provinces, various aboriginal governments will display marked inequalities of jurisdiction. Integration of that third governing order into the constitutional framework will be a demanding process.

Aboriginal peoples will have a different relationship to the traditional federal and provincial orders of government than other Canadians – differences that range from the trivial to the substantial. Aboriginal peoples, therefore, like the Québécois of the future, will not be citizens like the others. The federal and provincial governments will not hold the same significance for them as for ROC Canadians. Their constitutionally entrenched aboriginal governments, with their unique jurisdictional levers, will be focal points of identity and self-assertion. Such governments will be theirs in a way that can never be true of the federal and provincial governments. Their governments will be to them as Quebec's government already is and will increasingly be to the French-speaking majority of that province.

According to a recent study that pushed aboriginal self-government to the limit: "Their [aboriginals'] primary allegiance will be to native communities and governments. Since neither the federal nor provincial government reflects their communities, they will enjoy special, separate rights in all matters where cultural values count ... To the extent that they will look to their own governments to make decisions and provide services, aboriginal peoples will have no need to participate in other governments, either by way of voting or running for office."[38]

If the different relationship of Québécois and aboriginal peoples to the governments of Canadian federalism is reinforced by differential application of the Charter, the norm of a uniform citizenship based on the equality of the provinces and of citizens' Charter rights will no longer hold. Further, at some future breaking point, Quebec's enhanced jurisdiction, in law or in fact, may lead to challenges to the role of MPs and cabinet members from Quebec. It is too easily forgotten that the equality of the provinces is not just a norm of federalism but is simultaneously the essential support for the norm of equal status for MPs. Rough equality of provincial powers is an indirect way of saying that federal jurisdiction applies equally across the country, which, in turn, is the prerequisite for undifferentiated roles for MPs, regardless of their province of origin. Jurisdictional equality of the provinces, and the equal capacity of MPs to act in Parliament across the whole range of federal jurisdictions, are two sides of the same coin.[39] To offer to all what only Quebec is expected to take may blur the constitutional issue for a transition period, but if the long-run trend is for Quebec to leap ahead of the other provinces in powers and responsibilities, the obfuscation will be seen through and resisted.

The issue of aboriginal parliamentary representation is also likely to arise, given the premise that aboriginal governments will handle functions that are dealt with for other Canadians by federal and provincial governments. Somewhat paradoxically, however, the drive to remove aboriginal peoples, to a greater or lesser degree, from the jurisdiction of federal and provincial legislatures by self-government is accompanied by political pressures to strengthen aboriginal representation in both the Senate and the House of Commons. If aboriginal communities come to exercise special, extensive, entrenched powers, the constitutional appropriateness of aboriginal peoples exercising the same voting rights as other members of the electorate will emerge as an issue. If there is special separate aboriginal representation in Parliament, the participation of aboriginal members in discussions and voting over laws that do not apply to their people will have to be reconsidered.

At some upper limit, the extent of the powers wielded by aboriginal governments will erode the legitimacy of aboriginal senators or MPs playing vigorous parliamentary roles concerning policies that do not apply to their voters. In response, it can be argued that an apparently privileged role for aboriginal peoples and their representatives is simply a logical and just recognition of "their special constitutional position as peoples within the Canadian federation."[40] An apparent anomaly can thus be made legitimate by an encompassing historic exceptionalism. Alternatively, aboriginal parliamentarians could be viewed as akin to ambassadors who participate and vote only on explicitly aboriginal matters. Such a solution would stress their separate status in Canada at the expense of attributes shared with other Canadian citizens.[41]

Significant readjustments of the constitutional order to accommodate aboriginal peoples and Quebec nationalism go beyond rearranging the powers of governments to the creation of differentiated categories of citizens, possibly to differential application of the Charter and, depending on the extent of special jurisdictional powers, the emergence of differential status for MPs.

The stability of such a constitutional order will be maintained only by unceasing statecraft and self-restraint; it will not be held together by rights and civic identities held in common; the social obligations of responsibility for the disadvantaged will presumably weaken toward those who are outside the nation of one's primary membership. Such wide divergences among the citizenry will displace the sense of sharing and caring for one's own that is generated by a relatively uniform citizenship and replace it with the much less compelling requirement, outside of one's own group, of caring for and sharing with an ambiguous category halfway between fellow-citizens and strangers.

The voyage on which we are embarked is designed to make the constitutional order more sensitive to our coexisting nationalisms. It will necessarily make us less sensitive to other values linked to sharing common citizenship. This may be most serious for aboriginal peoples. Creation of a unique constitutional status that distances them unduly from majority conceptions of citizenship may conflict with their need for extensive financial resources from federal and provincial governments.[42]

Since the present disharmonious coexistence of a historic, now decentralized, federalism with the three nationalisms now struggling, if not warring, in its midst was not predicted by even the most learned of our predecessors, modesty cautions against the soothsayer role. The likelihood, however – assuming that a recognizable version of Canada survives – is that the future challenge to Canadianism will come not from centrifugal provincialism alone, but from its interaction with the powerful forces of internal nationalisms. Within that latter development, the least developed nationalism of all, that of ROC, retreating from a no-longer viable version of pan-Canadian nationalism that was its first choice, will be pushed by nationalist contagion toward a more coherent sense of itself. Since, numerically, ROC will possess the biggest battalions, the nature of its future transformation is one of the most crucial and unpredictable variables in Canada's constitutional evolution. Its present weakness reflects its residual status – an unsought condition thrust upon it by the more aggressive nationalism of Quebec and aboriginal peoples. For reasons already noted, however, its incoherence will not be easily overcome. It may become a fragmented, lurching, unpredictable giant, the raw material for ROC nationalist leaders preaching, to borrow a phrase, "Equality or Independence."

THE NEW DIVERSITY AND CITIZENSHIP[43]

The nationalisms of Quebec, aboriginal peoples, and ROC are not the only contemporary challenges to the idea of a single standard of citizenship. Another comes from the political articulation of various social, ethnic, and gender diversities of modern society. While the latter do not threaten the survival of the constitutional order, they do challenge the norms of a universal, common citizenship. This is especially evident with respect to the theory and practice of representation and makes increasingly difficult the task of the state, via the politician, of representing, accommodating, and transcending the diversities of Canadian society.

This difficulty reflects the convergence of three phenomena. (1) The ethnic, social, and cultural diversity of Canadian society is increasing. (2) These diversities, based on gender, ethnicity, lifestyle, and so on are now politicized and indeed, in some cases, constitutionalized. (3) The politicized identities and group self-consciousness building on these diversities support the assertion that 'X' cannot represent 'Y,' if 'X' does not share/possess the characteristics that Y considers essential to his/her identity and as necessary for the vigorous pursuit of Y's political goals.

The perceived inability of X may be attributed to either lack of empathy, derived from an absence of essential shared characteristics that limits understanding, or to a deficiency of trust that leads Y to believe that X, not being part of the Y group, will be ready to sacrifice the interests of Y more casually than Y would prefer.

The diversification of Canadian society is most dramatically evident in terms of race and ethnicity. Changes in the source countries of immigrants are pushing Canada in a multicultural and multiracial direction. The population of British and French background – the original European founding peoples – continues to decline in percentage terms, as does the population of European background in general. The British component, which was about 60 per cent at Confederation, fell below 50 per cent in 1940 and will soon be below 40 per cent. The segment of French origin fell below 30 per cent in the early 1960s and is now nearing 25 per cent. By 1981, the 'other' had passed the French, and in the 1986 census it amounted to 38 per cent of the Canadian total. The 'other' component is growing rapidly and by the turn of the century is projected to surpass 40 per cent. The great metropolitan centres of Vancouver, Toronto, and Montreal are already, in David Cameron's evocative phrase, "riotously multicultural."44 Within the ethnocultural category, the multiracial component – the visible minorities – constitutes a growing percentage. Whereas formerly almost 80 per cent of immigrants came from countries with a European heritage, now almost three-quarters come from Asia, Africa, and the Caribbean. Almost half of Canadian immigrants now come from Asia. Visible minorities, exclusive of aboriginal peoples, are expected to reach more than 10 per cent of the total by the end of the century, almost double their percentage in 1986. Nearly half of Vancouver school children have English as a second language, and they are predominantly of Asian background.

This ethnic transformation of Canada will almost certainly continue. Our immigration needs cannot be met from the traditional suppliers of our first century. Ethnic and racial minorities who are already here are advocates for those whom they left behind. Given the ethnic composition and distribution of the world's people and the exceptionally privileged position of the relatively small Canadian population, neither immigration nor border controls can prevent an influx, legal and illegal, of new arrivals that will add to Canada's ethnic heterogeneity.

The ethnic diversification has led to new labels – Third Force, visible minorities, allophones, multicultural peoples, and others – in the search for identities outside the French-English-aboriginal circle of "founding" or "first peoples." Thus Canadians are grappling with what L.S. Lustgarten, referring to the changed ethnic demography of Western nations, described as "irreversible ... [and] the dominant characteristic of twentieth century states: ethnic pluralism within the framework of a united polity."45

The articulation of diversity does not stop at the boundaries of race and ethnicity. It extends to women, the disabled, gays and lesbians, proponents of alternative life-styles, and others. Indeed, the phrase "coming out," initially self-applied to the gay community, can fit other minorities, including women (technically not a minority, of course), aboriginal peoples, Third Force Canadians, visible minorities, official-language minorities, and the disabled. In each case, their "coming out" challenged historic assumptions of what was acceptable, normal behaviour, and of who counted and why. In some cases, this adventure is accompanied by a sense of uniqueness and difference and by challenges to previously dominant ways of viewing the world. Thus, according to Jill Vickers, feminist scholarship has recently demonstrated "that knowledge, which is apparently unisex, neutral and universal, is in fact biased by the point of view of the knowledge creator ... few of us doubt that 'knowledge' about most human endeavours has been biased by the race, sex, and class of the dominant knowledge makers, not to mention their sexual orientation, their location in the northern hemisphere and other elements of their historical locatedness."[46]

In general, these groups have a sense of being marginal, of having been historically maltreated, or of having experienced wounding discrimination. They nurse a sense of grievance – their political language is replete with such phrases as "exploited," "overlooked," "left out," "dominated," "abused," "second class," and other negative rubrics used to describe their past experience. Thus Monture and Turpel note that it is impossible to threaten aboriginal people who "do not have anything to lose anymore."[47] Ovide Mercredi, national chief of the Assembly of First Nations, recently attacked the distorted view of Canada "as only consisting of French and English peoples," and he asserted that aboriginal languages, cultures, governments, and spirituality are "excluded by the Canadian constitution" and "continue to be despised and rejected," so that aboriginal peoples are "viewed as strangers in our own land."[48] Aboriginal and other marginalized groups speak the language of minorities, of those whose sense of status and recognition is precarious, who have been taught by history to be watchful lest their concerns be sacrificed by indifferent majorities.

Their suspicions are grounded in contemporary realities and historic memories. When they look at the contemporary state they do not see themselves proportionately represented. When women, for example, look at the gender distribution of political power within political parties they see the confirmation of Putnam's "law of increasing disproportion" – that is, "the higher one goes in party elites, the fewer women are to be found."[49] In 1984, 9.6 per cent of MPs were women; in 1982 only 6.2 per cent of the members of provincial legislatures were women.[50] The number of women legislators increased to 13.2 per cent for the House of Commons in 1988 and to 13.9 percent in provincial and territorial legislatures by 1989.[51] Women and others remember that they were not among the early recipients of the franchise – women in Quebec not receiving the provincial vote until 1940, and status Indians not receiving the federal vote until 1960. The recency of their acquisition of full citizenship status attests to the pejorative view of their civic capacities only a few decades ago. As Boyle notes, women's political history is different from that of men; they lack a long tradition of political activity: "In fact, their tradition is marked by the absence of political role models and by opposition to their efforts at emancipation."[52]

Thus the specific constitutional past of yesterday's constitutional outsiders is not of colony to nation but of historic events particular to themselves, a set of living memories that conditions their interactions with the state today. The 1929 *Persons case* occupies a prominent place in the feminist historical past and is the occasion for an annual commemorative breakfast organized by LEAF (Women's Legal Education and Action Fund). The exemption of section 28 of the Charter from the override is recalled with pride as a hard-won achievement by the women's movement.

Every ethnic association that appeared before the Joint Senate and House of Commons Committee on the Constitution of 1980–81 "began with a recitation of their members' arrival in Canada, their contribution to the development of the nation, and the trials and tribulations they endured along the way ... In every tale, ... there are epic heroes, early leaders of settler communities who saved their people from near catastrophe at the hands of ruthless villains – usually bigoted 'WASPs' who wanted to preserve the British character of Canada from the onslaught of foreign immigration."[53]

For aboriginal peoples, the Royal Proclamation of 1763 far surpasses the Constitution Act of 1867 as a statement of their constitutional significance. In a recent dialogue, M.E. Turpel and P.A. (Trisha) Monture respectively described 1867 as "a date which I hate to use" and said that "Canada's birth is not something I celebrate."[54] For Métis, inclusion in the Constitution Act of 1982 is a signal achievement – a lever of immense potential that will be wielded to enhance access to entitlements now normally restricted to status Indians. Particular ethnic groups recall when they got the vote, how long they were deprived of it, and other indicators of citizenship deprivation. For decades, the Franco-Ontarian sense of minority status and unjust treatment was nourished by the memory of the attack on French-language schooling embodied in the infamous Regulation 17 of 1912.

The constitutional history of some groups, especially visible minorities, focuses on changes in immigration law – punctuated by moves from stigmatic exclusion to universalism. Particular communities, or at least custodians of official memories, keep alive past instances of maltreatment for which contemporary redress and apology are sought and, with partial success, gained – Japanese Canadians and relocation and internment, Chinese Canadians and the head tax, and the internment of Ukrainian and Italian Canadians in the First and Second World Wars, respectively. These histories are stimulated by the overall salience of ethnicity, by a contagion effect, by their utility as tools of ethnic mobilization, and, of course, by the historical evidence.

The Canadian state of the 1990s governs a variegated assemblage of peoples who do not share a common past and whose historical memories are instruments of group affirmation and differentiation. 'Je me souviens' is a motto for more than francophone Québécois, and functional equivalents of the conquest are widespread.

Today's politicization of diversity is broadly based. It draws sustenance from basic changes in Western culture. The feminist movement, the aspirations of indigenous peoples, and the demands of gays and lesbians for acceptance of their preferred sexual practices and family patterns, for example, all have an international dimension. They are not ephemeral local phenomena, and they express themselves in many arenas. In universities, black studies, native studies, women's studies, and ethnic studies, with professors normally if not exclusively drawn from the group concerned, struggle to give recognition and voice to identities and experiences that it is claimed were overlooked when their representation was in the hands of outsiders. The connection of these phenomena with citizenship in Canada may not be immediately apparent, but they are integrally linked to political assertions that query the legitimacy, capacity, or propriety of a "non-A" to speak for, give voice to, or represent an "A." As a consequence, the nature of citizenship and representation is no longer straightforward in heterogeneous societies where personal civic identity is informed by patterned differences in assumptions, memories, and goals.

A recent paper by Iris Young severely and lucidly criticizes the ideal of a universal citizenship on the ground that different social groups with different life experiences necessarily bring different needs and perceptions to the analysis and advocacy of public policy.[55] Young's paper helps us to appreciate both the profound diversity of modern society, with the concomitant variety of world views in the electorate, and her conclusion that citizenship is or should be a many-splendoured thing – a status that does not hold everyone to precisely the same civic rights and duties.

Pressure for recognition of diversity contributes to the enhanced symbolic role of the constitution. It has become the vehicle that confirms (or not) one's acceptance by society and the relative status enjoyed by particular groups vis-à-vis others. The written constitution is no longer only or primarily a functional instrument for the management of federalism but also a powerful symbolic statement of inclusion or exclusion. Hence constitutional battles are now fought over status, and the language of constitutional politics is replete with emotionally powerful words – shame, dignity, honour, and so on. Historic offices of high symbolic value – most prominently governors-general and lieutenant-governors – are now employed to remind Canadians of, and accord public recognition to, diversities of sex, ethnicity, and aboriginality that had not previously been represented in such exalted offices of state.

A corollary of the view that modern society is more like a television set with many channels than a contest to determine whose voice will triumph and silence the losers is the pressure to diversify the representational basis of political authority. Bureaucratically, the contemporary Canadian state is honey-combed with particularistic portfolios and commissions devoted to official-language minorities, the disabled, the young, the old, ethnic groups, women, aboriginal peoples, and so on. Police forces across the country, especially in metropolitan centres, find their effectiveness and legitimacy challenged if their minority representation is inadequate. The insensitivity of legislatures is attributed to their lack of representativeness, leading to proposals for special guaranteed aboriginal representation in the Senate and the House of Commons and for electoral systems that will produce roughly proportionate male and female representation.[56] This latter goal explains the tendency for contemporary feminist scholars in Canada to advocate proportional representation or dual-member constituencies, because of their capacity to enhance women's representation.

A recent advocate of special aboriginal electoral districts described Parliament as "the exclusive domain of the settlers, a reflection no doubt, of the fact that the electoral system was designed by settlers, for settlers, and historically developed to exclude aboriginal peoples."[57] Aboriginal peoples are seriously under-represented, with the 900,000 aboriginal people south of the sixtieth parallel having only one MP of aboriginal descent to represent them. Accordingly, "Aboriginal people question the legitimacy of the electoral system and the capacity of Parliament to deal effectively with Aboriginal issues."[58] A similar argument was used by Christine Boyle, who concluded that the existing electoral system "developed by men for use by men" grossly underrepresented women. She recommended "a form of benign segregation [some form of separate representation of women], at least on a temporary basis, in order to ensure representation of women by women and, I hope, in the interests of women."[59]

Courts are criticized for not proportionately representing minorities in their ranks, which allegedly results in limited empathy for or understanding of the concerns of the underrepresented. Hence the steady pressure from feminist groups for more women on the Supreme Court and from ethnic organizations for judges outside the French-English "founding" stock.[60] Growing pressures for a separate system of justice for aboriginal peoples draw on the analogous assumption that cultural differences between aboriginals and whites generate insensitivity, misunderstandings, and injustice, when those who hold judicial office are culturally different from those on the receiving end.

Public hearings on the Meech Lake Accord provided graphic evidence of distrust toward elites that lacked the appropriate ascriptive or acquired characteristics. Presentations by a host of groups defined by for example, gender, ethnicity, race, disability, and indigenousness routinely and categorically denied that "eleven white able-bodied male" first ministers could or would represent the group's interests when they negotiated constitutional changes among themselves.

With suitable modifications to their own situation, most of the Meech Lake critics would agree with George Erasmus, then national chief of the Assembly of First Nations, who strongly repudiated the assertion that aboriginal peoples were appropriately represented by the first ministers that aboriginal voters had helped to elect. "This bland assertion that First Nations and their governments are represented by non-aboriginal politicians who have no interest, demonstrated or latent, in advocating our rights is bogus and is without foundation in fact or action."[61] Erasmus's thesis reflected the pervasive aboriginal belief that the existing system essentially represents non-aboriginal interests, either because aboriginal peoples are too scattered and numerically weak to have electoral influence or because only direct, unmediated aboriginal representation can effectively and sensitively represent aboriginal interests. The suggestion that aboriginal peoples should trust elected white leaders was scorned by two aboriginal law professors "'Trust us:' I mean what do you think we are, forgetful or just plain crazy."[62]

Many social groups support the proposition that dissimilar others cannot speak for or represent them, that their concerns will be overlooked or given scant consideration if one of their own is not at the bargaining table or in the decision-making body. The extent of this phenomenon was lucidly revealed in the reactions of the Métis National Council (MNC) to the federal proposals in *Shaping Canada's Future Together: Proposals*. The MNC requested guaranteed participation in "all constitutional matters," guaranteed seats in the Senate and the House of Commons, appointment of a Métis to the Supreme Court "at the government's earliest opportunity," a requirement of consent by Métis to all future amendments affecting them, and specific representation in the proposed Council of the Federation.[63]

The pressures lying behind demands for more mirror-like practices of representation lead to more fundamental structural demands; hence advocacy by the elites of New Brunswick Acadians, francophones outside Quebec, Indians, Inuit, and Métis for direct control over institutions explicitly sensitive to the groups concerned, and Quebec anglophones' objective of retaining control of their own institutions and keeping them viable. Minorities use voice to demand a form of opting-out, or institutional exit, in a complex version of the voice-and-exit strategies brilliantly described by Hirschman.[64]

The impact of diversity on public life acquired a special dimension in Canada because it coincided with a constitutional crisis and the federal government's support for a Charter of Rights as one of the responses to the crisis. As a result, various of the "coming out" groups became attached to the Charter at a time when Ottawa was seeking allies. The Charter's anti-majoritarian thrust added to its attractiveness for groups that had their own apprehensions about majority rule.

The Charter is more than an instrument that hands out abstract rights equally to all Canadians and is indifferent to their various statuses defined by gender, ethnicity, official language status, and the presence or absence of disabilities. In fact, it specifically mobilizes Canadians in terms of these categories. It encourages Canadians to think of themselves for constitutional purposes as women, as official-language minorities, as disabled, or as ethnocultural Canadians. Particular Charter clauses and the high profile of the constitution in recent years engender constitutional discourses organized around gender, ethnicity, indigenousness, and so on, which join the historic constitutional languages of federalism and parliamentary government. Organizations, often publicly funded, have developed to enhance the potency of Charter clauses relevant to their clientele. These clauses generate constitutional identities, formerly lacking, in those to whom they apply. The elites of the social categories concerned may be said to occupy constitutional niches, or to possess constitutional clauses. They also think of themselves as constitutional somebodies. The public profile of the social categories accorded such recognition is markedly enhanced, as is their sense of distinctiveness.

Much public discussion of particular Charter clauses is dominated by the clientele with a strong interest in an expansive definition of their clause – for example, women and section 28, non-founding peoples and section 27, aboriginals and section 25 of the Charter and section 35 of the Constitution Act, and section 15 and the groups mentioned in its equality provisions. This clustering of attention driven by self-interest largely reflects the normal gravitational pull that draws thirsty people to oases. In addition, however, there is a tendency to treat those who do not belong to the clientele group concerned as intruders or outsiders illegitimately entering into a discursive terrain that belongs to "insiders." This control by insiders and the cultural restraints inhibiting discussion by outsiders suggest that only those directly affected can understand or legitimately comment on a constitutional clause[65] – an assumption that lay behind much of the criticism of the Meech Lake process.

Charter clauses referring to "everyone," "every citizen," or "any person" are less likely to elicit political mobilization. From this perspective, the constitutional politics of the Charter responds to and mirrors the fragmentation of society. The Charter's diffuse contribution to a more democratic constitutional culture is supplemented, and perhaps undermined, by its stimulus to constitutional fragmentation. The Charter is a political battleground between supporters of competing clauses and between rival claimants to being the leading advocate for a particular clause.

The politicization and constitutionalization of diversity redefine groups previously excluded from the franchise on grounds of their difference – construed in the past as evidence of civic incapacity – as having unique voices, or vantage points, that justify their specific and explicit inclusion in public forums. The formerly excluded see their task as that of challenging a uniformity that is viewed as a mask for the hegemony variously of males, of whites, of non-aboriginals, of the historically privileged, or of those who do not live with disabilities.

Our steady progress toward a universal franchise has led to a more heterogeneous electorate, more self-conscious of its own internal differences than was true of earlier, more exclusive electorates. Indeed, earlier franchise restrictions on Indians, Asians, and women produced a relatively homogeneous electorate and a narrow range of views to be considered in policy determination, at the price of excluding the carriers of difference. Homogeneity was a code word for coercion and marginalization. As the formerly marginalized emerge from what Chantal Maillé, writing of women, describes as "a long culture of exclusion from politics,"[66] it is not surprising that they do not leave behind the sense of difference forged when they were left out as they enter political arenas shaped for less variegated electorates.

This politicized heterogeneity may pose problems for a representative system that presupposes that one representative can speak for the many who are different. Clifford Geertz recently noted how "the end of colonialism altered radically the nature of the social relationship between those who ask and look and those who are asked and looked at."[67] By analogy, the emergence from the audience or the background of the previously silenced or acquiescent female majority and of historical minorities, supplemented and invigorated by the ethnic diversity fostered by contemporary immigration patterns, alters the relationship between those who are represented and their representatives. It requires us to rethink citizenship.

CONCLUSION

The past is another country. Yesterday's constitution was able to contain the less aggressive nationalism of Quebec by federalism and various accommodative practices at the centre. This is no longer so. Some significant recognition of distinctiveness, of special status, so that Quebec and its people will not be precise counterparts of other provinces and provincial populations, appears unavoidable.

The indigenous peoples were relegated to the backwaters of Canadian life for most of our first century. The Inuit (then Eskimo) were isolated and ignored in northern Canada; Indians were mostly out of sight on reserves; and the Métis were technically Canadians like any others. The concepts of wardship, vanishing races, and assimilation conjured up various prospects for indigenous peoples but no recognition that they might develop unique constitutional voices in the service of distinctive constitutional futures. The rubric "aboriginal" did not exist to generate shared constitutional concerns among indigenous peoples. Aboriginal peoples are no longer in the background. They do not aspire to be citizens like the rest of us. Their distrust of the federal and provincial governments is so high, and their sense of difference so profound, that they seek not to be accepted by the majority as individuals on the former's terms but to achieve institutional and constitutional recognition of a special status that will contribute to their ongoing survival as distinct nations.

The nationalism of Quebec and of the aboriginal peoples induces ROC to think of itself, reluctantly, as some kind of national people, if only because to be both a majority and defined as residual, as rest-of-Canada, is psychologically debilitating.

The struggles today of these three national communities undermine the pan-Canadianism that anglophone Canadians, at least, thought of as a transcending identity. The norm of equal citizens' rights, crystallized by the Charter, and equality of provinces, as embodied in the amending formula and in the rhetoric of provincial ideologists of a federalism of principle, are both challenged by aboriginal and Québécois nationalism. Differential support for the Charter from the three national communities exerts pressure for its differential application or, at a minimum, for a differential in the willingness to override some of its clauses – presupposing that the (or perhaps a special) override is available to aboriginal governments. Both the special status sought by Quebec, and the third order of government sought by aboriginal peoples, are outside the norms of basic, everyday provincehood. Even if a partial accommodation of Quebec takes place that appears, by obfuscating constitutional mechanisms, to preserve the illusion of provincial equality, the de facto reality of future decades will not be a Quebec indistinguishable from the other provinces.

This, of course, may not be enough, and two or more successor Canadas may emerge by accident or design. Further, special status for Quebec, if it involves reduced roles for Quebec's MPs, reduced application of the Charter in Quebec, jurisdictions wielded by Quebec's government that are unavailable to the other provinces, and an asymmetrical citizenship, may be unstable and may not survive.

An additional fragmentation of citizens' consciousness occurs along the lines of such characteristics as sex, ethnicity, life-styles, and disabilities. The modernity that was to make us one has led instead to an explosion of particularistic self-consciousness that denies, in Iris Young's words, the idea of a universal citizenship.[68] The mosaic label applies not only to our ethnicity but also to other diversities whose spokespersons insist on recognition. Many of the latter represent the formerly excluded – those who were late in getting the vote or who in other ways felt mistreated or defined as second-class citizens. These historical memories contribute to distrust, suspicion, and reluctance to have one's fate determined by others devoid of the appropriate signifying characteristics. In a word, we lack fraternity and sorority within each of the three nations as well as across them.

We also, as Michael Bliss recently observed, no longer have a unified vision of Canadian history with which citizens can identify. Historians, at least in English Canada, have become specialists in minutiae, with Donald Creighton's grand if somewhat arrogant visions replaced by studies of "the history of housemaid's knee in Belleville in the 1890s."[69]

We are not alone in our fragmentation and wonderment about whether the centre can hold, or if we are still capable, occasionally at least, of thinking and acting as a single people. Hugh Heclo portrays the American political system as "much more open, fragmented, self-critical, nondeferential, and fluid in its attachments" than formerly. He describes a factionalism that "has shaped itself around a governmental presence that is doing so much more in so many different areas of life ... Factions ... now come to life across a huge spectrum of government activities touching almost everything about ourselves as a society."[70]

The crucial Canadian difference is that our most serious fragmentation is structured around competing nationalisms and is also entangled with the constitution. Hence our peril and our challenge are much greater.

This, then, is the fragmented human base we have to work with – the raw material of the variegated citizenship of the future that we must both respond to and then employ in the citizenship tasks of the twenty-first century. If we survive as one country, we must accommodate diversity without so destroying our interconnectedness that we shall be incapable of undertaking future civic tasks together. Since the latter will be more demanding than yesterday's challenges, we must hope that a citizen body lacking the bond of a standardized citizenship but nevertheless participating in common civic endeavours is not an oxymoron.

NOTES

1 The Report of the Special Joint Committee of the Senate and the House of Commons (Beaudoin-Edwards Committee), *The Process for Amending the Constitution of Canada* (Ottawa: Supply and Services Canada, 20 June 1991).

2 *Citizen's Forum on Canada's Future: Report to the People and Government of Canada* (Spicer Report) (Ottawa: Minister of Supply and Services Canada, 1991).

3 The "political vision, based on the Canadian Charter of Rights and Freedoms enshrined in the 1982 Act, perceives equality as having a strictly individual scope and applying uniformly across Canada: it does not make allowance for Quebec society to receive special constitutional recognition. The notion of a distinct Quebec society is thus understood as being a source of inequality and incompatible with the principle of equality of all Canadian citizens." Bélanger-Campeau Com-

mission, *Report of the Commission on the Political and Constitutional Future of Québec* (Quebec, 1991), 34.

4 For analysis of Canada from a three-nations perspective, see Peter G. White: "Understanding Canada's Cultural Reality: Accommodating Canada's Three Established Cultural-Linguistic Groups within the Canadian Federal System," Submission to the Special Joint Committee on a Renewed Canada, January 1992, mimeo.

 For recent advocacy of a three-nations view of Canada and a "National Covenant" negotiated and signed by their representatives, see "Speaking Notes by Ron George, President, NCC, to the Policy Conference on 'Identity, Rights and Values,'" 6–9 Feb. 1992, Toronto.

 Ten academics from the University of Toronto and York University and the writer Christina McCall have also supported a three-nations approach. See "Three Nations in a Delicate State," *Toronto Star*, 4 Feb. 1992.

5 See Sally M. Weaver, *Making Canadian Indian Policy: The Hidden Agenda 1968–1970* (Toronto, 1981) for an excellent analysis.

6 White, "Understanding Canada's Cultural Reality," 6.

7 André Siegfried, *The Race Question in Canada*, ed. Frank H. Underhill (Toronto, 1966) (original French edition published in 1906).

8 René Lévesque, "For an Independent Quebec," in J. Peter Meekison, ed., *Canadian Federalism: Myth or Reality*, 3rd ed. (Toronto, 1977), 491.

9 M.E. Turpel and P.A. (Trisha) Monture, "Ode to Elijah: Reflections of Two First Nations Women on the Rekindling of Spirit at the Wake for the Meech Lake Accord," *Queen's Law Journal* 15 no. 2 (1990) 345, and "The Myth of Canada's Dual Nationhood Was Stopped Dead in Its Tracks," 348.

10 For example, even the suggestion "that all of the Aboriginal people in Atlantic Canada could participate in one Aboriginal Electoral District" was described by a New Brunswick Chief as a "non-Indian thought process." The Committee for Aboriginal Electoral Reform, *The Path to Electoral Equality* (Ottawa, 1991), 31.

11 *Sparrow v. The Queen* [1990] 1 SCR 1075 at 1108.

12 *Report of the Aboriginal Justice Inquiry of Manitoba*, Vol. 1, *The Justice System and Aboriginal People* (Winnipeg: Queen's Printer, 1991); Law Reform Commission, *Report on Aboriginal Peoples and Criminal Justice: Equality, Respect and the Search for Justice* (Ottawa, 1991).

13 Government of Canada, *Shaping Canada's Future Together: Proposals* (Ottawa: Minister of Supply and Services, 1991), 8–9.

14 Committee for Aboriginal Electoral Reform, *Path*.

15 Deborah Wilson, "Loud, Clear Voice of the 'Other' Indians," *Globe and Mail*, 17 Dec. 1991, citing Ron George, President of the Native

Council of Canada. The Native Council describes the unacceptable divisions among aboriginal peoples as follows: "Ottawa has created separate classes of Aboriginal Peoples in a system of apartheid that presents little more than a choice of the form of cultural genocide: complete segregation or complete assimilation." Native Council of Canada, *Towards a New Covenant* (Ottawa, 1992), n.p. The Métis National Council also supports the interpretation that the federal government has, and should exercise, jurisdictional responsibility for Métis under section 91(24). "MNC Response to the Federal Proposal," mimeo, n.d., 3.

This goal may not be easily attained for the Métis. In a 1986 national survey, "even after pointed prompting in the interview only a small majority (55.5%) of the Canadian population classified the Métis as aboriginal people. Hence, it is difficult for the Métis to ride the political coattails of status Indians, if Métis leaders were so inclined." J. Rick Ponting, "Aboriginal Dilemmas of the Federal State in Canada," Paper presented to the Annual Meetings of the Association for Canadian Studies in the Netherlands, Hilversum, The Netherlands, 29 Nov. 1991, mimeo, 6.

16 Joe Clark, Minister Responsible for Constitutional Affairs, "Notes for a Speech ... at a Luncheon Hosted by the Saskatchewan Métis Assembly at the Saskatoon Inn," Saskatoon, 28 Sept. 1991, mimeo, 5.

17 Kim Campbell, Minister of Justice, "Aboriginal Constitutional Matters, Speech ... at University of Ottawa, Faculty of Law, Ottawa, November 1, 1991," mimeo, 8–9.

18 A recent paper by Robert K. Groves and Jean-Yves Assiniwi, "Aboriginal Peoples and the Division of Powers in a Reformed Federalism," mimeo, 10 Jan. 1992, 5, citing what are viewed as conservative figures from Statistics Canada gave a total of 950,000 aboriginal people as of 1991 – 247,000 non-status Indians, 148,000 Métis without lands, 5,000 Métis with lands, 35,000 Inuit, 311,000 status Indians on reserve, and 205,000 status Indians off reserve.

19 When the Mohawk warriors were asked to surrender their weapons to facilitate a negotiated solution to the 1990 Oka crisis, Ellen Gabriel, Mohawk spokesperson, stated: "One sovereign country does not surrender its weapons to another sovereign country."

A history textbook, used in Mohawk schools, teaches the students that "they are the original inhabitants of North America, and because of their aboriginal occupation of this hemisphere, have a special status above all of the European, Asian and African immigrants to North America." Stanley G. French, "Native Peoples and Quebec Sovereignty," Montreal, Dec. 1990, mimeo, 4.

Although the main aboriginal organizations have insisted that they are not pursuing complete independence, but self-government within Canada, "various aboriginal groups have argued that they are sovereign nations beyond the jurisdiction of Canadian governments." C. Radha Jhappan, "Aboriginal People and the Right to Self-Government: Response to the Government of Canada's proposals on Aboriginal Self-Government," Ottawa, 6 Nov. 1991, mimeo, 13–14.

20 Ponting recently noted the "Indians' demonstrated tendency to play the game of political embarrassment on the international stage" and that "Canadian aboriginals appear to have world public opinion on their side"; "Aboriginal Dilemmas," 4, 3. See also J. Rick Ponting, "Internationalization: Perspectives on an Emerging Direction in Aboriginal Affairs," *Canadian Ethnic Studies* 22 no. 3 (1990) 85–109.

21 Report of the Canadian Bar Association, *Rebuilding a Canadian Consensus: An Analysis of the Federal Government's Proposals for a Renewed Canada* (Ottawa 1991), 168. See Inuit Tapirisat of Canada, "Constitutional Position Paper – Inuit in Canada: Striving for Equality," mimeo, 6 Feb. 1992, Ottawa, 7–8, for elaboration of the Inuit demands for participation in the constitutional reform process, including a requirement for aboriginal consent to amendments in key areas of concern to aboriginal peoples.

22 Susan Delacourt, "Clark Offered Unity Plan Advice," *Globe and Mail*, 3 Oct. 1991.

23 Government of Canada, *Shaping Canada's Future Together*, 4–9.

24 The First Peoples Constitutional Review Commission, *Aboriginal Directions for Coexistence in Canada*, NCC Constitutional Review Commission Working Paper No. 1 (Ottawa, August 1991), 3.

25 Frank Cassidy and Robert L. Bish, *Indian Government: Its Meaning in Practice* (Halifax, 1989), 56.

26 See French, "Native Peoples and Quebec Sovereignty," for a discussion.

The conflict was clearly enunciated by National Chief Ovide Mercredi of the Assembly of First Nations. See his "Speaking Notes for ... Constituent Assembly on the Renewal of Canada: Identity, Rights and Values," Toronto, 7 Feb 1992, mimeo, 4, dealing with the tension between the proposed designation of Quebec as a distinct society and the "10 First Nations in the provincial boundaries of Quebec who do not have a tradition of French language, culture and civil law ... [They] ... cannot be made subject to French language, culture and civil law without their freely informed consent."

The Inuit Tapirisat proposed that section 25 of the Charter protecting aboriginal, treaty, or other rights from other Charter guarantees of rights and freedoms be amended to ensure that the federal government's 1991 distinct society constitutional proposals also do not abrogate or derogate from aboriginal rights. "Inuit in Canada: Striving for Equality," 7.

27 *Citizens' Forum on Canada's Future*, 4, 16, 24–5.

28 Ibid., 3, 53–4, 64.

29 Government of Canada, *Shaping Canada's Future Together*, vi.

30 Jean Chrétien, of course, now (1992) holds a seat from New Brunswick.

31 Charles Taylor, "Shared and Divergent Values," in Ronald L. Watts and Douglas M. Brown, eds., *Options for a New Canada* (Toronto 1991), 74–6.

32 See Alan C. Cairns, *Charter versus Federalism: The Dilemmas of Constitutional Reform* (Montreal: McGill-Queen's University Press 1992), 120–2 for a discussion of the Charter's reception in Quebec. Mary Ellen Turpel's "Aboriginal Peoples and the Canadian *Charter*: Interpretive Monopolies, Cultural Differences," *Canadian Human Rights Yearbook* 6 (1989–90) 3–45, is a passionate critique of the Charter's appropriateness for aboriginal peoples.

    The Law Reform Commission's *Report on Aboriginal Peoples and Criminal Justice* observed (p. 20): "The question of determining to what extent *Charter* rights are negotiable can hardly be avoided." As the *Globe and Mail* pointed out in a biting editorial, the Law Reform Commission ducked most of the tough issues that would attend aboriginal justice systems. "Defining the Terms of Native Justice" (26 Dec. 1991).

33 Justice Minister Kim Campbell stated recently: "I know Aboriginal women are pleased to see that the Federal Proposal provides for the protection of the Charter. There are traditional values in every society that should be sacred and there are traditional values in every society that should be held up to the light every now and then." "Aboriginal Constitutional Matters," 8.

    See also *Globe and Mail*, 11 Jan. 1992, "Canada Reconsidered: Aboriginal Rights," for the preference of the Native Women's Association of Canada to subject aboriginal governments to the Charter.

34 Inuit Tapirisat of Canada, "Inuit in Canada," 6.

    The Native Council of Canada also asserts that the Charter's sexual equality rights must apply to "any form of aboriginal self-government." This Charter support appears to extend only to sections 15 and 28, not to the whole document. Support is further qualified by the additional phrase "unless and until something more appropriate than the Charter is in place"; Ron George, "Speaking Notes ... Feb. 6–9, Toronto, 1992," mimeo, 10–11.

35 Tony Hall, "Aboriginal Issues and the New Political Map of Canada," mimeo, n.d., 7.

36 *Indian Self-Government in Canada, Report of the Special Committee,* (Penner Report) Minutes of Proceedings of the Special Committee on Indian Self-Government, No. 40, 12, 20 Oct. 1983, 63.

37 *Indian Self-Government in Canada,* 59. "The Committee recommends ... Legislation under the authority of Section 91 (24) of the *Constitution Act, 1867* designed to occupy all areas of competence necessary to permit Indian First Nations to govern themselves effectively and to ensure that provincial laws would not apply on Indian lands except by agreement of the Indian First Nation government."

38 Noel Lyon, *Aboriginal Self-Government: Rights of Citizenship and Access to Governmental Services* (Kingston, 1984), 5.

39 Hence, as Philip Resnick argues, "Quebec, I am convinced, is going to have to choose. It can have new powers – substantially more than the current federal proposals would allow, something a good deal closer, in fact, to Allaire – but on one condition. For every transfer of power to Quebec, there must be a corresponding reduction in the power of M.P.s, ministers, indeed civil servants from Quebec, where the rest of Canada is concerned. Quebec cannot have it both ways. It can have increased power, if it is prepared to pay the price with drastically reduced influence over central institutions and, thereby, over the rest of Canada. It cannot have its cake and eat it too." "Brief to the Special Joint Parliamentary Committee on a Renewed Canada," mimeo, n.d., 9.

   A.W. (Al) Johnson makes a similar proposal, employing the same reasoning, in "The Constitutional Proposals and the Canada-Quebec Dilemma, A Description, Analysis and Critique of the Government of Canada's Constitutional Proposals," mimeo, 12 Nov. 1991.

40 Canadian Bar Association, *Rebuilding a Canadian Consensus,* 142.

41 The "problem" of special aboriginal representation in the federal Parliament will be alleviated to the extent that aboriginal self-governing powers are modelled on provincial jurisdiction, as is likely to be the case for Nunavut. If, however, aboriginal provinces are carved out of the existing provinces, the issue of aboriginal voters and representatives in provincial politics will arise.

42 The future reliance of aboriginal governments on financial resources from federal and provincial governments is conceded by Ovide Mercredi. "We do not like it, but we are dependent on the rest of Canada for improving our socio-economic conditions. The right to self-government is only a means to an end." Rudy Platiel, "Mercredi Denies Grab for Power," *Globe and Mail,* 7 Nov. 1991.

43 Much of the material, including statistics, in this section is taken, with minor modifications, from an unpublished paper by the author, "Representation and the Electoral System: Some Possible Questions

for Research," an "Issues Paper" for the Royal Commission on Electoral
Reform and Party Financing, 28 March 1990, mimeo.

44 David R. Cameron, "Lord Durham Then and Now," *Journal of Canadian Studies* 25 no. 1 (Spring 1990) 17.

45 L.S. Lustgarten, "Liberty in a Culturally Plural Society," in A. Philipps Griffiths, ed., *Of Liberty* (Cambridge, 1983), 98.

46 Jill Vickers, "Why Should Women Care about Constitutional Reforms?" mimeo, Oct. 1991, 3.

47 Turpel and Monture, "Ode to Elijah," 358.

48 Mercredi, "Speaking Notes ... Constituent Assembly on the Renewal of Canada: Identity, Rights and Values," passim.

49 Sylvia B. Bashevkin, *Toeing the Lines: Women and Party Politics in English Canada* (Toronto, 1985), 55.

50 Ibid., 76.

51 Chantal Maillé, *Primed for Power: Women in Canadian Politics* (Ottawa: Canadian Advisory Council on the Status of Women, 1990), 6–12.

52 Christine Boyle, "Home Rule for Women: Power-Sharing between Men and Women," *Dalhousie Law Journal* 7, no. 3 (Oct. 1983) 795.

53 Jennifer Jackson, "The Symbolic Politics of Multiculturalism," graduate course essay, 16 Dec. 1991, University of British Columbia, 12–13.

54 Turpel and Monture, "Ode to Elijah," 346.

55 Iris M. Young, "Polity and Group Differences: A Critique of the Ideal of Universal Citizenship," in Cass R. Sunstein, ed., *Feminism and Political Theory* (Chicago and London, 1990), 250–74.

56 The National Action Committee on the Status of Women recently advocated putting mechanisms in place for a revised Senate to "ensure that women are represented politically in proportion to our presence in the population." Judy Rebick, Barbara Cameron and Sandra Delaronde, "Why We Want Half the Senate Seats," *Globe and Mail*, 28 Oct. 1991.

Another feminist scholar argues that Canada, like other nations, is "composed of two sexual groups which have different traditions and interests," that the strategy of electoral assimilation via single-member territorial constituencies has not really worked to represent adequately women, that at the present time men cannot represent women, and that accordingly the time has come to consider "some form of separate representation of women ... in our electoral system." Boyle, "Home Rule for Women," 790, 797, 808.

See also Susan Jackel's support for "post-modernist and post-colonial arguments against the coercive homogeneity of liberal democratic citizenship and legal regimes," leading her to recommend a complex but ingenious proposal to ensure 50 per cent representation of women in the total membership of both houses of a renewed parliament.

"Rethinking Equality and Citizenship," Text of presentation at "Conversations among Friends, 25 Oct. 1991, mimeo, 13 Nov. 1991, 6–9.

See also Jill Vickers, "Brief Submitted to the Royal Commission on Electoral Reform and Party Financing," Ottawa, 13 June 1990, mimeo, 4, 5, 6, 11, for advocacy of proportional representation (PR) or of designating half of each province's seats for women. She also suggests that "many Canadian women" support "descriptive representation theories which require an accurate correspondence between the characteristics of the people to be represented and the characteristics of the representatives."

Maillé, *Primed for Power*, 33, recommends either PR or dual ridings, each electing one man and one woman.

57 Presentation by Senator Len Marchand to the Royal Commission on Electoral Reform and Party Financing, 13 March 1990, 3.

58 Committee for Aboriginal Electoral Reform, *The Path to Electoral Equality*, 10.

59 Boyle, "Home Rule for Women," 791, 809.

60 The relevant issues are helpfully discussed in Ontario Law Reform Commission, *Appointing Judges: Philosophy, Politics and Practice* (Toronto, 1991).

61 Cited in Alan C. Cairns, "Citizens (Outsiders) and Governments (Insiders) in Constitution-Making: The Case of Meech Lake," in Alan C. Cairns, *Disruptions: Constitutional Struggles, from the Charter to Meech Lake*, ed. Douglas E. Williams (Toronto, 1991), 113. See 113–15 for a litany of such complaints.

A weaker version of the same point was recently made by the Committee for Aboriginal Electoral Reform. It advocated separate aboriginal electoral districts so that aboriginal MPs "could pursue the concerns and interests of Aboriginal people with concentrated attention and vigour ... They could do so without fear of alienating non-Aboriginal constituents, a problem that sometimes arises for Aboriginal people elected under the current system." *The Path to Electoral Equality*, 14.

62 Turpel and Monture, "Ode to Elijah," 350.

63 Métis National Council, "MNC Response to the Federal Proposal," 1, 3, 4, 5, 7.

64 Albert O. Hirschman, *Exit, Voice, and Loyalty* (Cambridge, Mass.: Harvard University Press, 1970).

65 I have discussed these and related "taboo" issues in "Ritual, Taboo, and Bias in Constitutional Controversies in Canada, or Constitutional Talk Canadian Style," in Cairns, *Disruptions*, 199–222.

66 Maillé, *Primed for Power*, 3.

67 Clifford Geertz, *Works and Lives: The Anthropologist as Author* (Stanford, 1988), 131.

68 Young, "Polity and Group Differences." See also Susan Jackel, "Rethinking Equality and Citizenship," 6–7, for a linking of the idea of asymmetrical citizenship postulated for Québécois with the idea of *"coexisting but not identical* citizen statuses [for the] ... oppressed or disadvantaged citizens in Canada, if that differential were explicitly designed ... to reduce oppression and move in the direction of equality."

69 J.L. Granatstein, quoted in Michael Bliss, "Privatizing the Mind: The Sundering of Canadian History, The Sundering of Canada," Creighton Centennial Lecture, Delivered as part of the University of Toronto History Department's 100th Anniversary Celebrations, 18 Oct. 1991, mimeo, 12.

70 Hugh Heclo, "The Emerging Regime," in Richard A. Harris and Sidney M. Milkis, eds., *Remaking American Politics* (Boulder, Col.: Westview Press, 1989), 309–10.

R O B E R T J. S H A R P E

Citizenship, the Constitution Act, 1867, and the Charter

This essay examines the treatment accorded citizenship by the Canadian constitution. It reveals a contrast between the rhetoric of citizenship as a metaphor for fundamental rights and privileges and the reality of the limited weight that citizenship carries in constitutional law and doctrine.

In ordinary discourse, the concept of citizenship is a broad one, identifying those shared values and fundamental rights and obligations that bind people together as a political community. It has become commonplace in Canada, particularly since the advent of the Charter of Rights and Freedoms in 1982, to identify the fundamental rights and freedoms accorded by the constitution as the bedrock attributes of citizenship. In the current round of discussion and debate on the country's constitutional future, there is much talk of the meaning of our citizenship and how our constitution should reflect those basic values. For example, in the federal government's proposals for constitutional change, *Shaping Canada's Future Together*, there is discussion of "The Rights of Citizenship and the Charter" and a proposed "Canada clause" which would identify a list of the country's fundamental characteristics and values, including "respect for the rights of its citizens and constituent communities as set forth in the Canadian Charter of Rights and Freedoms." This is but one example of the use of "citizenship" as a short-hand label to identify the most important characteristics and attributes of being a Canadian.

By contrast, when one looks to the text of the constitution and the manner in which it has been elaborated by the courts, one finds that the formal status of citizenship has limited scope as a legal or constitutional value. Attempts to identify with the status of citizenship a constitutional core of fundamental rights and privileges have failed. Any attempt to limit entitlement to most constitutional rights to citizens has been rejected, and indeed, under the Charter, laws that confer rights or benefits on the basis of citizenship are constitutionally suspect.

This may seem merely to reflect the poverty of the technical legal conception of citizenship in conveying the deeper meaning that the idea carries in a richer stream of political discourse. I suggest, however, that the minimal weight that citizenship possesses in constitutional law does reflect significant values important to an understanding of the Canadian constitution.

I shall examine the concept of citizenship at three different stages of Canada's constitutional development. First, I shall discuss citizenship in the context of federalism and the failed attempt in the early years of this century to derive a broad national legislative power in relation to citizenship in order to curtail discriminatory provincial legislation. Second, again in the context of federalism, I shall describe the attempt in the period of 1930 to 1960 to guarantee certain fundamental political freedoms through a rich conception of citizenship. Third, I shall discuss the role played by citizenship as a legal category under the regime of the Charter.

FEDERALISM AND DISCRIMINATION

Federalism and the division of powers between the Parliament of Canada and the ten provincial legislatures are a fundamental attribute of the Canadian constitution. This division of powers is contained in Canada's original constitution, the British North America Act, 1867, now known as the Constitution Act, 1867. Canada is geographically, culturally, and linguistically diverse, and the division of legislative power between a central national Parliament and ten provincial legislatures represents an attempt to accommodate that diversity. Our constitution enshrines not one political community but eleven, and even the most ardent centralist has to admit that our allegiance as citizens to a political community is accordingly divided.

The original written constitution made no express reference to citizenship. This is hardly surprising, as the concept of Canadian citizenship is very much a product of the twentieth century. Canadian nationals were British subjects only, and the status of Canadian citizenship did not emerge until the first Citizenship Act came into force in 1947.

The 1867 constitution did, however, reflect the fact that Canada was to be a land of immigrants. The provinces and the dominion government were given shared responsibility with respect to immigration,[1] while the Parliament of Canada was given exclusive legislative authority with respect to "naturalization and aliens."[2] This meant at a minimum that Parliament could determine the legal status of aliens in Canada and the terms on which newcomers could become British subjects. Ottawa's authority to create Canadian citizenship has never been doubted, but as the concept of citizenship was not current in Canadian or English constitutional discourse in 1867, it is not clear whether Parliament has legislative competence by implication, through the "naturalization and aliens" power, or whether that competence is derived from its general residual power to legislate for the "peace, order and good government" of Canada.[3]

The more difficult and contentious pre-Charter issue was to determine the scope of Parliament's naturalization and citizenship power. In particular, when conferring the status of subject or citizen, does Parliament also have the power to ensure the enjoyment of certain fundamental political and legal rights? Undoubtedly, Parliament could so act with respect to matters otherwise within federal jurisdiction, but did this head of federal power preclude the provinces from denying naturalized Canadians rights enjoyed by other subjects or citizens?

Union Colliery v. Bryden[4] was the first case to raise these issues at the highest level. It involved a challenge to BC legislation forbidding employment of "Chinamen" below ground in a coal mine. The prohibition had been added to a section that originally prohibited employment of all females and males under the age of fourteen. It was but one of a shockingly long list of legislative measures introduced in British Columbia to prevent or restrict settlement of Chinese immigrants in the province. Some of these measures were disallowed by the dominion government.[5] John McLaren's recent article[6] traces the early history of these provisions and examines a series of early BC decisions in which various measures were struck down as ultra vires the province. He shows how the judges "went further than deciding the straight constitutional issue, and examined and criticized the discriminatory character of the enactment in question,"[7] providing evidence "of an earlier acceptance in some judicial quarters of the notion, however limited and imperfect, of an irreducible core of legal rights which every resident of a jurisdiction claiming to be governed by British conceptions of justice should be entitled to enjoy."[8] However laudable in moral terms, the reasoning of these decisions was problematic, given the limitations of the scope of judicial review under the original 1867 constitution. There was no constitutional guarantee of equality, and there was nothing to permit a court to strike legislation down as invalid solely on the ground that it was racist in nature. In order to mount a constitutional challenge, one had to show that the legislation fell outside the powers allocated to the provinces in section 92 of the Constitution Act, 1867.

The *Bryden* action was brought not by a worker or a representative of the Chinese community but rather by a shareholder of the Union Colliery, seeking a declaration that by employing Chinese workers the company was violating the law. As there was a suspicion that the suit was collusive – with the real motive being to have the law struck down to make available a source of cheap labour – the province's attorney general intervened and successfully defended the legislation before the BC courts. Regulation of the terms and conditions of employment in a coal mine fell within exclusive provincial jurisdiction with respect to "local works and undertakings"[9] or "property and civil rights in the province,"[10] and, it was argued, any perceived injustice of racial barriers to employment provided no basis for a court to "second-guess" the legislature's decision. Provincial legislative power, however, had to be reconciled with the authority of Parliament, and if it could be shown that there was also a federal "aspect" and that the matter fell within one of the classes of subjects enumerated in section 91 of the Constitution Act, 1867, there would be grounds for holding the legislation invalid. The constitutional challenge focused on Parliament's exclusive power to deal with "naturalization and aliens."[11]

Lord Watson, writing the decision of the Judicial Committee of the Privy Council in London, doubted that the power to legislate with respect to "naturalization and aliens" conferred any powers with respect to natural-born Canadians (the BC statute applied to "Chinamen," whether alien, naturalized, or native-born), but he did enunciate a broad and significant conception of the scope of this head of power with respect to those who had been naturalized: "The subject of "naturalization" seems prima facie to include the power of enacting what shall be the consequences of naturalization, or, in other words, what shall be the rights and privileges pertaining to residents in Canada after they have been naturalized."[12]

While those defending the legislation argued that it bore no relation to this dominion head of power and merely established regulations governing the operation of underground coal mines and the conditions of employment in mines, the Privy Council refused to accept this characterization. Lord Watson saw the law for what it was – an attempt to limit the ordinary rights and privileges of a class of persons comprised largely of aliens and naturalized subjects, and this, he held, fell within exclusive dominion jurisdiction: "by virtue of s. 91, sub-s. 25, the legislature of the Dominion is invested with exclusive authority in all matters which directly concern the rights, privileges, and disabilities of the class of Chinamen who are resident in the provinces of Canada."[13]

Lord Watson concluded that "the whole pith and substance of the enactments ... consists in establishing a statutory prohibition which affects aliens or naturalized subjects, and therefore trench upon the exclusive authority of the Parliament of Canada."[14]

The Privy Council's opinion, though formalistic, provided a possible basis for elaboration of an important branch of dominion legislative power to ensure the rights and privileges attached to Canadian citizenship. While Lord Watson emphasized that it was not the function of the courts to assess the wisdom of legislation, there can be little doubt that the Privy Council was troubled by the racist nature of the statute challenged before it. The language of the constitution offered only limited scope for judicial review, but the Privy Council made the most of the tools available. Between the lines of the terse and narrowly legalistic text of the opinion, one reads a determination to locate in the Parliament of Canada sufficient legislative power to ensure that those admitted to the country were treated with the decency and respect due a subject of the British crown.

Admittedly, it would take some creative judicial law-making to overcome the apparent limitations of the language of the constitution if the expansive conception of legislative authority with respect to the protection of the rights of Canadian citizenship nascent in the *Bryden* opinion were to reach full bloom. In particular, the doubt expressed by Lord Watson with respect to Parliament's capacity to protect the rights of native-born Canadians would have to be resolved in favour of dominion authority, for it could hardly be that naturalized subjects were in a better position than the native-born. Moreover, the doctrine would at best act as a brake on provincial abuses and by its very nature could not prevent Parliament itself from derogating from the rights of citizenship. But at the time, the most significant threat of overtly racist legislation came from the provinces, and a constitutional barrier to such measures would have been significant.

Shortly after *Bryden* was decided in the Privy Council, a naturalized Japanese resident of British Columbia challenged the constitutional validity of the election law which denied the vote to all those of Japanese descent, whether naturalized or not. The plaintiff, Tomey Homma, relied on the expansive definition of the dominion's power over naturalization in the *Bryden* case and on the specific terms of the Naturalization Act of Canada which provided that a naturalized alien was entitled to all political and other rights, powers, and privileges to which a natural-born British subject is entitled in Canada.[15] The province's case rested on section 92 (1) of the British North America Act, 1867 (repealed in 1982), which gave the provinces exclusive legislative authority in relation to "The amendment from time to time, notwithstanding anything in this Act, of the Constitution of the province, except as regards the office of Lieutenant Governor."

The province contended that it was entitled to decide which British subjects resident in the province should enjoy the franchise. The franchise was a privilege conferred by legislation, not a right. Many subjects – women, those under the voting age, and certain office holders – did not have the vote. It was for the province to decide, as a matter of its own constitution, who should enjoy the privilege. A general provision in the dominion's law could not extend that benefit to all naturalized subjects and deprive the province of the legislative capacity given by the constitution to decide who should vote in provincial elections.

At trial,[16] Tomey Homma succeeded before Chief Justice McColl, who observed that "the residence within the Province of large numbers of persons, British subjects in name, but doomed to perpetual exclusion from any part in the passage of legislation affecting their property and civil rights would surely not be to the advantage of Canada, and might even become a source of national danger."[17] Chief Justice McColl seems to have thought that the appropriate remedy was disallowance of the provincial legislation but considered himself bound by the *Bryden* decision and conceded that the decision contained a significant restraint on provincial authority to the following effect: "that the Provincial Legislature has no power to pass any legislation whatever which does not, in terms at least, apply alike to born and naturalized subjects of Her Majesty, however its results may varyingly affect different classes or persons."[18]

The decision to strike down the discriminatory election law was upheld somewhat reluctantly on appeal, on the ground that *Bryden* governed.[19] The province appealed to the Privy Council, and when it decided the case in 1903,[20] it dashed any hope that the expansive vision of citizenship and the guarantee of legislative power to ensure its enjoyment might evolve from the assignment of legislative power in relation to "naturalization and aliens." The Privy Council swiftly abandoned the doctrine outlined by Lord Watson in *Bryden*, adopting in its place an analysis that emphasized, to the exclusion of other values, the protection of provincial legislative authority. It accepted the characterization of the franchise as a privilege that the province was entitled to grant or withhold, as the legislature saw fit. Its opinion zeroed in on what it perceived to be the weakness of the *Bryden* analysis. First, the actual language of the constitution's grant of dominion power was said to be too narrow to preclude discrimination on racial grounds. The BC law did not just discriminate against naturalized Japanese Canadians – even those who were racially Japanese but Canadian-born were denied the vote.

The Earl of Halsbury, lord chancellor, wrote that a power to legislate with respect to "naturalization and aliens" had no application with reference to those who were British subjects by birth. The very fact that the disenfranchisement of Japanese was overtly racist made it less vulnerable to attack. Race, like gender, was simply a category that the province was entitled to adopt in determining who should have the "privilege" of the franchise. Moreover, even discrimination in the terms of present or former alien status was not necessarily beyond the power of the province. Precluding legislative classifications based on alienage would, in the lord chancellor's view, lead to the absurdity that a province could not deny the vote to an alien. This was plainly a highly formalistic analysis which refused to consider the substance of the distinction, but it led to the conclusion that the province had the right, unqualified by dominion authority, to decide who could and who could not vote in provincial elections.

The Privy Council feared the capacity of a broad dominion power to protect the rights and privileges of citizenship to swallow huge areas of provincial jurisdiction. It thought that the only way to prevent this was to limit the office of section 91 (25) to granting the mere status of naturalization and not to include the power to deal with the consequences:

The truth is that the language of that section does not purport to deal with the consequences of either alienage or naturalization. It undoubtedly reserves these subjects for the exclusive jurisdiction of the Dominion – that is to say, it is for the Dominion to determine what shall constitute either the one or the other, but the question as to what consequences shall follow from either is not touched. The right of protection and the obligations of allegiance are necessarily involved in the nationality conferred by naturalization; but the privileges attached to it, where these depend upon residence, are quite independent of nationality.[21]

Bryden was said to rest on its "particular facts" and to have been based on the conclusion that the law at issue was aimed not at the regulation of coal mines but designed "to deprive the Chinese, naturalized or not, of the ordinary rights of the inhabitants of British

Columbia and, in effect, to prohibit their continued residence in that province, since it prohibited their earning their living in that province."[22]

Not only does this seem a strained reading of *Bryden*, but from a modern perspective, *Tomey Homma* seems a stronger case for judicial review. It represented an ideal fact situation for the courts to develop and expand on the concept of a broad dominion power to protect the rights of citizenship. Denying the province the capacity to disenfranchise naturalized subjects hardly destroyed a huge area of provincial legislative authority.

For a time, the courts continued to follow *Bryden* with respect to legislative barriers to employment on racial lines.[23] But even this narrow reading of the case suffered a setback with the decision of the Supreme Court of Canada in *Quong Wing v. The King* in 1914.[24] At issue there was the constitutional validity of a Saskatchewan law which created the following offence: "No person shall employ in any capacity any white woman or girl or permit any white woman or girl to reside or lodge in or to work in or, save as a *bona fide* customer in a public apartment thereof only, to frequent any restaurant, laundry or other place of business or amusement owned, kept or managed by any Chinaman." Quong Wing, described in the Supreme Court's decision as "a Chinaman and a naturalized Canadian citizen,"[25] was convicted of employing a white woman and challenged the law, relying on *Bryden*.

Only Mr. Justice Idington, dissenting, would have acquitted Quong Wing and found that the law was either invalid or that it could not be applied to a naturalized subject. Mr. Justice Idington offered a rationale for extending dominion competence to guarantee naturalized subjects protection from discriminatory provincial legislation. Canada, he observed, needed immigrants to settle and develop its vast spaces, and the power to guarantee immigrants a secure future once they were naturalized was a necessary incident of the "naturalization and aliens" head of power: "To define and forever determine beyond the power of any legislature to alter the status of such people and measure out their rights by that enjoyed by the native-born seems to me a power implied in the power over 'naturalization and aliens.'"[26] To read the word "Chinaman" as applying to a naturalized subject was, in Idington's view, a breach of faith to "a man who may have bid good-bye forever to his native land, induced to do so by the assurances offered him."[27]

The other judges were not persuaded, and the majority of the court preserved provincial power from qualification by an implicit dominion authority to secure the rights of naturalized subjects. Chief Justice Fitzpatrick saw the legislation as a valid exercise of provincial legislative capacity to establish proper conditions of employment for women and thought that "the difference between the restrictions imposed on all Canadians by such legislation and those resulting from the act in question is one of degree, not of kind."[28] Mr. Justice Davies (with whom Mr. Justice Anglin concurred) conceded that if *Bryden* were to be followed, Quong Wing would succeed. However, in the view of Mr. Justice Davies, *Bryden* had been seriously limited if not effectively overruled by *Tomey Homma*, and there was "no inherent right in any class of the community to employ women and children which the legislature may not modify or take away altogether."[29]

Mr. Justice Duff also saw the legislation as falling within exclusive provincial competence to determine appropriate terms and conditions of employment. The contention that the legislation was invalid as being in relation to naturalization and aliens could not be sustained as "it applies to persons of the races mentioned without regard to nationality."[30] Mr. Justice Duff pointed out that it was "impossible to say that the Act is, in its practical operation, limited to aliens and naturalized subjects,"[31] and hence it could not be seen as impinging on Parliament's power with respect to that subject. Again, the overtly racist classification adopted by the legislature saved it from constitutional attack. Mr. Justice Duff also observed that *Bryden* had to be read in light of *Tomey Homma*, and he read the latter case as limiting the reach of *Bryden* to laws that effectively prohibited naturalized subjects of the right to reside and earn a livelihood in the province. The provision in the Naturalization Act guaranteeing naturalized subjects the rights and privileges of native-born British subjects – one of the grounds for the *Bryden* decision – was read narrowly by Mr. Justice Duff, who wrote that it could not provide naturalized subjects immunity from the operation of provincial law.

The overt racism of the legislation challenged in these cases is shocking to the modern reader. Equally disturbing is the implicit acceptance by many of the judges of the racist assumptions underlying the legislation. Yet the failure of the courts to develop an expansive conception of basic rights of citizenship as implicit in the dominion power over "naturalization and aliens" is hardly surprising. The language of the constitution hardly led inexorably to that conclusion, and the constitution embodies values and principles that run the other way. The very function of our constitution is to provide a structure within which diverse political communities may define themselves and pursue their own local aspirations within the sphere of legislative authority allocated to them. While some citizens will identify more closely with the federal power and wish to see Parliament have the most important role in defining our political community, it cannot be denied that our citizenship is divided and that we are members of two political communities. It would have taken an exercise of judicial creativity and imagination of considerable magnitude to articulate a conception of citizenship that would embody at the dominion level the authority to define and protect the essential attributes of citizenship, while at the same time respecting the legitimate claims of provincial power.

FEDERALISM AND POLITICAL FREEDOMS

A second attempt to create a constitutional category to ensure the protection of certain fundamental rights within the structure of the 1867 constitution, based in part on an expansive conception of Canadian citizenship, occurred in the period 1930–60. The leading academic proponent was Bora Laskin,[32] while the principal judicial exponent was Mr. Justice Rand of the Supreme Court of Canada.[33]

In Laskin's view, to suggest that civil liberties were not a discrete "matter" within the allocation of powers between the federal and provincial governments was unthinkable: "Such a suggestion is repellent to our institutions and to our political and social traditions, and thus alien to the very sources of our constitutional law. It would amount to a rejection of civil liberties as an independent group of values in our society and reduce them to a parasitic position."[34]

Laskin rejected the more ambitious theory that the words of the preamble to the 1867 constitution proclaiming Canada to have "a constitution similar in principle to that of the United Kingdom" placed certain fundamental rights beyond the reach of Parliament as well as the provinces.[35] This, he felt, was inconsistent with both the doctrine of parliamentary supremacy and the theory that the Constitution Act, 1867, accomplished an exhaustive distribution of legislative authority embracing every possible legislative objective.[36] Laskin conceded that responsibility for egalitarian and economic rights and even certain legal rights (powers of arrest, search, and seizure) was shared by the federal and provincial governments. He was convinced, however, that certain fundamental civil liberties were within exclusive federal competence and beyond the reach of provincial legislatures. These were what he called political liberties, those rights "associated with the operation of our parliamentary institutions and which make Parliamentary democracy possible and tolerable."[37] These rights were freedom of association, assembly, expression, the press, and conscience and religion, and in Laskin's view, they fell within exclusive federal legislative competence.

In developing his theory, Laskin relied heavily on the notion that there were certain fundamental rights inherent in Canadian citizenship, drawing in particular on the judicial opinions of Mr. Justice Rand. In the *Winner* case,[38] (although the issue was not civil liberties but the right of the provinces to regulate the activities of an American engaged in interprovincial busing), Mr. Justice Rand offered the following statement of the rights of Canadian citizenship: "The first and fundamental accomplishment of the constitutional Act was the creation of a single political organization of subjects of His Majesty within the geographical area of the Dominion, the basic postulate of which was the institution of Canadian citizenship. Citizenship is membership in a state; and in the citizen inhere those rights and duties, the correlatives of allegiance and protection, which are basic to that status."[39]

Not dissuaded by the *Tomey Homma* decision from reverting to *Bryden*, Mr. Justice Rand found implicit in the constitution's allocation of power to the federal government over naturalization and citizenship a right of mobility to move about and work "as a constituent element of ... citizenship status."[40] While Mr. Justice Rand seems to have been concerned primarily with rights of mobility,[41] Bora Laskin inferred from his dictum in the *Winner* case the right to exercise political freedoms free from provincially imposed restraints: "It must follow that a provincial legislature may not inhibit movement out of or through a province, and, equally, that it may not limit a person in the province in his privilege of association with others outside the province. It is my submission, further, that apart from territorial limitation on the operation of provincial legislation, it is beyond the competence of the province to limit freedom of political association or of assembly or of speech or religion where sought to be exercised within the province."[42]

Support for the notion that there was a core of fundamental political freedoms beyond the reach of the provinces could be drawn from a series of cases in which the Supreme Court of Canada had struck down provincial legislation. *Reference re Alberta Statutes*[43] held the provinces incompetent to suppress debate on public issues; other cases struck down provincial laws on Sunday observance;[44] and an Ontario decision struck down provincial obscenity legislation.[45] One of the most significant cases was another decision in which Mr. Justice Rand participated, *Switzman v. Elbling*,[46] striking down Quebec's "padlock law" as invading exclusive federal jurisdiction over criminal law. Laskin thought that Mr. Justice Rand's opinion made him "the greatest expositor of democratic public law which Canada has known," and he described the opinion "as representing the crystallization of constitutional law on the political liberties".[47] Mr. Justice Rand had written as follows in *Switzman*:

Parliamentary government postulates a capacity in men, acting freely and under self-restraints, to govern themselves; and that advance is best served in the degree achieved of individual liberation from subjective as well as objective shackles. Under that government, the freedom of discussion in Canada, as a subject-matter of legislation, has a unity of interest and significance extending equally to every part of the Dominion ... This constitutional fact is the political expression of the primary condition of social life, thought and its communication by language. Liberty in this sense is little less vital to man's mind and spirit than breathing is to his physical existence. As such an inherence in the individual it is embodied in his status of citizenship.[48]

Was Mr. Justice Rand tending toward the view expressed by his colleague Mr. Justice Abbott that there were certain freedoms beyond the reach of even the Parliament of Canada,[49] or was he taking the Laskin position which placed the subject within federal control? The ambiguity was never resolved, but it seems clear that there was an underlying ideal of inherent and inalienable attributes of citizenship motivating his judgments.[50]

In 1959, Mr. Justice Rand decided *Roncarelli v. Duplessis*.[51] The premier of Quebec, Maurice Duplessis, had ordered the cancellation of Roncarelli's liquor licence because Roncarelli had made it a practice to furnish bail to Jehovah's Witnesses arrested for distributing religious tracts. The judgment, vindicating the rule of law and the control of abuse of power by government officials, focused again on what Mr. Justice Rand saw to be fundamental attributes of citizenship: "To deny or revoke a permit because a citizen exercises an unchallengeable right totally irrelevant to the sale of liquor in a restaurant is equally beyond the scope of the discretion conferred. There was here not only revocation of the existing permit but a declaration of a future, definitive disqualification of the appellant to obtain one: it was to be "forever". This purports to divest his citizenship status of its incident of membership in the class of those of the public to whom such a privilege could be extended."[52]

While there was a coincidence of purpose between the academic writing of Laskin and the judicial writing of Mr. Justice Rand, the thinking of each was motivated by a distinct underlying theory. Laskin was a positivist. His concern was to elaborate a theory that could be accommodated within the existing text and doctrine of the constitution. He saw Parliament as the protector of liberty against the vicissitudes of provincial politics, and he became convinced that the constitution allocated exclusive legislative competence to Parliament in relation to political liberties. Mr. Justice Rand, in contrast, was motivated by a theoretical ideal of citizenship, something that was natural and inherent and existed quite apart from positive law. He thought that the constitution embodied those values in spirit and that it was the task of the judiciary to implement those overarching values in deciding concrete cases.

Again, however, an expansive conception of citizenship proved incapable of sustaining the constitutional protection of fundamental rights. Despite the powerful combination of Mr. Justice Rand's judicial opinions and Bora Laskin's academic argument, neither Rand's ideal of natural and inherent citizenship rights nor Laskin's doctrine of the exclusivity of federal authority over political liberties was accepted. Rand's views could only collide with the doctrine of parliamentary supremacy. Citizenship and the rights attached thereto were what Parliament and the provinces, each acting within their own competence, said they were. The inherent rights of the citizen might find a home in political theory, but they could not be accommodated in the pre-Charter constitution which had as one of its pillars parliamentary supremacy. Laskin's attempt to accommodate the theory within the existing positive law of the constitution depended on a highly centralist conception of the division of powers which failed to attract significant support.

While Laskin asserted as late as 1962 "that the Provinces have no competence to limit such traditional freedoms as speech, assembly, association, and religion, and that the Parliament of Canada may legislate to protect them,"[53] the cases were more ambiguous than he was prepared to admit. While participation in the federal electoral process was held to be beyond the reach of provincial legislation in 1965,[54] the courts were simply not prepared to accept that provincial legislative power was to be limited in the name of protecting the fundamental attributes of citizenship and political participation.[55] Indeed, after his appointment to the Supreme Court of Canada, Laskin did not avail himself of opportunities to advance the theory.[56] He dealt specifically with the citizenship power in the *Morgan* case,[57] where he upheld the right of the province of Prince Edward Island to restrict the rights of non-residents, including Canadian citizens, to own land there. While he did allow that provincial legislation aimed at aliens or naturalized persons and striking at their very capacity would be beyond the powers of the provinces, he rejected the contention that the law offended the equality of status of citizenship, holding that federal power could not be invoked "to give aliens, naturalized persons or natural-born citizens any immunity from provincial regulatory legislation, otherwise within its constitutional competence, simply because it may affect one class more than another or may affect all of them alike by what may be thought to be undue stringency."[58]

The constitutional law of federalism could not, then, accommodate a theory of citizenship that would embrace certain fundamental values and ensure their protection by the courts. On the one hand, the doctrine of parliamentary supremacy required that any limitation of legislative power to define, limit, or remove the rights inherent in citizenship be explicit. The only available form of judicial review concerned the division of legislative power between the federal Parliament and provincial legislatures. Neither the text of the constitution nor the political reality of the distinctive political communities that comprise Canada made possible allocation to Parliament of exclusive responsibility for defining the rights of citizenship.

CHARTER OF RIGHTS AND FREEDOMS

The amendment of the Canadian constitution in 1982 to include the Charter of Rights and Freedoms brought about a fundamental change in Canadian law and politics. The Charter enshrines certain rights and freedoms and explicitly provides that the courts have the duty to declare invalid those laws that infringe the rights and freedoms so protected. The doctrine of parliamentary supremacy which protected legislative choices from judicial review has been overcome, and the constitution now unambiguously proclaims certain rights and freedoms as supreme. The Charter rests on ideals that determine the relationship between the governed and those who exercise state power and, in that sense, appeals to a rich, liberal vision of citizenship. However, as will be seen, the formal legal status of citizen is not an indicator of entitlement to most rights, and the principles of human dignity and respect on which the Charter is founded preclude conferring privileges or imposing restrictions based on citizenship.

The Charter identifies and enshrines six broad categories of rights: (1) the so-called fundamental freedoms of conscience, religion, thought, belief, opinion, expression, assembly, and association;[59] (2) democratic rights, including the right to vote and the guarantee of regular elections and Parliamentary sessions;[60] (3) mobility rights to enter and leave the country and the right to reside in and gain a livelihood in any province;[61] (4) legal rights, particularly those pertaining to the criminal process such as the right against unreasonable search and seizure, habeas corpus, and the right to counsel, to a trial within a reasonable time, and to be presumed innocent until proven guilty;[62] (5) the right to equality before and under the law and to the equal protection and equal benefit of the law;[63] and (6) language rights.[64]

Only three Charter rights are expressly given to "citizens." These are the right to vote and be qualified for membership in the House of Commons or a provincial legislature,[65] mobility rights,[66] and minority-language education rights.[67] Other rights are conferred variously on "everyone," "any person," "every individual," or "any member of the public in Canada." The Supreme Court of Canada has held that the right to "life, liberty and security of the person" guaranteed to "everyone" by section 7 of the Charter extends to "every human being who is physically present in Canada and by virtue of such presence amenable to Canadian law."[68] As will be explained below, non-citizens have been held entitled to assert claims to equality rights, guaranteed to "every individual" by section 15, and there can be little doubt that other Charter rights, except where specifically reserved to citizens by the text of the constitution, are similarly extended to non-citizens.

The Charter was plainly inspired by a desire to ensure respect for certain universal principles of human rights and dignity. It conditions the legitimacy of the exercise of state power on respect for those fundamental values and principles to which all individuals who are subject to the exercise of state power are entitled. To accord such rights only to those who enjoy the formal status of citizenship would be a denial of the Charter's very foundation.

If one looks to the rights extended only to citizens one finds, first of all, political rights, which are indicative of the individual's full integration into the Canadian political community. Significantly, the rights attached to citizenship are not subject to the possibility of legislative override.[69] The franchise constitutes recognition of one's entitlement to full participation in the governance of the community. Governments can indeed withhold this right from some of those who are subject to Canadian law, according it only to those who have a demonstrated attachment and commitment to Canada (i.e. citizens). Mobility rights include "the right to enter, remain in and leave Canada." The right freely to enter and leave the country is one that sovereign nations typically reserve to their own nationals, and extension of the right to a person is indicative of full and unqualified membership in the community. It is instructive to note that individuals who have the right to remain in Canada permanently but are not citizens acquire mobility rights within Canada. The right to move to, take up residence in, and earn a livelihood in any province is extended to both citizens and those who have "the status of a permanent resident of Canada."

Minority-language education rights are restricted to "citizens of Canada" who meet certain further qualifications and fall into a special category. By restricting these rights to citizens, the Charter allows provinces to attempt to integrate and assimilate new Canadians into the dominant linguistic culture of the province in which they settle. Once citizens, they are entitled to the same education rights as anyone, but until they acquire that status, they are subject to provincial linguistic policy.

The Charter, however, goes well beyond extending most rights to non-citizens. As a result of the guarantee of equality in section 15 and the decision of the Supreme Court of Canada in *Andrews v. Law Society of British Columbia*,[70] the Charter significantly constrains governments' capacity to confer benefits or impose restrictions on the basis of citizenship. In other words, not only is citizenship eliminated as a prerequisite for asserting a claim to most Charter rights: citizenship itself is rendered a highly suspect legislative classification.

Andrews was the first section 15 case to reach the Supreme Court. At issue was the constitutionality of a provincial law, the British Columbia Barristers and Solicitors Act,[71] which required citizenship for entry into the legal profession. The plaintiff satisfied all other entry requirements but was not a Canadian citizen. He alleged that the citizenship requirement infringed his right to equality, guaranteed by section 15 of the Charter: "Every individual is equal before and under the law and has the right to the equal protection and equal benefit of the law without discrimination and, in particular, without discrimination based on race, national or ethnic origin, colour, religion, sex, age or mental or physical disability."

The key issue of interpretation was how to identify those classifications that offend the promise of equality and non-discrimination. The Supreme Court rejected the suggestion that all differences in treatment between individuals should be subject to Charter scrutiny under section 15 and held that "consideration must be given to the content of the law, to its purpose, and its impact upon those to whom it applies, and also upon those whom it excludes from its application."[72] In determining which distinctions or classifications would infringe on the guarantee of equality, the court held that one had to pay heed to the underlying spirit and purpose of section 15 – "the promotion of a society in which all are secure in the knowledge that they are recognized at law as human beings equally deserving of concern, respect and consideration."[73]

A central concept in section 15 is discrimination, defined by the court as follows:

discrimination may be described as a distinction, whether intentional or not but based on grounds relating to personal characteristics of the individual or group, which has the effect of imposing burdens, obligations, or disadvantages on such individual or group not imposed upon others, or which withholds or limits access to opportunities, benefits, and advantages available to other members of society. Distinctions based on personal characteristics attributed to an individual solely on the basis of association with a group will rarely escape the charge of discrimination, while those based on an individual's merits and capacities will rarely be so classed.[74]

The court held that while the enumerated grounds in section 15 were not exclusive, they did reflect the "most common and probably the most socially destructive and historically practiced bases of discrimination"[75] and that to qualify for consideration as a prohibited ground of discrimination, another category would have to be analogous in nature to one of the enumerated grounds.

What is contemplated by the definition of equality and discrimination adopted by the Supreme Court is a substantive assessment of the law and its impact on particular individuals or groups. Only those differences based on historic patterns of discrimination or disadvantage, such as those listed in section 15 itself, will constitute a denial of equality.

All judges agreed that denying the plaintiff entry into the legal profession because he was not a citizen constituted discrimination and a denial of section 15 rights. The legislature had adopted a classification which excluded the members of a group on the basis of a characteristic analogous to those set out in section 15 and without regard to the qualifications or merits of the members of the group. Madam Justice Bertha Wilson emphasized that non-citizens were a disadvantaged group in that they lacked political power and were accordingly vulnerable to having their interests overlooked and the right to equal concern and respect violated: "Non-citizens, to take only the most obvious example, do not have the right to vote. Their vulnerability to becoming a disadvantaged group in our society is

238 Robert J. Sharpe

captured by John Stuart Mill's observation in Book III of *On Liberty and Considerations of Representative Government* ... that "in the absence of its natural defenders, the interests of the excluded is [sic] always in danger of being overlooked ..." I would conclude therefore that non-citizens fall into an analogous category to those specifically enumerated in s. 15."[76]

Mr. Justice La Forest referred to the sorry history of discriminatory legislation of the type at issue in *Bryden* and *Quong Wing* and added: "Discrimination on the basis of nationality has from early times been an inseparable companion of discrimination on the basis of race and national or ethnic origin, which are listed in s. 15."[77]

While he was prepared to accept that "citizenship is a very special status that not only incorporates rights and duties but serves a highly important symbolic function as a badge identifying people as members of the Canadian polity," he thought it irrelevant as a qualification for most functions: "By and large, the use in legislation of citizenship as a basis for distinguishing between persons, here for the purpose of conditioning access to the practice of a profession, harbours the potential for undermining the essential and underlying values of a free and democratic society that are embodied in s. 15. Our nation has throughout its history drawn strength from the flow of people to our shores. Decisions unfairly premised on citizenship would be likely to [undermine the faith of newcomers in Canadian political and social institutions]."[78]

As an infringement of section 15 was found by the court, the next question was whether that infringement could be justified as a reasonable limit that could be "demonstrably justified in a free and democratic society" under section 1 of the Charter. Two members of the court, Messrs. Justice McIntyre and Lamer, would have upheld the barrier to non-citizens practising law on this ground, but the majority of the court found that the restriction could not be so justified and struck it down.

The Charter itself says very little if anything about how limitations on rights are to be justified, but the Supreme Court of Canada set out the basic framework for analysis in *R. v. Oakes*.[79] In that case, it was established that the initial burden of proving a violation of rights rests with the individual asserting a Charter claim. As soon as a prima facie violation is proved, as was the case in *Andrews*, the burden shifts to the party attempting to justify the infringement. It is at the justification stage that the court must consider the collective interest in limiting a right or freedom and weigh that collective interest against the right of the individual. Reconciliation of the collective interest against individual rights is achieved through "proportionality" review. Is there an objective "of sufficient importance to warrant overriding a constitutionally protected right or freedom"?[80] In *Oakes*, the Supreme Court of Canada said that the objective must "relate to concerns which are pressing and substantial in a free and democratic society."[81]

Next, the court asks, is there a rational, non-arbitrary, non-capricious connection between the objective and the law that is challenged? Was there some other way for the legislature to satisfy the objective that would not impair the right or freedom at issue or that would have less impact on the right or freedom than does the law under review?

In *Andrews*, Madam Justice Wilson wrote that as the court had interpreted section 15 narrowly, catching only those distinctions that impinge on groups that suffer social, political, and legal disadvantage, the burden on those seeking to uphold such distinctions under section 1 would be onerous. It was argued that the citizenship bar fulfilled three important purposes – that citizenship ensures familiarity with Canadian institutions and customs, that it is indicative of a strong commitment to Canadian society, and, that as lawyers play an important role in the administration of the law and in the Canadian system of democratic government, they should be citizens.

The Supreme Court's negative assessment of citizenship as a sufficient indicator of these qualities is revealing. Madam Justice Wilson, with whom both Chief Justice Dickson and Madam Justice L'Heureux-Dubé agreed, accepted the desirability of lawyers being familiar with Canadian institutions and customs but found that the citizenship requirement was not carefully tailored to achieve that objective. Citizenship, she wrote, provided no assurance of such familiarity, and whether the prospective lawyer had the requisite knowledge could better be determined by a test specifically designed for the purpose. She adopted the reasoning of Madam Justice Beverley McLachlin (now a member of the Supreme Court of Canada but then on the BC Court of Appeal) in finding that citizenship was inapt as an indicator of a commitment to Canadian society: "Only those citizens who are not natural-born Canadians can be said to have made a conscious choice to establish themselves here permanently and to opt for full participation in the Canadian social process, including the right to vote and run for public office. While no doubt most citizens, natural-born or otherwise, are committed to Canadian society, citizenship does not ensure that that is the case. Conversely, non-citizens may be deeply committed to our country."[82]

Finally, she doubted the extent to which lawyers should be considered part of government but added: "even if lawyers do perform a governmental function, I do not think the requirement that they be citizens provides any guarantee that they will honourably and conscientiously carry out their public duties. They will carry them out, I believe, because they are good lawyers and not because they are Canadian citizens."[83]

Mr. Justice La Forest also rejected the citizenship requirement as a reasonable limit on the guarantee of equality, and consequently the majority of the Supreme Court of Canada found that the citizenship requirement could not be justified as a reasonable limit on the right to equality under section 1.

The *Andrews* case indicates that respect for human dignity and respect will ordinarily preclude according privileges or imposing restrictions on the basis of the formal status of citizenship. Indeed, it identifies preferences or restrictions based on citizenship with the most invidious forms of discrimination based on race, nationality, and religion. Moreover, even where it is legitimate to establish preferences or restrictions on the basis of familiarity with Canadian customs and institutions or a commitment to Canada, the formal status of citizenship is found wanting as an indicator of such attributes. This devastating assessment reveals the weakness of the formal status of citizenship as an indicator of rights and the overwhelming strength of the fundamental and universal principles of human dignity and respect on which the Charter is based.

Charter challenges have also been directed against citizenship requirements or preferences for employment in the public service. In the only reported case to date, a trial judge in British Columbia held that a general prohibition in the provincial Public Service Act[84] prohibiting appointment of non-citizens was contrary to the Charter.[85] On the authority of *Andrews*, the petitioner was easily able to establish a violation of section 15, and the government's contention that the measure could be justified as a reasonable limit under section 1 was rejected. The argument that the "symbolism" of citizenship as a prerequisite to employment in the public service was a pressing and substantial objective was found wanting. The court also found that even if that were accepted as an objective of sufficient importance to justify limiting the right of equality, the legislation was too broad, as it applied to all public servants. This case and the majority opinion in *Andrews* suggest that the section 1 hurdle will be a difficult one for governments to surmount. Unless the citizenship requirement is focused on particular positions for which citizenship is a demonstrably justifiable qualification, it would seem likely that the courts will strike it down.

CONCLUSION

The Constitution Act, 1867, rested on the principle of parliamentary supremacy, qualified only by the division of powers between the dominion Parliament and the provincial legislatures. It did not include formal recognition of the ideals of the essential attributes of citizenship, and the elected representatives of the people were free to define the rights of citizenship as they saw fit. Attempts were made to qualify legislative choice through judicial review by linking the concept of citizenship with an exclusive head of dominion power, first to constrain racist provincial legislation and later to protect fundamental political rights. These attempts met with little success. The values of citizenship were unable to overcome the twin hurdles of parliamentary and provincial sovereignty.

The Charter of Rights and Freedoms overcomes the limitations of federalism and parliamentary sovereignty by making an appeal to certain universal principles of human dignity and respect applicable to all individuals and all communities. The Charter embodies a rich vision of the relationship between the individual and the state, but that vision is not linked to the status of citizenship. The Charter draws a sharp distinction between those few rights accorded exclusively to citizens, which are indicative of full membership in the political community, and most rights which are available to all who are subject to Canadian law. One of the rights available to all, the right to equality, reinforces this distinction by rendering suspect legislative classifications based on citizenship.

I do not suggest we should abandon the attempt to identify those shared values and fundamental rights and obligations that bind us together as a political community. We should recognize, however, that the constitution consciously transcends the interests of those who are full members of our political community and that one of the fundamental rights that we enjoy forbids us from preferring our fellow citizens to the detriment of strangers.

NOTES

1 Constitution Act, 1867, s. 95.
2 Ibid., s. 91 (25).
3 Hogg, *Constitutional Law of Canada*, 2nd ed. (Toronto: Carswell, 1985), 668; *Morgan v. A.G. Prince Edward Island* (1975), 55 DLR (3d) 527 at 531–2; *Winner v. S.M.T. (Eastern) & A.G. of New Brunswick*, [1951] SCR 887 at 919.
4 [1899] AC 580.
5 Lefroy, *Canada's Federal System* (Toronto: Carswell, 1913), 312; Ryder,

"Racism and the Constitution: The Constitutional Fate of British Columbia Anti-Asian Immigration Legislation, 1844–1909" *Osgoode Hall Law Journal* 29 (1991) 619.

6 McLaren, "The Early British Columbia Supreme Court and the "Chinese Question": Echoes of the Rule of Law" *Manitoba Law Journal* 20 (1991) 107.

7 Ibid., 108.

8 Ibid., 146–7.

9 S. 92 (10).

10 S. 92 (13).

11 S. 91 (25).

12 [1899] AC at 586.

13 Ibid., 587.

14 Ibid.

15 RSC 1886, c. 113, s. 15.

16 (1900), 7 BCR 368.

17 Ibid., 372.

18 Ibid., 372.

19 (1901), 8 BCR 76.

20 [1903] AC 151.

21 Ibid., 156–7.

22 Ibid., 157.

23 Re Coal Mines Regulation Act (1904), 10 BCR 408 (CA).

24 (1914), 49 SCR 440.

25 Ibid., 443, per Fitzpatrick CJ.

26 Ibid., 454.

27 Ibid., 458.

28 Ibid., 445.

29 Ibid., 447–8.

30 Ibid., 463.

31 Ibid.

32 See Sharpe, "Bora Laskin and Civil Liberties," *University of Toronto Law Journal* 35 (1985) 632, from which I have drawn freely in this section.

33 See Price, "Mr. Justice Rand and the Privileges and Immunities of Canadian Citizens," *University of Toronto Faculty of Law Review* 16 (1958) 16.

34 Laskin, "Our Civil Liberties – The Role of the Supreme Court," *Queen's Quarterly* 61 (1954) 463.

35 *Switzman v. Elbling & A.G. of Quebec*, [1957] SCR 285 at 328 per Abbott, J.

36 *Canadian Constitutional Law*, 2nd ed (1960), 938; "An Inquiry into the Diefenbaker Bill of Rights," *Canadian Bar Review* 37 (1959) 102.

37 "Inquiry," 80.
38 *Winner v. S.M.T. (Eastern) & A.G. of New Brunswick*, [1951] SCR 887 (varied on other grounds [1954] AC 541).
39 Ibid., 918.
40 Ibid., 919.
41 In some quarters, opening this unsettled area to judicial review caused concern: see McWhinney, "Constitutional Law – Provincial Regulation of Commerce – Mr. Justice Rand and the Inherent Rights of the Canadian Citizen," *Canadian Bar Review* 30 (1952) 832.
42 "Inquiry," 112–3.
43 [1938] SCR 100.
44 *A.G. Ontario v. Hamilton Street Railway Co.*, [1903] AC 524; *Henry Birks & Sons (Montreal) Ltd. v. Montreal & A.G. Quebec*, [1955] SCR 799.
45 *A.G. Ontario v. Koynok*, [1941] 1 DLR 548.
46 *Switzman v. Elbling*.
47 "Inquiry," 124.
48 *Switzman v. Elbling* 306.
49 Ibid.
50 See Conklin, *Images of a Constitution* (Toronto: University of Toronto Press, 1989), 220–2.
51 [1959] SCR 121.
52 Ibid., 141.
53 "Canada's Bill of Rights: A Dilemma for the Courts?" *International Comparative Quarterly* 11 (1962) 523.
54 *McKay v. The Queen* (1965), 53 DLR (2d) 532.
55 See, for example, *Saumur v. The City of Quebec*, [1953] 2 SCR 299; *Oil, Chemical & Atomic Workers International Union, Local 16-601 v. Imperial Oil Ltd.*, [1963] SCR 584; *Nova Scotia Board of Censors v. McNeil*, [1978] 2 SCR 662; and *A.G. Canada & Dupond v. Montreal*, [1978] 2 SCR 770.
56 For a full discussion of Laskin's approach as an academic and then as a judge, see Sharpe, "Bora Laskin."
57 (1975), 55 DLR (3d) 527.
58 Ibid., 538–9.
59 S. 2.
60 SS. 3–5.
61 S. 6.
62 SS. 7–14.
63 S. 15.
64 SS. 16–23.
65 S. 3.
66 S. 6.
67 S. 23.

68 *Re Singh and Minister of Employment and Immigration* (1985), 17 DLR (4th) 422 at 456.

69 S. 33.

70 *Andrews v. Law Society of British Columbia* (1989), 56 DLR (4th) 1.

71 RSBC 1979, c. 26, s. 42.

72 Ibid., 13, per McIntyre, J.

73 Ibid., 15.

74 Ibid., 18.

75 Ibid.

76 Ibid., 32.

77 Ibid., 39.

78 Ibid., 40.

79 *R. v. Oakes*, (1986), 26 DLR (4th) 200.

80 *R. v. Big M Drug Mart* (1985), 18 DLR (4th) 321 at 366, per Dickson, J.

81 *R. v. Oakes* at 227, per Dickson, CJC.

82 *Andrews* at 36, quoting from 27 DLR (4th) 600 at 612–3.

83 Ibid., 36.

84 SBC 1985, c. 15, s. 12.

85 *Austin v. British Columbia (Ministry of Municipal Affairs, Recreation and Culture)* (1990), 66 DLR (4th) 33.

WILLIAM KAPLAN

Who Belongs? Changing Concepts of Citizenship and Nationality

Historically, citizenship has meant membership in a nation-state and demanded allegiance as a condition for that membership. Allegiance to a membership ideal – whether national, racial, linguistic, democratic, cultural, or otherwise – was considered unique. It created a socially consequential status which demanded loyalty to one's country. Thus, not long ago citizenship was readily, if not always easily, defined. This is no longer so.[1]

The mass migrations of this century, from the Old World to the New, from developing to industrialized countries, have challenged traditional notions about citizenship, not to mention the nation-state. Borders no longer serve as barriers, and all over the world countries have been forced to consider who will be welcome and who will not. The reasons are many. As the imperial powers, most notably Britain and France, shed their overseas responsibilities, imperial subjects and citizens returned in great numbers to former mother countries to claim their "birthright." As they did, questions concerning citizenship as a common status transcending a particular sovereign state became increasingly apparent, and citizenship law was reformed to keep out the unwanted. Those European countries that invited foreigners in to work also passed laws to ensure that they did not stay or, if they did stay, to preclude their assimilation. Guest workers, and refugees, arrived by the tens of thousands, and once settled they became difficult to send home. Nevertheless, today citizenship has been extended only to a very few, and all over western Europe legal, social, and political barriers separate and often segregate in "guest worker communities" those who belong from those who do not. The latter group includes second- and third-, and sometimes fourth-, generation descendants of the original migrants. These people know no other home but have no claim to the citizenship of their birthplace. The only thing surprising in these circumstances is the relatively limited expressions of racial and other social discontent.

This phenomenon is by no means unique to Western countries. In Japan, for example, innumerable Koreans and Filipinos born and raised in Japan are denied any claim to the citizenship of their birth, of their parents' birth, and in many cases of their grandparents' birth. Their economic power is extremely limited, and lacking a vote, they have little political power. (Japanese leaders, however, have repeatedly pointed to their nation's racial homogeneity as a critical factor in that country's economic success. Likewise South Korea and Germany – two countries that are actively hostile to the integration of foreigners – are similarly prosperous, while countries ethnically and racially heterogenous to a significant degree, such as India, Nigeria, and Brazil, have been economically less successful.)

Even where citizenship itself is not in issue, difficulties in integrating outsiders arise. The "oil bust" sent millions packing from the Persian Gulf, and where guest workers remained, as in Kuwait, they did so at the price of continuing debate, antipathy, and ultimately expulsion from the receiving state. Similarly, the spectacle of thousands of Ghanaians being expelled from Nigeria in the mid-1980s indicated how insecure foreigners really are, particularly when the host state's economy is in decline. Recent experiences in Fiji and Malaysia demonstrate that even integration to the point of citizenship hardly guarantees acceptance in society. A case in point is the centuries-old experience of the Volga Germans, who are now returning "home" to Germany in droves.

"Immigration countries" such as Canada, Australia, and the United States have not been unaffected by these and other developments. Citizenship has always been relatively easy to obtain there – particularly when compared to western Europe and Japan – but liberalized access has not been problem free. Until recently, citizenship legislation in Canada, Australia, and the United States has been riddled with prejudice of one kind or another – favoritism for designated racial or ethnic groups or discrimination based on gender – and has preferred individuals from designated groups. By and large the discriminatory features of earlier acts have been repealed, but the New World must still confront the same questions faced in the Old: who is to be let in, and who is to be kept out? Contemporary debates about multiculturalism, the place of immigrants in society, and the meaning of citizenship all seek to answer this fundamental question.

Throughout the world, citizenship has become a matter of urgent public policy and growing debate. It is not hard to understand why. Behind the rhetoric, citizenship represents our aspirations for ourselves and our society. It tells us who we are and where we, as a given country, wish to go. But more so than at any other time in the past, it is a troubling concept because the world, not to mention accepted standards of justice and fair play, has so radically changed. For citizenship to continue to have meaning, we must draw a line between "them" and "us"; but how can we justify a citizenship which, for whatever reasons, discriminates between people? Citizenship laws set out the legal rules that enable us to draw a line and make a justification. But like many laws, those governing citizenship provide, at best, an unsatisfactory means for resolving a fundamental social and political question: who belongs?

CITIZENSHIP LAW

Citizenship is the status of being a citizen. In its original sense, the term referred to a member of a free or jural society (*civitas*), who possessed all the rights and privileges that could be enjoyed by any person under its constitution and government. Citizenship also encompassed the duties owed by the citizen to the society. While many societies had a concept of citizenship, it was in the Greek city-states that the status was first defined.

Athens was the best known of the Greek city-states, and it was a democracy in the sense that all citizens participated in government, as electors and as officials. However, not all persons could become citizens. Women, slaves, foreigners, and resident aliens were denied this status and enjoyed only limited membership in the community.

The status of citizenship was further refined in Rome. Citizenship was more widely granted than had been the case in the Greek city-states but was still quite restrictive. The Roman Republic distinguished between civil rights, meaning equality before the law without participation in government, and political rights, or membership in the sovereign body with full political participation. Only persons who had both civil and political rights had citizenship rights, also referred to as "freedom of the city." As the boundaries of Rome, and then the Roman Empire, expanded and grew, citizenship was extended to the conquered peoples: "It is interesting to note that initially it was citizenship as the right of membership within the City of Rome, and only subsequently did it become citizenship in the wider sense of being a member of the Empire. At that time being a citizen of Rome was not only a grant of the Empire, it was also a feeling of unity more widespread than before or since, and perhaps even equivalent to the feeling of 'nationality' ... With the break-up of the Roman Empire, and a period of several centuries of wars, invasions, and movements of whole groups of people who were subsequently to settle more permanently in relatively stable territories and become 'nations,' the status of 'citizen' disappeared."[2]

The concept was revived during the later Middle Ages and Renaissance in the sense of membership in a free town or city. It became more widespread than ever before, but the distinctions between citizens and others remained. Only citizens could participate fully in all aspects of community life. Between the sixteenth and eighteenth centuries, the free towns and cities gradually developed into the nation-states and empires of Europe, and the notion of citizenship again went into abeyance. It re-emerged at the time of the French and American revolutions.

The term "citizen" came into wide use during the French Revolution when the title "citoyen" was adopted instead of the more conventional "monsieur" and "madame." "Feeling a kinship with, and assuming a succession to the republican tradition of the Greek and Roman city-states, the leaders and supporters of the Revolutionary forces felt that this term, and its connotation in the sense of free and equal participation in government, seemed best suited to describe how the people felt about their new situation."[3] At the same time, and for quite similar reasons, the term was adopted in the newly formed United States. The American constitution speaks of "citizens" rather than "subjects" and of "citizenship" rather than "nationality," – an important change.

While "citizenship" describes a status that can be conferred, "nationality" means membership in a "nation." The latter has come to be defined not just as a political entity but also as an ethnological and sociological one. Prior to the French and American revolutions, the relationship between the individual and the state was generally signified by a personal bond of allegiance between the sovereign and the subject. The French and American revolutions fashioned republican forms of government which were ultimately derived from Lockean notions of allegiance. Locke's theories emphasized that the relationship between the people and their government was consensual and contractual.

In the same way that the French and American revolutions revived the concept of citizenship, they also introduced the idea that persons having a common language and culture formed a nation. It followed that such a nation ought to be recognized as entitled to self-government and independence. The state came to be identified with the nation, and individuals belonging to the nation owed allegiance to the state: "Thus, with the rise of the nation state and the emergence of the idea that those who lived within its boundaries were members of an 'imagined community' with collective interests grounded in a common heritage, the possession of common characteristics and the universalization of political rights, there developed a dichotomy between *national* and *alien* (or *foreigner*). The former, as citizens, were considered to have the right of residence and political participation within the nation state while the latter could enter only with the permission of the state which assumed sovereignty over the nation."[4]

Nationality, therefore, both as a legal and as a political ideal, is of modern origin,[5] as is the intermingling and synonymous use of the terms "citizenship" and "nationality." Indeed, citizens are referred to as "nationals" when they travel abroad. While "citizenship" and "nationality" are used interchangeably, they may mean different things and can describe a very different status. In the United States, for instance, all citizens are American nationals, but some American nationals, such as people born in American Samoa, are not citizens. Prior to the Civil War, many American nationals, slaves in particular, were not citizens. The examples in other national contexts are virtually endless.

The term "nationality" also belongs to public international law. In that context, it connotes the quality of being permanently within the jurisdiction of a state, whether within or without the territory of that state: "Thus the 'nationals' of a State are all those persons, natural or artificial, whom it has the right to protect abroad, with respect to whose conduct abroad it has the right to legislate, and whom it is under a duty to receive back into its territory if a foreign State desires to deport them. Thus more than one State may claim a single individual as a national. And a State may well draw distinctions between different categories of its nationals."[6]

It is a state's domestic law that determines who is a citizen and what rights and obligations flow from that status. In most legal systems, no ordinary law is higher than any other ordinary law. However, acts defining a country's citizens are generally considered of fundamental, often constitutional importance. In many cases, the rights of citizens can be found described in the constitution, with the United Kingdom being a significant exception.

Domestic law also determines the rights and obligations of aliens within a state. According to Article 1 of the Hague Convention of 1930, "It is for each state to determine under its own law who are its nationals."[7] It is generally accepted that the power to confer citizenship, and to admit and exclude aliens, is inherent in sovereignty and is essential for any political community.[8] As one commentator has observed: "Since the ideal of nationhood first fired the human imagination, a country's power to decide unilaterally who may enter its domain, under what conditions, and with what legal consequences has been regarded as an essential precondition to its independence and sovereignty."[9] Article 1 of the Hague Convention further provides that "nationality law is recognized by other states in so far as it is consistent with international conventions, international custom and the principles of law generally recognized with regard to nationality." It is fair to say that the most fundamental principle underlying all legal entitlements to citizenship is the existence of a connection with the state.[10]

Connection is established by legal title, and most nationality legislation is based on one of the following titles, or on a combination of them: (a) jus soli; (b) jus sanguinis; (c) marriage; (d) incorporation of territory; (e) option in special circumstance; (f) adoption, legitimation, and recognition of paternity; or (g) naturalization. Of these, jus soli, jus sanguinis, and naturalization are the most common methods of acquiring citizenship in a state.

Jus soli is the rule under which nationality is acquired by the mere fact of birth within the territory of the state (although by international custom, it does not apply to the birth of children of diplomatic staff, and so on, born on the territory of the receiving state). Depending on the particular country, the nationality of the parents may or may not be relevant. Jus sanguinis provides that nationality is acquired by descent wherever the child is born. Application of this rule varies considerably from one country to the next. Historically, jus sanguinis has been limited to transmission of the nationality of the father only or, where the mother was unmarried, to allow for transmission of her nationality. Most countries have now amended their domestic legislation so as to do away with this discriminatory characteristic.[11]

Naturalization also plays a major part in every citizenship system, and it is the process by which a person who was formerly an alien becomes a subject or citizen of the state. Naturalization confers on a person all political and other rights, powers, and privileges, as well as obligations, to which natural-born members of the state are entitled:[12] "Naturalization, in its more technical and restricted meaning, as a specific title to nationality, is the admission of an alien to the nationality of a state as a result of a voluntary application or a formal act on his part equivalent to such application, and normally at the complete discretion of the state. The connections invariably selected as a basis for individual naturalization are a substantial period of residence, service under the government of the naturalizing state, or exceptional public services to the state."[13] While domestic law (or municipal law, as it is sometimes called) determines state citizenship, customary international law also plays a part. For example, the International Court of Justice has said that for a nation to exercise diplomatic protection, the legal bonds of nationality must reflect a real connection between the state and the individual concerned.[14] Nationality also determines the rights and obligations of states in matters as diverse as claims made by one state against another on behalf of an individual, returnability of deportees, and treatment of aliens.

International law generally regards questions of nationality as matters for the determination of the particular state, but there are some notable qualifications. For example, domestic law may be subject to treaty obligations. The Universal Declaration of Human Rights[15], for example, provides that everyone has a right to a nationality and that no one should be arbitrarily deprived of nationality. Similarly, the International Covenant on Civil and Political Rights[16] provides that every child has the right to acquire a nationality. There are United Nations conventions on the conflict of nationality laws, and the Treaty of Rome (1958) and the European Social Charter (1961)[17] provide for freedom of movement for work and related rights. There are also provisions on nationality and freedom of movement in conventions of the International Labour Organisation and in UN and other conventions dealing with the rights of refugees and aliens. Under the UN Convention on the Nationality of Married Women,[18] a wife now has independent status with respect to her nationality, and neither marriage nor divorce automatically affects the nationality of a married woman. In addition, the UN Convention on the Reduction of Statelessness (1961)[19] requires states to grant nationality to persons born in their territory who would otherwise be stateless and the Fourth Protocol of the European Convention on Human Rights[20] provides that people are free to leave any country, including their own, and that no one may be arbitrarily deprived of the right to enter the country of which he or she is a national.

All these international conventions and agreements[21] set international standards against which nationality laws can be assessed, and along with their domestic counterparts they establish the legal means for determining who is a citizen and who is not. Citizenship status, as the plethora of citizenship legislation and international conventions suggests, is not something to be taken lightly.

WHY CARE ABOUT CITIZENSHIP?

Citizenship and nationality are clearly matters for legal definition (as well as for legal dispute), but they are also intensely political and social issues, defining as they do a person's place in the world. Citizenship decides more than the passport that a traveller carries or which state will afford protection to an individual abroad. Nationality and citizenship are related to participation in the community, democracy, access to certain types of employment, residence, land-ownership, who a people are, and what their country is all about.

Not all who possess citizenship share equally in the economic, political, and social bounty of their society. Nevertheless, it does confer certain essential rights: "People who lack security of residence, civil and political rights are prevented from participating fully in society. They do not have the opportunity of deciding to what extent they want to interact with the rest of the population, and to what extent they want to preserve their own culture and norms. The choice is pre-empted by legal disabilities, which lead to isolation, separatism and alienation. The option of becoming a citizen may not lead to equality and full participation, but it is a pre-condition for it."[22]

Citizenship has become crucial in western Europe because of the European Community and the increasing free movement of people and goods. But it is important in western Europe for another reason as well. In the 1960s and 1970s there was a huge labour migration to that area, as foreign workers arrived to do the jobs that domestic workers eschewed:

Something like 30 million people entered the Western European countries as workers or workers' dependents in the post-war period, making this one of the greatest migratory movements in human history. Many did indeed return to their countries of origin after a while, but others stayed: altogether, the population of Western Europe increased by about 10 million between 1950 and 1975 as a result of net migration ... Immigration of workers was not of course the only migratory current of Western Europe in this period. In the late forties and the fifties there was considerable overseas migration, leading to a net loss for the whole of Europe of 3 million people ... The aftermath of the Second World War and the beginning of the cold war caused large-scale refugee movements. But labour migration was the largest factor in the development of immigrant populations.[23]

Moreover, until restrictions on immigration were imposed by the former colonial powers, there was virtually unhindered access to the mother country by subjects and overseas citizens alike, and they were joined by refugees who sought haven under both domestic and international law. These mass migrations have brought the meaning and scope of citizenship sharply into focus, resulting in a battle between the political right and left over the place of "foreigners" in European society, paradoxically, just as Europe moves closer to complete economic, if not political integration.

Large-scale labour immigration to western Europe ceased in the early 1970s, but millions of "guest workers," not to mention the innumerable refugees, remained. By and large, their prospects for naturalization are rather bleak. What rights do these foreigners enjoy? They may enjoy the right of residence by virtue of their work permits, but no real political rights (notwithstanding protestations to the contrary), and so have little if any input into the political process which often affects them profoundly. Many of these "foreigners" and their organizations have been demanding (often through strikes or riots) recognition and, ultimately, participation in the community.[24] This has clearly created some pressure for reform of citizenship laws, but it does not appear to have led to any positive change.[25] It may have fostered the opposite result – fanning the fire of anti-immigrant discontent.

There are some positive signs on the horizon. The beginning of a change can be traced to a speech in Stockholm in 1974. President Urho Kekkonen of Finland expressed his nation's interest in reform, and two years later Finland gave all non-Finnish Nordics with a minimum of three years' residence in the country municipal voting rights. Sweden then gave municipal voting rights to Finnish citizens, and Denmark and Norway gave the same to all foreigners who met a three-year residency requirement. The Council of Europe and the European Conference of Ministers of Migration have both expressed interest in the development of this franchise and the new Union Treaty makes further significant advances in this direction.[26] A related development was the creation of local advisory councils, elected and appointed, in both Germany and France. These organizations theoretically represent non-citizens' interests to government. Needless to say, there is controversy about whether they "co-opt" non-citizens or foster communication and ultimately integration.[27] But all of this is just window dressing. The prize, still out of reach for many, is citizenship, whatever that might come to mean.

Very few countries, and Canada is probably the one exception of note, give permanent residents a "right" to citizenship when stated conditions are met. "Hence, decisions about naturalization are, in most states, made only when this process would be in the interest of the country."[28] In 1980, of a foreign population of 909,000 in Switzerland, only 18,100 were naturalized, or some 2 per cent. In that same year, of a foreign population of 3,500,000 in France, only 120,000 were naturalized, or some 3.4 per cent. These statistics have not changed, although the size of the "foreign" population in western Europe continues to grow.

At some point, the European countries will have to reform their laws and extend their citizenship:

The citizens of Western Europe no longer have the choice of whether they wish to live in multi-ethnic and multi-cultural societies. They already do. The issue yet to be decided is whether the ethnic minorities are going to be pushed to the margins of society by racism and discrimination, or whether they can succeed in their struggle for equality without loss of identity. Marginalization and oppression of minorities has a long and unsavoury tradition in Europe. Minorities have become scapegoats and objects for persecution during crises, oppression of minorities has paved the way for the destruction of democracy and the labour movement. The alternative – equality and self-determination of the new ethnic minorities – could enrich our cultures and give our social life a new quality. The choice is still open.[29]

In determining the direction of reform, does British experience provide any guide? Unfortunately, not very much.

In the United Kingdom, citizenship laws have recently been reformed, although the British move to jus sanguinis from jus soli leaves much to be desired. Britain may not consider itself a nation of immigrants any more than Germany does, but it has a sizeable immigrant and ethnocultural population. The decision to remove automatic acquisition of citizenship by birth caused widespread alarm within Britain's ethnic communities:

At one level the legislation has been seen as a move towards the Powellite doctrine that the accident of the place of birth gives no claim to citizenship, a concept that denotes a common historical and cultural heritage to which mere birth in the United Kingdom cannot give access. This argument is not confined to the realm of political philosophy; its clear policy implication is that it would enable the state to deport large numbers of British-born descendants of immigrants of West Indian and Asian origin, a measure that [some believe] may be necessary in the future to prevent the racial strife that they have so frequently predicted as the inevitable consequence of a multi-racial and multi-cultural society, many of whose members' ultimate loyalties are owed to another country or culture. It is hardly surprising, therefore, that legislation which appears to endorse in any way such notions has provoked the deepest anxieties amongst those who already often have good reason to doubt that they have been accepted as equal members of British society. It has also been pointed out that the Act will, in an immediate sense, discriminate between citizens on grounds of race and colour because proof of citizenship, in addition to the production of a birth certificate, is likely to be required by officials only of those who belong to a visible minority: applicants for passports, for example, may have to provide proof of the citizenship or immigration status of parents, or length of residence in the United Kingdom.[30]

At some point Britain had to close the door. That is any nation's right, and the only thing that is surprising is how long the British maintained the fiction of an imperial citizenship otherwise known as British-subject status. It is the method that they chose to redefine their citizenship that was questionable, not that they chose to do so. Creating classes of citizenship (with only some putative "citizens" having the right of British abode), which is what the United Kingdom's Parliament effectively chose to do, is antithetical to the concept itself. When those classes appear to be based on racial lines, the enterprise becomes even more questionable. The fact that British legislation still does not clearly define who is a British national and who is not illustrates the fundamentally problematic nature of the process. The fact that some British nationals are entitled to enter Britain and others are not confirms it.

The British government took the first steps toward restricting colonial migration with the Commonwealth Immigrants Act, 1962,[31] which was followed by further restrictions in the late 1960s and introduction in 1971[32] of significant limitations on the entry of dependants. France soon followed suit with restrictions on migration from Algeria and its other African ex-colonies. In general, the position of migrants from colonies or former colonies is virtually indistinguishable today from that of other foreigners. Those migrants who have obtained citizenship are obviously in a less precarious legal position than those who have not. But it would be incorrect to suggest that citizenship necessarily brings with it social, political, and economic equality, even when it brings security of residence. Ethnically and racially distinct people still find themselves victims of discrimination. "The result is frequent harassment and victimization of non-Europeans"[33] – as with Le Pen and his followers in France and the recent rise of the neo-nazis in Germany.

Changing demographics will affect the future of citizenship. In Australia, for example, the change has resulted in cries of concern that the multicultural fabric of that country threatens its identity and stability. This expression of concern has, for Canadians, a familiar ring. In the United States, the dramatic nature of the demographic change is reflected in the prediction that by 2010 white non-Hispanics will represent less than half of the American population. Nevertheless, Australia, Canada, and the United States have succeeded, where Europe has obviously failed, in better integrating newcomers within society.[34]

It is clear that there are important differences in the developments in European countries and those of the New World. Immigration is one of the national myths of Australia and the United States (and Canada to a somewhat lesser extent), helping to forge a common identity; similarly, citizenship is seen as a logical evolution in the process of nationhood. Nevertheless, some have expressed concern that extension of citizenship has helped diminish a national sense of community.

The case is made that if a state makes no distinction between citizens and non-citizens, then citizenship will become meaningless, and some suggest that erosion of differences has led to exactly that result. In typical US presidential elections, for instance, only 50–60 per cent of those eligible to vote actually do so. In western Europe, approximately 80–90 per cent of citizens vote in elections. Do these statistics tell us anything about the value of citizenship in Europe as compared to the United States? Probably not much. More telling are the statistics indicating that US naturalization rates are falling:

The precise causes of so many aliens' lack of interest in naturalizing remains uncertain. Doubtless, some of it reflects many aliens' continuing hope to return to their native lands to live. This hope is a realistic one for many individuals, like Mexicans, whose countries are nearby and whose domestic policies are relatively stable. For others, such as Cambodians and Vietnamese who have migrated great distances and whose homelands are firmly controlled by brutal regimes, that hope – the so-called "myth of return" – is unlikely to be fulfilled. The reluctance to acquire American citizenship may also reflect property restrictions and other disadvantages to which those who naturalize here and thus renounce their foreign nationalities might be subjected were they to return to their native lands. Finally, INS backlogs and administrative priorities have impeded some naturalization.

To these well-understood motives for resisting American citizenship, another less-discussed one may be added: the courts, by interpreting the equality and due process principles more expansively, have substantially reduced the value of citizenship to legal resident aliens. Today, the marginal benefits to most aliens of moving from legal resident status to full membership are slight. Indeed they have never been smaller.[35]

Historically, there has also been a low rate of naturalization in Australia by British subjects. Since there was no advantage to be gained by becoming an Australian, many of these privileged settlers chose not to. The law was subsequently changed to establish advantages to citizenship, but British subjects already resident were protected by a "grandfather" clause. In Canada, dual citizenship is explicitly permitted, and (especially given the country's liberal naturalization regime) Canada has one of the highest naturalization rates in the world. There is everything to be gained and absolutely nothing to be lost in becoming a Canadian citizen.

Whatever the cause, there are obvious dangers to a society's devaluing of citizenship, particularly in multicultural, polyglot nations such as Canada and the United States and in emerging multicultural societies such as Australia. Race, religion, ethnicity, and gender are characteristics not easily changed. "Citizenship, in contrast, is a status that can enable us to transcend these more enduring differences and achieve some common ground. If citizenship is to perform this special office, it must be accessible to all. But if it becomes too readily accessible, it may lose much of its capacity to bind us together in a meaningful, emotionally satisfying community."[36] If the differences between citizenship and resident-alien status disappear, or are rendered meaningless, the same result is likely. There are also real dangers in emphasizing difference. For the European countries under review – not to mention Japan, with its premise that citizenship is for those of the Japanese race – excluding large numbers of people from citizenship denies newcomers and long-term residents this "transcendental status" and segregates them on the basis of ethnicity and race. It splits society between those who belong and those who do not. The strong assimilationist thrust of both German and French naturalization laws, for those lucky enough to qualify, clearly distinguishes "them" from "us".

Contemporary debates about citizenship raise difficult questions about access and meaning. Exclusionists argue that for citizenship to have meaning, access must be restricted and citizenship must grant citizens rights not enjoyed by others. Inclusionists argue that citizenship should be open if not free and that all members of society, whether citizens or not, should be treated the same.

In many countries, the vast array of social programs characteristic of the welfare state are offered equally to citizen and non-citizen alike. Likewise, there are in western Europe, Canada, the United States, and Australia limited economic restrictions on permanent residents, with some citizenship requirements for public-service employment being among the few. There have been other pressures on traditional notions of citizenship in recent years. Multiculturalism may be a term invented in Canada, but its proponents are world-wide and share a common belief in and allegiance to pluralism as the mainstay of democracy.[37] These inclusionists reject categorically ideas about assimilation as a necessary pre-condition to citizenship. Communitarian and egalitarian notions about justice have also gained ground. "Is it 'just' to treat people differently because of their place of birth?" is the question often asked:

Men and women are either subject to the state's authority, or they are not; and if they are subject, they must be given a say, and ultimately an equal say, in what that authority does ... No community can be half-metic,[38] half-citizen and claim that its admissions policies are acts of self-determination or that its politics is democratic.

The determination of aliens and guests by an exclusive band of citizens (or of slaves by masters, or women by men, or blacks by whites or conquered peoples by their conquerors) is not communal freedom but oppression. The citizens are free, of course, to set up a club, make membership as exclusive as they like, write a constitution, and govern one another. But they can't claim territorial jurisdiction and rule over the people with whom they share the territory. To do this is to act outside their sphere, beyond their rights. It is a form of tyranny. Indeed, the rule of citizens over non-citizens, of members over strangers, is probably the most common form of tyranny in human history ... The denial of membership is always the first of a long train of abuses. There is no way to break the train, so we must deny the rightful-ness of the denial. The theory of distributive justice begins, then, with an ac-count of membership rights. It must vindicate at one and the same time the (limited) right of closure, without which there could be no communities at all, and the political inclusiveness of the existing communities. For it is only as members somewhere that men and women can hope to share in all the other social goods – security, wealth, honour, office and power – that com-munal life makes possible.[39]

WHAT IS TO BE DONE?

Whether or not it is just to treat people differently, all over the world, people have questioned the numbers of immigrants and their ability to adapt. It does not matter whether the country encourages immigration and citizenship or not.

By and large, however, the New World welcomes immigrants and has over the years systematically dismantled barriers to citizenship which stood in the way of equal participation, at least in theory. This is hardly the case in many other countries. Immigrants, and migrants, even those who have obtained citizenship, are still, to a considerable extent, treated as second class. Obviously, the roots of this problem run deeper than a determination of legal entitlement to citizenship. Cultural and linguistic barriers, not to mention the two evils of nationalism and racism, as well as institutional and systemic discrimination, inhibit full community participation, even for those with citizenship papers. The fact that citizenship is generally exclusive only exacerbates the problem, which is the presence of a huge underclass of visible minorities, many of whom are foreign workers, few of whom have any realistic hope of integration in the country that they consider home. In this context, citizenship based on jus sanguinis alone is hopelessly out of date and a recipe for little more than statelessness through the generations.

However, can jus soli serve as a title, in and of itself, to citizenship? Just because someone is born in a country, why should they become a citizen if they have no other connection to it?

In Texas towns along the American-Mexican border, women frequently appear at the local public hospitals just as they are about to give birth. Their child is an American, and soon after birth mother and child return to Mexico. The child is also a Mexican, but one, if he or she wishes, with an American future. "Do these children really have links to the American political community? What differentiates them from the Mexican children, not born in the United States, with whom they grow up? What principles of citizenship and community can lie behind the rule of automatic birthright citizenship to anyone born in the United States? Are these principles and concepts ones that Americans should continue to endorse?"[40] However, for the "guest workers" in Germany, citizenship at birth is seen as an indispensable part of political integration, and its absence promises to create an underclass of workers who will never be allowed to participate fully in German economic, political, and social life. The same can be said with respect to migrants in other countries where citizenship status clearly matters. But the fact remains that citizenship does not make a big difference everywhere. Indeed, the concept itself is under attack.

Has globalization transformed the meaning of citizenship? Have the rise of collective security, free trade, GATT, environmental protection, and economic interdependence, not to mention the end of the Cold War, and perhaps of history, changed it permanently? The internationalists argue that in the late twentieth century, the nation-state and its citizenship are anachronistic. They proudly proclaim that we are all citizens of the world. Moreover, and more to the point, they believe that in many cases citizenship means only the right to vote and to be considered first for some government jobs. Has citizenship as a concept outlived its usefulness? Is it out of step with the times?

Assuming these arguments to be valid, how does one reconcile national and global responsibilities? Even more problematic is the resolution of conflicts between national and international interests.[41]

"World citizenship," whatever that might mean, is hardly an idea whose time has arrived, much less one that has been satisfactorily defined. If it is difficult for the citizens of one nation to articulate a national identity, what are the prospects for a global identity? The experience of the British, who redefined and reconceptualized their status from subjects to de facto citizens illustrates the difficulties involved in articulating a national identity in a multinational state. From a broader perspective, articulating an identity in a global state would likely be impossible.[42] The legislative process leading to Britain's 1981 act is noteworthy if only for the absence of any soul-searching about who the British were and what they wanted their society to be all about. But then again, maybe it was so obvious that it did not need mention.

Nationalism is clearly enduring. One has only to look at the emerging nations of eastern Europe for evidence of the strength and depth of national feeling. Quebec is another case in point. There are many values that all people share, and historically one means of expression of these values has been allegiance to a state represented by citizenship in that state. Citizenship, however, means different things for different people: "What does citizenship mean for Christians and Moslems in Lebanon, for Blacks in South Africa, for Jews and dissidents in the Soviet Union, for ethnic and language groups in India, Sri Lanka, China or Nigeria, for new immigrants to the United States?"[43] Clearly, it means something different to everyone, and to some people it means nothing at all.

DOES CITIZENSHIP HAVE A FUTURE?

Fundamentalists defend the traditional model of the nation-state, stressing in particular the idea that state-membership presupposes nation-membership. Multicultural pluralists, on the other hand, deny any validity to this model, arguing for new forms of political membership that would mirror an emerging postnational society. Fundamentalists demand of immigrants either naturalization, stringently conditioned upon assimilation, or departure; multicultural pluralists demand for immigrants a full citizenship stripped of its sacred character and divorced from all nationality. Neither position is particularly nuanced. Fundamentalists treat the nation-state as something frozen in social and political time; theirs is a profoundly anachronistic interpretation. Multicultural pluralists, in their haste to condemn the nation-state to the dustbin of history, underestimate the richness and complexity of the nation-state model. If suitably reinterpreted to take account of the changing economic, military, and democratic contexts of membership, the nation-state model may have life in it yet.[44]

Citizenship will endure and probably will not change significantly. To be sure, there is no stopping globalization. But there appear to be spatial limits to the human capacity for communal spirit, and the lines are logically drawn at the nation-state. People need refuge from universalizing impulses, such as GATT, the Canada–United States Free Trade Agreement, Europe 1992, and the United Nations, and for the most part they find a haven in family, friends, religion, and ethnic and social organizations. But national citizenship has an important role to play, for it can provide a "focus of political allegiance and emotional energy on a scale capable of satisfying deep human longings for solidarity, symbolic identification, and community."[45]

The law is an unsatisfactory tool for many things, including determination of who "belongs." If citizenship is to endure – and all indications are that it will – lines will continue to be drawn. How this is to be done must be answered by every nation in its own way. The major challenge for many countries will be to transform their long-settled immigrants and residents and their illegal aliens and guest workers – their "foreigners" of many stripes – into full and equal members of the community. Social justice and common sense demand no less, but it would be a mistake to think that granting citizenship is the end of that success – it is quite clearly only the beginning.

Citizenship is important, although perhaps for different reasons than those traditionally given: "Citizenship can be considered as a resource in the continual bargaining that characterizes all social processes. It is one of many sources of power, but differs from other sources, such as social class or social status, in that, theoretically at least, it does not divide the society. Again, theoretically, it recognizes all under a common definition of citizen."[46] Citizenship is a status that can be shared. Moreover, it is the one status in the modern world that can allow everyone in a community to participate individually, collectively, and equally in national projects that transcend race, religion, language, ethnicity, and region. Citizenship can be a unifying force – for everyone in a society. Instead of keeping people out, citizenship, reconceptualized in this way, must seek to bring people in. The people who live and work in a country are people who are entitled to belong and participate if they wish. Citizenship and citizenship laws must continue to draw lines, but in doing so they must ensure that everyone has an equal right to participate and, ultimately, to belong.

NOTES

1 I would like to acknowledge, with thanks, the assistance of Chi Carmody in the research of this paper.
2 This section is based on *Citizenship* (Citizenship Registration Branch, Secretary of State, April 1984.) For a sociological, historical, political, and theoretical history of citizenship see D. Heater, *Citizenship: The Civic Ideal in World History, Politics and Education* (London: Longman, 1990) 1–2. See also F.H. Cramer, "The Evolution of Citizenship," *Current History* 13 no. 74 (1947) 193.
3 Heater, *Citizenship*, 2.
4 R. Miles, "Nationality, Citizenship, and Migration to Britain, 1945–1951" *Journal of Law and Society* 16 no. 4 (1989) 428.
5 This section is in part derived from J.M. Jones, *British Nationality Law* (Oxford: Clarendon Press, 1965).
6 C. Parry, *British Nationality* (London: Stevens & Sons, 1951), 4.
7 Convention on Certain Questions Relating to the Conflict of Nationality Laws, 12 April 1930, Can. TS 1937 No. 7 (hereinafter the Hague Convention).
8 For a contrary view, see J.H. Carens, "Aliens and Citizens: The Case for Open Borders," *Review of Politics* 48 (1986) 251–73.
9 P.H. Schuck, "The Transformation of Immigration Law," *Columbia Law Review* 84 (1984) 1.
10 An alien, therefore, is a subject or national of one state resident in another state.
11 The same can be said with respect to laws granting the nationality of a husband to his foreign-born wife, but not the nationality of a wife to her foreign-born husband, although here the general tendency has been to remove marriage as an automatic title to nationality.
12 On the status of aliens in Canada see I.L. Head, "The Stranger in Our Midst: A Sketch of the Legal Status of the Alien in Canada," *Canadian Yearbook of International Law* (1964) 107.
13 Jones, *British Nationality Law*, 16. Collective naturalization is also known to the law, whereby a state naturalizes a group of aliens. See ibid., 25.
14 See *Nottebohm Case (Preliminary Objection) (Liechtenstein v. Guatemala)*, [1955] *I.C.J. Rep* 4.

15 10 December 1948, U.N. Doc. A/811.

16 16 December 1966, Can. T.S. 1976 No. 47, 999 U.N.T.S. 171.

17 18 October 1961, 529 U.N.T.S. 89, Europ. T.S. No. 35.

18 20 February 1957, 309 U.N.T.S. 65.

19 30 August 1961, 989 U.N.T.S. 175.

20 Protocol 4, Securing Certain Rights and Freedoms Other Than Those Included in the Convention and in Protocol 1, 16 September 1963, Europ. T.S. No. 46.

21 See generally P. Weis, *Nationality and Statelessness in International Law* (Alphen aan den Rÿn, Netherlands: Sijthoff and Noordhoff, 1979).

22 S. Castles, *Here for Good: Western Europe's New Ethnic Minorities* (London: Pluto Press, 1984), 161.

23 Ibid., 1–2.

24 See generally P.G. Brown and H. Shue, eds., *Boundaries: National Autonomy and Its Limits* (Totowa, NJ: Rowman & Littlefield, 1981).

25 See M.J. Miller, *Foreign Workers in Western Europe: An Emerging Political Force* (New York: Praeger, 1981).

26 New Zealand gives voting rights to immigrants.

27 See generally M.J. Miller, "Political Participation and Representation of Noncitizens," in W.R. Brubaker, ed., *Immigration and the Politics of Citizenship in Europe and North America* (Lanham: German Marshall Fund of the United States, 1989), 129.

28 T. Hammar, "Dual Citizenship and Political Integration" *International Migration Review* 19 (1985) 440.

29 Castles, *Here for Good*, 229.

30 J.M. Evans, *Immigration Law* (London: Sweet & Maxwell, 1983), 79.

31 10 & 11 Eliz. II, c. 21.

32 Immigration Act (U.K.), 1971, c. 77.

33 Castles, *Here for Good*, 93.

34 It may be easy to integrate newcomers when there is little to integrate them into. Fitting "foreigners" into centuries-old societies is completely different, some would claim, and the very difficulty of integration arguably infuses citizenship with meaning for newcomers and the community alike.

35 P.H. Schuck, "Membership in the Liberal Polity: The Devaluation of American Citizenship," in Brubaker, ed., *Immigration*, 57.

36 Ibid., 62.

37 As do many opponents of official government-funded multiculturalism.

38 This is a reference to the Athenian metics who served as "guest workers" in ancient Athens. While they and their descendants were denied political rights, metics were required to share some of the other responsibilities of citizenship, such as defence of the city. The analogy with the "guest workers" of modern Europe is self-evident.

39 M. Walzer, *Spheres of Justice: A Defense of Pluralism* (New York: Basic Books, 1983), 61.

40 J.H. Carens, "Who Belongs? Theoretical and Legal Questions about Birthright Citizenship in the United States," *University of Toronto Law Journal* 37 (1987) 413.

41 See Council for the Advancement of Citizenship, *The Meaning of Citizenship* (Washington, DC: Council, 1990), 15.

42 See L.C. Green, "Is World Citizenship a Legal Practicality?" *Canadian Year Book of International Law* (1987) 151.

43 R.F. Butts, "Civic Education in an Interdependent World" in Council for the Advancement of Citizenship, *The Meaning of Citizenship*, 8.

44 Brubaker, ed., *Immigration*, 6.

45 Schuck, "Membership," 65.

46 A.P. Maingot, "Ideology, Politics, and Citizenship in the American Debate on Immigration Policy: Beyond Consensus," in M. Kirtz, ed., *US Immigration and Refugee Policy* (Lexington, Mass.: Lexington Books, 1983), 369.

MICHAEL A. WALKER

The Costs and Benefits of Being Canadian

The title of this essay conveys an impression of both consummate arrogance and complete hopelessness. Fortunately, having had the title imposed on me, I can, with some comfort, note that the arrogance is not mine. The concept of costs and benefits, when applied in the current circumstances, yields, however, an infinite variety of outcomes, corresponding to the unlimited imaginations of Canadians who re-create this type of analysis every day.

An assessment of the costs of being Canadian might dwell on the harsh climate or the long distances that separate our centres of population and our economic resources. Or it might focus on the fact that our attempts to deal with climate and distance and the desire, in spite of these, to make a nation have, together with the fact that many of our ancestors emanated from the environs of Glasgow, Scotland, left us with a predilection for impracticality. Our constitutional arrangements are a manifestation of that weakness.

A calculation of benefits might include the ability to travel in this immense nation without the necessity of sharing intimate personal details with an aneuronic customs official. We can experience the sunset in the Bay of Islands or the sunrise on the Bras d'Or Lakes, Saskatoon in September, the Gatineau in sugaring-off time, the glacial outcroppings in the Rockies, and the incomparable serenity of a forest in British Columbia. (Following further research, later versions of the essay will also contain a reference to a pleasant experience in Ontario.)

This essay will not attempt to assemble a list of costs and benefits of this kind.

The question of costs and benefits of current arrangements also begs the interesting question of "compared to what?" – that is to say, compared to being an American, for example, or Japanese, or even a citizen of ROC (the rest of Canada), in the event that Canada's current structure should be changed by the exit of one or more of the constituent provinces.

The fact that the core of the current unrest in Canada is about the system of government embedded in our constitution suggests that the appropriate focus of the first section of this essay is the costs and benefits associated with our governmental arrangements. Constitutions are about the relationship between the individual and the state. The state is a manifestation of the desire of individuals to co-operate for the pursuit of certain objectives which, if obtained, will improve their lives, but which they cannot attain alone. The achievement of these benefits entails certain costs which individuals bear. This essay assesses the net benefit, if any, generated by the relationship between Canadians as individuals and the state through the apparatus of government.

The Canadian constitution has the additional twist that it sets down the relations among the semi-autonomous provinces and their relationship to the federal government. It seems sensible also, therefore, to question the net benefits or costs associated with that relationship. That is, how do provinces as distinct entities bear costs or receive benefits from the constitutional arrangements into which they have entered? This essay analyses the costs and benefits for provincial groupings in their dealings through the federal government.

The second section of this essay deals with the relationship between the individual and the Canadian state in its various governmental manifestations. The cost, at least the measurable tax cost, of that relationship is calculated, and its distribution among the population is shown. I also calculate the benefits received by Canadians from the various levels of government, either directly in the form of transfer payments or indirectly in the form of public services or expenditures on infrastructure. I also present a net-benefit distribution within the population according to means.

The third section of the essay presents the distribution of taxes and net benefits by province and offers a net-fiscal-balance calculation showing those provinces that are net losers and those that are net winners in the distribution of costs and benefits among the provinces.

THE COSTS AND BENEFITS OF BEING CANADIAN

In this section we calculate the costs and benefits faced and enjoyed by Canadians. The unit of analysis is the average-income family.

The (Tax) Costs of Being Canadian

"The art of taxation consists in so plucking the goose as to elicit the least amount of hissing" (Jean Colbert, minister of finance to Louis xiv of France). Under the Canadian constitution, the federal government and the provincial governments are essentially given unlimited powers of taxation. The British North America Act, the immediate predecessor of the Constitution Act, limited the provinces to collecting taxes paid directly by the person being taxed – so-called direct taxes. But because of the broad judicial interpretation given to the meaning of "direct," the provinces have been able to levy all sorts of taxes except import duties and taxes on sales that cross provincial borders. Given the unlimited scope for taxation and the hundred years of ingenuity that have elapsed, Canada now has a very complicated tax system.[1] The average Canadian family faces some twenty-two different categories of tax and a much larger number of individual kinds of taxes.

Table 1 outlines these taxes by province. In addition to income taxes and sales taxes, the average family also faces liquor, tobacco, amusement, and other excise taxes, auto fuel and motor vehicle licence taxes, social security, pension, medical, and hospital taxes, natural resource taxes of various kinds, as well as import duties and twelve other categories of tax ranging from dog licence fees through municipal business licence fees through to other federal excise taxes. Social security, pension, medical, and hospital taxes include things such as Canada Pension Plan payments and unemployment insurance payments, as well as medical insurance levies in certain provinces.

Natural resource taxes are paid by Canadians in some provinces because of the peculiar ownership arrangements that exist with regard to natural resources. Natural resources are deemed to belong to the crown – that is, the government – on behalf of the people. Fees and payments collected from users of natural resources such as oil royalties or stumpage fees, in the case of forestry, or of water rights, in the case of hydro-electric facilities, are collected by the crown on behalf of the people. Strictly speaking, these revenues belong to the people, not to the government, and under an alternative set of arrangements these payments would be collected by the crown and dispersed to the population, reflecting its ownership. The government could then collect a portion of this income through the tax system for support of public programs. In Canada these resource revenues are collected directly into the treasury without the prior laundering of them through the hands of the resource owners, and this hides the extent of taxation being levied. In my calculations I ex-

Table 1
Taxes ($) of the average Canadian family, 1991*

Province	Average cash income	Profits tax	Income tax	Sales tax	Liquor, tobacco, amusement, and other excise taxes	Auto, fuel, and motor vehicle licence taxes	Social security, pension, medical, and hospital taxes	Property tax	Natural resources taxes	Import duties	Other taxes	Total taxes
Nfld	44,500	883	5,667	4,097	1,134	656	2,107	917	188	275	674	16,598
PEI	42,000	885	5,991	3,278	1,300	674	1,941	981	18	272	171	15,512
NS	45,500	1,321	7,389	3,468	1,211	612	2,440	1,426	28	333	445	18,672
NB	45,000	1,412	6,757	3,765	1,176	749	2,316	1,830	240	307	217	18,769
Que.	45,500	1,461	7,371	3,572	789	602	3,714	1,823	36	332	527	20,226
Ont.	59,500	1,993	11,890	4,168	1,252	740	4,467	2,554	83	476	972	28,595
Man.	45,500	1,674	5,994	2,715	1,149	569	2,182	2,772	277	327	416	18,074
Sask.	48,500	1,665	7,708	3,480	1,347	832	2,256	2,101	1,057	365	586	21,397
Alta	51,000	1,753	8,622	1,613	1,427	723	3,208	2,189	3,446	395	430	23,807
BC	50,500	1,635	8,613	3,182	1,328	606	3,188	1,956	880	380	575	22,342
Canada	52,000	1,649	9,263	3,538	1,149	677	3,679	2,090	544	395	661	23,645

Sources: Statistics Canada data on taxes and income; federal and provincial government budgets and estimates; and Fraser Institute Canadian Tax Simulator (CANTASIM).

* Preliminary estimates.

Table 2
Tax rates as percentage of cash income, 1991

Nfld	37.3
PEI	36.9
NS	41.0
NB	41.7
Que.	44.5
Ont.	48.1
Man.	39.7
Sask.	44.1
Alta	46.7
BC	44.2
Canada	45.5
Without resources	
Sask.	41.9
Alta	39.9
BC	42.5
Canada	44.4

plicitly allocate to Canadians the natural resource revenues that are their due and regard their extraction from them, even though indirectly, as a tax.

I include taxes on profits in the calculation because corporations, strictly speaking, can bear no tax. Only people who own, work for, or buy from a corporation can meaningfully bear the tax burden assessed on the corporation. I therefore calculate the profit taxes paid by Canadians when these taxes are levied on corporations. Profit taxes are deemed here to be paid by those who are recipients of income from capital, and this includes a surprising array of Canadians who typically would not regard themselves as capitalists, including many trade unionists whose pension funds hold the shares of Canadian corporations.

Who Bears the Tax Cost of Being Canadian?

Table 1 reveals wide variation in families' average income in Canada, from a low of $42,000 in Prince Edward Island to a high of $59,500 in Ontario. This range in incomes, together with different provincial sales and income taxes, produces extensive variation in the tax bill paid by the average-income family in each province – from $15,512 in Prince Edward Island to $28,595 in Ontario. Table 2 displays tax rates as a percentage of cash income for 1991, and this

Table 3
Decile distribution (%) of taxes by province, 1990

	Lower-income groups			Middle-income groups				Upper-income groups		
	1st	2nd	3rd	4th	5th	6th	7th	8th	9th	10th
Nfld	0.6	1.7	3.4	4.6	6.7	9.3	11.8	13.8	23.0	25.0
PEI	0.7	1.9	3.3	4.0	6.7	8.3	10.9	14.6	20.8	29.0
NS	0.6	1.3	2.9	4.5	6.7	9.6	12.0	14.3	24.1	24.1
NB	0.6	1.6	3.2	4.9	6.8	9.2	11.2	14.1	23.5	25.0
Que.	0.4	1.2	2.7	4.6	6.9	8.9	11.7	15.3	24.2	24.1
Ont.	0.6	2.1	4.3	5.7	8.1	9.7	14.3	18.5	18.5	18.2
Man.	0.4	1.8	3.3	5.0	6.9	8.9	11.7	15.4	23.3	23.3
Sask.	0.5	1.9	3.0	4.8	6.8	8.5	11.6	14.0	24.4	24.5
Alta	0.4	2.3	4.0	6.0	7.8	9.4	10.9	17.4	20.9	20.9
BC	0.8	1.9	3.6	5.3	7.7	9.7	11.5	17.5	21.1	20.9
Canada	0.5	1.6	3.3	5.5	7.3	9.4	11.5	18.5	21.2	21.2

Source: Fraser Institute Canadian Tax Simulator (CANTASIM).

reveals a similar pattern – from 36.9 per cent in Prince Edward Island to 48.1 per cent in Ontario.

Table 3 indicates how the tax burden is distributed among income groups. The lowest 10 per cent of the Canadian family income distribution bore 0.5 per cent of the tax burden in 1990 (the most recent calculations available). Generally speaking, the tax burden is borne proportionally more by higher-income groups than by lower-income groups, with some variation among provinces in the degree of progressivity. Progressivity is strongest in provinces with the lowest average incomes. For example, in Prince Edward Island fully 29 per cent of the total tax burden is carried by the top 10 per cent of income earners.

Table 4 shows the tax rate faced by individuals in different income groups in the various provinces. This table uses not the cash income concept of Table 1 but a theoretical income measure, total income before tax, the calculation of which is provided in the Fraser Institute's volume Tax Facts 7. (The results, therefore, are not comparable with those in Table 2.) These tax rates reveal that overall progressivity beyond the middle-income group is not very pronounced, except in some lower-income provinces.

Evidently the tax cost of being Canadian is that you surrender a very significant fraction of your total income to government and you begin to do so at a relatively low level of income. While it would take me beyond the scope of this essay to delve deeply into the mat-

Table 4
Tax rate (%) by decile by province, 1990

	Lower-income groups			Middle-income groups				Upper-income groups		
	1st	2nd	3rd	4th	5th	6th	7th	8th	9th	10th
Nfld	8.2	12.9	18.5	20.9	24.6	27.0	30.2	31.0	34.8	35.3
PEI	10.9	15.2	19.6	20.4	24.9	25.0	26.2	28.6	29.5	31.0
NS	10.4	12.4	18.3	22.1	26.2	28.8	31.2	31.9	33.5	33.5
NB	9.5	14.6	19.7	23.0	25.5	27.7	29.7	31.0	32.8	33.0
Que.	8.9	13.7	19.3	24.5	28.2	30.1	32.0	33.1	35.1	35.1
Ont.	13.4	21.1	27.0	29.1	31.9	33.1	32.8	33.3	33.3	33.3
Man.	8.0	15.3	19.9	23.3	26.0	26.9	29.6	29.0	29.7	29.7
Sask.	14.7	14.7	17.9	21.0	23.2	25.4	27.4	27.8	27.5	27.5
Alta	11.3	21.1	26.0	30.0	30.6	30.8	32.5	31.5	31.6	31.6
BC	17.1	19.3	24.4	27.7	31.3	32.1	32.7	33.0	33.3	33.3
Canada	10.9	17.2	22.6	27.5	29.4	31.4	32.3	32.9	33.2	33.2

Source: Fraser Institute Canadian Tax Simulator (CANTASIM).
Income measure = total income before tax.

ter, it is also the case that Canadian taxes are high by comparison with other countries. The interested reader can pursue this in the *OECD* special-country study on France (1991), which compares Canada's tax burden with other countries.

Other Taxes

This tax picture is incomplete from a number of points of view. First, it ignores deferred taxation – the extent to which governments are incurring obligations that imply future taxes. Governments do so by incurring deficits that enable them to convey benefits to current electors while not confronting those electors with the cost of providing these benefits. Table 5 repeats information of Table 2 but adjusts for deferred taxation in the form of deficit spending and thus shows that the 1991 tax rate is considerably higher than it appears. The total average Canadian tax rate in 1991, excluding the deficit, was 45.5 per cent. Including it boosts the rate to 53.9 per cent of cash income.

There are in addition a wide range of regulatory taxes. The most obvious is a prohibition against imports which raises the Canadian price of products. As widespread discussion of the General Agreement on Tariffs and Trade (GATT) negotiations regarding agriculture has made clear, Canadians pay a high price for the system of marketing boards which artificially raise the price of agricultural

Table 5
Tax rates as percentage of cash income, 1991,
adjusted for deferred taxes

Province	Tax rates as percentage of cash income	Tax rate, including deferred taxes, as percentage of cash income
Nfld	37.3	44.9
PEI	36.9	42.1
NS	41.0	50.4
NB	41.7	49.5
Que.	44.5	51.9
Ont.	48.1	58.5
Man.	39.7	46.9
Sask.	44.1	50.6
Alta	46.7	52.1
BC	44.2	51.6
Canada	45.5	53.9

products and keep foreign-produced products out of the Canadian marketplace. Regulations on foreign ownership which are imposed in some provinces and generally through the activities of Investment Canada continue to depress the price of Canadian assets and therefore impose a tax on capital owners in Canada. The exclusion of alcoholic beverages, beer in particular, from the free trade agreement with the United States is imposing taxes on Canadian alcohol users, in addition to the large quantity of taxes already collected, in the form of higher prices.

Generally speaking, regulations are designed to impose a tax on one group of Canadians in order to convey a benefit to another group. The fact that this tax and that benefit are not explicitly accounted for and do not therefore have to be enumerated in the budgeting process makes them often a politically preferred route to assign costs and distribute benefits. Moreover, the precise costs associated with these regulations are difficult to measure, and no measurement of them is included in the total tax cost used in this paper.

THE BENEFITS OF BEING CANADIAN

The taxes collected by all three levels of government are spent on many programs and activities. I have gathered these into fifteen categories, and Table 6 shows the total amount spent by all govern-

Table 6
Total government spending ($ million), by function

Function	1970	1975	1980	1985	1988
Culture and recreation	584.2	1,797.2	3,101.6	4,627.8	5,341.4
Education	5,894.3	10,393.0	17,906.9	27,383.9	31,294.6
General services	1,973.4	4,447.6	8,782.8	13,073.7	15,605.9
Health	4,227.9	9,486.1	16,625.8	29,132.9	36,558.0
Housing	366.0	928.5	1,792.8	2,575.7	2,947.0
Interest charges	2,617.7	5,729.7	14,161.3	39,798.4	49,408.7
Labour	407.9	942.4	1,619.5	2,775.8	3,765.3
Natural resources	1,089.6	2,983.6	5,254.1	9,647.9	11,018.9
Oil and gas	4.9	1,686.2	4,625.6	4,123.8	1,757.4
Other	435.3	1,372.5	2,595.6	6,651.1	5,927.1
Protection	3,121.6	5,802.7	10,472.6	18,275.4	21,640.2
Research establishments	395.2	526.6	1,137.2	1,340.4	1,344.9
Social security	5,836.1	16,177.4	28,113.4	51,688.4	60,890.5
Trade and industry	1,162.6	2,894.5	4,649.9	7,889.6	10,179.2
Transportation and communication	2,802.0	5,834.5	9,201.7	12,273.2	13,669.5
Total	30,918.8	71,002.6	130,040.9	231,258.0	271,348.5

ments for a number of years. The most recent year for which complete data are available is 1988.

Social security accounted for $60.8 billion, or 22.4 per cent, of total government spending. Interest payments absorb $49.4 billion – 18.2 per cent of the total. Health is next, at $36.5 billion, or 13.5 per cent, followed by education and by protection of persons and property, at 11.5 and 8.0 per cent, respectively. The relative composition of spending and how it is has changed over time may be seen in Table 7.

Who benefits from all this spending? Or, more precisely, on whose behalf are these expenditures made?

Benefits v. Spending

There is a distinction to be made between benefits and spending; they are not, strictly speaking, interchangeable. We can, by an analytical process, estimate particular expenditures made on behalf of particular people. For example, we find in Table 8 that families with incomes between $25,000 and $30,000 were engaged in educational programs that resulted in expenditures amounting to $2.442 billion. So we can say that this $2.442-billion expenditure was made on behalf of those individuals in that income class. Whether or not the individuals benefited from that expenditure is difficult to say. The expenditures were not made in a voluntary, individual market-purchase arrangement where the individual making the purchase could reasonably have selected alternative services. The supplier, for the most part, received the funding for the expenditure directly from the treasury and was not, therefore, required to win the support of "customers" in the normal way. Thus the benefit created may have been less, the same, or greater than the amount of spending. (This is apart from the question of cost of service delivered, which might also affect the calculation. For example, could the educational service be provided at lower cost? If so, the total spending on education includes some benefit creation and some waste.) The same is true of most government expenditures. They are made on behalf of individuals or on behalf of achieving a certain objective without there being any direct way of ascertaining the utility that individuals derive from the expenditure.

In the statistical analysis used to produce the allocations in this paper, I have attempted to allocate expenditures according to a number of criteria, as reported in *Government Spending Facts*, which I wrote with Isabella Horry for the Fraser Institute in 1991. The criteria are too extensive to report here. In some instances I can do no

Table 7
Composition (%) of total government spending

Function	1970	1975	1980	1985	1988
Culture and recreation	1.9	2.5	2.4	2.0	2.0
Education	19.1	14.6	13.8	11.8	11.5
General services	6.4	6.3	6.8	5.7	5.8
Health	13.7	13.4	12.8	12.6	13.5
Housing	1.2	1.3	1.4	1.1	1.1
Interest charges	8.5	8.1	10.9	17.2	18.2
Labour	1.3	1.3	1.2	1.2	1.4
Natural resources	3.5	4.2	4.0	4.2	4.1
Oil and gas	0.0	2.4	3.6	1.8	0.6
Other	1.4	1.9	2.0	2.9	2.2
Protection	10.1	8.2	8.1	7.9	8.0
Research establishments	1.3	0.7	0.9	0.6	0.5
Social security	18.9	22.8	21.6	22.4	22.4
Trade and industry	3.8	4.1	3.6	3.4	3.8
Transportation and communication	9.1	8.2	7.1	5.3	5.0
Total	100.0	100.0	100.0	100.0	100.0

Table 8
Total government spending ($ million) by function, by income group ($ 000), 1988

Function	10	10–15	15–20	20–25	25–30	30–35	35–40	40–50	50+	Total
Culture and recreation	105	190	280	285	412	472	446	847	2,304	5,341
Education	799	1,620	1,686	2,011	2,443	2,836	2,795	5,177	11,928	31,295
General services	1,817	1,505	1,455	1,312	1,184	1,169	1,127	1,845	4,193	15,606
Health	1,658	1,996	2,203	2,795	3,029	2,498	3,711	6,640	12,028	36,558
Housing	324	410	402	311	267	241	209	281	501	2,947
Labour	26	44	85	143	186	232	268	568	2,213	3,765
Natural resources	1,283	1,062	1,027	926	836	826	795	1,303	2,960	11,019
Oil and gas	205	169	164	148	133	132	127	208	472	1,757
Other (net of interest)	87	72	69	62	56	56	54	88	200	743
Transfer payments to own enterprises	603	500	483	436	393	388	374	613	1,393	5,184
Protection of persons and property	2,519	2,087	2,018	1,819	1,642	1,621	1,562	2,558	5,814	21,640
Research establishments	157	130	125	113	102	101	97	159	361	1,345
Social security	7,284	9,248	9,300	6,199	5,076	4,556	3,843	5,444	9,941	60,890
Trade and industry (includes agriculture)	254	479	723	699	803	654	679	1,105	4,782	10,179
Agriculture	− 102	117	380	383	468	353	371	600	2,838	5,407
Transportation and communication	439	640	761	801	1,040	1,006	1,179	2,185	5,620	13,669
Total	17,561	20,151	20,782	18,059	17,604	16,786	17,266	29,020	64,711	221,940

better than distribute the expenditures in proportion to the number of households – that is, assign the same benefit to each household without distinction. This is true of expenditures for protection of persons and property or for research establishments or for general services. In most instances, as in education, it is possible to make a more or less sensible allocation of the "benefits."

Total Government Spending Received by Income Class

The data produced by the assumptions are displayed in Tables 8 through 11, for 1988. Table 8 provides a distribution of total government expenditure by income class and shows the total dollar amounts estimated to have been expended on behalf of groups with incomes in the ranges noted. In Table 9, this gross flow of money is divided by the number of families in the income class to give an impression of the dollar amount of benefit enjoyed by the average family within each income class.

The data in Table 9 reveal the tendency for the major expenditure items, health and education, to generate increasing benefits on average for families as annual income increases up to the $40,000-to-$50,000 range. At income levels above $50,000, there is a modest tailing off. Social security expenditures in total generate the single biggest benefit flow for low-income families, with the highest transfer payments being made to the second- and third-lowest income classes.

The group for which total benefits reach a peak is the $35,000-to-$40,000-per-year family, which received average benefits of $23,649. This figure is well above the overall average of $21,945 and considerably greater than the benefits enjoyed by families in the lowest income classes, who nevertheless received significant benefit. Benefits of $23,816 on average for the top income class – $50,000 or more – are somewhat below the peak level but still above the average level of $21,945.

Distribution of Benefits by Income Decile

The distribution of expenditures by income class reveals something about which families benefit from government expenditures. However, since there are varying numbers of families within each income class, it is not clear from the income class distribution how benefits are distributed among groups of people of different income levels. Table 10 therefore provides a distribution of government expenditures by deciles within the population. That is, if one imagined the

Table 9
Total government spending per family ($) by function, by income group ($ 000), 1988

Function	10	10–15	15–20	20–25	25–30	30–35	35–40	40–50	50+
Culture and recreation	90	194	297	335	537	622	611	708	848
Education	679	1,662	1,788	2,366	3,182	3,743	3,828	4,329	4,390
General services	1,543	1,543	1,543	1,543	1,543	1,543	1,543	1,543	1,543
Health	1,409	2,046	2,336	3,288	3,946	3,297	5,083	5,553	4,427
Housing	275	421	426	365	348	318	286	235	184
Labour	22	45	91	168	242	306	367	475	815
Natural resources	1,090	1,090	1,090	1,090	1,090	1,090	1,090	1,090	1,090
Oil and gas	174	174	174	174	174	174	174	174	174
Other (net of interest)	73	73	73	73	73	73	73	73	73
Transfer payments to own enterprises	513	513	513	513	513	513	513	513	513
Protection of persons and property	2,140	2,140	2,140	2,140	2,140	2,140	2,140	2,140	2,140
Research establishments	133	133	133	133	133	133	133	133	133
Social security	6,187	9,483	9,863	7,292	6,613	6,013	5,264	4,553	3,659
Trade and industry (includes agriculture)	216	492	767	822	1,046	864	930	924	1,760
Agriculture	–87	120	403	450	610	466	508	502	1,045
Transportation and communication	373	656	807	942	1,354	1,327	1,615	1,827	2,068
Total	14,916	20,664	22,040	21,244	22,934	22,154	23,649	24,271	23,816

Table 10
Total government spending ($) by decile, per family, 1988

Decile	1	2	3	4	5	6	7	8	9	10
Culture and recreation	90	177	284	352	566	616	696	804	848	848
Education	679	1,500	1,772	2,412	3,373	3,793	4,264	4,371	4,390	4,390
General services	1,543	1,543	1,543	1,543	1,543	1,543	1,543	1,543	1,543	1,543
Health	1,409	1,942	2,299	3,295	3,726	4,352	5,492	4,780	4,427	4,427
Housing	275	397	426	367	338	299	242	200	184	184
Labour	22	41	85	171	264	342	461	708	815	815
Natural resources	1,090	1,090	1,090	1,090	1,090	1,090	1,090	1,090	1,090	1,090
Oil and gas	174	174	174	174	174	174	174	174	174	174
Other (net of interest)	73	73	73	73	73	73	73	73	73	73
Transfer payments to own enterprises	513	513	513	513	513	513	513	513	513	513
Protection of persons and property	2,140	2,140	2,140	2,140	2,140	2,140	2,140	2,140	2,140	2,140
Research establishments	133	133	133	133	133	133	133	133	133	133
Social security	6,187	8,942	9,814	7,381	6,409	5,571	4,646	3,939	3,659	3,659
Trade and industry (includes agriculture)	216	446	731	841	984	903	925	1,498	1,760	1,760
Agriculture	−87	86	367	463	561	490	502	874	1,045	1,045
Transportation and communication	373	610	788	974	1,345	1,497	1,799	1,993	2,068	2,068
Total	14,916	19,721	21,864	21,459	22,669	23,037	24,189	23,959	23,816	23,816

Table 11
Distribution (%) of total government spending across deciles, 1988

Deciles	1	2	3	4	5	6	7	8	9	10	Sum
Culture and recreation	1.7	3.4	5.4	6.7	10.7	11.7	13.2	15.2	16.1	16.1	100.0
Education	2.2	4.8	5.7	7.8	10.9	12.3	13.8	14.1	14.2	14.2	100.0
General services	10.0	10.0	10.0	10.0	10.0	10.0	10.0	10.0	10.0	10.0	100.0
Health	3.9	5.4	6.4	9.1	10.3	12.0	15.2	13.2	12.2	12.2	100.0
Housing	9.5	13.6	14.6	12.6	11.6	10.3	8.3	6.9	6.3	6.3	100.0
Labour	0.6	1.1	2.3	4.6	7.1	9.2	12.4	19.0	21.9	21.9	100.0
Natural resources	10.0	10.0	10.0	10.0	10.0	10.0	10.0	10.0	10.0	10.0	100.0
Oil and gas	10.0	10.0	10.0	10.0	10.0	10.0	10.0	10.0	10.0	10.0	100.0
Other (net of interest)	10.0	10.0	10.0	10.0	10.0	10.0	10.0	10.0	10.0	10.0	100.0
Transfer payments to own enterprises	10.0	10.0	10.0	10.0	10.0	10.0	10.0	10.0	10.0	10.0	100.0
Protection of persons and property	10.0	10.0	10.0	10.0	10.0	10.0	10.0	10.0	10.0	10.0	100.0
Research establishments	10.0	10.0	10.0	10.0	10.0	10.0	10.0	10.0	10.0	10.0	100.0
Social security	10.3	14.9	16.3	12.3	10.6	9.3	7.7	6.5	6.1	6.1	100.0
Trade and industry (includes agriculture)	2.1	4.4	7.3	8.4	9.8	9.0	9.2	14.9	17.5	17.5	100.0
Agriculture	−1.6	1.6	6.9	8.7	10.5	9.2	9.4	16.4	19.5	19.5	100.0
Transportation and communication	2.8	4.5	5.8	7.2	10.0	11.1	13.3	14.7	15.3	15.3	100.0
Total	6.8	9.0	10.0	9.8	10.3	10.5	11.0	10.9	10.9	10.9	100.0

Table 12
Government spending benefit (%) going to bottom 30 per cent of income earners
and top 30 per cent of income earners

	Bottom 30 per cent	Top 30 per cent
Culture and recreation	10.5	47.4
Education	12.7	42.5
General services	30.0	30.0
Health	15.7	37.6
Housing	37.7	19.5
Labour	4.0	62.8
Natural resources	30.0	30.0
Oil and gas	30.0	30.0
Other (net of interest)	30.0	30.0
Transfer payments to own enterprises	30.0	30.0
Protection of persons and property	30.0	30.0
Research establishments	30.0	30.0
Social security	41.5	18.7
Trade and industry (includes agriculture)	13.8	49.9
Agriculture	6.9	55.4
Transportation and communication	13.1	45.3
Total	25.8	32.7

population lined up from lowest income to highest income and then
divided it into tenths, we can then calculate a distribution of expenditures among each of these ten groups. The seventh decile received
the most benefit, with an average expenditure per family of
$24,189. The lowest-benefiting group was the first decile, with an
average of $14,916.

Table 11 presents the distribution of total benefits among deciles,
confirming the impression gained from Table 10.

Table 12 further collapses the data to compare the relative position of the bottom 30 per cent and the top 30 per cent of income
earners and their participation in the benefits generated. For the top
30 per cent, one of the benefits of being Canadian is that one gets a
disproportionate share of spending on culture and recreation, on
education, on health care, on labour services, and on agriculture and
transportation and communication, as well as subsidies to trade and
industry. In the bottom 30 per cent, one gets a disproportionate
share of social security spending and expenditures on housing.

Net Receipts from the Government Sector

The assessment of spending by income decile makes it clear that the
principal beneficiaries of the operation of all levels of government in

Table 13
Government spending benefits ($) and tax paid ($) per family,
by income level, 1988

Income group	Average income	Government spending per family	Tax paid per family	Net benefit per family	Deferred tax per family	Net benefit less deferred tax per family
< 10,000	5,000	14,916	1,210	13,706	208	13,497
10,000–15,000	12,500	20,664	3,989	16,675	687	15,988
15,000–20,000	17,500	22,040	7,350	14,690	1,266	13,424
20,000–25,000	22,500	21,244	11,448	9,796	1,972	7,824
25,000–30,000	27,500	22,934	13,935	9,000	2,400	6,600
30,000–35,000	32,500	22,154	16,984	5,170	2,925	2,245
35,000–40,000	37,500	23,649	20,641	3,008	3,555	−547
40,000–50,000	45,000	24,271	24,109	162	4,153	−3,991
50,000 and over	74,703	23,816	42,694	−18,878	7,354	−26,232

Canada are those in the top income deciles. In 1985 they received 56.9 per cent of the total benefits of government spending, and in 1988 54.2 per cent. However, this information may not show the extent to which government may nevertheless play the role of Robin Hood, redistributing benefits from those with high incomes to those with low incomes. In order to establish the profile of expenditures from that point of view, it is necessary to compare them to the estimated tax burden assessed to families with different incomes. Table 13 compares the expenditure profile for 1988 with total taxes for that year. The data suggest a number of comparisons.

First, total spending and spending per family do not include interest spending by government, since we are here concerned only with total program spending, or distribution of current benefits to citizens, during the current year. Interest payments on the public debt reflect payment for past expenditures: if the government spends more than it takes in tax revenue, it finances the difference by borrowing, and the interest costs are reflected in current government spending. No current program benefit is being delivered for that interest cost, except to the extent that capital structures such as highways and public buildings were financed with the deficit spending. Education too is a form of investment, which, like highways and buildings, will produce a flow of services over time which ought appropriately to be paid for over time and reflected in interest charges. Thus there is a benefit flow from past spending which is not picked up in total spending if that total is reduced by the amount of interest expense.

Who Bears the Burden of the Public Debt?

The tax figures presented in Table 13 also underestimate the total tax burden implied by current spending, even excluding interest payments. Insofar as expenditures are financed by deficits, an implied future or deferred tax burden ought to be included in the analysis. Use of deficit finance allows governments to produce an aggregate program expenditure and an expenditure per family greater than the apparent tax liability. In order to ascertain the actual position of families, I have calculated the deferred tax burden per family by income level. Evidently, although we talk about the deficit as burdening all Canadians equally, since taxes vary with family income the actual burden depends on the level of income. So, for example, the deferred tax is only $208 for a family earning less than $10,000 a year but $4,153 for a family with an income of $40,000 to $50,000.

Net Benefits of Being Canadian

There are a number of fascinating aspects of the distribution of taxes and expenditures provided in Table 13. First, for a very large number of Canadians there is a net benefit flow: total program expenditures are greater than the tax burden borne. Excluding deferred taxes, that is true for all families up to an income of $45,000 per year. Beyond that figure, the total tax cost exceeds expenditures by a fairly wide margin. Including deferred taxes, the point of zero net benefit is reached at an income of $37,000 per year. Below that level, families enjoy an apparent net benefit, while above it they bear a net cost.

These data on net benefits also provide some potentially useful information about the choices that Canadians make electorally and how they might respond to choices that are provided to them in the future. The total number of families earning less than $37,000 is 5.763 million, and the number earning more than that is only 4.35 million. In other words, the majority of citizens actually benefits from the current structure of expenditures; in particular, a majority benefits from current deficit spending, which may explain the apparent unwillingness of the political process to come to grips with this problem.

There has been some suggestion that at base our current constitutional difficulties are really fiscal problems. Some provinces, including Quebec, are increasingly disgruntled by the federal government's extraordinarily large deficits. The costs of the deficits are going to be borne by the provinces in proportion to their share of federal tax, and the distribution of benefits is determined by the federal government. Fifty-one per cent of Canadian adults are in the less-than $37,000 income group, and 63.5 per cent are below $45,000 – the net beneficiary group if deferred taxes in the form of deficits are ignored.

While this is not the place to explore these ramifications, it is clear that the distribution of benefits and the disproportionate sharing in particular programs by people of different incomes imply that political dynamics may militate against resolution of certain economic problems. For example, it is not clear how a political constituency can be forged that would "do something" about the national deficit, even though the average family is imperilled and loses as a consequence of it. This distribution of benefits obscures the array of constitutional accommodations that may be thought to be optimal. Thus, for example, the fact that a majority of Canadians are net beneficiaries from income transfer programs implies that these are always likely to be, at least overtly, sacred trusts. High income groups are particular beneficiaries from health and education spending and will therefore be the biggest losers if decentralization implies less funding. They can be expected to fight against decentralization if only for that reason.

The analysis also sharply underlines the point that one's attitude toward the costs and benefits of being Canadian is likely to depend strongly on where one is in the income distribution. Of course, as has been noted, there is a relationship between income distribution in Canada and province of residence, for average incomes in the so-called have not provinces do tend to be, by definition, below those in other parts of the country. The fact that one's attitude may vary by income level, together with the fact that the sorting out of the Confederation puzzle will have to be done explicitly along provincial lines because of the voting provisions in the amendment formula, suggests that it would be useful here also to examine net benefits on a provincial basis.

In order to make the analysis interprovincial, however, we must move from consideration of total government expenditures (federal, provincial, and municipal) to look only at federal expenditures. In the context of Confederation, it is the relative expenditures and tax policies of the federal government that determine the allocation of net benefits within the federal system. In the next section, therefore, I provide a compilation of the expenditures of the federal government by province and a comparison of total federal expenditures in each province with revenues raised there by Ottawa.

THE COSTS AND BENEFITS OF CONFEDERATION

The economic benefits of Confederation are in general the expenditures made in each province by the federal government. The economic costs of Confederation are, roughly speaking, the taxes collected in each province by Ottawa. The difference between these two conveys a net benefit to the province in the same sense as we could identify net benefits generated for individuals in different parts of the income distribution. As before, the spending levels that I use as proxy for benefits may not convey an accurate impression about benefits realized.

First, let us consider the total level of expenditure. In doing so, we have to distinguish between who spends the money and who funds the spending of the money. While taxpayers ultimately fund all expenditures of government, different levels of government engage in the taxing activities that produce the revenue. The government that raises the money may be different from the one that spends it. This section attempts to identify the amount of money that the federal government provides, either from tax revenue or from borrowing, to fund expenditures of different kinds in the provinces. The total of spending by province sums to total federal spending. (However, since most of the analysis concerns the ten provinces and ignores Yukon and Northwest Territories, the total of provincial expenditures does not add up to the federal total.)

Spending Distribution by Province

Table 14 provides a province-by-province distribution of total federal funding of all government expenditures. From 1970 to 1988, total federal expenditure increased from $14.5 billion to $132.6 billion. While Table 14 gives a sense of how the aggregate federal funding of expenditures has changed over time in each province, trends in particular provincial figures are obscured by movement in the overall totals. Accordingly, Table 15 presents calculations of the distribution of gross federal funding of total expenditures across each of the provinces. The entries in Table 15 provide the percentage of total federal funding that went to each province in each year. Thus, for example, 2.6 per cent of total federal funding in 1988

Table 14
Gross federal funding ($ million) of total government spending, by province

Year	Nfld	PEI	NS	NB	Que.	Ont.	Man.	Sask.	Alta	BC	Canada
1970	416.2	126.9	816.7	528.9	3,177.2	5,427.3	737.2	619.5	968.0	1,370.0	14,497.4
1975	1,014.4	272.2	2,112.4	1,479.3	8,195.7	12,272.1	1,695.8	1,428.9	2,193.4	3,256.7	34,495.9
1980	1,824.6	439.2	4,212.2	3,087.5	15,193.0	21,568.7	2,941.7	2,421.1	3,876.2	5,777.5	63,043.4
1985	3,328.5	840.6	5,856.9	4,120.4	25,516.2	42,466.8	5,095.9	4,726.3	8,943.0	11,319.3	115,712.5
1988	3,419.4	967.3	6,773.3	4,316.1	28,022.3	50,275.2	6,143.8	5,702.5	9,628.3	13,216.8	132,599.9

Table 15
Distribution (%) of federal funding of total government spending across Canada

Year	Nfld	PEI	NS	NB	Que.	Ont.	Man.	Sask.	Alta	BC	Canada
1970	2.9	0.9	5.6	3.6	21.9	37.4	5.1	4.3	6.7	9.4	100.0
1975	2.9	0.8	6.1	4.3	23.8	35.6	4.9	4.1	6.4	9.4	100.0
1980	2.9	0.7	6.7	4.9	24.1	34.2	4.7	3.8	6.1	9.2	100.0
1985	2.9	0.7	5.1	3.6	22.1	36.7	4.4	4.1	7.7	9.8	100.0
1988	2.6	0.7	5.1	3.3	21.1	37.9	4.6	4.3	7.3	10.0	100.0

went to Newfoundland. In the same year, 37.9 per cent went to Ontario and 10.0 per cent to British Columbia.

Common Perceptions Not Validated

The historical perspective on the distribution of federal funding provided by Table 15 does not conform to the usual impressions that people have about this spending. First, there is no evidence of any change over the period 1970–88 in the extent to which federal funding has accrued to the benefit of the residents of Quebec. Federal expenditures in Quebec comprised 21.9 per cent of the total in 1970 and nearly the same percentage in 1988. We shall look at changing population distribution below.

Another widespread belief about government expenditure also is not borne out by the distribution table – namely, concerning the Atlantic region over the period. In 1970, Newfoundland, Prince Edward Island, Nova Scotia, and New Brunswick together received 13.0 per cent of the total federal funding made available. By 1988, those four provinces received in total only 11.7 per cent, a decline of 1.3 per cent. Over that period, the percentage going to the Atlantic provinces rose to 15.2 per cent in 1980 and then fell to 11.7 per cent by 1988. Equally surprising, both Alberta and British Columbia enjoyed an increase over the same period. From 9.4 per cent in 1970, British Columbia grew to 10.0 per cent by 1988, and Alberta moved from 6.7 per cent in 1970 to 7.3 per cent in 1988.

Provincial Distribution per Capita

Part of the reason for the evolving distribution of expenditures as seen in Table 15 is the changing population structure of the country. Average expenditure per capita in 1988 was $5,118, and as can be seen from Table 16, there is considerable variation among provinces. Nova Scotia received the highest per capita expenditure in

Table 16
Federal funding ($) of total government spending per capita

Year	Nfld	PEI	NS	NB	Que.	Ont.	Man.	Sask.	Alta	BC	Canada
1970	805.0	1,153.9	1,044.3	843.6	528.4	718.7	750.0	658.3	606.9	643.8	680.7
1975	1,847.3	2,324.5	2,577.6	2,223.8	1,326.4	1,501.7	1,673.0	1,574.7	1,233.5	1,338.5	1,519.8
1980	3,226.0	3,576.5	4,984.2	4,439.9	2,379.1	2,516.9	2,870.2	2,523.5	1,810.8	2,167.1	2,622.2
1985	5,824.1	6,671.5	6,724.3	5,804.2	3,917.0	4,715.2	4,789.4	4,686.9	3,808.0	3,943.9	4,598.1
1988	6,020.0	7,527.7	7,680.3	6,042.4	4,219.7	5,330.8	5,667.1	5,626.5	4,030.8	4,434.9	5,117.9

1988, and indeed over the period from 1975, with $7,680 per person. Alberta was lowest, with $4,031. Provinces enjoying above-average rates include Newfoundland, Prince Edward Island, Nova Scotia, New Brunswick, Ontario, Manitoba, and Saskatchewan. Lower-than-average expenditures were enjoyed by Alberta, British Columbia, and Quebec. Later in the essay we shall compare these figures with per capita taxation numbers to gain a better sense of net federal activity in each province.

Table 17 displays the distribution of federal expenditure by function by province. The per-capita figures reveal interesting differences in federal spending by province. The category with most variance is expenditures on interest on the public debt. These outlays, often considered "unproductive," are nevertheless received as income by Canadians and are thus properly considered a "benefit," even though there is no creation of a current program benefit. They are, moreover, an important aspect of federal spending across the provinces. Because of their sheer size, their provincial distribution helps determine per-capita allotment of federal spending.

For example, the $1,870-per-person spent on interest payments in Ontario boosted federal expenditure there above the per-capita average in the country. Interest distribution is based on figures provided by Statistics Canada for the estimates of gross provincial product. The fact that a significant portion of that interest is paid into pension accounts and on holdings of debt by the Bank of Canada allocated to Ontario because of the location of the national capital suggests that it may be more useful to view total expenditure distribution by province excluding interest from the expenditure distribution profile.

As can be seen in Table 18, subtracting interest payments from total federal expenditure by province produces a profile that more nearly matches what one would have expected. That is to say, Quebec, Ontario, Alberta, and British Columbia have expenditure levels below the national average, and Newfoundland, Prince Edward Island, Nova Scotia, New Brunswick, Manitoba, and Saskatchewan have levels above.

However, Quebec receives the lowest per-capita level, considerably below the national average for any other province. One potential explanation is the structure of the compensation that provinces receive under federal-provincial fiscal arrangements. Broadly speaking, Ottawa historically has agreed to provide the provinces funds for program spending in areas of provincial responsibility where it sought to encourage national standards of service or national coverage for a program. Some funding for these programs is in the form

Table 17
Federal funding ($) of government spending by function, per capita, 1988

Function	Nfld	PEI	NS	NB	Que.	Ont.	Man.	Sask.	Alta	BC	Canada
Culture and recreation	57.5	82.2	94.9	54.9	33.4	40.7	45.8	27.9	27.5	32.3	41.0
Education	489.9	460.7	364.3	419.9	229.0	130.5	322.9	249.5	160.0	168.2	207.2
General services	287.1	491.1	517.0	365.8	207.4	281.7	276.4	169.9	162.2	222.8	260.0
Health	343.7	333.0	357.0	341.0	271.1	297.0	396.9	386.6	292.8	325.5	307.0
Housing	56.8	73.9	65.6	69.9	60.8	51.1	126.9	265.7	83.5	38.7	68.5
Interest charges	689.0	780.0	1,173.7	687.0	907.8	1,870.3	895.6	534.4	624.5	819.8	1,207.2
Labour	107.3	141.4	159.7	108.7	92.4	102.2	104.0	77.4	78.9	76.9	98.8
Natural resources	189.0	181.3	183.7	130.7	73.7	77.7	81.4	55.0	60.2	64.3	86.3
Oil and gas	210.1	1.0	62.3	0.8	0.5	0.9	3.8	35.2	10.3	3.6	17.0
Other (net of interest)	117.2	32.0	75.8	106.1	130.2	79.6	172.7	87.7	37.6	28.6	92.6
Protection of persons and property	340.0	899.4	1,645.5	737.3	293.8	462.9	536.7	248.0	406.0	411.0	541.6
Research establishments	33.5	25.1	79.0	44.3	29.4	44.0	40.0	32.8	33.7	36.9	40.5
Social security	2,642.1	2,870.5	2,362.0	2,486.5	1,611.7	1,594.3	1,951.2	1,830.3	1,549.1	1,993.0	1,749.8
Trade and industry	155.9	765.8	219.5	216.5	146.4	159.9	505.2	1,387.5	379.6	98.2	240.8
Transportation and communication	300.9	390.3	320.6	273.1	132.4	138.1	207.6	238.8	125.1	115.1	159.6
Total	6,020.0	7,527.7	7,680.3	6,042.4	4,219.7	5,330.8	5,667.2	5,626.5	4,030.8	4,434.9	5,117.9

Table 18
Federal funding ($) of expenditure per capita,
net of interest charges, 1988

Nfld	5,631.7
PEI	6,936.6
NS	6,669.6
NB	5,500.8
Que.	3,379.1
Ont.	3,462.6
Man.	4,899.6
Sask.	5,138.6
Alta	3,414.8
BC	3,618.0
Canada	3,954.9

of cost sharing, and some is provided on a fixed cash-transfer basis.
More recently, the federal government has vacated, in favour of the
provinces, a certain amount of "tax room" in the form of percentage
points of personal income tax. Quebec, for example, elects to receive
tax transfers for the hospital portion of insured health services as
well as for the Canada Assistance Plan and youth allowances. The
total amount of such transfers for fiscal 1987–88 has been estimated
by the Canadian Tax Foundation to be about $1.6 billion, or $239
per capita (*The National Finances, 1987/88*, p. 1,525, Table 15.2, note
b). These amounts must be added to the total per-capita figure reported in the table to make the figure for Quebec comparable with
those of other provinces. However, even with this adjustment, the
former is less than the national average.

Social security expenditures per capita display more or less the
kind of pattern that would be expected. The Atlantic provinces, with
their above-average reliance on transfer income, have much higher
participation than the national average. British Columbia also enjoys
a higher-than-average amount, largely because of the greater proportion of people there receiving Old Age Security.

In trade and industry, Saskatchewan receives per-capita expenditure of nearly six times the national average. The province traditionally obtained more support in this category than other provinces,
largely as a result of payments to agriculture. While payments recently have been nearly six times the Canadian average, in 1970 they
were only about twice as large. The payments tended upward stead-
ily during the 1970s and 1980s. Expenditures on agriculture in Saskatchewan constitute a considerable fraction of total federal funding
for this purpose – in 1988, 23 per cent of the national total. By com-

parison, Ontario got 24 per cent, Quebec 16 per cent, Manitoba 9 per cent, Alberta 15 per cent, and the other provinces insignificant fractions.

Federal expenditures on protection of persons and property reflect the allocation of defence installations. Prince Edward Island, Nova Scotia, and New Brunswick gain more in this category than other provinces. Nova Scotia gets $1,645 per capita, more than three times the national average. While Nova Scotia and Prince Edward Island benefit significantly, they obtain only 11.2 per cent of total expenditures.

Federal Taxes Compared to Federal Spending by Province

Of course, the federal government does not create the benefits analysed in Tables 17 and 18; it transfers them from taxpayers. To what extent can Ottawa spend taxes raised in one province in another? I shall examine this issue province by province.

Table 19 presents a distribution of total federal tax levied on the provinces, ignoring that portion raised by taxing non-residents of Canada and therefore looking only at domestic distribution. It is evident that there is an imbalance in sharing of the total federal tax burden and total distribution of expenditures. Newfoundland receives 2.9 per cent of total federal expenditure and pays just over 1 per cent of the total federal tax burden. In fact, all the Atlantic provinces bear a smaller fraction of tax burden than they receive in expenditures. The only provinces for which that is not true are Ontario, Alberta, and British Columbia.

This differential distribution is also reflected in Table 20, which provides a per-capita statement of federal spending and taxation by province. The first line repeats the per-capita federal expenditure by province from Table 16. The second line reports estimates of total federal taxes paid, on average, by residents of each province, according to the calculations provided in the Fraser Institute's biennial study of taxation, *Tax Facts*. The third line reports the apparent current benefit enjoyed by individuals in each province – the difference between total spending by the federal government and total taxes raised by it in the province. For example, on average a resident of Newfoundland receives $3,743 more in benefits than he or she pays in federal taxes. The average Albertan receives $422 less in current benefits than the amount paid in taxes.

The fourth line in the table reports the amount of tax per capita deferred by federal deficits. Every dollar of deficit is a dollar of fu-

Table 19
Distribution of current and deficit taxes, 1970 and 1988

	Nfld	PEI	NS	NB	Que.	Ont.	Man.	Sask.	Alta	BC
1970										
Distribution of total federal tax ($ million)	181.2	37.4	376.4	266.7	3,066.1	6,693.9	616.8	400.9	1,142.1	1,694.2
Percentage distribution	1.2	0.3	2.6	1.8	21.1	46.1	4.2	2.8	7.9	11.7
Distribution of deficit taxes ($ million)	9.7	2.0	20.2	14.3	164.6	359.5	33.1	21.5	61.3	91.0
Deficit taxes per capita ($)	18.8	18.2	25.8	22.8	27.4	47.6	33.7	22.9	38.5	42.8
1988										
Distribution of total federal tax ($ million)	1,293.6	321.5	2,693.3	1,955.8	20,249.2	45,254.1	3,500.3	2,977.4	10,637.4	11,787.6
Percentage distribution	1.3	0.3	2.7	1.9	20.0	44.8	3.5	2.9	10.5	11.7
Distribution of deficit taxes ($ million)	367.7	91.4	765.5	555.9	5,755.2	12,862.1	994.8	846.2	3,023.4	3,350.3
Deficit taxes per capita ($)	647.3	711.1	868.0	778.2	866.6	1,363.8	917.7	835.0	1,265.7	1,124.2

Table 20
Federal net spending benefits (nominal dollars per capita) by province, 1970 and 1988

	Nfld	PEI	NS	NB	Que.	Ont.	Man.	Sask.	Alta	BC
1970										
Federal government services	805	1,154	1,044	844	528	719	750	658	607	644
less taxes paid	350	340	481	425	510	886	627	426	716	796
equals gross current benefit	455	814	563	418	18	−168	122	232	−109	−152
less taxes deferred	19	18	26	23	27	48	34	23	38	43
equals net current benefit	436	796	537	395	−9	−215	89	209	−148	−195
1988										
Federal government services	6,020	7,528	7,680	6,042	4,220	5,331	5,667	5,627	4,031	4,435
less taxes paid	2,277	2,502	3,054	2,738	3,049	4,798	3,229	2,938	4,453	3,955
equals gross current benefit	3,743	5,026	4,626	3,304	1,171	532	2,438	2,689	−422	480
less taxes deferred	647	711	868	778	867	1,364	918	835	1,266	1,124
equals net current benefit	3,095	4,315	3,758	2,526	304	−831	1,521	1,854	−1,688	−645

Sources: Tables 3-3, 3-6, and calculations by the authors.

ture taxes to pay the interest on the debt. Since deferred taxes also generate interest expense at the current government bond rate, it is appropriate to regard the current deficit as the liability associated with future tax burdens.[2] The deferred taxes are distributed among the provinces according to the share of actual federal tax revenue collected in that province. Subtracting deferred taxes from current benefits produces the net current benefit for residents and is the barometer of net federal activities in taxing and spending.

The last line of the table reveals that seven provinces are net fiscal beneficiaries and three are net fiscal losers. Newfoundland, Prince Edward Island, Nova Scotia, New Brunswick, Quebec, Manitoba, and Saskatchewan all receive more per capita in current expenditures than they pay in terms of current or deferred tax liabilities. The range is from $304 in Quebec to $4,315 in Prince Edward Island.

Deferred taxes can also be regionally distributed by two other methods, as can be seen in Table 21. In the first case we assume that only money not already earmarked for a particular transfer program to the provinces will be available to pay interest on the public debt. This figure is approximated by the regional distribution of federal tax collected net of transfer payments to provincial and municipal governments. In the second case, we further exclude payments to the Canada Pension Plan from the tax total, as is done in other fiscal-flow studies such as that of M.A. Raynauld[3]. British Columbia, Alberta, and Ontario are all net fiscal losers: total current and deferred taxes exceed the fiscal flow from Ottawa in transfers or expenditures. The loss ranges from $645 per capita for British Columbia to $1,688 in Alberta.

The movement from line three to line five in Table 20 (deducting deferred taxes) swings Ontario and British Columbia from net beneficiaries to net losers. The fact of this swing and the importance of deficit financing suggest another calculation – provincial distribution of inflows and outflows associated with interest on the federal public debt (Table 21).

Who Pays the Interest on the Debt?

The first row in Table 22 provides the total tax cost of federal interest payments – the distribution, according to the average distribution of total federal revenue, by province, of interest paid during 1988. Each province is assumed to bear the cost of interest payments in proportion to the percentage of total federal revenue that it provides. The second line provides the per-capita distribution of these

Table 21
Federal net spending benefits ($) per capita, by province

	Nfld	PEI	NS	NB	Que.	Ont.	Man.	Sask.	Alta	BC
Method 1										
Taxes deferred regionally allocated by share of federal tax revenue collected in each province	3,095	4,315	3,758	2,526	304	–831	1,521	1,854	–1,688	–645
Method 2										
Taxes deferred regionally allocated by share of federal tax revenue collected less transfer payments to provincial and municipal governments in each province	3,738	4,902	4,095	2,966	435	–1,035	1,708	1,960	–1,788	–712
Method 3										
Taxes deferred regionally allocated by share of federal tax revenue less CPP payments less transfer payments to provincial and municipal governments in each province	3,743	4,976	4,152	3,032	376	–1,022	1,754	1,988	–1776	–645

Table 22
Distribution of tax and expenditure flows associated with interest on the federal public debt, 1988

	Nfld	PEI	NS	NB	Que.	Ont.	Man.	Sask.	Alta	BC
Tax cost of interest ($ million)	385.8	95.9	803.2	583.3	6,038.6	13,495.5	1,043.8	887.9	3,172.3	3,515.3
Dollars per capita	679.2	746.1	910.8	816.5	909.3	1,431.0	962.9	876.1	1,328.0	1,179.5
Interest paid ($ million)	220.6	76.1	893.4	386.9	5,580.7	17,618.2	832.5	493.4	1,479.1	2,437.7
Dollars per capita	388.4	592.0	1,013.0	541.7	840.4	1,868.1	767.9	486.8	619.2	818.0
Net flow ($ million)	−165.1	−19.8	90.2	−196.4	−457.9	4,122.7	−211.3	−394.5	−1,693.1	−1,077.6
Net flow ($ per capita)	−290.8	−154.0	102.2	−274.9	−68.9	437.1	−194.9	−389.3	−708.8	−361.6

figures. Line three presents total interest paid out in the province, and line four the per-capita amount of interest. The fifth line provides the calculation of the net flow of money into or out of the province, which is determined by the payment of interest on the public debt and the taxes that must be raised to pay for it.

The figure for Newfoundland is minus $165 million: residents receive fewer dollars in interest payments than the total that they are assessed in taxes in order to pay for interest on the public debt. The latter figure is calculated by simply observing the percentage of total federal tax collected in Newfoundland and assuming that any taxes levied to pay the interest on the debt would be obtained in the same way in which current revenues are raised. Most provinces are losers. Ontario is a significant net beneficiary in interest on the public debt. It receives $4.1 billion more in interest payments than would be attributed to it, but some financial institutions, such as pension funds, hold Government of Canada debt in Ontario on behalf of residents in other provinces. Statistics Canada is compiling data on the issue.

Some Insights on Old Issues

The data in Table 22 cast some light on two statements that are part of everyday conversation and that deserve closer scrutiny. One is that we do not have to worry about the national debt because we owe it to ourselves. As the net flows associated with the public debt outstanding make quite clear, for the most part the public debt is something that the rest of the country owes to Ontario. Total interest payments from the federal government received by residents of Ontario exceed by more than $4.1 billion the total expenses incurred by residents of Ontario associated with interest on the debt in the form of higher taxes. Ontario receives 58 per cent of all the interest paid on the outstanding public debt, but it bears only 44.8 per cent of the total taxes paid to the federal government.

The other statement implies that Quebec, by quitting Confederation, can rid itself of a very significant liability in the form of interest payments on the public debt. The story goes that the $364 billion in gross federal public debt outstanding means that Quebecers have a $93-billion incentive (their share of the total) to quit Confederation and rid themselves of this encumbrance. Such an analysis implicitly assumes that all residents of Quebec regard the public debt as a burden and a future tax liability. It fails to recognize that $5.6 billion in 1988 was paid to Quebecers as holders of that same debt in the form of government bonds. It is, however, true for Quebec, as for all provinces save Nova Scotia and Ontario, that the public debt is a net burden, amounting to an annual flow of $0.5 billion out of Quebec, or $69 per capita.

Several issues associated with these calculations bear further discussion. First and most important, it is inappropriate to regard payment of interest on the public debt as creating a net benefit. Obviously, all provinces and the country as a whole would be better off if there were no pulic debt. The public debt is an expense incurred because of past spending by the federal government. There are no current program benefits conferred by paying interest on the debt. Interest payments on the public debt are a transfer from current taxpayers to past recipients of government program expenses. For example, payments made to program beneficiaries in 1984, when the federal deficit amounted to $38 billion, are now being paid for by current taxpayers in the form of the interest on bonds that the government issued in 1984 to enable it to make those payments. That having been said, given a national debt and interest payments on it, the holders of the debt receive the interest and current taxpayers pay it. To the extent that on average those who receive and those who pay are resident in different provinces, interest payments on the public debt are regionally redistributed.

Second, the "net benefits" enjoyed by provinces that hold above-average amounts per capita of government debt are directly determined by the choice of residents of the province to hold Government of Canada bonds. So, for example, Quebec, a net loser, could change its standing by buying more Government of Canada bonds. This fact places in sharp relief the tendentious nature of the calculation and its sensitivity to variables that have nothing to do with Ottawa's proclivity to spend money in one province or another.

SUMMARY AND CONCLUSIONS

These then are calculations of the costs and benefits of being a Canadian from the point of view of the governmental apparatus. It is not evident that any conclusions are appropriate other than the distributions of net benefit themselves, except to note that this structure of benefits may be one of the most significant costs of being a Canadian. Distribution of benefits within the income distribution to individual families creates a strong interest in maintaining the fiscal problems that beset our country. In particular, there is no political constituency interested in doing anything about the size of the public deficit. We do nothing about the national deficit because we want to do nothing about it. Now, to the extent that the decay of fiscal circumstances and economic performance generally lies at the base of our current constitutional crisis, the distribution of the benefits of being a Canadian may also be a crucial obstacle in resolving the problem.

Establishment of a second house in Parliament or creation of an effective Senate with equal distribution of seats among provinces could dramatically affect the distribution of benefits and costs within Confederation. At the moment the "have-not" provinces are significant net beneficiaries, even though they have together less than a majority of seats in the House of Commons. These seats are of course divided along party lines, in the same way that seats in the "have" provinces are, meaning that there is no clear and unambiguous thrust to enhance net flows into the regions. Clearly, however, an effective Senate with equal representation from each province might well increase distribution of net benefits to the "have-not" provinces.

NOTES

1 A survey of the evolution of the Canadian tax system, with emphasis on the sharing of tax revenues between the provinces and the federal government, can be found in the chapter "The Tangled Tale of Taxes and Transfers" in M. Walker, ed., *Canadian Confederation at the Crossroad* (Vancouver: Fraser Institute, 1979).

2 This is because of a concept which economists refer to as "present value." If deferred taxes bear interest at the government bond rate and we discount the future interest on those taxes at the same rate, the force of interest cancels out over the period. So the current deficit is a good estimate of the present value of the tax liability associated with the extra spending.

3 André Raynauld, *Les enjeux économiques de la souveraineté* (Quebec: Conseil du Patronat du Québec, 1990).

PART FOUR

Individuals and Groups

DARYL T. BEAN

Citizenship and the Trade Union Movement

The Canadian trade union movement is concerned, above all else, with the promotion of collective rights. Individual unions, and their central labour bodies, give expression to this concern in many tangible ways. The rules governing the rights and responsibilities of union members, normally enshrined in constitutions and by-laws, give concrete expression to this reality. So too does the negotiation process, whereby terms and conditions of employment are enumerated in collective – as opposed to individual – agreements.

Normally this posture prevails without public controversy. Occasionally, however, it becomes a flashpoint, because promotion of collective rights inevitably gives short shrift to individual rights or choice. In terms of public profile, two recent examples highlight the clash between individual and collective rights within the union movement – the Mervyn Lavigne case, and union discipline of members who worked during last fall's strike by the Public Service Alliance of Canada (PSAC).

Mervyn Lavigne, a teaching master at the Haileybury School of Mines, was remunerated pursuant to a collective agreement negotiated between the Ontario Council of Regents for Colleges of Applied Arts and Technology and the Ontario Public Service Employees Union (OPSEU). Lavigne, who had never joined the union, was nonetheless required to pay to OPSEU an amount equivalent to the dues paid by OPSEU members. He argued unsuccessfully in the Supreme Court of Canada that his Charter rights were infringed because, in addition to the money collected and paid by OPSEU for matters related to collective bargaining, OPSEU collected money that it subsequently paid to the New Democratic Party and campaigns such as those for disarmament and choice respecting abortions. The Supreme Court decided in essence that unions could spend membership dues and money collected from non-members on these and other issues notwithstanding the individual beliefs of contributors.

The second example, involving the PSAC, also relates to the conflict between individual choice and collective rights. Pursuant to the PSAC constitution, and as a basic principle of union membership, individuals who choose to work during a strike by their bargaining unit are likely not only to be shunned by their colleagues but to be subject to punitive sanction. This is as it should be, because the benefits secured by the union apply to all members (and employees), whether they choose to participate in union activities or not.

Within the union movement, other examples abound. It is not unusual, during the collective bargaining process, for unions to refuse to advance a position that would benefit a few members, if the benefit would hurt a majority of members. Similarly, before a grievance is advanced to arbitration or adjudication, a determination must be made as to whether or not winning the individual grievance would erode the acquired rights of other members. Should that be the case, the rights of the individual must be assessed in relation to collective rights.

People who challenge this concept, particularly with regard to its expression within unions, often argue that it is undemocratic. They argue, in essence, that individual rights are paramount and that individual choice is sacrosanct. They cite the Charter of Rights and Freedoms and its explicit recognition of the rights of individuals as justification for challenging protection of collective rights.

The Canadian labour movement brings its concept of collective rights to its analysis of the state in general, and particularly to its analysis of the constitution. While the Canadian Constitution, especially the Charter, is viewed increasingly as protecting the individual from the state and even outside organizations (as in Lavigne's Charter challenge against OPSEU and the Council of Regents), many of the benefits of Canadian citizenship have evolved from the collectivist nature of Canadian society.

Hence, the conflict between individual and collective rights within the Canadian union movement is also present in society at large. Pursuant to the Charter of Rights, the government can argue, and has done so, that while a particular policy, action, or piece of legislation infringes on the Charter rights of an individual, the policy, action, or legislation is necessary to protect the collective rights of society. In such cases, it argues that notwithstanding a finding that it has infringed a Charter right, its actions are "demonstrably justified in a free and democratic society."

Thus the protection of individual rights and choice is not absolute. Citizens cannot choose to act individually if the expression of their individual choice undermines the integrity of the collective. For example, as an individual in Canada today, you can choose to use medical services that are outside the public system, but you cannot choose to withhold the tax revenues that pay for the public system. Similarly, even if you have never flown on a plane, you are required to contribute to the development and maintenance of an air transport infrastructure and the various regulations and mechanisms that ensure air worthiness and passenger safety. If you live in a prosperous province, you must contribute to the equalization of services in the less wealthy provinces; likewise, you must contribute to social service programs whether you are likely to be a recipient or not.

There is no opting out; this is not a cafeteria where you can pick the items that you like and ignore the rest. This is appropriate, because the decisions to implement these programs – and a great many others – were made both collectively and democratically.

The importance of collective rights within the Canadian constitutional context is not enigmatic – far from it. The recognition of collective rights is fundamental to any society that considers itself democratic. Consequently, the Constitution Act of 1982 included freedom of association as one of four fundamental rights of all Canadians. In many respects, freedom of association is or should be the glue that binds economic and social rights with political rights and freedoms. Should be, because in Canada today, the judicial interpretation of freedom of association is not only lacking but destructive.

Whatever one may think of the role and power of unions in Canada, the individual right to join and form a trade union and to engage in free collective bargaining is the hallmark of democracy. Wherever and whenever one identifies an authoritarian regime, one can be assured that its workers are denied freedom of association, the right to join and form independent unions, and the right to negotiate collectively. Although Canada's constitution explicitly recognizes freedom of association, the federal and many provincial governments have gone to great lengths to demean its value for Canadian workers and undermine its constitutional validity.

During the debate leading to the Constitution Act of 1982, the Canadian government defined freedom of association, as it should have, as including the right to strike. On 22 January 1981, the acting minister of justice, Robert Kaplan, provided the following interpretation to the Special Joint Committee of the Senate and the House of Commons:

Our position on the suggestion that there be specific reference to freedom to organize and bargain collectively is that that is already covered in the freedom of association that is provided already in the Declaration or in the Charter; and that by singling out association for bargaining, one might tend to diminish all the other forms of association which are contemplated – church associations; associations of fraternal organizations or community organizations. If one tears apart that general freedom of association, it may diminish the general meaning – freedom to associate.

Subsequently, on 9 April 1987, a majority of justices of the Supreme Court of Canada upheld, as constitutional, the federal government's "six and five" inflation-restraint legislation – Bill C-124, the Public Sector Compensation Restraint Act. In addition, it upheld separate but similar labour legislation affecting the rights of Saskatchewan dairy workers and the Alberta public sector.

All three cases had been referred to the court by unions arguing that the laws were contrary to the Charter. They argued specifically that the freedom-of-association provision within the Charter – section 2 (d) – included the right of workers to bargain collectively, as the former acting minister of justice had said, and further that it included, as a corollary, the right to strike. Not only was such an interpretation not novel, but it recognized Canada's obligations as a signatory of various conventions of the International Labour Organization (ILO), which has held repeatedly that freedom of association must include the right to bargain and its essential tool, the right to strike. Notwithstanding Canada's long-standing commitment to the ILO, a majority of the court concluded that the Charter guarantees unions neither the right to bargain collectively nor the right to strike. "I am of the opinion that the guarantee of freedom of association in Section 2 (d) of the Canadian Charter of Rights and Freedoms does not include a guarantee of the right to bargain collectively and the right to strike" (Mr. Justice Le Dain). Messrs. Justice Beetz and La Forest concurred, and Mr. Justice McIntyre stated: "I am of the opinion that Section 2 (d) of the Charter does not include a constitutional guarantee of a right to strike. My finding in that case does not, however, preclude the possibility that other aspects of collective bargaining may receive Charter protection under the guarantee of Freedom of Association."

Two members, including Chief Justice Brian Dickson, dissented from the majority, concluding in effect that freedom of association must be given a broad interpretation. The chief justice's dissent reads in part: "If freedom of association only protects the joining together of persons for common purposes, but not the pursuit of the very activities for which the association was formed, then the freedom is indeed legalistic, ungenerous, indeed vapid." He added: "I believe that freedom of association in the labour relations context includes the freedom to participate in determining conditions of work through collective bargaining and the right to strike."

Subsequent to this 1987 decision, federal and provincial governments have introduced arbitrary and capricious measures denying workers, particularly those in the public sector, the right to bargain collectively and strike. They have devalued freedom of association to the point that it has become a more or less meaningless charade for Canadian workers.

The government of Canada is no stranger to back-to-work legislation. From 1950 until the end of 1991, it introduced such legislation on twenty-five separate occasions. Before 1991, two separate bills relating to two separate disputes were the most frequent use in any one year; in 1991, the government introduced and passed four bills relating to four separate disputes.

In and of itself, the cavalier attitude of the current government vis-à-vis such legislation is alarming. Ottawa has come to view it as an integral part of collective bargaining. Rather than encouraging the parties to a dispute to resolve issues, the government has indicated, by its actions, that it is prepared routinely to legislate an end to disputes. Without a doubt, the knowledge that the government is prepared to do so and thereby impose terms and conditions of employment is contributing to employers' growing reluctance to negotiate. The situation is that much worse when an employer (the government) has the ability to legislate an end to disputes to which it is itself a party.

In light of the 1987 Supreme Court ruling, Canadian unions are looking increasingly to the international community for protection of freedom of association. In November of this year, the ILO is expected to rule on a number of complaints filed on behalf of the National Union of Provincial Government Employees and the PSAC, to the effect that provincial wage-control legislation and the federal act that ended the 1991 PSAC strike violated freedom of association, contrary to various ILO conventions.

In the closing paragraphs of its complaint to the ILO, the PSAC stated: "Individually and collectively, the 155,000 members of the PSAC are looking to the ILO to tell the Canadian Government that while it has the legislative majority necessary to impose its will, it does not have the moral authority to do so. Individually and collectively, the 155,000 members of the PSAC are looking to the ILO to tell the Canadian Government that its actions do not enjoy international sanction."

At the same time, Canadian unions are participating more forcefully in the current constitutional debate than they did in either 1981 or 1987. On 21 January 1992, The Canadian Labour Congress will appear before the Special Joint Committee on a Renewed Canada and argue that trade union rights, including the right to organize, bargain collectively, and strike, should be given explicit constitutional sanction.

Such constitutional protection would not prevent governments from introducing wage controls or ending strikes. The main difference between explicit constitutional recognition of these rights and the Supreme Court's current (1987) interpretation of freedom of association is that governments intent on abrogating these rights, through wage control or back-to-work legislation, would have to show that their actions were "demonstrably justifiable in a free and democratic society," pursuant to section 1 of the Charter. In other words, the government could not simply say that it was introducing controls to arrest inflationary pressures or stem the growth in the deficit but would actually have to prove that the measures were necessary.

Without explicit constitutional recognition of freedom of association, governments can continue the downward spiral of living standards and social conditions that have come to be the everyday reality of millions of Canadians. It is this reality that has placed a social charter on the constitutional agenda. It is this reality that has made a social charter essential if the right of Canadian citizenship is to have lasting social and economic significance for Canadians.

Citizenship is not simply the right to inhabit a country. It confers certain rights, responsibilities, and privileges on people that are, or should be, beyond the arbitrary whims of the government of the day. It protects individuals from such things as arbitrary or unlawful arrest, and in the Canadian context, it should include the right to medicare, education, social assistance, and so on. These and a great many other public services are the ties that bind Canadians together and set us apart from citizens of other North American countries.

In light of what has been happening in Canada over the last eight years, it is crucial that the collective economic and social rights of Canadian citizenship be given explicit constitutional sanction. Nor is this a novel approach, for in reality, a constitution should simultaneously reflect the historical evolution of the country, understand the present, and attempt to define the country's destiny. A constitution should not be used, as the current government is attempting, to entrench an economic agenda that goes against the grain of public sentiment.

Over the past eight years, the current government has embarked on a comprehensive campaign to deregulate the economy, privatize and contract out public services, institute free trade, and increase the profitability of private capital by reducing employment incomes and the social wage enjoyed by all citizens. For all but a few Canadians, a job is absolutely essential if they are to participate in society. Yet, under the current government, workers have seen their jobs permanently disappear. The employment restructuring precipitated by the Conservative government through free trade and other equally insidious aspects of the big business agenda has been accompanied by severe cuts to unemployment insurance. In fact, no aspect of the social safety net has been immune to the axe. The federal commitment to medicare and other social programs has been reduced.

In essence, many of the ties that bind Canadians together and provide us with a collective sense of self have snapped – not accidentally, but brutally severed by a government endeavouring to reduce expectations and enforce a declining standard of living on the overwhelming majority of Canadians. It is important, when reflecting on this situation, to understand that the government is not acting alone. Since the first day of its tenure in September 1984, it has been taking its cues from the Business Council on National Issues. From free trade to the Goods and Services Tax, from patent protection for pharmaceutical companies to privatization, from contracting out to expenditure cuts for health, education, and social services, the business wish list and the government's willingness to comply are almost endless. With increasing vitriol, senior business and government representatives are asserting that Canadians have to do more with less, that there is no free lunch, and that Canadians must become more self-reliant.

During the current constitutional round, the federal government appears intent on enshrining its economic agenda in the constitution. Its proposals related to property rights, federal-provincial budgetary harmonization, the Bank of Canada, and free trade within Canada are aimed at strengthening business to the detriment of Canadians. Entrenching property rights will further erode the fundamental right of freedom of association, making it even easier for corporations to prevent picketing of their premises. At the same time, property rights will make it harder for the nation, as a collective, to protect the environment from corporate excess, to say nothing of what will happen to provinces dominated by a single corporate entity.

The government's proposals relating to federal-provincial budget harmonization will make it easier for future federal governments to impose wage controls and have the program emulated by the provinces. As has been shown, the current government's disregard for freedom of association, particularly in the public sector, is almost absolute. The proposals will, if implemented, complete the circle. The attack on the public service is, in reality, an assault on all citizens. A federal government that boasts that the federal civil service is smaller today than it was in 1973 fails to mention that it now takes three months to respond to a routine pension inquiry.

All of this, and much more, are done under the guise of fiscal responsibility. For many people, fiscal responsibility has come to be strictly a justification for government cutbacks and anything even remotely connected to deficit reduction. We are at the point where some people, aided and abetted by the current government and the business community, are tallying the cost of the relationship between citizens and the state and concluding that it is just too expensive.

But Canadians see things differently. In the current climate of "fiscal responsibility," they see the importance of public services to individuals and society at large when disaster strikes. The problem can be as explosive as a woman fleeing an abusive relationship; as threatening to human life as a toxic waste spill or airplane crash; or as individual as the suffering of a person losing his or her job or being forced into poverty because of inadequate pension income.

When a government citing fiscal responsibility or deficit reduction lays off or fails to hire adequate numbers of inspectors to check the air worthiness of airplanes, the chances that a plane will crash increase. The inquiry into the March 1989 Air Ontario crash in Dryden, for example, uncovered evidence that the flight was a victim of failure in Canada's aviation safety system. Clearly, it is not "fiscally responsible" to maintain staff levels inadequate to ensure the safety of the Canadian public. From a purely financial perspective, the Dryden air crash cost far more than would have been spent providing adequate inspection of the company's planes. Nor is it "fiscally responsible" to cut back on the inspection of food and other consumer products that can cause serious illness and injury if not properly produced and inspected.

Examples can easily be cited throughout the range of government services that dramatically and often tragically bring home the point. It could be questioned, for example, whether it is "fiscally responsible" to force unemployed workers or pensioners to wait an inordinate period of time to have a legitimate claim for social benefits processed.

Another favoured ploy of governments facing deficits is to transfer their responsibilities to other levels of government and individuals. In 1991, we saw a vicious circle of cutbacks passed down the line from Ottawa to the provinces, from the provinces to local governments and school boards, and, finally, from municipalities to property taxpayers.

We see, as well, indirect transfers that are equally insidious, as in the transfer that occurs when a provincial or municipal government, citing fiscal restraint, deliberately decides to allow a road to deteriorate to the point that an unsuspecting motorist damages his or her car. It could be argued that it is fiscally irresponsible to save a million dollars in this way when motorists will pay two or three times that amount in needless repairs. More important, the declining infrastructure is placing the health and safety of Canadians at risk – leading ultimately to higher health care costs, not to mention the personal trauma experienced by the victims of fiscal responsibility.

It needs to be repeated that the perquisites of Canadian citizenship and the collective good are devalued every time a cut is made to public services. It has been argued, frequently correctly, that the rights of citizenship in Canada are not always equal. Aboriginal Canadians have not been treated fairly in their relationship with the state. White males are better served by our democracy than women. Opportunities of English-speaking Canadians may exceed those available to francophones. Whites usually fare far better than citizens from visible minority communities. Residents and citizens from one region may enjoy greater benefits than those who happen to inhabit another region. The discrimination faced by many of these groups is deplorable and cries out for immediate remedy.

In many respects, the discrimination faced by public-sector workers pales in comparison. Yet discrimination against them as a class of citizens does exist. It is probably true that such discrimination emanates from the unique relationship that these workers have with the state.

The Canadian government routinely disregards the fundamental right of freedom of association when it is convenient to do so. In addition, successive governments have refused to introduce legislative reform that would give public-sector workers the same rights in collective bargaining and employment practices that it believes fair for private-sector workers and employers. As a result, public-sector workers are denied the right to negotiate such fundamental issues as pensions and job classification. Through much of Canadian history, the government of the day, adding insult, has treated its work-force with a degree of paternalism that has no place in developed society.

As part of its agenda to make Canadians do more with less, the current government is proposing to revamp the public service. The so-called revitalization process, known as PS2000, seeks to entrench this paternalism well into the next century. The authors of PS2000 want public-sector workers to be, among other things, non-partisan. They reaffirmed this "age-old" value of public service subsequent to the Supreme Court's determination that legislation enforcing non-partisanship was an unconstitutional infringement of section 2 (b) and (d) and section 15 of the Charter. If an election were to be called today, the government would quickly advise federal public-sector workers that their employment would become tenuous if they had the audacity to work visibly or show support for a candidate or party of their choice.

Similar situations abound. Pursuant to legislation, public-sector unions are prevented from affiliating with political parties, even though private-sector unions and corporations are encouraged to do so. The double standard vis-à-vis public-sector workers serves to devalue the citizenship rights of these workers.

In promoting collective rights, the Canadian labour movement in no way seeks to devalue the individual rights that Canadian citizens enjoy pursuant to the Charter. In fact, the union movement has championed, and will continue to do so, the rights of all citizens, especially those who have been treated unfairly or been discriminated against in the past. The individual rights of citizens are normally enhanced by strong protection of collective rights, such as freedom of association. It is only where a clash occurs between an individual and a collective right that the labour movement may appear insensitive to the rights of the individual.

In increasing numbers, Canadian trade unionists have adopted the slogan "an injury to one is an injury to all." This is a reflection of principle rather than a rhetorical pronouncement. I believe that while the coupling of individual rights with a clearly defined collective consciousness makes trade unionists, and the trade union movement, unique, it does not undermine the value that unions and their members place on citizenship. On the contrary, the dichotomy created by our strong support for both individual and collective rights forces us to assess situations, policies, legislation, and even the Canadian constitution from several points of view.

I believe that our assessment of the relative advantages and disadvantages of a particular policy from an individual and collective perspective provides us with a balanced view that all Canadians and our governments would do well to emulate. This is particularly the case because the relationship between individuals and the state is not one-sided.

MAUREEN O'NEIL

Citizenship and Social Change: Canadian Women's Struggle for Equality

"Citizen" is defined by the Funk and Wagnalls *Canadian College Dictionary* as "a native or naturalized person owing allegiance to and entitled to protection from a government."

For very good reason, women have often wondered about the nature of protection they have received from their governments. For centuries laws discriminated against them. In Canada, there was a gap of five decades between Confederation and women winning the vote. And in 1992, seventy years after women's suffrage was introduced, women are less than 20 per cent of legislators. Women are still petitioners, not lawmakers. Ironically, in a world that is fast embracing the form and rhetoric of democracy, women actually seem to be losing ground in the transition from dictatorship. Both the democrats of eastern Europe and the mullahs of the Middle East are prepared to wipe out hard-won advances.

Why is real citizenship so illusory for women? The philosophers are not much assistance in helping us find an answer. Lorenne Clark and Lynda Lange pose the following question in their introduction to *The Sexism of Social and Political Theory*:

What would be the effect of assuming that one criterion of the present interest or relevance of any political theory is whether or not sexual equality is a feature of it? We believe that political theory in the past neither made this assumption nor generated theories compatible with it. This resulted from its failure to recognize that the manner of reproduction in human societies requires as thorough an understanding as do other matters with which political philosophy has traditionally been concerned, such as the manner of production or the basis of authority. We contend that traditional political theory is sexist, not merely because women have been deemed to have an inferior nature or social role but, more importantly, because women literally have not been considered 'political animals' in the major theoretical models of political society."[1]

Just as Diane Elson took up this issue (ten years later) in her analysis of male bias in economic policy, Clark and Lange refer to the need for "an adequate theory of the relation between production and reproduction" to compensate for traditional political theory which is "utterly bankrupt" in any equality perspective.[2] Philosophers who shaped Western thought did not think about women. Women were rooted in the private sphere, while philosophers were animated by the public sphere.

A small industry has grown up to shake this notion of women hemmed in by reproduction, particularly in considering what women do in Third World countries. There, analysts have dissected gender (the socially constructed relations between men and women) even more thoroughly than in industrialized countries. Public policy in North America and Europe requires equal scrutiny.

However, as Diane Elson says, "conscious and unconscious male bias in thought and action is frequently buttressed by economic and social structures which make such practices seem rational, even to those who are disadvantaged by them."[3]

Marilyn Waring, a New Zealand ex-politician, economist, and sheep farmer, has written extensively about the invisibility of women's labour. Her book, *If Women Counted: A New Feminist Economics*, has contributed to a statistical redefinition of women's work, to take account of all that happens in the non-formal sphere.[4] In Canada, that usually means work in the home. The venerable (Canadian) National Council of Women has been making this point for decades, arguing that Statistics Canada should keep track of what women do *without* pay.

For most women, having babies and looking after them have until very recently overshadowed all else. Not only did these responsibilities take up most of their lifetime – no matter what other work they did in addition – for centuries it took their lives. Until 1926 in Canada, women's probability of dying in childbirth was 5.7 per 1,000 births. This is considerable, compared to 1989 figures where there were only 0.4 maternal deaths per 10,000 births.[5] Women in developing countries, in the South, are at least twelve times more likely to die from causes related to pregnancy and childbirth than are women in the North.

Camille Paglia says in her controversial study, *Sexual Personae*:

It is precisely in advanced western society, which attempts to improve or surpass nature and which holds up individualism and self-realization as a
model, that the stark facts of women's condition emerge with painful clarity.
The more woman aims for personal identity and autonomy, the fiercer will
be her struggle with nature ... Political equality for women, desirable and
necessary as it is, is not going to remedy the radical disfunction between
sexes that begins and ends in the body. The sexes will always be jolted by violent shocks of attraction and repulsion.[6]

Paglia is right about there being a constant struggle. Even Mary
Wollstonecraft, author of *A Vindication of the Rights of Women*, spent
a distressing period of her life in self-destructive behaviour (she attempted suicide), all for the unrequited love of Gilbert Imlay, ex-
officer in the American Revolutionary Army. "Much of her political
ardour had evaporated into infatuation for this one man – and he
had tired of her ... It was the worst of a woman's lot to be emotionally
beholden, like her, to a faithless man (physically too, with the child)
until both her pride and her freedom were lost."[7] In the end, poor
Mary died after giving birth.

To quote Paglia again, "Political equality will succeed only in political terms. It is helpless against the archetypal. Kill the imagination,
lobotomize the brain, castrate and operate: then the sexes will be the
same. Until then, we must live and dream in the daemonic turbulence of nature."[8]

The magnificent enterprise of women's struggle has tried to tame
"the daemonic turbulence of nature" – or at least to ensure that
women do not continue to suffer economically, socially, and politically, simply because they are women. The feminist rallying cries
have been: give women the means to control their bodies, to control
their reproduction; give women the means to earn their living outside their homes, beyond the control of their fathers and the fathers
of their children; give women the voice to proclaim their views in
public places, to contribute as lawmakers and regulators of the public sphere, to be politicians.

Women are making progress toward citizenship, to the right of
some protection by government and to their own representation in
government. For women to be full citizens they must first actively
want to be. They need to feel able to participate – whether as an
armchair (or kitchen-chair) follower of public events, as a member
of a group pushing for change, as a member of a political party, or
as a person with a full-time career in the public policy-making circle
(as a politician, a senior public servant, a journalist, a judge, an industrial or trade union leader consulted by government, or in aca-
deme, on an advisory council, or in a think-tank).

PREREQUISITES

Then there are the requirements of time, money, and support at home.

Do women have the time for politics? Virtually all time-budget studies show that men and women have different amounts of leisure time – time not taken up by work or family obligations. Women have far less leisure time than men, and this is not changing very quickly.

Do women have the money? True, more women have their own incomes now. However, do their incomes and the kinds of jobs that they hold permit them the luxury of venturing into the uncertain terrain of politics? The proportion of the Canadian labour force made up by women has increased from approximately one-third in 1970 to 44 per cent in 1988, with large gains in work-force participation for married women and women with young children.[9]

Indeed, the increasing income of female spouses accounted for much of their families' real income growth in the 1970s and softened the decline in the early 1980s. Still, there are income inequalities – the female-male earnings ratio for university graduates was 70 per cent in 1987, up from 61 per cent in 1971. And the growing proportion of women living without spouses resulted in more women and children on low incomes by the mid-1980s. Women with full-time jobs still earned only 66 per cent of men's incomes in 1987.[10]

Clearly, there is still a long way to go.

As Virginia Woolf once said, "The history of men's opposition to women's emancipation is more interesting perhaps than the story of that emancipation itself."[11] To add community activism or a life in politics to the time-consuming enterprise of managing work, a home, children, and a spouse requires help. It means as little (or as much) as a husband or lover not made jealous or feeling inconvenienced by these interests "beyond the private sphere." (He must be willing to share in looking after children and house.) It means as much (or as little) as affirmative action measures by political parties to increase women's candidacies. It requires "permission" and resources for women to roam further from home than women usually do – particularly since participation in politics in Canada, except at the municipal level, almost always means moving and commuting. Even judging requires time away from home.

WOMEN AND PUBLIC POLICY

Whether or not women are actually direct participants in the political process, the major issues of concern have been a part of the Canadian political fabric for some time. In Canada the struggle for women's equality has been an element of public policy discussion for more than twenty years. There are a number of reasons for this. First, and probably foremost, was timing.

The Royal Commission on the Status of Women (1970) reported to Parliament at just the right time – a new women's movement was emerging, and then, unlike now, government saw itself as a key actor in the transformation of Canadian society. The "Just Society" and "Participatory Democracy" were political objectives in 1970 – a year of turbulence in relations with Quebec – but clearly an exciting and path-breaking time in the evolution of Canadian public policy-making.

The federal government made the prescient decision to ensure follow-up to the royal commission; it set a precedent in establishing an office within the Privy Council Office to prepare the government's response and also analyse, on a continuing basis, the impact of its policies on women. (Later this became Status of Women Canada.) It was probably one of the first, if not the first national government to recognize formally that all policies had differential effects on women and men. (This does not mean that the "right decisions" were always taken or even the key policies acted on). Later, departmental advisors, an Advisory Council, the Women's Program at the Department of the Secretary of State, and a Human Rights Commission were added. The Women's Bureau in the Department of Labour, which antedated all of these, changed its function as new centres of activity and new legislation reshaped the bureaucratic landscape.

From 1970 on, the Citizenship Branch of Secretary of State was the crucible for experimentation with the very particular relationships between "social movements" and government itself.[12] This expanded notion of "citizenship," which was derived from the political objectives of participatory democracy, was used to increase women's access to government funds through the creation of the Women's Program at Secretary of State.

Support for voluntary groups had been called for in the royal commission's report. The purpose of the Women's Program (officially born in 1973) was "to promote greater participation by women in all aspects of society particularly in decision making and the political process and to increase the capability and effectiveness of women's organizations working to improve the status of women."

The program's mode of operation was clearly within the mandate established earlier for citizenship grants. Its style of operation – with program officers feeling "accountable to the women's movement" and seeing themselves as "radicals" – fitted with the style of the times. Sue Findlay, the first director, has written about these early days. As one commentator said, referring to the establishment of the Company of Young Canadians, "the radicals were, increadibly, the government officials."[13]

The eight "permissible bases for grants"[14] from the Citizenship Branch at the time demonstrate how easy it was for the women's program to find a home in that program:

(1) increase participation by people in the affairs of society and ... decrease alienation. Participation assumes the potential for behavioural change in the persons concerned;

(2) make persons more socially aware in the sense of what happens to people;

(3) provide a voice for people who have not had a voice in their affairs;

(4) increase self-help, i.e., grassroots programs for grassroots people by grassroots people;

(5) are concerned with the values of human life and dignity (quality of life);

(6) that articulate the reality of the developmental process toward participation;

(7) that have a research component built in (Action-research);

(8) stimulate the emergence of local community leaders.

The notion that government itself could take on the revolutionary spirit and become bold – to paraphrase Ian Hamilton, who wrote a history of the Company of Young Canadians, Canada's version of the Peace Corps – has had important consequences for women's equality, for women's citizenship. It has meant that Canada has finely tuned "national machinery" for analysing the effect of public policy on women and carefully crafted political rhetoric on women's equality as well as a significant financial investment in women's groups which lobby for change.

Sadly, more than twenty years after the commission, women in Canada are still under-represented in politics – the most salient affirmation of their citizenship. They lag behind women in the Nordic social democracies, not only in their levels of political participation but also in wage differences with men, crucial social security (maternity benefits at full salary), and affordable child care. Indeed, in the UN *Human Development Report* of 1991, Canada, though ranked second in the world with respect to the Human Development Index, is ninth when gender indicators are incorporated.[15]

Sue Findlay has always seen the state as "maintaining women's inequality." "The State," she said, " ... cannot deny the accumulation of almost two decades of contradictions between political commitments (the rhetoric) and the persistence of women's inequality."[16] But she is probably too negative. Whatever the contradictions – and of course they exist – there *have been* public policy victories. Nonetheless, the achievement of women's equality requires a transformation both in women's relations with men and in thinking about public policy.

For public policy to transform, it must be based on a full understanding of the nature of the socially structured relations between women and men. And policy-makers must be committed to making changes possible for women. That means political parties first must incorporate in their platforms the policy changes needed to advance women's equality. Then, governments must ensure that ministers and the public service know what that means for their legislative policy and programs.

In 1976, the federal cabinet decided that all ministries must take into consideration the effects of their policies and programs on women. In new policies coming to cabinet for decision, the implications for women were to be spelled out.

At that time there were fewer than a dozen people working at Status of Women Canada, the "central agency" which replaced the post–royal commission Status of Women office within the Privy Council Office in 1976. Status of Women reported then to a powerful minister in cabinet, Marc Lalonde, who, over the years he held the portfolio (1974–79) was also variously minister of health and welfare, minister of state for federal-provincial relations, and minister of justice.

A major preoccupation of the Status of Women office during 1976–78 was preparation of the National Action Plan, a series of undertakings that set out proposals for change "where realistic progress toward women's equality can be made by 1985." Changes were to take place in federal legislation, policy, research, and programs. This initiative was part of Canada's "compliance" with UN-mandated activities, part of the UN Women's Decade, 1975–85.

There were changes to the maternity benefits section of the Unemployment Insurance Act, the sexual assault provisions of the Criminal Code, the Divorce Act, and a host of other legislative initiatives. These built on the earlier omnibus bill of 1975 (and other legislative changes) which removed blatant discrimination from federal statutes. Policy initiatives were agreed to: to increase trades training for women in non-traditional occupations; to produce guidelines for the elimination of sex-role stereotyping both in government publications and in the media; to examine ways to end sexual harassment in

the workplace; to examine the role of women in economic development; to increase the accessibility of language and orientation programs for immigrant women; to re-evaluate government support
for women's voluntary associations; and to require management ac-
countability for equal opportunities in the public service. Some research initiatives were launched in new territory – for example,
violence against women.

Since the late 1970s, there has been considerable evolution in
federal-provincial discussion of Status of Women issues. In developing the national action plan, the Status of Women offices and councils in the provinces were brought together. Then, only Quebec had
a structure similar to the federal government and only Quebec put
out a comprehensive document, *Indépendance et égalité*. Ontario's office had died on the vine but was soon rapidly and enthusiastically
put into place when the federal government began scheduling annual federal-provincial meetings of ministers responsible for the
Status of Women. The first was held in 1982 under the Status of
Women minister, Judy Erola. However, it took almost ten years before all the provinces and territories had the bureaucratic resources
to support the hastily named ministers. Now ministers and officials
meet regularly.

Status of Women Canada has often had to spend as much time
working to defeat policies that would have harmed women as putting together the bureaucratic coalitions necessary to advance the
positive policies. For example, in the early 1980s there were proposals for "family based UI" that clearly would have hurt women. They
did not move forward, largely because of Status of Women Canada's
intervention early in the policy discussions.

More recently, the office was heavily involved in trying to get the
best of the bad proposals on abortion legislation accepted. (In this it
was the abortion bill's defeat in the Senate that saved the day.)

But neither the bureaucrats nor the ministers have ensured that a
good child-care package came forward. Judy Erola established the
Task Force on Child Care under Katie Cooke, in May 1984, but the
Liberals were out of power before the work was completed. The
Conservatives redid this work, through a parliamentary committee,
and prepared a legislative package but lost it before the next election
– the child-care advocates of "the best" ensuring that the merely
"good" proposals went down to defeat.

There has never been another five-year plan. However, a two-year
agenda was tabled by the prime minister at the first ministers' conference in Vancouver in November 1986. In 1989, an update on
that work was published. The device of a forward-looking plan is

still useful to focus bureaucratic and ministerial attention. Some issues that were research questions in the first plan – such as violence against women – sadly continue as a major preoccupation.

In February 1991, Mary Collins, the minister responsible for the Status of Women, announced a $136-million initiative to prevent family violence and help support victims and their families. This was followed in August by a Panel on Family Violence "to heighten public awareness, enable participants to seek solutions related to root causes of violence against women and to focus on preventative measures."

However, there have been setbacks over the last few years. First, the transformation of the decision-making system of government overall has made it more difficult for Status of Women to have policy leverage. From 1978 to 1984 there were two umbrella organizations called ministries of state co-ordinating sectoral policies in two areas, economic and social policy. These agencies operated as secretariats to the relevant cabinet committees, and they came to dominate and determine both the agenda and the direction of cabinet discussion on many of their issues. As Maureen O'Neil and Sharon Sutherland have written: "This process was a boon for Status of Women Canada. The Coordinator attended the weekly DM meetings at the Ministry of State for Social Development and, as necessary, the Ministry of State for Economic Development. On really major issues, the staff of Status of Women Canada worked in advance with the staff of two other departments ... it was humanly possible (or almost) to comment on any or all of the documents going forward to cabinet in the area and to put forward, argue and even win with an alternative analysis."[17]

However, it is much more difficult now. Not only have there been changes in the central machinery of government, but there has been in Canada a loss of consensus regarding social policy directions, and there is the contemporary economic malaise.

Over the last several years the attack on the status quo and the accepted direction of change from the culturally fundamentalist anti-choice women's groups such as REAL Women constituted a serious blow. There have been substantial reductions in core funding for change-oriented women's groups by the Women's Program, whose very existence came under parliamentary scrutiny.

On the economic front, the "fiscal crisis of the state" has prompted supply-side responses: less progressivity in rates of income tax, more indirect taxation, lower corporate taxes, accelerated depreciation of capital assets, more subsidies, and more capital assistance to business. These policy shifts have been more than a sop to the dominant political ideology in Anglo-Saxon countries of "less is better" where government is concerned. As Sutherland and O'Neil say: "This is clearly not a set of policies destined to improve the economic position of the average woman, nor is it one that is conducive to the kind of government action necessary to improve social benefits for women ... since the 1970s, the working poverty of women has grown about five times as much as that of men."[18]

It is useful to consider again the Scandinavian countries. Economic progress for women there came about not from "women-oriented" policies (with the exception of maternity leave) but because of social and income policies that stressed the reduction of social and economic inequalities between people. Women as lower wage earners benefited.

If a government really intends to seek equality between women and men, the macroeconomic policies adopted must reflect an understanding of gender relations and commitment to change. So far this has not happened – and it would be truly surprising if it did. However, women's ability to make the necessary arguments for macroeconomic policy change is improving.

Diane Elson has written clearly and eloquently about the need for a "feminist economics": "Effective challenges to male bias in theoretical reasoning need to demonstrate how supposedly gender-neutral theories are in fact imbued with male bias and how gender awareness improves the theory."[19] In the literature of women and Third World development, these issues are rising in prominence. But not much progress has been made so far in their analysis, and even less in influencing policy. However, it is easy to agree with the 1986 *World Survey on the Role of Women in Development*, "Of all issues belonging to the field of money and finance, the social impact of monetary and fiscal policies appears to be most relevant to women, especially in the context of world recession and budgetary retrenchment."[20] However, monetary and fiscal policies have been the least amenable to intervention on equality grounds.

These negatives of the last few years have obscured the positive changes of the last twenty: women's greater control of their fertility, increased access to higher education, increased (legal) equality in marriage, progress in closing the wage gap (by admittedly small steps). However, there have been changes in the climate, in government's interest in listening to women's groups.

Some think that this tendency to listen is diminishing. In Doris Anderson's new book, *The Unfinished Revolution*, her chapter on Canada is titled "Canada and Women – too little, too slow and always a compromise."[21] She quotes Sylvia Gold, like Ms. Anderson a former president of the Advisory Council on the Status of Women. Gold watched public policy from this vantage point from 1984 to 1990 and concluded: "In spite of all the briefs and work, the government doesn't listen. Today women have made almost no inroads on policy making."

THE WOMEN'S LOBBY

What has happened to the women's lobby, those who hacked a path through the forest of culture and tradition that impede the advancement of women's equality?

I have already noted that in one part of the federal government, at one time at least, there were radical bureaucrats in the Women's Program, who saw their loyalty more to the women's movement than to their minister or the government. The program contributed to the success of the women's lobby. It made a myriad of community initiatives possible and was not halted in its growth until 1986, when REAL Women[22] attacked, successfully, through their sympathizers in the Conservative caucus.

It would be useful to look briefly at the growth of women's groups dedicated to women's equality in Canada over the last two decades. Women who are part of this movement are active in using citizenship rights for women's benefit generally. In 1972, the National Action Committee on the Status of Women (NAC) was born at the "Strategies for Change" conference in Toronto (financed by the Women's Program and immortalized on film, financed from the same source).

Jill Vickers's study of NAC will soon be published. Her paper "Politics as if Women Mattered" is a partial preview:

Women's movement institutions with their umbrella structures allow the creation and expansion of coalitions among groups of quite different ideological positions, thus avoiding the fragmentation so often the fate of social movements with a project of long duration ... the creation of innovative political structures such as the National Action Committee on the Status of Women (NAC) was an essential element in the Canadian movement's political success which has resulted in the establishment of equality-seeking as a key dynamic of federal politics.[23]

NAC brought together the "new" women's groups from the post-1960s women's liberation movement with the liberal/reform groups revitalized by the royal commission in a way quite different from either the American or the European experience, where each political strain is likely to have its own organization. Vickers outlined the Canadian women's movement's success from the establishment of the royal commission to the equality rights and sex-equality guarantees in the Charter of Rights. She pointed out that this lobby helped ensure that *The Equality for All Report* of the Conservative-dominated parliamentary committee legitimized a number of the movement's key demands. As well, the Secretary of State's Women's Program was saved from the worst ravages of an attack by right-wing Conservatives responding to appeals from REAL Women to shut it down because the women's lobby turned out in force.

The Canadian women's movement is a multi-partisan mass movement. As Vickers points out, in 1986, more than 700 groups were receiving funding from Secretary of State. Over 570 were affiliated with NAC. In Quebec, some 40,000 individuals and groups are affiliated with the Fédération des femmes du Québec. The Canadian women's movement is multi-partisan, not non-partisan. It has advocated a broad, results-oriented definition of equality and has pushed for development of a "feminist policy analysis."

There has always been tension within NAC on the question of Quebec. Québécois feminists, of course, have many hundreds of provincial organizations focusing on the provincial government. (They are more extensive in provincial focus than is the case in any other province. Many women's groups in other provinces traditionally have seen Ottawa as more progressive on policy issues than their provincial governments – although that may no longer be true today.) In NAC's 1988 organizational review, it was clear that Quebec affiliates viewed NAC policy resolutions directed toward provincial governments as "improper."

The women's lobby's clearest success in the 1980s was in the minefield of constitutional reform where, given a very particular set of circumstances, it crafted the language of equality in the Charter of Rights and Freedoms. However, it was not NAC per se (which saw the FFQ, representing more than 100 Quebec groups, leave over constitutional debates) that led the effort. An ad hoc lobby group took charge, formed in outrage at a minister's alleged interference in the Canadian Advisory Council on the Status of Women's decision to hold a conference on the constitution, a conference already postponed once because of a translators' strike.

Doris Anderson, president of the Advisory Council, fed up by what she saw as temporizing by her executive over rescheduling the conference, requested a meeting with the minister responsible, Lloyd Axworthy. The minister, when asked by Ms. Anderson whether the Advisory Council should hold the conference, answered in an academic fashion – very much "on the one hand, on the other hand" – but said clearly that it was up to the council to decide. he certainly did not "interfere" – it was the council's president who asked *him* for the meeting to help *her* decide what to do, given what must have been a range of views on her executive. In any case, the president resigned.

The women's movement had its martyr – the best-known president that the Advisory Council has ever had, given her previous post as editor of the widely read *Chatelaine* magazine. The press had a field day, the Conservatives jumped on the bandwagon to embarrass the Liberals (and add to the numbers at the Ad Hoc Committee's Constitutional Conference). (This was helpful to the Conservatives who had very few credentials in women's equality battles, aside from the personal popularity of some of their stars, such as Flora MacDonald.) And Lloyd Axworthy was unfairly tagged as the minister who interfered with an independent council.

This combination of circumstances focused a spotlight on the constitutional equality issues. Probably the level of interest would not have been there so emotionally without the Anderson-Axworthy debacle. At the next stage of constitutional talks, the Ad Hoc Committee received considerable support from the next minister, Judy Erola. She allowed her phone-lines to be used (free) by the lobbyists. Shortly after the equality provisions became law, Madam Justice Bertha Wilson became the first woman appointed to the Supreme Court of Canada.

The battle over constitutional equality not only spawned new groups but also pushed to the fore the careful formulation of legal strategies to use the Charter in the fight for equality. The Women's Legal Education and Action Fund (LEAF) has been central to this work, as it endeavours to enhance women's legal rights, defined as widely as possible. The Charter has been used against women, too, as Brodsky and Day pointed out in their 1987 study for the Advisory Council.[24]

Another important source of new ideas to nourish the policy debate emerged from the Royal Commission on Equality in Employment, headed by Judge Rosalie Silberman Abella. Her report was tabled in October 1984. The commission had been established by the Liberal government on the recommendation of Lloyd Axworthy, with strong support from Judy Erola. It was acted on by the Conservative minister for employment and immigration, Flora MacDonald, who successfully moved the Employment Equity bill through cabinet, against the privatization and deregulation tide of her party's economic agenda. This somewhat controversial bill, which depends on the Human Rights Commission for enforcement, fell short of women's groups' hopes but was a major accomplishment, given the policy climate of the time.

The definition of the women's policy agenda and the success in moving items onto the broader political agenda have occurred even in the absence of significant political representation for women. Women in Canada are still unlikely to be members of Parliament and to exercise their citizenship as legislators. Indeed, they are unlikely to play significant roles in the public policy circle – in "think-tanks." There are now, however, women heading the Economic Projects Group (reconstituted after the 1992 federal budget killed the Economic Council of Canada), the Institute for Research on Public Policy, and the North-South Institute.

WOMEN IN POLITICAL CIRCLES

Women in Political Parties

No matter how much improvement there has been, it is still shocking to see how absent women are from the corridors of power. Just because we see some, we can be lulled into thinking that there are many. As the numbers show, those who do not make a career as public servants but tempt fate and enter the uncertain world of politics are still going very much against the grain.

All political parties have had women's caucuses, specific policies, and small election funds to increase women's representation. Women's caucuses in all parties are probably envious of the Scandinavians who were able, given the structure of their political institutions, to use female quotas in the list of party members put forward to the electorate. (Only in Nordic countries do women make up nearly 50 per cent of legislators.)

The NDP has very recently agreed to an affirmative action policy which attempts to graft "goals and objectives" onto our much less amenable system of constituency-controlled nominations and "first-past-the-post" parliamentary system. The policy reflects "a genuine desire within the New Democratic Party" that candidates for election and the subsequent NDP federal caucus reflect the gender and ethnic diversity of Canada. Ridings with NDP incumbents seeking re-election are exempt from this somewhat complex, mandatory process.

It is an ambitious policy. The goal is to have women running as NDP candidates in 50 per cent of all federal ridings, with women running in a minimum of 60 per cent of ridings where the NDP has a reasonable chance of winning. As well, they will aim for visible-minority, disabled, or aboriginal candidates in 15 per cent of win-nable ridings. There will be special attention to ensure that women and other affirmative-action candidates run for the NDP where elected New Democrats decide not to run again. (Ridings in this cat-egory will be under the direct scrutiny of the federal secretary.) The policy also provides some support for financing nomination fights.

It will be fascinating to watch what happens – and whether the other two parties follow suit. It was the Labour party that led the way in Norway in setting quotas for women on election lists – but the other parties soon followed.

Women as Legislators

In November 1990, the Canadian Advisory Council published a background paper entitled (optimistically) *Primed for Power: Women in Canadian Politics*, by Chantal Maillé. As Maillé explains, it was not until the 1980s that Canadian women began to make breakthroughs in politics – and their success has been greater in municipal and pro-vincial arenas than in the federal Parliament.

However, if we compare the last federal election in 1988 with the 1972 election – the first following the royal commission – we do see progress. Then only 6.4 per cent of candidates were women, and only 1.8 per cent of women were elected. In the 1988 election, 19.2 per cent of candidates were women, and women won 13.2 per cent of the House of Commons. Clearly we are still a long way from 50 per cent!

Women were least likely to run for the Conservative party. How-ever, given the politics of the time, if they did run as Conservatives, they were likely to win. Nineteen of the 23 who did won their seats. Only five of the 47 who ran for the Liberals won, three of 64 New Democrats, and none of the 83 "other."

There has been even greater improvement in provincial legisla-tures during the last decade, except for still-dismal showings in New-foundland (3.8 per cent), Nova Scotia (5.7 per cent), Saskatchewan (7.8 per cent), and NWT (8.3 per cent). In the 6 September 1990 elec-tion in Ontario, the total number of women candidates fell from 96 to 85, but their success rate improved from 20.8 per cent to 32.0 per cent. Twenty-eight women (21.5 per cent) were elected, up from 21 (16.5 per cent) in 1987. There are 11 women in cabinet. "Gender parity" has been instituted in two of the most senior cabinet commit-tees: Policy and Priorities Board and Management Board. In Manitoba, the 1990 election saw women's participation increase from nine to 11 (15.7 per cent to 19.2 per cent).

Maillé's statistics show that in municipal politics in larger urban centres, women have significantly higher representation than at either the provincial/territorial or federal level. In Edmonton in 1989, for example, more than half of the councillors were women. In Montreal and Toronto, 25 per cent were women.

Women in the Public Service

One year after the royal commission's report (1971), women numbered less than 1 per cent of senior executives in the federal government. Now they are 19.7 per cent. (Even if the current definition of senior management is broader, that is still a big jump.)

There have also been significant increases in women's appointments to boards and commissions. This is much easier to accomplish than increasing managers in the public service. It requires a political decision and good staff work to turn up suitable nominees in different fields. Candidates may not require long years of incremental managerial experience, as they do in the federal public service.

Women in the Judiciary

Women are still only 15 per cent of any provincial or territorial court. Of the nine federal Supreme Court Justices, two are women. (There were three before Madam Justice Bertha Wilson retired, and none before her appointment in 1982.)

For the last several years, women have made up at least half of law students. There will be a large pool to choose from when these women have acquired the ten years of experience necessary for judges.

Women in Journalism

The under-representation of women in politics and in the senior ranks of the bureaucracy is mirrored in journalism.[25] The Southam Newspaper group (owner of seventeen daily newspapers – representing the largest circulation in Canada) tabled the results of a two-year study on women's opportunities, including recommendations for action, in April 1990. As Russell Mills, president of Southam, said when the report came out, there obviously had been "some barriers in place that have been preventing the merit system [of promotion] from operating properly ... it's about time we made some changes so that women have the same access to the merit system as men had." At about the same time, the *Toronto Star*, the country's largest-circulation (independent) newspaper, posted a policy statement regarding employment equity for both women and visible-minority representatives.

There has already been action at Southam. Women senior managers (publishers, those reporting to publishers, and head office managers) have increased from six to eight out of 126 (still only 6 per cent). In December 1991, Southam appointed its first woman publisher (Linda Hughes of the *Edmonton Journal*). Each newspaper now has an employment-equity co-ordinator, and most have sexual harassment policies in place. Encouraged by action at Southam, there have been two national conferences of women in the media. Women journalists were very concerned at the most recent conference in Vancouver about "male backlash."

Now women students constitute more than 50 per cent of the country's main journalism programs. Still, in spite of "heightened sensitivity" in the industry, just one-quarter to one-third of newsroom employees are women.

CONCLUSION

Why is it taking Canadian women so long to move into elected politics and, indeed, into the wider political circle? Clearly, the low percentage of Canadian women in politics is not an aberration – with the Nordic exception, there are very few women anywhere in politics and the higher ranks of bureaucracies.

Maillé offered the usual explanations in her short study for the Advisory Council – political parties still seem to be controlled by "old boys' networks." For political life, personal characteristics such as wealth, prestige, influence, success, and education are sought after – but women are still a very small part of the elite. However, it is probably (at least in my view) what Maillé calls "the lifestyle demands of political life" that are the greatest hurdle.

If women do have the self-confidence, organizational skills, communication abilities, financial resources, and thirst for intellectual combat that are all required in politics, then, particularly if they have children, they must also have a partner willing to do more than just "help out" at home. They need someone who really is a partner – and there are still not very many men around who are interested in playing that kind of role. This is as true for senior public servants and journalists as politicians, where workdays are routinely twelve hours long and work frequently involves travel. Without changes at home, women in the public sphere must be either without partners or small children – or very rich and with excellent domestic help, like the Queen. Most of us are not.

Women in Canada are still some way from claiming their full citizenship. In addition to the average woman's persistent economic inequality and the undervaluing of her "non-economic" contribution in raising the next generation, women are still less than a quarter of federal legislators and senior public servants. They are still a minority in the press too, that crucial dimension of democratic political life. There are certainly significantly increasing numbers of women elected officials in municipalities and some provinces. These are encouraging signs for the future – particularly for women who choose their partners well.

NOTES

1 Lorenne Clark and Lynda Lange, eds., *The Sexism of Social and Political Theory: Women and Reproduction from Plato to Nietzsche* (Toronto: University of Toronto Press, 1979), vii.
2 Ibid., xvi.
3 Diane Elson, ed., *Male Bias in the Development Process* (Manchester: Manchester University Press, 1991), 8.
4 Marilyn Waring, *If Women Counted: A New Feminist Economics* (New York: Harper & Row, 1988).
5 Statistics Canada, *Vital Statistics for 1926*, Health Report Supplement, *Deaths* (Ottawa: Dominion Bureau Statistics, Queen's Printer, 1989).
6 Camille Paglia, *Sexual Personae* (Princeton, NJ: Yale University Press, 1990), 10, 23.
7 Jane Robinson, *Wayward Women: A Guide to Women Travellers* (Oxford: Oxford University Press, 1990), 251–2.
8 Paglia, *Sexual Personae*, 23.
9 Statistics Canada, *Women in Canada* (Ottawa: Queen's Printer, 1990).
10 Ibid.
11 Virginia Woolf, *Room of One's Own* (London: Hogarth, 1926).
12 Department of Secretary of State of Canada, *Public Interest Groups in the Policy Process* (Ottawa: Centre for Policy and Program Assessment, School of Public Administration, Carleton University, 1990).
13 R. Van Loon and M. Whittington, *The Canadian Political System*, 3rd ed. (Toronto: McGraw-Hill Ryerson, 1981), 418, quoted in Secretary of State, *Public Interest Groups*, 34.
14 Secretary of State, *Public Interest Groups*, 35.
15 UNDP, *Human Development Report 1990* (1991), 15–17.

16 Sue Findlay, "Facing the State: The Politics of the Women's Movement Reconsidered," in Heather J. Maroney and Meg Luxton, eds., *Feminism and Political Economy: Women's Work, Women's Struggles* (Toronto: Methuen, 1987), 49.

17 Maureen O'Neil and Sharon Sutherland, "The Machinery of Women's Policy: Implementing the RCSW," Paper prepared for the conference Women and the Canadian State, 1–2 November 1990, 25.

18 Ibid., 27.

19 Elson, *Male Bias*, 197.

20 United Nations, *World Survey on the Role of Women in Development*, A/CONF.116/4/Rev.1 ST/ESA/180, United Nations, 1986, 129.

21 Doris Anderson, *The Unfinished Revolution: The Status of Women in Twelve Countries* (Toronto: Doubleday Canada, 1991), 213.

22 An American-style, anti-abortion, anti–women's equality group reminiscent of Phyllis Schafly's Eagle Forum.

23 Jill Vickers, "Politics as if Women Mattered: The Institutionalization of the Canadian Women's Movement and its Impact on Federal Politics 1965–1988," Paper presented to ACSANZ '88, Canadian Studies Conference, Canberra, 23 June 1988, 1.

24 Gwen Brodsky and Shelagh Day, *Canadian Charter Equality Rights for Women: One Step Forward or Two Steps Back?* (Ottawa: Canadian Advisory Council on the Status of Women, 1989).

25 Letter from Shirley Sharzov, Coordinator, Editorial Training and Development, Southam Newspaper Group, 3 January 1991.

GLENDA P. SIMMS

Racism as a Barrier to Canadian Citizenship

I, Too
I, Too, sing Canada.
I am the darker sister.
They send me to eat in the kitchen
When company comes,
But I laugh,
And eat well,
And grow strong.

Tomorrow, I'll be at the table
When company comes.
Nobody'll dare
Say to me,
"Eat in the kitchen,"
Then.

Besides,
They'll see how beautiful I am
And be ashamed –
I, too, am Canadian.

With apologies to Langston Hughes

The highest status that a state can bestow on its inhabitants is that of citizenship. Out of its history as part of the British empire and later the (British) Commonwealth, Canada has been a part of "British citizenry" for most of its existence. Nevertheless, something called "Canadian citizenship" did emerge in 1947 with the passage of the Canadian Citizenship Act. At this point Canada was still – as it continues to be, although the equation is changing – a country dominated by white immigrants and white values. The immigrants came mainly from Europe, and the values were predominantly white, Anglo-Saxon, Protestant. Indeed, Canada was a country that for many years protected its white face-scape (in spite of the presence of the First Nations) with racist tendencies and immigration rules that worked against East Indians, Blacks, and all other people of colour.

Gradually, economic and socio-political concerns caused radical shifts in immigration patterns following the new Immigration Act of 1967. The "coloured" countries of the West Indies, Asia, and Africa replaced "white" Europe as the main source of immigrants. This shift is significant to the growth of non-European Canadians, especially in large, urban centres such as Vancouver, Toronto, and Montreal. This growth added to populations that had existed for centuries but still did not affect the status of Aboriginal peoples who were never included whenever the term "Canadian" – with its purely white ascriptive value – was used.

Indeed, we may now speak of the Canadian population as having three components: "Canadians" (white Canadians), "Canadian citizens" (non-white Canadians), and Aboriginals. It is these other Canadians – "Canadian citizens" and Aboriginals – that this essay is about. These are the people whose definition as "non-white," "immigrant," or "visible minorities" subjects them to racism which renders them less than "Canadian."

For the purposes of this discussion, racism is described as the application of discrimination based on skin colour or the identification of groups of people as belonging to racial categories. The scientific basis of such identification is largely suspect, but the concept of "race" is socially accepted. With the climate of the acceptance of racial groups of human beings there exists a basic assumption that a Canadian is "white." To bolster this assumption, Canada's immigration policies for many years were devoted to keeping Canada white. Thus, the concept "Canadian" has been steeped in a tradition of racism and exclusion.

THE NATURE OF CITIZENSHIP

From the time of the earliest nation states, citizens attracted a most-favoured status. The word "citizen," from the Latin "civitas," means inhabitant of a city; the notion of citizenship was rooted in the Greek polis, or city-state, and the early philosophers of the Western tradition had clear ideas of what qualified people to become citizens of their particular city or state. It was generally accepted that not all people would be granted full citizenship or even the same level of citizenship. For instance, in Athens, "slaves, foreigners and resident aliens were denied citizenship."[1] Likewise, Aristotle distinguished between the active, or full citizen and the reduced, or passive citizen. He also believed that women were not entitled to citizenship in the same way as men. Thus, a gender factor was part of the earliest discussion on the concept of the citizen and the rights that accompanied this status. In the modern sense, the word "citizen" gained popularity during the French Revolution, which began in 1789.

In the Roman Empire one needed both civil and political rights to have the rights of citizenship. Under the concept of jus sanguinis, a child inherited the citizenship of one or both parents at birth. Later, during the feudal era, the concept of jus soli emerged – the child became a citizen of the country of birth, regardless of the parents' allegiance. Thus it is clear that citizenship, from its earliest manifestations, connoted rights, privileges, and responsibilities. But above all, it connotes identity. In a real sense, the statement "I am a Canadian" operates on the legal as well as on the psychological level. The speaker subscribes to a certain set of values and even to a particular way of seeing the world. But above all, the person distinguishes herself from the American, the Mexican, the European, and all others who gain their identity from their geographical location.

RACISM IN CANADIAN IMMIGRATION POLICY

In order to examine the assertion "I am a Canadian" within a sociopolitical and historical tradition we need to recognize that, as Daiva K. Stasiulis points out, non-European workers such as the Chinese, East Indians, and Blacks have been subordinated over the years through a series of restrictive immigration policies and legislation.[2] Such policies were steeped in racism – a concept whose "themes originate deep in Canada's past, reverberate through the country's development and ring clearly in many of our contemporary practices."[3]

These restrictive and clearly racist state policies resulted in laws which, in 1840, imposed a head tax, or landing tax, on immigrants or their vessels. Ostensibly, these measures were to minimize public burden, and this preoccupation with the notion of immigrants as a possible public burden led to enactment of more restrictive legislation between 1851 and 1864. On 1 January 1870, an Immigration Act was proclaimed establishing immigration offices in the United

Kingdom and Europe, imposing a head tax of $1.00 or $1.50 on immigrants, and requiring a bond of $300 to be posted for people who could be a public charge. The governor in council also excluded paupers or destitute immigrants.

In 1885, the Chinese Immigration Act made Chinese the only people subjected to "restrictive legislation rather than regulations."[4] For them a "Head-Tax" was set at $50, and there was a limit of one Chinese immigrant per every fifty tons of vessel tonnage. Chinese Canadians needed a certificate of residence to remain in the country. By 1903 the head tax was increased to $500. The Chinese Immigration Act remained in force until 1947. In January 1908, an order-in-council known as the "Continuous Journey Stipulation" gave the minister the authority to accept only those immigrants who "come from the country of birth or citizenship by continuous journey and on a through-ticket, purchased before leaving the country of their birth or citizenship."[5] Before this policy was revoked in 1947, it led to a remarkable incident.

On 23 May 1914, the *Komagata Maru*[6] anchored in Vancouver's Burrard Inlet with 376 passengers. The captain, Gurdit Singh Sarhali, had chartered the vessel for a period of six months and had hoped to help aspiring Canadian immigrants to make the journey to Canada while respecting the regulations set forth by that government. In the years preceding this undertaking, very few South Asians had been let into Canada. In 1911 and 1912 there had been nineteen migrants per year. The number had risen to eighty-eight in 1913. In 1914 the *Komagata Maru* set sail for Canada with 165 passengers on board. Along the way it stopped to pick up 111 passengers in Shanghai, 86 in Moji, and a final 14 passengers in Yokohama. The ship arrived in Victoria's quarantine station on 21 May 1914.

When the ship arrived, armed guards surrounded it to ensure that no one except an official party could either board or land. The official party decided that twenty-two returnees would be allowed to land in Canada but the rest would have to return to the Far East once deportation orders had been filed. Until then they would be confined to the boat. A letter from the boat was smuggled to Mit Singh Pandori, a leader in the Vancouver community, who began organizing a committee to work on the case.

The government declared that 90 of the people on the ship had trachoma and therefore were ineligible immigrants. Not wanting to create a negative image internationally, the government opted to examine one person rather than all 354 and to use the result of that case to determine the fate of all 354 passengers. This decision was met by much opposition from Gurdit Singh. Consequently, a stalemate developed. On board conditions got worse. Immigration officials refused to remove garbage from the ship, food and water provisions were running low, and by 10 June many were ill and one had died. Eventually Munshi Singh, a young Sikh farmer, was chosen for a court test to stand for all on board. On 28 June he was ruled an inadmissible immigrant. The next day an appeal was disallowed, and by 5 July the legal battle was over. On 17 July the passengers were served with deportation orders. The *Komagata Maru* set sail for the Far East on Thursday morning, 23 July 1914.

This incident is cited in most discussions on state racism in Canada and serves as a reminder of the many past actions in which the country takes no pride.

In 1910 Canada had a definition of citizenship and Canadian domicile, as well as immigrant and non-immigrant categories that could be based on nationality, occupation, or country of origin. Privileged status was given to "agriculturalists, British subjects, and usa citizens."[7] The policy clearly set out to encourage some (Europeans) and discourage others (Asians) on the basis of nationality or country of origin (race) and occupation. For instance, while some immigrants needed to produce $25 or $50 in "landing money," Asians were required to produce $200. By 1923, the monetary requirement was lifted for all except Asians, who had to pay $250 per head. In 1930, Asian immigration was limited to the wife of any Canadian citizen resident in Canada and unmarried children under eighteen years of age.

The Canadian Citizenship Act came into force on 1 January 1947, but many African and Asian countries at the United Nations were labelling Canada "a racist country."[8] In 1951, bowing to international pressure, Canada permitted 150 Indians, 100 Pakistani, and 50 Ceylonese yearly to immigrate, as well as dependants of non-white Canadian citizens. The regulations gave "Special Inquiry Officers" authority to determine who could be readily assimilated and to bar entry to those whom they felt could not. New regulations in 1962 removed discrimination in respect to admissible classes of immigrants based on national or ethnic origin, but the government was still recruiting mainly whites. By 1964 Canada had thirty-two immigration offices around the world, but only four were in non-white countries and the country's so-called open immigration policy was described as being more a farce than reality.[9] In 1976, for the first time, an Immigration Act came into force that did not discriminate on the basis of race, national or ethnic origin, colour, religion, or sex.

FOREIGN (BLACK) DOMESTIC
WORKERS

Like most other developed countries, Canada has adjusted to changing priorities and economic and social pressures. For instance, during the 1950s and 1960s a shortage of available domestic workers
caused the Canadian government to enter into a special agreement
with the governments of certain Caribbean countries. Under the Domestic Immigration Service Agreement of 1955, Canada imported
280 to 300 English-speaking women yearly to meet the demand for
household workers. The women came predominantly from Jamaica; some came also from Barbados and Trinidad. While these
women were able to apply for permanent-resident status after one
year as a domestic helper in Canada, it was very difficult to sponsor
their male partners. If and when partners were allowed to come to
Canada it was on the clear understanding that they had to be married within thirty days of their arrival.

According to a McGill University study, most of the women came
from white-collar, middle-class backgrounds in their own country.
They were teachers, postal clerks, and so on, and in their own
country many of them had their own domestic workers.[10] Thus,
in coming to Canada many suffered a drop in status. The foreign-
domestic-worker scheme reinforced the hierarchy of women and reinforced stereotypes of Black women which originated during the
era of slavery. As the program expanded, Canada began issuing
temporary work permits which allowed these workers to remain in
the country for a specified period (usually a year), doing a specific
type of work for a specific employer. This new employment-visa system was a form of indentured labour. Foreign domestic workers
came as guest workers instead of immigrants, and they had "no
rights to stay in Canada or claim social benefits."[11]

The precarious situation of these Third World domestic workers
was described by one of the women featured in a recent National
Film Board production, *Older, Stronger, Wiser*. Eva Smith, who was
recruited for the Foreign Domestic Worker Program in 1955, said
that sometimes when the employers were out for the evening and
you were babysitting, "even if till six o'clock in the morning, you better be sitting up when they arrive and you must be up also at seven
o'clock to get breakfast." According to Ms. Smith, the average salary
for a domestic worker at that time was $60 a month, or $15 a week.
It was not uncommon for a domestic worker's passport and clothes
to be confiscated by her employer in order to accentuate the worker's relative powerlessness. In a real sense, then, the price for achiev-

ing Canadian citizenship had major negative psychological and social consequences for this group of women.

The controversial issue of the working conditions of foreign domestic workers continues to be a topic of debate in Canada. The majority of such women now come from the Philippines, and they continue to argue that racism is still a factor in the dynamics of the discourse around their status within Canada and the conditions under which they work.

RACISM AS A BARRIER TO CANADIAN CITIZENSHIP

Citizenship is not only a legal definition; it is testimony to how one is treated in a given society. When the concept of racism clashes with that of citizenship, racism, not citizenship, emerges victorious. White people who are born in Canada, even if they are Nazis, are automatically given the right to Canadian citizenship. But Aboriginals, new citizens, and Blacks who are born in Canada do not achieve citizenship in any automatic way. The following real-life experiences of persons who should have had the right to all the systems that protect the Canadian citizen are instances of how racism affects citizenship. Each incident is an example of why the debate on racism and the Canadian state is a contemporary preoccupation.

Helen Betty Osborne

In a story captured in the 1991 CBC documentary *Conspiracy of Silence*, and fully documented by the Report of the Aboriginal Justice Inquiry of Manitoba, Canadians in the Manitoba town of The Pas remained silent for sixteen years although they knew the four (white) men who abducted, assaulted, battered, and murdered a nineteen-year-old high-school student, Helen Betty Osborne, early in the morning of 13 November 1971. Indeed, only a few months later, Royal Canadian Mounted Police officers concluded that four identifiable young men were involved in her death. Yet it was not until December 1987 that one of them, Dwayne Johnston, was convicted and sentenced to life imprisonment for the murder.

For a long time the police had found it impossible to gather enough evidence to support a murder charge against any of the men. By the end of 1972, the investigation stalled. In July 1983 an extensive review of the file was begun by Constable Robert Urbanoski of the Thompson RCMP, who interviewed many of the original informants. In response to a newspaper advertisement by the

RCMP, many people came forward to recount comments about the murder made over the years by two of the suspects who were eventually charged with murder in October 1986.

On 12 August 1991, the Report of the Aboriginal Justice Inquiry of Manitoba, dealing with the deaths of Helen Betty Osborne and John Joseph Harper, was turned in to Manitoba's minister of justice. The inquiry had heard testimony that The Pas was a troubled town, with segregation at the movie theatre, at least one of the bars, and in the school lunch-room. An RCMP officer told the inquiry that while inter-racial violence was not common, when it did occur it was usually a case of an assault by a white man on an Aboriginal man. The RCMP itself discriminated when dealing with Aboriginals, stopping them for no apparent reason and requiring them to account for their actions while white youth in similar situations were neither stopped nor questioned. The clear verdict of this murder inquiry was that the act of abduction itself was racist and that the sixteen-year silence was based on the fact that since Ms. Osborne was an Aboriginal woman, the townspeople considered the murder unimportant because Aboriginal people were considered to be less than human.

A lasting image from the CBC documentary has a white woman screaming, "We are no more racist here than anywhere else in Canada." She is probably right, but her cries do not obscure the fact that this is a clear case of racism interfering with Helen Betty Osborne's rights under the law.

Minnie Sutherland

In a similar vein, the disturbing scenario involving Minnie Sutherland is worthy of consideration. Constables Denis Regimbald and Guy Vincent of the Hull, Quebec, police, came up on Minnie Sutherland, a Cree woman, lying motionless in the street on the early morning of 1 January 1989. The police claimed that a nurse who was already on the scene told them that the woman was fine. They also claimed that Joyce Wesley, Ms. Sutherland's companion and cousin, told them that the woman had fallen down because she was drunk. The police also said that there were some "arrogant and rude" men on the scene who claimed that Ms. Sutherland had been in an accident. The constables decided that Ms. Sutherland did not require medical treatment or an ambulance. Constable Regimbald did radio for a taxi but later called back to say, "Cancel the taxi; the squaw has decided otherwise." Ms. Sutherland died ten days later from a head fracture apparently suffered in the accident.

A coroner's inquest heard that the men told the police that a car had hit Ms. Sutherland. According to the *Globe and Mail* of 24 February 1989, the police nevertheless "dragged her over to the snow bank at the side of the road, her head dangling." The men protested this treatment, but one policeman replied, "You better walk away or the same thing's going to happen to you." The inquest found that the constables were negligent but were not racially motivated. Despite this finding, it recommended that Hull set up a multicultural training course for police. According to the *Ottawa Citizen* of 1 September 1990, Ovide Mercredi, then a vice-chief at the Assembly of First Nations, wondered why the multicultural course was suggested if indeed racism was not a factor.

Donald Marshall, Jr.

The story of Donald Marshall was perhaps the most widely publicized and readily recognizable case of racism affecting the human rights and life chances of a Canadian. A MicMac Indian of Nova Scotia, Donald Marshall, Jr., was arrested, tried, and sent to jail for a murder committed in 1975 by a white man, Roy Ebsary. Marshall spent eleven years in jail before Ebsary confessed, thus rendering his incarceration untenable. But even at this stage, even after he was ordered freed, the recalcitrance of the Nova Scotia justice system to acknowledge fully its weaknesses and failures was again publicly instructive as to the inferior treatment accorded non-"Canadians." According to the *Spectrum* of 15 March 1991, two research studies for a royal commission that examined the Marshall case said that Blacks and Indians in the province had been kept poor and powerless by a white society that "has repeatedly shown them prejudice and discrimination." The studies also said that prejudice against both the province's 11,000 Natives and its 13,000 Blacks is prevalent and leads to discrimination against them in the justice system.

These examples put faces on the problem of exclusion and oppression of Aboriginal people in a racist environment.

SLAVERY: THE PRECURSOR TO THE BLACK EXPERIENCE IN CANADA

In order to understand fully the historical forces that conspired to rob Black Canadians of their rights of citizenship, we need to revisit the legacy of slavery. One of the most shameful and demeaning phenomena of inter-racial activity was the British slave trade, in which millions were taken from Africa and shipped forcibly to the Caribbean and North America to work as slaves. Although some of these people were brought to Canada, the first Black person on record in Canada was a free man. Matthew Da Costa came to Canada with Samuel de Champlain on his third trip in 1606. Champlain chose him because he knew the language of the Acadian MicMac, which suggests that he had been to Canada before.[12] It would be twenty-two years before the first Africans arrived in New France to work as slaves. Although it was never officially proclaimed, the "Code noir" of 1685 was used as a customary law in New France for slave ownership. Not only were the expensive African slaves used as "labour-saving devices," they were also considered valuable property that functioned as symbols of social status among the elite.[13] In the eighteenth century, Black slaves escaped to Canada from the southern United States, and they settled as free men and women in Ontario and Nova Scotia.

In his book *Blacks in Deep Snow*, Colin Thomson notes that the abolition of slavery in the British empire in 1833 ended the enslavement of Blacks in Canada, but it also marked the beginning of a new version of oppression which rendered them second-class citizens. As long as they were slaves, Blacks posed no threat to the dominant white society, since they were absolutely without rights. If Canadians could not have Blacks as slaves, they did not want them at all. Canadian Blacks received sporadic, badly financed, "separate but equal" education which emphasized practical subjects and concerns that would "better fit the mind" of the Black student. There was also an attempt to develop something called an "Ultimate Canadian Race," and the Black person was not considered a part of the emerging national character. It was believed that Blacks could not be assimilated but that if they could be, they would leave a "tinge" of coloured blood in the "Ultimate Canadian Race" – "a race which should be bred from the best 'stock' that can be found in the world."[14] Vigorous efforts were therefore made to keep Blacks out. The climate, it was said, was too harsh for them to endure, although, as slaves, they had endured it for two centuries. Neither did it make any difference to this pervasive argument that Matthew Henson, who was Black, discovered the North Pole in 1909.

Henson's ability to endure and survive harsh physical and social conditions is a lasting feature of the reality of Black people's history. The earliest experiences of these people who helped in the development of Canada are generally not known. In many instances these were not recorded, or they were distorted because they were not described and interpreted by the people themselves. Generally, these experiences were ignored because they were not considered important to the interpretation and recording of Canadian history. In spite of this situation, there are enough narratives, oral history, and recorded incidences, such as the destruction of Africville in Halifax, to substantiate the insidious effects of racism on the life chances and outlook of significant numbers of Canadians at every period in several areas of the country.

For instance, I discovered an interesting account of what life was like for a number of Blacks who settled the inhospitable frontiers of what is now Saskatchewan at the turn of the century. This account was found in a document housed in the provincial archives in Regina. It was a simple, early version of a school magazine, and the article may have been written by one of the senior students. The language and style are not sophisticated, but the voice is unmistakeably clear and contemporary. The following are excerpts as recorded in the archival document:

Longford School 1908–1955

O keep us building, Master
May our hands never falter
When the dream is in our heart.
Longford's motto: A place for everything and every thing in its place.
Longford's colours: red and white.
Longford's Junior Red Cross: Shooting Star.
Location of school: On the N.E. quarter, section 8, township 15, range 12, west of the 3rd meridian.

Early Settlers

The early settlers of Longford District came from the United States and Europe. The negroe settlement coming in 1908 from the United States. We think from slavery. There were five or six families living north of the coulee. They built their homes and farmed the land. These Negroes were musical and fun-loving. One young chap was especially fond of fried chickens which caused his neighbours to keep locks on their chicken coops and blame the poor fellow every time a hen was missing.

They also enjoyed many joyful get togethers where the fiddles were played and enjoyed by all.

In 1918 the district was stricken with a disease which probably was the 'flu. Mr. Sutton's little son, a Negro boy, died at this time. One Negro woman who had some nurse training took care of the stricken Sutton family. Mr. MacLaughlin visited the family to see if he could help them. At first they refused to let him in. After some persuasion from Mr. MacLaughlin they agreed to let him in. After entering the house he saw the little boy laying dead on the floor. Mr. MacLaughlin wrapped the boy in blankets and brought him to Mr. Charles Warren. He was later buried in the Mount Pleasant Cemetery ...

This particular recording of everyday life by an anonymous Longford student who is obviously white, as opposed to the Black families that he or she described, is more important than the efforts to house school documents in an archive. It is almost frightening to recognize that the stereotype of the fun-loving, fried-chicken-eating Black male is recorded in such an obscure Canadian settlement. It is also very clear from the passage that the Black settlers were segregated north of the coulee (a place for everything, and everything in its place) and that they were expected to take care of themselves. One cannot help but wonder why Mr. MacLaughlin was not a welcome neighbour. Did the Black community recognize the level of racism that affected their lives? One can only guess, because this archival document obscures their view and muffles their voice since their story is told by others.

Africville

At times, though, Black people have had opportunities to tell their story. Many remember Africville. The rise and demise of Africville are a classic case of citizenship denied on the basis of colour. Africville was founded by Black refugees of the War of 1812 who escaped slavery in the United States and fled to Nova Scotia with the help of the British military. The settlement was home to almost 80 Black families – approximately 400 people. Despite the richness of life in Africville, essential services such as water, garbage pick-up, and sewage were not provided for these citizens. Rather than provide these services to the community, Halifax city officials decided to force the residents of Africville to relocate. The excuse was the pressing necessity to build a highway through the middle of the community. That highway has still not been built. The last family was moved out and Africville died in 1964, putting an end to years of an oral tradition of story-telling and to a whole communal way of life.

These Blacks in Halifax were treated as second-class citizens, and the situation does not appear to be changing. A report by the Institute of Public Affairs in Dalhousie University in 1962 said that Blacks "earn less than the mean income, are unemployed for many more weeks than the average and occupationally they are concentrated far more in manual or menial jobs and virtually are unrepresented in the professions." The report continued, "White employers may for personal reasons, or in deference to the wishes of others on the staff, or of customers, decline to hire negroes or else employ them only on less skilled jobs far away from the public view. Negroes themselves may anticipate rebuffs that they will meet if they try for a more desirable position – indeed, they may anticipate rebuffs even where they might not exist – and so resign themselves to the bottom rungs of the employment ladder."[15]

The question of whether racism or other factors is the basis on which sectors of Canadian citizenry are denied their rights is ongoing. Today, like Helen Betty Osborne, J.J. Harper, and Donald Marshall, Black men and women in Canada are finding that their "citizenship" comes up short of full Canadian citizenship. In recent years fourteen Black men and one Black woman have been shot by policemen in Ontario and Quebec, six of them in 1991 alone, according to Ewart Walters, writing in the *Ottawa Citizen* of 16 January 1992. Most of these people were unarmed when they were shot. In many cases, the policemen were not arrested and charged until after protracted delays prompted public outcry. Remarkably, not one policeman has yet been convicted for any of these shootings. The public has had the impression of the same kind of inadequate police investigation that was evident in the J.J. Harper case, where the Aboriginal Justice Inquiry of Manitoba found police intent more on accepting the story of the accused policeman and offering him protection and accommodation than on conducting a proper, full, and impartial investigation.

LABELLING

In order to maintain racial distinctions, hierarchies, and value systems that relegate significant numbers of Canadians to second-class citizenship or the periphery of society, the age-old practice of labelling is constantly being applied and renewed. In demonstrating how labelling is used to deny justice and citizenship rights, I offer the following discussion that first appeared in *Women's Education des femmes* and which I entitled "Coming to Terms with 'Visible Minority.'"

Recently I began to pay closer attention to the large numbers of Canadians who, like myself, are opposed to being labelled 'visible minorities.' I now wonder if the problem of 'self-identification' which is reputedly preventing both government and private sector employers from adequately implementing employment equity programs lies partially in the use of the label 'visible minority' or partially in the lack of political will to address some of the most serious social and institutional barriers of the Canadian society. Those of us who have raised these concerns find the 'visible minority' label demeaning, anonymous, and psychologically distressing.

As a Black Canadian woman, I object to the term on a number of grounds. Firstly, it denies my identity. I am not a 'visible minority.' I define myself as a Black woman who was born in Jamaica and is now a proud first-class citizen of Canada. Secondly, it undermines my ability to define myself and forces me to accept an externally imposed definition. This is psychologically unacceptable. It is an assault on my psyche and is part of the historical process of denying my inherent human right to seek the essence of selfhood within my being and in the context of my personal history.

I have no idea of the genesis of the term 'visible minority.' I became aware of its acceptance at the official governmental level when the document "Equality Now!", the report of the Special Committee on Visible Minorities in Canadian Society, was released in March 1984. In this document, the term 'visible minority' was sanctioned as the appropriate label for 1,864,000 or 7 per cent of the Canadian population. Included in this definition are those with origins in Africa, China, India, Pakistan, Japan, Korea, South East Asia, Latin America, the Pacific Islands, the West Indies, the Philippines, and the Arabic countries.

As a Black woman, I am very aware of the political and social use of labelling. Back a few years, my people were part of the 'nigger/nigra/negro' continuum. Later on, they were 'the darkies'; still later, they were rendered 'coloured'. In the turbulent sixties and seventies they became 'Black'. Contemporary writings inform us that they are 'people of colour', Afro-Americans/Canadians, or 'the most visible of the visible minorities'.

In spite of the variety of labels and regardless of the social and political reason for the change in definitions, it is undeniable that the Canadians who are now marginalized have paid their dues to our society. These people descended from ancestors who helped to break the frontiers of Eastern, Central, and Western Canada, worked on the railroads, fished in the coastal waters, ploughed and gathered in wheatfields, potato plots and fruit vineyards, farmed in obscure communities in some of the harshest climatic conditions, and gave unconditional love to generations of 'white' Canadian children. In more recent times, many of the 'visible minorities' have come to Canada as students, domestic workers, professionals, skilled trades people, sponsored spouses and relatives, and as refugees. In short, these people are old and new Canadians and they have served and they continue to serve this country in very positive ways.

Given this perspective, the questions that need to be answered include the following: Why does Canadian society find it difficult to create a climate in

which all its citizens find justice? Why is it necessary to have employment equity programs for women, the disabled, Native Canadians and the so-called
'visible minorities'? Does the definition of so many Canadians as 'visible minorities' obscure the real problems of injustice and racism in Canadian society? Does the targeting of such diverse peoples as one group result in equity,
or does it create 'a hierarchy of the oppressed'? Who are truly the most disadvantaged people in Canadian society?

I have no answers to these questions. What I do know however, is that Canadian society is changing at a very rapid rate. Whether we live in isolated
Northern communities, in rural townships, or in teeming urban centres
such as Toronto, Montreal, Vancouver or Winnipeg, we cannot escape the
following documented facts: more and more Native peoples are becoming
urban dwellers; one in three Canadians is neither English nor French; one
in four Canadians fills the category of 'visible minority'; immigration rates
will rise in line with the government's plans and projections; and the majority of new immigrants will be from Asia, Latin America, and South America.

Given these facts, it is important for the society to concentrate on less exotic definitions and more on solutions to the social and economic inequalities
that cause so many Canadians to seek redress for historical wrongs. The
challenge is to pay attention to the sons and daughters of the 'visible minorities'. These are the youth of tomorrow and they are Canadians who know
no other land. They expect justice; they will demand justice; they will fight
for justice. They will challenge the society in ways that it has never before
been challenged.

Let us plan for the future and come to terms with injustice rather than
spend too much effort in the creation of new and meaningless categories of
Canadian citizens.

The issue of labelling is very instructive about the way in which the
dominant society marginalizes groups of people and keeps them effectively disadvantaged.

Obviously, we cannot allow ourselves to continue this marginalization in Canada. In "I, too" we echo the sentiments of the Black
American poet Langston Hughes which represent the possibility of
hope and change, even through a strategy of defiance. Society benefits from all its citizens producing a more and more humane and
productive entity. It is the responsibility of every citizen to ensure
that he or she commits to a struggle to overcome racism and achieve
the full fruits of citizenship.

Canada needs the best skills of all its citizens if it is to move into the
next century as a prosperous and progressive country. Policy-
makers and those who control the institutions need to make sure

that they do not continue to re-create in their practices the historical and contemporary practices that have denied and continue to deny many Canadians their citizenship rights.

NOTES

1 William Kaplan, *The Evolution of Citizenship* (Ottawa: Citizenship Registration and Promotion Branch, Department of Multiculturalism and Citizenship, 1991), 5.
2 Daiva K. Stasiulis, *Theorizing Connections: Gender, Race, Ethnicity and Class*, 277; also Bolaria, B. Singh, and Peter S. Li, *Racial Oppression in Canada*, 2nd ed. (Toronto: Garamond, 1988), 177.
3 Daniel G. Hill and Marvin Schiff, *Human Rights in Canada: A Focus on Racism*, 2nd ed. (Ottawa: Canadian Labour Congress and the Human Rights Research and Education Centre, University of Ottawa, n.d.).
4 O.P. Dwivedi, Ronald D'Costa, C. Lloyd Stanford, and Elliot Tepper, eds., *Canada 2000: Race Relations and Public Policy* (Guelph: Guelph University Press, 1989), 48.
5 Ibid., 47.
6 Norman Buchignani and Doreen M. Indra, with Ram Srivastiva, *Continuous Journey: A Social History of South Asians in Canada* (Ottawa: McClelland and Stewart in association with the Multiculturalism Directorate, Secretary of State, and the Canadian Government Publishing Centre, 1985), 55–8.
7 Dwivedi et al., *Canada 2000*, 47.
8 Hill and Schiff, *Human Rights in Canada*.
9 Ibid., 15.
10 D.W. Williams, *Blacks in Montreal 1628–1986: An Urban Demography* (Quebec: Les Éditions Yvon Blais Inc., 1989), 63.
11 Sedef Arat-Koc, "Foreign Domestic Workers," in *Studies in Political Economy: A Socialist Review* 28 (Spring 1989) 46.
12 This is taken from "400 Years: African Canadian History," a display by Sheldon Taylor, curator, Multicultural History Society of Ontario, Toronto, 1990.
13 Ibid.; Williams, *Blacks in Montreal*, 7.
14 Colin A. Thomson, *Blacks in Deep Snow: Black Pioneers in Canada* (n.p.: J.M. Dent & Sons, 1979), 21.
15 Institute of Public Affairs, Dalhousie University, *The Condition of the Negroes of Halifax City, Nova Scotia*, Publication No. 27 (Halifax, 1962), 9.

DARLENE JOHNSTON

First Nations and Canadian Citizenship

Citizenship. The very word conjures up notions of freedom and autonomy, the right to participate, a sense of belonging. The Western political tradition regards the evolution of citizenship as its crowning democratic achievement. However, for the First Nations over whom Canada asserts jurisdiction, the experience of Canadian citizenship has been somewhat less than ennobling.

The political status of the First Nations within the Canadian Confederation has never been satisfactorily resolved. The prevailing Canadian mythology portrays a transition from ally to subject to ward to citizen. In First Nations circles, this is often referred to as "the Big Lie." This theory of transition constitutes a denial of the inherent right of First Nations to be self-governing. Such denial is characteristic of the practice of colonialism.

I take as the benchmark of colonialism the settler community's systematic deprivation of the political, economic, and cultural rights of indigenous people. From this perspective, the history of the denial and gradual extension of Canadian citizenship to First Nations is a study in colonialism. It entails the alteration of status and rights without consent of the people concerned. It is relatively easy to recognize as non-consensual the exclusionary aspects of Canadian assertion of jurisdiction over First Nations. Paradoxically, the measures designed to remedy this exclusion were likewise coercive. This history of exclusion and inclusion must be recounted from a First Nations perspective. Only then can the ambivalence and resistance that First Nations display toward Canadian citizenship begin to be understood.

OF ANCIENT COVENANTS AND
FRIENDSHIPS

Contrary to popular belief, the history of the so-called New World does not begin in 1492. Turtle Island has always been home to the First Nations. Long before the Europeans began leaving their home-lands, First Nations were living in their territories, governing them-selves. Not only did the Europeans not discover America, they did not invent democracy or citizenship. There were, in fact, some very elaborate constitutional structures created by First Nations before the arrival of the Europeans.

Perhaps the best-known example is the Confederacy of the Haudenosaunee, the People of the Longhouse. The founding of their federation can be traced to nearly a thousand years ago. At that time, according to the traditional account, a messenger was sent by the Creator to bring an end to several generations of warfare among the Seneca, Onondaga, Oneida, Mohawk, and Cayuga nations. The messenger, Deganwidah, established the Great Law of Peace, the Kaianerekowa, as the constitution of the Haudenosaunee confeder-acy.[1] The Great Law provided an intensely democratic decision-making process, replete with checks and balances. No measure could be decided without the consent of all five represented nations. Each decision had to be unanimous. The fifty civil chiefs who sat on the confederate council were nominated by clan mothers. The chiefs could also be removed by the clan mothers if they failed to abide by the rules of the Great Law. An appreciation of the richness of this democratic tradition prompted Felix Cohen to write: "Politically, there was nothing in the Empires and kingdoms of Europe in the fif-teenth and sixteenth centuries to parallel the democratic constitu-tion of the Iroquois Confederacy, with its provisions for initiative, referendum and recall, and its suffrage for women as well as for men."[2]

The Haudenosaunee conception of citizenship is symbolically captured on the Covenant Circle Wampum.[3] The intertwining strands that form the circle represent the fifty chiefs of the confed-eracy. Their hands are bound together so firmly and so strongly that, if a tree should fall on the circle, it could not break it. Inside the circle, the clans, laws, ceremonies, ways, and traditions of the con-federacy are protected. The people and their future generations re-main in security, peace, and happiness. People are free to leave the circle – that is, to submit to the law of a foreign nation – by passing under the arms of the chiefs. But to stand outside the circle is to stand without a language, without a culture. The drastic consequences of leaving the circle were explained by Chief John Buck, Fire-keeper, in 1897: "if at any time one of the Confederate Lords choose to submit to the law of a foreign people, he is no longer in but out of the Confederacy, and persons of this class shall be called 'They have alienated themselves'. Likewise such persons of this class who submit to the laws of foreign nations shall forfeit all birthrights and claims on the Five Nations Confederacy and territory."[4] The tenet that Haudenosaunee identity exists only inside the circle influenced the relationships that developed between the Confederacy and European powers.

The alliance that the Haudenosaunee formed with the British was modelled on the ideals of mutual respect and autonomy. The spirit of this alliance is depicted on the Gus-Wen-Qah, the Two Row Wampum Belt. The first of these belts was delivered and explained at the Treaty of Fort Albany, in 1664, marking the commencement of formal relations between the British and the Confederacy.[5] It has remained an integral feature of Haudenosaunee diplomacy into the twentieth century. The Special Committee on Indian Self-Government received an explanation of the import of the Gus-Wen-Qah by an authorized representative of the Confederacy at a hearing in May 1983:

[W]hen your ancestors came to our shores, after living with them for a few years, observing them, our ancestors came to the conclusion that we could not live together in the same way inside the circle ... So our leaders at that time, along with your leaders, sat down for many years to try to work out a solution. This is what they came up with. We call it Gus-Wen-Qah, or the two row wampum belt. It is on a bed of white wampum, which symbolizes the purity of the agreement. There are two rows of purple, and those two rows have the spirit of our ancestors; those two rows never come together in that belt, and it is easy to see what that means. It means that we have two different paths, two different people. The agreement was made that your road will have your vessel, your people, your politics, your government, your way of life, your religion, your beliefs – they are all in there. The same goes for ours ... They said there will be three beads of wampum separating the two, and they will symbolize peace, friendship, and respect.[6]

The vessel metaphor characterized the distinct jurisdictions: the British vessel and Confederacy canoe. The two were to coexist as independent entities, each respecting the autonomy of the other. The two rows of purple wampum, representing the two governments, run parallel, never crossing. The two vessels travel together as allies, but neither nation tries to steer the other's vessel.

In the relationship envisioned by the Two Row Wampum, neither government has the authority to legislate for the other. The vessels are always separated by the three white beads symbolizing peace, friendship, and respect. The principles captured by the Two Row Wampum formed the basis of the alliance between the British and the Confederacy. Perhaps the most striking feature of the Haudenosaunee vision of diplomatic relations with the British is its consistency. For over three centuries, the Confederacy has abided steadfastly in its "canoe" and has reminded the British of their obligation to do the same.[7]

This is simply one example of the alliances that the British formed with the First Nations. There were many others. Each First Nation had its own territory and system of government; the people had their own allegiances, rights, and responsibilities. Owing to their influence in trade and defence, the First Nations were much sought after as allies. In forging their alliances, the British were conciliatory and respectful of First Nations customs and usages, and they acknowledged their independence. These alliances proved especially important during the Seven Years' War.

When the conflict between the European powers ended in 1763, the victorious British were quick to honour their obligations to their First Nations allies. The Royal Proclamation of 1763 declared that "it is just and reasonable, and essential to our Interest, and the Security of our Colonies, that the several Nations or Tribes of Indians with whom We are connected, and who live under our Protection, should not be molested or disturbed in the Possession of such Parts of our Dominion and Territories as not having been ceded to or purchased by Us, are reserved to them, or any of them, as their Hunting Grounds."[8] Recognizing that "great Frauds and Abuses have been committed in purchasing Lands of the Indians, to the great Prejudice of our Interests, and to the great Dissatisfaction of the said Indians," the proclamation established a formal policy for the surrender of lands. King George III did "strictly forbid, on Pain of our Displeasure, all our loving Subjects from making any Purchases or Settlements whatever, or taking Possession of any of the Lands above reserved, without our especial leave and Licence for that purpose first obtained." Implicit in this document is the concept that, while the First Nations were under the protection of the British crown, their citizens were not among the monarch's subjects.

Canadian courts have recognized that the proclamation has the force of statute and that it has never been repealed.[9] Testimony to its continuing relevance may be found in section 25 of the Canadian Charter of Rights and Freedoms: "The guarantee in this Charter of certain rights and freedoms shall not be construed so as to abrogate or derogate from any aboriginal treaty or other rights or freedoms that pertain to the aboriginal peoples of Canada including (a) any rights or freedoms that have been recognized by the Royal Proclamation of October 7, 1763."[10] Not surprising, First Nations regard the proclamation as a guarantee of non-interference with their territorial rights, including the right of self-government.

THE ASSUMPTION OF SOVEREIGNTY

As long as the First Nations maintained their military influence, British respect for their autonomy was assured. British officials were especially deferential in the decades surrounding the War of 1812. However, as colonial security became a less pressing concern, the rights and powers of the First Nations were accorded increasingly less respect. The expediency of the British approach has been described in the following manner:

As British power (and the power of Britain's successors, the United States and Canada) increased, the use of Indian procedure and conventions decreased. This paralleled a decrease in respect for the sovereignty of the Indian nations, and an increase in the use of assumed powers by the Europeans. It is safe to state that the degree of independence and sovereignty recognized by the United States, Canada and Great Britain in their Indian allies, associates and enemies, has varied in almost direct proportion to the military value or threat that these nations represented.[11]

The loss of military prominence was reflected in the administrative history of Britain's Indian Department. When it was established for America in 1755, the department was considered an operational arm of the military. In 1830, however, it ceased to be part of the military and became a branch of civil service as the Department of Indian Affairs. As such, it was concerned primarily with transactions involving the surrender and sale of Indian lands in Upper Canada. Eventually, the local legislatures (Upper Canada's in 1839) enacted protective legislation designed to supplement departmental efforts.[12] This early act did not presume to govern the internal affairs of the First Nations. Rather, it prohibited British subjects from trespassing on Indian lands, from despoiling Indian resources, and from engaging in liquor trade with the Indians.[13]

The United Province of Canada, however, adopted a far more interventionist approach. In 1857, it passed an act purporting to alter the status of First Nations. The title of the statute, An Act to Encourage the Gradual Civilization of the Indian Tribes in this Province,[14] reveals the extent to which the colonial authorities had become disrespectful toward the customs and usages of the First Nations. The preamble is even more revealing: "Whereas it is desirable to encourage the progress of Civilization among the Indian Tribes in this Province, and the gradual removal of all legal distinctions between them and Her Majesty's *other* Canadian subjects, and to facilitate the acquisition of property and of the rights accompanying it, by such Individual Members of the said Tribes as shall be found to desire such encouragement and to have deserved it" (emphasis added).

This text assumes that the Indian tribes are included among her majesty's Canadian subjects. The legal distinctions referred to, such as their exemption from taxation and their immunity from civil suits, were an acknowledgment of the special constitutional relationship between the British crown and First Nations. However, it seems that once the province became accustomed to regulating relations with the Indians, it presumed to regulate the affairs of the Indians as well. According to J.R. Miller: "The Province now found itself on the slippery slope that led from the moral heights of protection to the depths of coercion."[15]

There is still an element of respect for the autonomy of the Tribes, since the provisions applied only to those individuals "who may desire to avail themselves of this Act."[16] An examination of the provisions reveals, however, that the act was designed to undermine the authority of the tribes and to dismantle their reserves. Under section 3, any Indian man could be "enfranchised" provided that he could meet certain education and language requirements (English or French), was of "good moral character," and was free from debt. The result was that all "enactments making any distinction between the legal rights and abilities of the Indians and those of Her Majesty's other subjects, shall cease to apply to any Indian so declared to be enfranchised, who shall no longer be deemed an Indian within the meaning thereof." The act also required that the enfranchised individual "shall cease to have a voice in the proceedings" of his tribe. This is hardly a decision that the province was entitled to make. This, however, was the price to pay for the "privilege" of British colonial citizenship.

The legislation contained both property and monetary incentives for enfranchisement. Under section 7, every Indian that became enfranchised was entitled to "a sum of money equal to the principal of his share of the annuities and other yearly revenues receivable by or for the use of such Tribe ... and such sum of money shall become the absolute property of such Indian." In addition, the individual could receive "a piece of land not exceeding fifty acres out of lands reserved or set apart for the use of his Tribe."[17] This allotment was to be made not by tribal authorities but by the superintendent general of Indian affairs! It amounted to a disposition of reserve lands without the consent of the Tribe: a blatant contravention of the royal proclamation, not to mention First Nations' land-holding systems.

The enfranchised individual could receive only a life estate in the land allotted to him, but, under the terms of the act, his children (who were automatically enfranchised, along with his wife) would inherit the land in fee simple.[18] Therefore, the allotted land would be susceptible to alienation to non-Indians within the span of one generation. The potential for dismantling the reserves was heightened by the fact that allotted lands became liable to taxes and "all other obligations and duties under the Municipal and School Laws of [the] Province."[19]

This assault on the constitutional status of the First Nations and their territories did not go unnoticed. First Nations protests, and colonial reactions, have been described by J.S. Milloy:

Immediately upon publication of the act, tribal councils recognized its intent and rejected it. Surely, one tribal leader noted accurately, it was an attempt "to break them to pieces." It did not, he continued, "meet their views" since it was inconsistent with their desire to maintain tribal integrity within customary forms most recently expressed by their insistence on group rather than individual tenure of reserve land. On their part, civilizers were coldly unsympathetic to these views. The head of the Indian Department, Civil Secretary R.J. Pennefather, replied to tribal objections with the curt phrase "the Civilization Act is no grievance to you."[20]

Although the potential disintegrative effect of this legislation was enormous, it appears that the would-be civilizers had presumed too much. Individuals did not come forward in great numbers to be enfranchised. The promise of British colonial citizenship was not as alluring as the province had anticipated. The offer of fifty acres of land and a lump-sum payment could not compensate for mandatory exclusion from the tribal community. As it turned out, the enfranchisement provisions were engaged on just one occasion, with rather unhappy results: "Only one Indian was enfranchised under that Act, and when the Government had granted him his share of the principal money, and desired to allot him his portion of land they found they could not lay it off. He was in the position of being neither an Indian nor a white man. He applied as a last resort to the Department to make him an Indian again, but they found although they had the power to make an Indian a white man, they had no power to make him an Indian again.[21]

Obviously, the tribe in question had prevented the allotment of its reserve. Such resistance should have been expected. However, the province had overestimated the attractiveness of assimilation and had underestimated the intensity of allegiance within First Nations. These errors of judgment would be repeated by its political successors well into the next century.

THE FEDERAL REGIME

In 1867 the Province of Canada, Nova Scotia, and New Brunswick were federally united by imperial statute. Section 91 (24) of the British North America Act, 1867,[22] purported to assign jurisdiction over "Indians, and Lands reserved for the Indians" to the Parliament of Canada. The provinces had become so accustomed to interfering in the affairs of First Nations that the question had become one of allocation rather than legitimacy.

There is little direct evidence concerning the decision to place the Indians within the jurisdiction of the dominion government. What is painfully clear is that the First Nations, the subjects of this assignment, were in no way involved. Their representatives were not invited to any of the conventions, they did not participate in any of the debates, they were afforded no opportunity to consider, let alone consent to, the imposition of dominion jurisdiction. Surely this is the height of colonialist behaviour.

The "Fathers of Confederation" felt little compunction to justify their gross interference with the constitutional status of the First Nations. The Quebec Resolutions of 1864 placed the heading of "Indians, and Lands reserved for the Indians" within the power of the General Parliament, but no discussion of the assignment is to be found in the minutes of the conference.[23] The Confederation Debates of the Province of Canada from the summer of 1865, though exhaustive, make no reference to the fate of the First Nations.[24] In various drafts of the bill, the category was juggled from one subsection to another but always remained within the dominion's jurisdiction. As far as these colonial politicians were concerned, the First Nations, their territories and governments, could be objectified, reduced to a heading or category that could be shuffled about.

In the absence of any contemporaneous explanation for the dominion's assumption of jurisdiction, several hypotheses have been offered. Suggested motivations range from paternalistic benevo-

lence through to blatant expansionism. The argument for benev-
olence harkens back to the imperial attitude, articulated in 1837,
that "the protection of the Aborigines ... is not a trust which could
conveniently be confided to the local Legislature."[25] The suggestion
is that the drafters intended to shield the Indians from direct competition with local interests. This generous interpretation glosses
over the fact that the British government had abandoned the First
Nations to the vagaries of colonial administration anywhere from
seven to eighty-three years preceding Confederation.[26] Benevolent
is not the adjective that First Nations choose in describing this unilat-
eral and illegitimate assertion of jurisdiction by the new Canadian
state.

Another explanation for the assumption of jurisdiction relates to
the territorial ambitions of the would-be dominion government.
The Canadian desire to annex Rupert's Land and the North-
Western Territory was a primary motivation in the campaign for
Confederation. As early as 1858 the advocates of Confederation expressed the opinion that "the powers of the Federal Legislature and
Government should comprehend the ... government of unincorpo-
rated and Indian territories."[27] The goal of annexation naturally
raised the issue of relations with the western First Nations. If the national government intended to control westward expansion, then responsibility for Indian affairs would be a vital prerequisite.

There is a perspective from which this latter explanation could be
validated. If the dominion government had intended to approach
Indian affairs on a nation-to-nation basis, much like its current jurisdiction for external affairs, then First Nations autonomy would not
have been compromised by section 91 (24). Any changes to the constitutional status of the First Nations would have been a matter for
negotiation and consent. Regrettably, the dominion government did
not perceive its authority as being constrained by the inherent rights
of the First Nations. From its earliest exercise of powers assumed
under section 91 (24), it embarked on a course of alien domination.

ENFRANCHISEMENT: THE DOMINION VERSION

Following Confederation, the dominion government decided that
the Indian Department should form a branch of the Secretary of
State. To this end, An Act Providing for the Organization of the Department of the Secretary of State of Canada, and for the Management of Indian and Ordinance Lands,[28] was passed in May 1868.
Section 5 provided that "The Secretary of State shall be the Superin-

tendent General of Indian Affairs, and shall as such have the control and management of the lands and property of the Indians in Canada." Again, there is no hint of participation or consent by the First Nations to this arrangement.

The dominion government was not satisfied with becoming the controller of Indian lands. It was determined to proceed with the deculturation campaign of the would-be civilizers from the previous regime. Section 33 continued the provisions of An Act respecting the Civilization and Enfranchisement of certain Indians.[29] Ottawa soon realized, however, that this enfranchisement policy had been singularly unsuccessful. The First Nations leadership was perceived as the source of resistance. Rather than respecting the strong ties that bound individuals to their communities, the Indian Department attempted to undermine traditional First Nations government. Its rationale has been summarized as follows: "If the various systems of development [i.e. Christianity and agriculture] were ever to produce the civilized Indian amenable to enfranchisement, then native self-government had to be abolished. It had to be shouldered aside and replaced by new institutions allowing unchallengeable departmental control."[30]

The product of this rationale was introduced to the House of Commons in 1869 as a bill for the gradual enfranchisement of Indians and the better management of Indian affairs.[31] According to H. Langevin, superintendent general of Indian affairs: "experience had shown that a number of Indians, by their education, good conduct, and intelligence, could be entrusted with the same privileges as white men, but as the law stood – at least in Quebec and Ontario – for Indians to obtain the franchise was so difficult that not one of them had ever been able to obtain it. The Government had thought, therefore that they should provide for the gradual enfranchisement of the Indians by a mode that would be less difficult."[32]

The new act empowered the governor in council to grant a life estate to "any Indian who from the degree of civilization to which he has attained, and the character for integrity and sobriety which he bears, appears to be a safe and suitable person for becoming a proprietor of land."[33] As with the earlier act, the tribe was not acknowledged as having any authority over this allotment procedure.

The process was to be gradual: Indians enfranchised under the new law would remain protected from the liquor trade, and their personal property and allotted lands were to be exempt from seizure.[34] Their enfranchised children, however, would inherit estates in fee simple, and these would be subject to seizure or other forms of alienation.[35] Once again, the enfranchisement procedure was designed to facilitate the erosion of First Nations territories.

The "better management" aspect of the bill was conceived entirely from the perspective of the Indian Department. As the superintendent general explained to the House: "An attempt was also made in the direction of giving them the benefits of municipal government. It was proposed to give them certain powers to pass by-laws, subject to confirmation by the Governor in Council, as to the care of public health, observance of order and decorum in their meetings, encouragement of temperance, &c."[36] The arrogance and Euro-centrism are unbearable. This intrusion into the internal affairs of First Nations, this denial of the inherent right to self-government, is presented as "giving the benefits of municipal government." So begins the myth of delegated authority. Under the act, chiefs were to be elected by male members over the age of twenty-one[37] – so much for the voice of First Nations women. Any action taken by the chiefs was subject to disallowance by the dominion government. Perhaps the most coercive aspect of the legislation was the authority that it gave to the governor in council to remove elected chiefs from office "for dishonesty, intemperance or immorality."[38] It does not require much imagination to foresee the use of the removal power against traditional leaders resistant to dominion intrusions. With this degree of assumed control, the government anticipated widespread enfranchisement and corresponding diminution in "Indians, and Lands reserved for Indians."

Much to the government's annoyance, the rush to enfranchise never materialized. By 1876, dominion officials had decided that a modified approach was necessary. That spring, the minister of the interior, Mr. Laird, introduced a bill to amend and consolidate the laws respecting Indians.[39] He admitted that under the existing enfranchisement provisions, "the inducement has been so small that very few Indians have asked for the privilege."[40] The bill envisioned a three-stage process: the individual, now termed a "probationary Indian" would receive an allotment of reserve land under a location ticket; after three years of good behaviour, he would be granted the land in fee simple; after an additional three years, he could receive his share of the tribe's moneys. The result of this process was described by the minister: "thus after six years of good behaviour they will receive their land and their share of the moneys in the hands of the Government, and will cease in every respect to be Indians according to the acceptation of the laws of Canada relating to Indians. We will then have nothing more to do with their affairs, except as ordinary subjects of Her Majesty."[41]

In an attempt to overcome community resistance to the process, the government suggested a more "cooperative" approach. According to Laird, "it had been deemed advisable to obtain the consent of the band, and unless this was done it was considered that there would be a great deal of trouble, and discontent would result."[42] Not only did the band council have to consent to the initiation of the process, it was also charged with the allotment of lands. Some honourable members, anticipating continued resistance to the allotment of reserve lands, demanded an amendment vesting final authority in the superintendent general.[43] The minister replied that if the new procedure proved ineffective, "the law would easily be amended."[44]

Another aspect of Laird's conciliatory approach had to do with the effect of enfranchisement. Section 88 provided that, following the receipt of letters patent, "any Indian[s] ... so declared to be enfranchised ... shall no longer be deemed Indians within the meaning of the laws relating to Indians, except insofar as their right to participate in the annuities and interest moneys, and rents and councils of the band of Indians to which they belonged is concerned."[45] The government was contemplating something akin to dual citizenship. The enfranchised Indian could participate fully in the affairs of the Canadian state without having to sever ties to his own nation. Of course, the flaw with this analogy was the extent to which the Canadian state interfered with the internal affairs of the First Nations. Nonetheless, this provision did reflect an element of tolerance.

This sentiment was not universally shared. The honorable member for Brant, a riding adjacent to the Six Nations reserve, was of the opinion that "National distinctions should not be perpetuated in this country."[46] According to Mr. Paterson, "The endeavour to perpetuate the Indian in the Canadian nation was an anomaly."[47] He insisted that "it was impossible at the same time to preserve the tribal relations and facilitate the enfranchisement of the Indians."[48] On this latter point he would probably have received the concurrence of First Nations, had any been included in the debate. Their resolution of the inconsistency, however, would be to abolish enfranchisement and preclude any interference with traditional government.

The Indian Act, 1876, as it became known, was full of contradictions. The government appeared committed to overcoming the legal disabilities that previous administrations had imposed on First Nations. At the same time, incidents of exclusion continued. For instance, Indians in Manitoba and the North-West Territories were prohibited from obtaining homesteads.[49] And although the enfranchisement provisions required the consent of the individual and the community, there was one glaring exception. Section 86 (1) provided: "Any Indian who may be admitted to the degree of Doctor of Medicine, or to any other degree by any University of Learning, or who may be admitted in any Province of the Dominion to practice law ... or who may enter Holy Orders ... shall *ipso facto* become and be enfranchised under this Act." It seems that, for the legislators, a well-educated Indian was a contradiction in terms.

Another clause deserves mention. In the definition section, paragraph 12 provides: "The term "person" means an individual other than an Indian, unless the context clearly requires another construction." The drafting is devastatingly revealing. The settler governments had become so accustomed to interfering that they were no longer cognizant of the basic humanity and inherent rights of the First Nations. Having created the legal category Indian, they added the subcategories probationary Indian and enfranchised Indian, as rungs on the ladder to becoming non-Indian. How could any government, with respect for personhood, purport to transform First Nations individuals into British colonial subjects by the mere expedience of issuing letters patent and paying out a specified sum of money?

To its dismay, the dominion government saw no immediate returns on its conciliatory approach to enfranchisement. Once again, the First Nations leadership was regarded as the source of resistance. In 1884, the government introduced an amendment to the enfranchisement provisions designed to overcome this resistance. In introducing the measure, Sir John A. Macdonald explained: "One of the obstructions to enfranchisement is that the majority of the band do not like an intelligent Indian to become enfranchised. Under the present law, an Indian has to obtain the consent of his band to be enfranchised. The amendment provides that the probationary ticket may issue on the authority of the Superintendent-General [Macdonald himself], after an enquiry as to moral character and intelligence."[50] The amendment prompted little debate. It was seen as an "improvement." The propriety of displacing the community's authority over the disposition of its land was never questioned by those in the House.

Over the next several decades, the enfranchisement provisions remained unchanged. However, the attempted circumvention of First Nations authority did not produce a flood of applications for enfranchisement. In the fifty-three years between Confederation and 1920, only 102 individuals became enfranchised.[51] Successive governments were perplexed by this sustained resistance. Perhaps they did not try to understand the matter from a First Nations perspective.

What did enfranchisement entail for a First Nations individual? At the most basic level, it required self-alienation. The power of the Canadian state to determine one's identity had to be accepted. The

Creator's gift of identity as an aboriginal person had to be rejected – cast aside as inferior to that of a British colonial subject. Enfranchisement also involved denial of community autonomy and rejection of the values that community membership represented. It meant standing outside the circle that contained one's ancestors, language, traditions, and spirituality. For what? To escape the humiliating disabilities that the Canadian state had imposed in the first place. To acquire a separate allotment of land, in contravention of the tradition of communal stewardship of land. To be able to alienate one's allotment, ignoring the needs of future generations. The statistics reveal that the hardships imposed by the Indian Act proved more tolerable than the renunciation of identity that enfranchisement necessitated.

As the term suggests, enfranchisement removed the disqualifications in relation to the dominion franchise. For a time, however, this result was redundant. From 1885 until 1898, adult male Indians, living east of Manitoba and possessed of separate allotments and property worth $150, were eligible to vote in dominion elections.[52] In 1898, the disqualification of unenfranchised Indians was reinstated, and it remained intact until 1960.[53] Although this fact may come as a shock to firm believers in the Canadian democratic tradition, the issue is more complicated than it first appears.

The question of whether to seek participation in dominion elections posed a dilemma for many First Nations. Their lack of representation in the House of Commons was consistent with their own sovereignty. However, the dominion government insisted on interfering with First Nations autonomy through its Indian legislation. Perhaps the Indian agents and the superintendents could be held accountable to communities that exercised the franchise. However, even if individuals were convinced of the benefits of representation, few were willing to pay the price of enfranchisement. So few, in fact, that by 1920 the Indian Department decided that it was time for sterner measures.

THE FINAL SOLUTION: COMPULSORY ENFRANCHISEMENT

In 1920, the government introduced an amendment to the enfranchisement provisions that would give the superintendent general the power to enfranchise individuals against their will. The bill was sent to a special committee of the House of Commons, and several witnesses were called. Duncan Campbell Scott, deputy superintendent general and author of the amendment, was a key witness. When

asked why he proposed to enfranchise Indians by compulsion, he replied:

I want to get rid of the Indian problem. I do not think as a matter of fact,
that this country ought to continuously protect a class of people who are able
to stand alone. That is my whole point. I do not want to pass into the citizen's class people who are paupers. This is not the intention of the Bill. But
after one hundred years, after being in close contact with civilization it is en-
ervating to the individual or to a band to continue in a state of tutelage,
when he or they are able to take their positions as British citizens or Canadian citizens, to support themselves, and stand alone. That has been the
whole purpose of Indian education and advancement since the earliest
times. One of the very earliest enactments was to provide for the enfranchisement of the Indian. So it is written in our law that the Indian was eventually to become enfranchised.

... Our object is to continue until there is not a single Indian in Canada
that has not been absorbed into the body politic, and there is no Indian
question, and no Indian Department, that is the whole object of this Bill.[54]

The message could not have been plainer. There was simply no
room in Canada for First Nations. As soon as they were sufficiently
deculturated under the auspices of the Indian Department, they
were to be absorbed into Canadian society, by compulsion if necessary. Although the amendment was unanimously opposed by the Indian witnesses who appeared before the committee, it was carried.[55]
And so compulsory Canadian citizenship became a "privilege" reserved for Indians only.

The compulsory enfranchisement provisions were repealed in
1922,[56] only to be restored in 1933.[57] Although the mandatory procedure was finally repealed in 1951,[58] voluntary enfranchisement
remained a fixture of the Indian Act until 1985.[59] As such, it was a
constant reminder to First Nations people that continued membership in their own communities was inconsistent with participation in
Canadian society; that they could only have a place in Canada if they
renounced their heritage and denied their identity.

In 1969, this message was reiterated by Prime Minister Pierre
Trudeau. Referring to his government's now infamous "White
Paper,"[60] Trudeau suggested the following solution to the so-called
Indian problem:

We can go on treating the Indians as having special status. We can go on
adding bricks of discrimination around the ghetto in which they live and at
the same time perhaps helping them preserve certain cultural traits and cer-

tain ancestral rights. Or we can say you're at a crossroads – the time is now to decide whether the Indians will be a race apart in Canada or whether it will be Canadians of full status. And this is a difficult choice. It must be a very agonizing choice to Indian peoples themselves because, on the one hand, they realize that if they come into society as total citizens they will be equal under the law but they risk losing certain of their traditions, certain aspects of a culture and perhaps even certain of their basic rights.[61]

The message had not changed since Scott's time, indeed since the first enfranchisement legislation back in 1859. It was still an either/or proposition. Either Indians or Canadians; either outside or inside; either subject to discrimination and coercion or stripped of aboriginality and community.

CONCLUSION

If this condensed history of enfranchisement contains an alternative message, it must be that First Nations identity and autonomy will not be sacrificed for participation in Canadian citizenship.

We are indeed at a crossroads. The current constitutional debate provides a crucial opportunity to address the status of First Nations within Canadian Confederation. Before First Nations can be expected to embrace Canadian citizenship, there must be assurances of respect, acceptance, and the right to be different.

NOTES

1 This law was transmitted orally from generation to generation, remaining untranscribed into English until 1880. For a text of the Great Law see Arthur C. Parker, *The Constitution of the Five Nations*, William M. Fenton, ed. (Syracuse: Syracuse University Press, 1968).

2 As quoted in Johansen, *Forgotten Founders: Benjamin Franklin, the Iroquois and the Rationale for the American Revolution* (Cambridge, Mass.: Harvand Common Press, 1982), 14.

3 Wampum beads, fashioned from conch and clam shell, are sewn into intricate patterns on hides. Each design carries a universe of meaning. Wampum belts are integral both to spiritual ceremonies and to council meetings. Ancient laws were preserved by being "talked into" strings and belts of wampum.

4 As quoted in W.N. Fenton, *Parker on the Iroquois* (Syracuse, NY: Syracuse University Press, 1968), 45.

5 Paul Williams, "The Chain," unpublished LLM thesis, Osgoode Hall Law School, York University, 1982, 96.

365 First Nations and Canadian Citizenship

6 Canada, Parliament, House of Commons, 1 Sess., 32 Parl., 1983, *Minutes of Proceedings and Evidence of the Special Committee on Indian Self-Government*, Issue No. 31, 13.

7 For a detailed discussion of the Confederacy's claim to sovereignty, see D. Johnston, "The Quest of the Six Nations Confederacy for Self-Determination," *University of Toronto Faculty of Law Review* 44 (1986) 1.

8 Royal Proclamation of 1763, reprinted in RSC 1985, App. II, No. 1, 4–5.

9 *R. v. Lady McMaster*, [1926] Ex. C.R. 68 at 72.

10 Canadian Charter of Rights and Freedoms, Part I of the Constitution Act, 1982, being Schedule B of the Canada Act 1982 (UK), 1982, c. 11.

11 Williams, "The Chain," 3.

12 SUC 1839, c. 15; D. Smith, ed., *Canadian Indians and the Law: Selected Documents, 1663–1972* (Toronto: McClelland and Stewart, 1975). See section B: Pre-Confederation Legislation.

13 I employ the term "Indian" when referring to statutory usage. It should be regarded as a legal construct, not a self-designation.

14 20 Vic. (1857), c. 26.

15 J.R. Miller, *Skyscrapers Hide the Heavens: A History of Indian-White Relations in Canada*, rev. ed. (Toronto: University of Toronto Press, 1991), 110.

16 20 Vic. (1857), c. 26, s. 3.

17 Ibid., s. 7.

18 Ibid., s. 10.

19 Ibid., s. 14.

20 J.S. Milloy, "The Early Indian Acts: Developmental Strategy and Constitutional Change," in I.A.L. Getty and A.S. Lussier, eds., *As Long as the Sun Shines and the Water Flows: A Reader in Canadian Native Studies* (Vancouver: Nakoda Institute and University of British Columbia Press, 1983), 59 (footnotes omitted).

21 Canada, Parliament, *House of Commons Debates*, 3 Sess., 3 Parl., 1876 (Ottawa: Maclean, Roger & Co., 1876), 750: Mr. Paterson, 21 March 1876. According to Miller, *Skyscrapers*, 61, the unfortunate Indian was Elias Hill.

22 Constitution Act, 1867, (UK), 30 & 31 Vic., c. 3 (RSC 1985, App. II, No. 5).

23 G.P. Browne, ed., *Documents of the Confederation of British North America: A Compilation Based on Sir Joseph Pope's Confederation Documents, Supplemented by Other Official Material*, Carleton Library No. 40 (Toronto: McClelland and Stewart, 1969), document 34: The Quebec Resolutions, Oct. 1864, 159.

24 J.S. Patrick, ed., *Index to Parliamentary Debates on the Subject of Confed-*

eration of the British North American Provinces, as compiled by M.A.
Lapin (Ottawa: King's Printer, 1951).

25 1837, "Report of the Select Committee of the [British] House of
Commons on the Aborigines of the British Settlements," as cited in
"1845 Report of the Affairs of the Indians in Canada," section III,
App. 96, *Journals of the Legislative Assembly of Canada*, 1847, App. T.

26 Imperial control over Indian affairs in the Atlantic region lapsed
in 1784. In Upper Canada, it continued until 1860.

27 Browne, *Documents*, document 11: G.E. Cartier et al. to Sir Edmund
Bulwer Lytton, 25 Oct. 1858, 18. Although the Confederation Debates
make no direct reference to Indian affairs, there is much discussion
of the general government's plans for "opening up" the North-Western
Territory. See Patrick, *Index*.

28 SC 1868, c. 42.

29 CSC 1859, c. 9.

30 Milloy, "Early Indian Acts," 61.

31 *Debates*, 2 Sess., 1 Parl., 1869, 83–5.

32 Ibid., 83.

33 SC 1869, c. 6, s. 13.

34 Ibid., ss. 16, 20.

35 Ibid., ss. 13, 20.

36 *Debates*, 2 Sess., 1 Parl., 1869, 83–4.

37 SC 1869, c. 6, s. 10.

38 Ibid.

39 *Debates*, 3 Sess., 3 Parl., 1876, 342.

40 Ibid.

41 Ibid.

42 Ibid., 749.

43 Ibid., 1038.

44 Ibid. In fact, in 1884 the law was changed so that band consent was
no longer required, and the allotment power reverted to the
superintendent general: see SC 1884, c. 27, s. 16.

45 SC 1876, c. 18, s. 88.

46 *Debates*, 3 Sess., 3 Parl., 1876, 750.

47 Ibid.

48 Ibid., 1049.

49 SC 1876, c. 18, s. 70.

50 *Debates*, 2 Sess., 5 Parl., 1884, 1403.

51 Canada, Parliament, *Annual Report 1921*, Sessional Paper No. 27,
13.

52 Electoral Franchise Act, SC 1885, c. 40; repealed by SC 1898, c. 14.

53 For a thorough discussion of the Indian franchise, see R.H. Bartlett,
"Citizens Minus: Indians and the Right to Vote," *Saskatchewan Law
Review* 44 (1970–80) 163.

54 National Archives of Canada, RG 10, vol. 6810, file 470–2–3, vol. 7: Evidence of D.C. Scott to the Special Committee of the House of Commons examining the Indian Act amendments of 1920, 55 (L–3) and 63 (N–3).

55 *Debates*, 23 June 1920, 4040. See SC 1919–20, c. 50, s. 3.

56 *Debates*, 15 June 1922, 2991; SC 1922, c. 26, s. 1.

57 SC 1932–33, c. 42, s. 7.

58 Of course, Indian women continued until 1985 to be subject to involuntary enfranchisement on marriage to non-Indians under s. 12 (1)(b) of the Indian Act.

59 To date, I have been unable to verify the number of Indians enfranchised, either on voluntary application or under the mandatory provisions. Between 1918 and 1950, about 5,000 of a status population of 130,000 were enfranchised. Between 1959 and 1969, nearly 1,500 Indians were enfranchised on application. In 1973, the last year in which statistics were published, 13 Indians applied for enfranchisement while 538 Indian women were involuntarily enfranchised. See Bartlett, "Citizens Minus," 188. Since 1985 it has been possible for enfranchised Indians and their children to regain their Indian status, and tens of thousands have done so.

60 Canada, Department of Indian Affairs and Northern Development, *Statement of the Government of Canada on Indian Policy, 1969*. The White Paper advocated abolishing Indian status, parcelling out the reserves to individual Indians, and winding up the Indian Department, all within five years.

61 P.E. Trudeau, excerpts from a speech given 8 August 1969, in Vancouver, as reproduced in Cumming and Mickenberg, eds., *Native Rights in Canada*, 2nd ed. (Toronto: Indian-Eskimo Association of Canada, 1972), 331.

NEIL BISSOONDATH

A Question of Belonging: Multiculturalism and Citizenship

3. (1) It is hereby declared to be the policy of
the Government of Canada to (a) recognize
and promote the understanding that
multiculturalism reflects the cultural and racial diversity of Canadian society and acknowledges the freedom of all members of
Canadian society to preserve, enhance and share
their cultural heritage.

Canadian Multiculturalism Act

The early seventies, York University, Toronto.

The cafeteria in Central Square was large and brashly lit. It was institutional, utilitarian, a place for *feeding* oneself rather than enjoying a meal. The sounds of trays and cutlery roughly handled
clanged from among the busyness of students grabbing a bite between classes. Off to one side, others too harried to pause for long
fed quarters to the coffee machines.

I was new to the country, the city, and the university, still foun-
dering around in the unfamiliarity of my surroundings.

The cafeteria seemed a benign atmosphere, friendly in an imper-
sonal way. Inserting oneself here, into the midst of the controlled
chaos, would not be difficult. As the eye got used to it, though, other
aspects emerged, and it eventually became clear that the apparent
chaos was in fact subtly ordered.

A map could be drawn of the cafeteria, with sections coloured in
to denote defined areas. To mark out, for instance, the table at
which always buzzed quiet Cantonese conversation; or the tables
over in one corner from which rose the unsubtle fervour of West Indian accents; or the table more subtly framed by yarmulkes and
books decorated with the Star of David. And there were others.

To approach any of these tables was to intrude on a clannish exclusivity. It was to challenge the unofficially designated territory of tables parcelled out so that each group, whether racially or culturally or religiously defined, could enjoy its little enclave protected by unspoken prerogatives.

This idea of sticking with your own was reinforced by various student organizations, many of them financially assisted by the university. Controversy arose at one point when an application for membership in the Black Students' Federation was received from a student – in fact, a staff member of the campus newspaper – whose skin colour seemed to disqualify him. The question arose: did one have to be black to belong to the Black Students' Federation? Was not a commitment to the issues raised by the association enough to justify belonging? Just how relevant was skin colour? The final decision was to admit him – on the grounds not that race was irrelevant but that, as an organization financially assisted by the university, it had to respect York's regulations prohibiting discrimination on the grounds of race and colour.

I did not belong to the federation, but the resolution was pleasing anyway, even though there was a tincture of discomfort at the way in which it had come about: through technicality, not through the application of principle.

Another moment remains with me. One day a Jewish friend with whom I was going to have coffee insisted that I accompany him to the Jewish Students Federation lounge. As he fixed us each a coffee he said in a voice clearly intended for others in the room that I should feel free to help myself from the coffee-maker at any time. And then he added in strained tones that the lounge, provided by the university, was open to everyone: I was to ignore anyone who tried to stop me. It was in this way that he sought to make me part of unsuspected internecine tensions – while publicly declaring his own position.

The issues made me wary: I neither joined the Black Students' Federation nor revisited the Jewish Students' Federation lounge. I learned, instead, to keep my distance from the tables that would have welcomed me not as an individual but as an individual of a certain skin colour, with a certain accent, the tables that would have welcomed me not for *who* I was and for what I could do, but for *what* I was and what I represented. I had not come here, I decided, in order to join a ghetto.

Segregated tables, notions of belonging, invitations to parties that would offer ephemeral visions of "home": alone in a new land, I faced inevitable questions. Questions about my past and my present, about the land left behind and the land newly found, about the na-

ture of this society and my place in it. At eighteen, about to embark
on a new life, I felt that these were weighty issues.

For many at those tables, though, these were questions of no great
import. Their voices were almost aggressive in dismissing any discomfort that they might have experienced by flaunting the only government policy that seemed to cause no resentment: Canada as a
multicultural land. Officially. Legally. Here, they insisted, you did
not have to change. Here you could – indeed, it was your obligation
to – remain what you were. None of this American melting-pot non-
sense, none of this remaking yourself to fit your new circumstances:
you did not have to adjust to the society, the society was obliged to
accommodate itself to you.

An attractive proposal, then, a policy that excused much and required little effort. It was a picture of immigration at its most
comfortable.

And yet I found myself not easily seduced.

The problem was that I had come in search of a new life and a new
way of looking at the world. I had no desire simply to transport here
life as I had known it: this seemed to me particularly onerous baggage with which to burden one's shoulders. Beyond this, though, the
very act of emigration had already changed me. I was no longer the
person I had been when I boarded the flight in Trinidad bound for
Toronto: I had brought to the aircraft not the attitudes of the tourist
but those of someone embarking on an adventure that would
forever change his life. This alone was a kind of psychological
revolution.

Multiculturalism, as perceived by those at whom it was most explicitly aimed, left me with a certain measure of discomfort.

A year later I returned to Trinidad to visit my parents. After two
weeks, I was itching to get back to Toronto. This had nothing to do
with my parents or Trinidad or the old friends already grown distant. It had to do instead with me and Toronto: already I had made
new friends – only a few of them from among "my own kind" – and
in this way had established the beginnings of a fresh life in a city that
I found to be friendly and welcoming.

Sharing this with those who wished me to bolster their ethnic bas-
tion made me distinctly unpopular. I was seen as a kind of traitor,
unwilling to play the game by indulging in a life best described as
Caribbean North. If there was any alienation, it came not from the
society at large but from those who saw themselves as the front-line
practitioners of multiculturalism. By establishing cultural and racial
exclusivity, they were doing their bit to preserve the multicultural

character of the country, while I, seeking to go beyond the confines of my cultural inheritance, was seen as acting counter to those interests.

To put it succinctly, they coveted the segregated tables of the cafeteria while I sought a place at tables that would accommodate a greater variety.

BEGINNINGS

[Prime Minister Pierre Elliott] Trudeau's imperative, post-1972, changed from doing what was right, rationally, to doing what was advantageous politically.

So Trudeau had been criticized for ignoring the Queen; in 1973, the Queen came to Canada twice ... with Trudeau at her side every step of the royal progress. So he had been accused of sloughing off the ethnics; up sprang a trebled multiculturalism program that functioned as a slush fund to buy ethnic votes.

Richard Gwyn, *The Northern Magus*[2]

Many have long suspected that multiculturalism, proclaimed official policy in 1971, was initially boosted into the limelight not as a progressive social policy but as an opportunistic political one, not so much an answer to necessary social accommodation as a response to pressing political concerns. If the emphasis on federal bilingualism had seemed to favour francophone Quebec at the expense of the rest of the country, enhanced multiculturalism could be served up as a way of equalizing the political balance sheet. As René Lévesque once commented, "Multiculturalism, really, is folklore. It is a 'red herring.' The notion was devised to obscure 'the Quebec business,' to give an impression that we are *all* ethnics and do not have to worry about special status for Quebec."[3]

But even a program born of manipulative cynicism does not necessarily have to be bereft of a certain amount of heart and sincerity. The Act for the Preservation and Enhancement of Multiculturalism in Canada, better known by its short title, the Canadian Multiculturalism Act, offers up – as do all such documents – gentle and well-meaning generalizations.

The act recognizes "the existence of communities whose members share a common origin and their historic contribution to Canadian society" and promises to "enhance their development"; it aims to "promote the understanding and creativity that arise from the interaction between individuals and communities of different origins" and commits the federal government to the promotion of "policies and practices that enhance the understanding of and respect for the diversity of the members of Canadian society." It talks about being "sensitive and responsive to the multicultural reality of Canada."

Recognition, appreciation, understanding; sensitive, responsive, respectful; promote, foster, preserve: these words and others like them occur time and again in the Multiculturalism Act, repeated in the thicket of legalistic phrasing like a mantra of good faith.

Beyond this, the act goes from the general to the concrete by authorizing the minister responsible to "take such measures as the Minister considers appropriate to ... (a) encourage and assist individuals, organizations and institutions to project the multicultural reality of Canada in their activities in Canada and abroad; ... (c) encourage and promote exchanges and cooperation among the diverse communities of Canada; ... (e) encourage the preservation, enhancement, sharing and evolving expression of the multicultural heritage of Canada; ... (h) provide support to individuals, groups or organizations for the purpose of preserving, enhancing and promoting multiculturalism in Canada."

The Multiculturalism Act is in many ways a statement of activism. It is a vision of government, not content to let things be, determined to play a direct role in shaping not only the evolution of Canadian – mainly *English*-Canadian – society but the evolution of individuals within that society. As a political statement it is disarming, as a philosophical statement almost naive with generosity. Attractive sentiments liberally dispensed – but where in the end do they lead?

The act, activist in spirit, magnanimous in accommodation, curiously excludes any ultimate vision of the kind of society that it wishes to create. It never addresses the question of the nature of a multicultural society, what such a society is and what it means. Definitions and implications are conspicuously absent, and this may be indicative of the political sentiments that prompted adoption of the act in the first place. Even years later, the act – a cornerstone of federal social policy – shows signs of a certain haste. In its lack of long-term consideration, in its delineation of action with no discussion of consequence, one can discern the opportunism that underlay it all. One senses the political hand, eager for an instrument to attract ethnic votes, urging along the drafting – and damn the consequences.

In its rush the act appears to indulge in several unexamined assumptions: that people, coming here from elsewhere, wish to remain what they have been; that personalities and ways of doing things, ways of looking at the world, can be frozen in time; that Canadian cultural influences pale before the exoticism of the foreign. It treats newcomers as exotics and pretends that this is both proper and sufficient.

Nor does the act address the question of limits: how far do we go as a country in encouraging and promoting cultural difference? How far is far enough, how far too far? Is there a point at which diversity begins to threaten social cohesion? The document is striking in its lack of any mention of unity or oneness of vision. Its provisions seem aimed instead at encouraging division, at ensuring that the various ethnic groups have no interest in blurring the distinctions among them.

A cynic might be justified in saying that this is nothing more than a cleverly disguised blueprint for a policy of "keep divided and therefore conquered," a policy that seeks merely to keep a diverse populace amenable to political manipulation.

The Canadian Multiculturalism Act is in many senses an ill-considered document, focused so squarely on today that it forgets about tomorrow. And it is this short-sightedness that may account for the consequences that it has brought about for individuals, for communities, for the country and people's loyalty to it.

CONSEQUENCES

The Simplification of Culture

The consequences of multiculturalism policy are many and varied, but none is as ironic – or as unintended – as what I would call the simplification of culture.

The public face of Canadian multiculturalism is flashy and attractive, emerging with verve and gaiety from the bland stereotype of traditional Canada at festivals around the country. At Toronto's "Caravan," for instance, various ethnic groups rent halls in churches or community centres to create "pavilions" to which access is gained through an ersatz passport. Once admitted – passport duly stamped with a "visa" – you consume a plate of Old World food at distinctly New World prices, take a quick tour of the "craft" and "historical" displays, then find a seat for the "cultural" show, traditional songs (often about wheat) and traditional dances (often about harvesting wheat) performed by youths resplendent in their traditional costumes.

After the show, positively glowing with your exposure to yet another slice of our multicultural heritage, you make your way to the next pavilion, to the next line up for food, the next display, the next bout of cultural edification. At the end of the day, you may be forgiven if you feel you have just spent several long hours at a folksy Disneyland with multicultural versions of Mickey, Minnie, and Goofy.

This in fact is all you have really done. Your exposure has been not to culture but to theatre, not to history but to fantasy: enjoyable, no doubt, but of questionable significance. You come away knowing nothing of the language and literature of these places, little of their past and their present – and what you have seen is usually shaped with blatantly political ends in mind. You have acquired no sense of the everyday lives – the culture – of the people in these places, but there is no doubt that they are each and every one open, sincere, and fun-loving.

Such displays are uniquely suited to seeking out the lowest common denominator. Comfortable only with superficialities, they reduce cultures hundreds, sometimes thousands, of years old to easily digested stereotypes. One's sense of Ukrainian culture is restricted to perogies and Cossack dancing: Greeks, we learn, are all jolly Zorbas, and Spaniards dance flamenco between bouts of "Viva España"; Germans gulp beer, sauerkraut, and sausages while belting out Bavarian drinking songs; Italians make good ice-cream, great coffee, and all have connections to shady godfathers. And the Chinese continue to be a people who form conga lines under dragon costumes and serve good, cheap food in slightly dingy restaurants.

Our approach to multiculturalism thus encourages the devaluation of that which it claims to wish to protect and promote. Culture becomes an object for display rather than the heart and soul of the individuals formed by it. Culture, manipulated into social and political usefulness, becomes folklore – as Lévesque said – lightened and simplified, stripped of the weight of the past. None of the cultures that make up our "mosaic" seems to have produced history worthy of exploration or philosophy worthy of consideration.

I am reminded of the man who once said to me that he would never move into an apartment building that housed any East Indian families because the building was sure to be infested with roaches: East Indians, he explained, view cockroaches as creatures of good luck, and they give live ones as gifts to each other. I had known the man for some time, was certain that he was in no way racist – a perception confirmed by the fact that he was admitting this to me, someone clearly of East Indian descent. His hesitation was not racial but cultural. I was not of India: he would not hesitate in having me for a neighbour. So searching for an apartment, he perceived the neighbours not as fellow Canadians old or new but as cockroach-lovers, a "cultural truth" that he had accepted without question. But what would he have done, I wondered later with some discomfort, had he seen me emerging from a building that he was about to visit?

The vision that many of us have of each other is one of division. It is informed by misunderstanding and misconception: what we know of each other is often at best superficial, at worst malicious. And multiculturalism, with all of its festivals and its celebrations, has done nothing to foster a factual and clear-headed vision of the other. Depending on stereotype, ensuring that ethnic groups will preserve their distinctiveness in a gentle form of cultural apartheid, multiculturalism has done little but lead an already divided country down the path to further social divisiveness.

Divided Loyalties

TORONTO – John Sola, a Liberal member of the Ontario legislature who is of Croatian descent, has rejected demands that he apologize for telling a CBC television interviewer: "I don't think I'd be able to live next door to a Serb." Mr. Sola said that he made the comment to stress that he cannot accept arguments of Serbian extremists that they will not feel secure until they eliminate all Croatians. The Canadian Serbian Council is demanding his resignation.

Globe and Mail, 7 December 1991[4]

It has become a commonplace that we who share this land – we who think of Canada as home – suffer an identity crisis stemming from a fragile self-perception.

Certain segments of the population profess a dogged loyalty to the monarchy, a manifestation of mental colonialism hardly in evidence in other parts of the former British empire. Other groups, in contrast, have evolved a sense of self independent of their colonial origins, one that, coalescing around language and distinctive culture, at times hints at a kind of besieged tribalism. There are even some, emerging from both groups, who quietly yearn for a kind of wider continentalism, the self as simply North American: the anglophone who professes to see no difference between Canadians and Americans; the francophone who holds that his rights would be more respected under the American constitutional umbrella.

To such fracturing must now be added a host of new divisions actively encouraged by our multiculturalism policy and aided and abetted by politicians (a cheque here, a cheque there) of every ideological stripe.

When, a few months ago, Yugoslavia was beginning its inexorable slide into horror, a CBC news report stated that an estimated two hundred and fifty sons of Croatian immigrants, young men of able body and (presumably) sound mind, had left this country to take up arms in defence of Croatia. The report prompted a question: how did these young men define themselves? As Canadians of Croatian descent? As Croatian Canadians? Or as Croatians of Canadian birth? And I wondered which country they would choose if one day obliged to: the land of their parents, for which they had chosen to fight, or the land of their birth, from which they had chosen to depart?

It seems an unfair question. Not only does federal law accept the concept of dual citizenship – which implies dual loyalties – but Canadians have a long and honourable history of inserting themselves into foreign wars. Norman Bethune is just one among hundreds of Canadians, for instance, who enlisted in battle on the republican side of the Spanish civil war.

But Yugoslavia is not Spain: the situation is different in its essentials. While Spain saw foreign youth taking up arms in defence of an idea, in Yugoslavia foreign youth have taken up arms in defence of ethnicity. While Spain's was an ideological conflict, a clash of ideas, Yugoslavia's is tribal: the distinction is vital.

To leave one's country, to commit oneself to conflict in the land of one's forbears for ideals not intellectual but racial, is at best to reveal loyalties divided between country and ethnicity. The right to decide on the distribution of one's commitments is of course fundamental: freedom of belief, freedom of conviction, freedom of choice. It says much about the new country, however, that its command of its citizens' loyalties is frequently so tenuous.

Divided loyalties reveal a divided psyche, and a divided psyche, a divided country. For these young Canadians of Croatian descent are not alone in their adulterated loyalty to Canada. Others, too, find it impossible to make a wholehearted commitment to the new land, the new ideals, the new way of looking at life.

Imported Old World feuds – ethnic, religious, and political hatreds – frequently override loyalties to the new country. If the aiming of a gun at one's Old World enemies breaks the laws of Canada, so be it: the laws of Canada mean little against the older hatreds. And multiculturalism, in encouraging the wholesale retention of the past, has done nothing to address what is a serious – and has at times been a violent – problem. In stressing the differences between groups, in failing to emphasize that this is a country with its own ideals and attitudes that demand adherence, the policy has instead aided in a hardening of hatreds. Canada, for groups with resentments, is just another battleground. Mr. Sola, the Liberal MPP, does not see other Canadians when he assesses potential neighbours; he sees Serbs. He does not see fellow Canadian citizens; he sees, instead, ancient European enemies.

And this insistent vision, passed down to the next generation, has already led – and will continue to lead – to suspicion, estrangement, vandalism, physical attack, and death threats; it is yet another aspect of the multicultural heritage that we seek to preserve, promote, and share.

Marginalization

One never really gets used to the conversation. It will typically go something like this:

"What nationality are you?"
"Canadian."
"No, I mean what nationality are you *really*?"

To be simply Canadian untinged by the exoticism of elsewhere seems insufficient, even unacceptable, to many other Canadians. This fact clearly stems, in part, from the simple human attraction to the exotic. But it seems to me that it also has much to do with a wider issue: the uncertainty that we feel as a people.

We reveal this uncertainty by that other quintessential (and quite possibly eternal) Canadian question: who are we? The frequent answer – Well, we're not like the Americans ... – is insufficient; a self-perception cast in the negative can never satisfy. Lacking a full and vigorous response, we search for distinctiveness – exoticism – wherever we can find it. And we find it most readily in our compatriots more recently arrived.

For professional ethnics – they who enjoy the role of the exotic and who depend on their exoticism for a sense of self – this is a not unpleasant state of affairs. For those who would rather be accepted for their individuality, who resent having their differences continually pointed out, it can prove a matter of some irritation, even discomfort. The game of exoticism can cut two ways: it can prevent you from being ordinary, and it can prevent you from being accepted.

The finest example of this remains the sprinter Ben Johnson. Within a shattering twenty-four–hour period, Mr. Johnson went in media reports from being the "Canadian" who had won Olympic gold through effort to the "Jamaican immigrant" who had lost it through use of drugs. The only thing swifter than Johnson's drug-enhanced achievement was his public demotion from "one of us" to "one of them." The exotic multicultural concept of the ever-lasting immigrant has come to function as an institutional system for the marginalization of the individual: Ben Johnson was, in other words, a Canadian when convenient, an immigrant when not. Had he, success or failure, been accepted as being simply Canadian, it would have been difficult for anyone to distance him in this way. Thus the weight of the multicultural hyphen, the pressure of the link to exoticism, can become onerous – and instead of its being an anchoring definition, it can easily become a handy form of estrangement.

There is also evidence of this in the infamous Sikh turban issue that keeps bubbling up on the placid surface of our cultural mosaic. The two well-known controversies – turbans in the RCMP and turbans in Canadian Legion Halls – are in themselves indications of the failure of multiculturalism to go beyond superficiality in explaining us to each other. To view the turban as just another kind of hat, with no significance beyond sheltering the head, is to say that a cross worn on a chain is of no significance beyond a decoration for the neck: it is to reveal a deep ignorance of the ways and religious beliefs of others. To ban either is to revel in that ignorance and to alienate the other by rejecting a fundamental part of his or her self.

Of greater interest, however, is what these controversies reveal about our idea of ourselves and our traditions. We are not a country of ancient customs, and multiculturalism seems to have taught us that tradition does not admit change: that traditions, in Canada, turn precious and immutable. This helps explain why, although RCMP headgear has changed throughout the years, there are those passionate in their opposition when faced with the possibility of seeing a turban among the stetsons. It also explains, in part, why a Legion Hall's desire to honour Canadian military men by banning headgear cannot make room for turbans. (In Britain, which is often seen as a tradition-bound society, turbans have long been accepted as part of the military and London police uniforms.)

But if, in our cultural insecurity, we have decided that tradition is immutable, what happens when two contradictory traditions come together? Only conflict can result, the natural outcome of our inflexible view of tradition and multicultural heritage: so that protests with distinctly racist overtones are raised against turbans in the RCMP; so that a Sikh wishing to enter an Alberta Legion Hall is told to use the back door.

A final consequence of the marginalization to which we can so easily subject one another comes frequently in times of economic hardship. The stresses of unemployment – the difficulty of the present and the invisibility of a future – create a need for scapegoats: we need something or someone to blame. We can rail against politicians, taxes, corporations – but these are all distant, untouchable in

their isolation. But no one is more easily blamed for the lack of opportunity than the obvious "foreigner" who is cleaning tables in the
local doughnut shop. Maybe he has brown skin, maybe he speaks
with an accent: clearly he is out of place here, filling a paid position
that should by rights have gone to a "real" Canadian. All differences,
always so close to the surface, are seized upon; are turned into objects of ridicule and resentment, the psychology of exoticism once
more cutting both ways.

Encouraging people to view each other as simply Canadian would
not solve this problem – humans, in times of pain and anger, have a
unique ability for seeking out bull's-eyes in each other – but it may
help redirect the resentment, so that in expressing the hurt we do
not also alienate our fellow citizens. Differences between people are
already obvious enough without their being emphasized through
multiculturalism policy.

THE LIMITS OF
MULTICULTURALISM

In the West Indies long and boisterous parties, on the whole, incon-
venience no one. They are held at houses, both inside and outside.
Neighbours tend to be invited, children sleep where they fall. Food
and drink are in plentiful supply, music is loud and lively, meant not
as backround filler but as foreground incentive to dance. There is
nothing sedate about the archetypal West Indian party. So central is
"a good time" to the West Indian sense of self that someone – not a
West Indian – once wryly commented that she had the impression
that parties, and not calypso or reggae, were the great West Indian
contribution to world culture. Booming music, the yelp and rumble
of excited voices, the tramp of dancing feet are accepted as an integral part of the region's cultural life.

Transfer this to, say, Toronto – not to a house surrounded by an
extensive yard but to an apartment hemmed in by other apartments.
Transfer the music, the dancing, the shouting – everything but the
fact that the neighbours, here unknown and uncommunicative, are
not likely to be invited. It takes little imagination to appreciate the
tensions that may, and do, arise.

A simple lack of consideration for the rights of others? Yes – but
it may be, as some claim, that everything is political. The view has
been expressed to me more than once that, in view of the importance of parties in West Indian culture, and considering the official
policy of multicultural preservation in Canada, complaints about
noise or demands that stereo volumes be lowered can be viewed as

a form of cultural aggression. Changing the tone of the party, the argument goes, results in a lessening of its Caribbean character – and is therefore a sign of cultural intolerance. Implicit in this view is the idea that everything deemed cultural is sacred – as well as the idea that the surrounding society must fully accommodate itself to displays, no matter how disruptive, of cultural life. In this atmosphere, a party is no longer just a party; it becomes a form of cultural expression and therefore a subject of political and legal protection.

This is an admittedly aggressive interpretation of the workings of multicultural policy, but it is neither farfetched nor fully indefensible. Open-ended political policy is, almost without exception, subject to an endless stretching of the envelope: there will always be someone – or some group – attempting to go farther than anyone else has gone before.

The Multiculturalism Act suggests no limits to the accommodation offered to different ethnic practices, so that a Muslim group in Toronto recently demanded, in the name of respect for its culture, the right to opt out of the Canadian judicial system in favour of Islamic law, a body of thought fundamental to the life and cultural outlook of its practising members. In the opinion of its spokesmen, this right should be a given in a truly multicultural society.

More recently, the Ontario College of Physicians and Surgeons expressed concern over a rise, unexplained and unexpected, in the number of requests for female circumcision. According to a report in the *Toronto Star* on 6 January 1992, the procedure, long viewed in Western culture as a kind of mutilation, involves "cutting off a young girl's external genital parts, including the clitoris. In some countries, it includes stitching closed the vulva until marriage, leaving a small opening for urination and menstrual flow ... Various health risks have been linked to it, including immediate serious bleeding, recurring infections, pain during intercourse, hemorrhaging during childbirth and infertility ... Charles Kayzze, head of Ottawa's African Resource Centre, believes it is being performed here by members of the community. In some cases, he says, families are sending their children to Africa to have it done."[5] The result is the reduction of the woman to the status of machine, capable of production but mechanically, with no pleasure in the process.

It is curious that such ideas can be brought to this land, survive, and then present a problem to doctors for whom policy guidelines, never before necessary, are now being established. ("The policy," the report states, "is likely to say Ontario doctors should not perform the operation.") Yet one awaits with bated breath calls for public performance of the ancient Hindu rite of suttee in which widows are cremated alive on their husband's funeral pyres.

There is a certain logic to all of this, but a logic that indicates a certain disdain for the legal and ethical values that shape, and are shaped by, Canadian society – and therefore for Canadian society itself.

And why not, given that the picture that the country transmits of itself is one that appears to diminish a unified whole in favour of an ever-fraying mosaic? If Canada, as a historical, social, legal, and cultural concept, does not demand respect, why should respect be expected?

ON BECOMING A CITIZEN

I swear (or affirm) that I will be faithful and bear true allegiance to Her Majesty Queen Elizabeth the Second, Queen of Canada, Her Heirs and Successors, and that I will faithfully observe the laws of Canada and fulfil my duties as a Canadian citizen.

Citizenship Act[6]

A friend had set me at ease about the first part of the citizenship process. It was easy, he said. Answer a few simple questions about the country, display a knowledge of the language, chat a bit with the kindly examiner, and watch as he or she signs your papers with a flourish worthy of royalty. And, hell, even those rules were not hard and fast: his own aged mother had spent over twenty years in Canada, had managed to acquire none of the language, but had nevertheless been given citizenship by a kindly examiner who sympathized with her wish to die as a citizen of the country that had been good to her family.

It was indeed as he had said: the simple questions, the friendly banter, the regal flourish.

The second step, three months later, was slightly more difficult, but only because it veered so close to farce. We were a large group, strangers united in the solemnity of a courtroom by our impending citizenship. After an uneasy wait, we were treated to a lengthy speech by a black-gowned citizenship judge, a man of dignity and a certain friendly charm, the only problem being that his words were so concealed by a heavy Italian accent that one could hardly begin to guess at the pearls of wisdom that he was trying to transmit to us. Then came the oath of citizenship itself, followed by a rendition of "O Canada," everyone standing with gaze directed at a colour photograph on the wall, the dress-uniformed mountie ramrod-stiff as he

directed a salute toward the same photo, of Elizabeth II, queen of
Canada. It seemed, as we worked our way through the words familiar from hockey games, a kind of idolatry.

There was no cheering at the end, no sense of occasion as we, at
the urging of the judge, shyly shook each other's hands in congrat-
ulations. And then we were free of the courtroom, back out in the
street among the traffic, changed by the papers that attested to our
new status but hurrying back to jobs and obligations with a curious
sense of anti-climax.

The reasons for taking that final step toward full citizenship are
many and varied. They emerge from the realization that all of one's
intellectual and emotional loyalties have come, through the years, to
commit themselves to Canada. One makes a life, puts down roots.
And from this feeling of belonging comes the wish to be as fully part
of the country as possible.

However, the diminishing value of Canadian citizenship – the creation of the hyphenated Canadian with divided loyalties, the perception that immigration policy now allows the rich to buy their way into
the country, the idea that citizenship is a natural right and not an
earned privilege – means that the exact opposite has also come to be
true. The acquisition of Canadian citizenship is frequently seen not
as a means of committing oneself to the country but as a way of leaving it with an assurance of safety.

Few passports are safer than a Canadian one, and for many people citizenship implies merely access to a passport that allows return
to the comforts of the former homeland with the assurance of safe
haven should plans go awry, or should political instability necessitate
flight. There is no way to prevent this, and those who wish to acquire
only a passport of convenience enjoy the right. But the implications
for the country cannot be ignored. I would suggest that any country
that does not claim the full loyalty of its citizens old or new, any
country that counts citizens old or new who treat it as they would a
public washroom – that is, as merely a place to run to in an emergency – accepts for itself a severe internal weakening. It is perhaps
inevitable that for many newcomers Canada is merely a job. It is desperately sad, though, when, after many years, they see Canada as
only that. Multiculturalism, with its emphasis on the importance of
holding on to the former homeland, with its insistence that *There* is
more important than *Here*, serves to encourage this attitude.

In a democracy, any legislation to address such a problem must be
viewed as anathema, for it cannot help but be a gesture of tyranny.
So although there is no role here for the legislator, there is a vital

role for the policy-maker. Multiculturalism, if it is in fact aimed at shaping Canadian society in a cohesive way, should seek out policies that would encourage engagement with the society rather than exploitation of it. From this point of view, multiculturalism has served us badly.

A VISION OF THE OTHER

In a radio interview not long ago, the novelist Robertson Davies talked of the difference between two words that are often – and erroneously – used interchangeably: acceptance and tolerance. Acceptance, he pointed out, requires true understanding, recognition over time that the obvious difference – the accent, the skin colour, the crossed eyes, the large nose – are mere decoration on the person beneath; it is a meeting of peoples that delves under the surface to a knowledge of the full humanity of the other. Tolerance, in contrast, is far more fragile, for it requires not knowledge but wilful ignorance, a purposeful turning away from the accent, the skin colour, the crossed eyes, the large nose; it is a shrug of indifference that entails more than a hint of condescension.

The pose of tolerance is seductive, for it requires no effort; it is benign in that it allows others to get on with their lives free of interference – and also free of a helping hand. The problem of course is that tolerance – based as it is on ignorance – can, with changing circumstances, give way to a perception of threat. And such a perception is all that is required to cause a defensive reaction to kick in – or lash out. Already in this country we are seeing the emergence of reaction from those who feel themselves and their past, their beliefs and their contribution to the country, to be under assault. People "put up with" in the good times assume aspects of usurpers in the bad. Notions of purity – cultural or racial – come to the forefront as the sense of self diminishes under the assault of unemployment, homelessless, a growing sense of helplessness.

This tolerance can very quickly metamorphose into virulent defensiveness, rejecting the different, alienating the new. Understanding, in contrast, requires effort, a far more difficult proposition, but may lead to acceptance and, for the new, a sense of belonging. Multiculturalism, with its emphasis on the superficial, fosters the former while ignoring the latter.

Canada has long prided itself on being a tolerant society, but tolerance is clearly insufficient in the building of a cohesive society. A far greater goal to strive for would be an *accepting* society. Multiculturalism seems to offer at best provisional acceptance, and it is with some difficulty that one insists on being a full – and not just an associate – member. Just as the newcomer must decide how best to accommodate himself or herself to the society, so the society must in turn decide how it will accommodate itself to the newcomer. Multiculturalism has served neither interest; it has highlighted our differences rather than diminished them, has heightened division rather than encouraged union. More than anything else, the policy has led to the institutionalization and enhancement of a ghetto mentality. And it is here that lies the multicultural problem as we experience it in Canada: a divisiveness so entrenched that we face a future of multiple solitudes with no central notion to bind us.

ENDINGS

In an article in the *Globe and Mail* on 18 July 1991, Dr. Suwanda Sugunasiri, a former member of the Ontario Advisory Council on Multiculturalism and Citizenship, called for the abolition of the federal Secretary of State's multiculturalism directorate and proposed that its functions be incorporated into the Ministry of Culture and Communications, with an emphasis on countering racism. He called for the disbanding of multicultural advisory councils, an end to heritage-language programs, and the abolition of the monarchy (which he deems a racist institution). Pointing to an Angus Reid poll which suggested that only one in ten Canadians supports multiculturalism, he suggested that the policy, which he characterized as having entered its adolescence, had, in its present form, outlived its usefulness. As he pointed out, the policy "was useful in giving multicultural communities a presence, but we know they're there now."[7]

Certainly, at this point in our development (or lack of it), ethnic communities have little to gain from multiculturalism, a policy that now serves to make them, more than anything else, simply privy to political manipulation from both inside and outside their communities.

At a more visceral level, we run the risk of falsifying ourselves. It would be untrue, it seems to me, to pretend to continue being what one has been in the past, or what one's parents have been – just as it would be false, under the assimilative US model, to pretend that one is no longer what one has been, that one has completely remade oneself. The human personality is not static; it is altered fundamentally, but not wholly, by circumstance and experience. And while the US approach is untrue to the individual, the Canadian approach is untrue to both the individual and the state. For if many who emigrate to the United States eventually come to think of themselves as simply "American," strengthening the social fabric, too few who come to Canada end up accepting themselves – and one another – as simply "Canadian," thereby weakening the social fabric.

Furthermore, indulging in the game of heightened ethnicity entails the risk of excessive fantasy. It is human to edit the past, to gloss even a harsh reality into a coveted memory: "We were starving, but we were happy." But such memory of a retreating past ever more golden frequently leads to acute personal dissatisfaction. It is easy, in the comforting grip of edited memory, to forget that everything has changed; easy, too, to embrace the miscalculation that arises from an acute yearning for the perfection which, in memory, used to be. Multiculturalism, with its stress on theatrical display, helps concretize such fantasy, and, once more, both the individual and the state lose – the one by clinging to and at times acting on a fantasy, the other by paling before golden fantasy taken for reality.

In his article, Dr. Sugunasiri suggests also several ways in which minority communities can help in "building a just society": he warns them against "crying racism at every turn" and urges that they "look inward at the racism and discrimination within [their] own ranks." He encourages them to seek greater co-operation with legal authorities and calls for an effort to "get rid of the dehumanizing aspects" of their culture. He also insists that historical injustices be left in the past, that they not be allowed to poison the present and, thus, the future – an elegant way of pleading with people to get rid of the chips on their shoulders. Finally, Dr. Sugunasiri offers what seems a radical policy: "Intermarriage must be promoted; it's perhaps our best hope for security and stability. More than 32 per cent of Canadians are the products of mixed marriages; the Japanese-Canadian figure is 50 per cent. Rejuvenate the gene pool."

While I endorse many of Dr. Sugunasiri's suggestions, I would not go quite as far as he does in his final recommendation. So long as it does not adversely affect others, what people do in their private lives is their own business, whether it be what they choose to eat, which foreign languages and heritage dances they choose to teach to their children, whom they choose to marry. State intervention in private affairs (as opposed to, say, intervention in private companies engaged in profit-making through public enterprise) is rarely benign.

Failing the abolition of the multiculturalism directorate as recommended by Dr. Sugunasiri – a task that, despite the unpopularity of the policy and because of the influence of interest groups, might prove politically risky – the entire sphere of multiculturalism should be removed from the political arena. It should either be incorporated into the Ministry of Culture and Communications, as suggested, or established as an arm's-length agency of the federal government in the manner of the Canada Council, funded by the government but not controlled by it.

The substantial funds involved could be put to far better use than the building of community halls and social facilities for specific, ethnically defined groups. (Should such facilities be needed, let them be aimed at the community as a whole, with no possibility for exclusion.)

More funds must also be dedicated to battling racism. Too often, highlighting the exoticism of ethnicity obscures the larger, Canadian background in the flash of colour. Aiming to establish understanding and inclusion, seeking to diminish racism by exposing Canadians to other Canadians, the government should concentrate on funding school or community programs that sensitize children to each other, stressing not the differences that divide them but the similarities that unite them. Despite the varying pasts that have formed us, we are all in the final analysis Canadians, with a common country and common interests that can lead to a common future. Children of Serbian and children of Croatian descent, for instance, may come to realize that here, in this country, they have more to gain by leaving aside Old World feuds than by joining in them; they may come to realize that Canada really does provide a second chance – but that it is up to them to take advantage of it. As Peter Gzowski, the avuncular host of CBC radio's "Morningside," has written in his thoughtful and heart-felt introductory essay to *The Fourth Morningside Papers*: "It probably *is* time, at least in government policy, to back off from the emphasis on differences that subsidized multiculturalism implies and begin to work a lot harder at seeking the similarities – Mike Pearson's common ground. But backing off from the aggravations doesn't have to mean denying the values that have led to them."[8]

Heritage belongs to the individual. It seems to me possible to instruct an individual child in his or her heritage without erecting ghetto walls by enlisting in communal endeavour. Emphasizing the "I" and de-emphasizing the "we" may be the only way to avoid the development of cultural chauvinism – the idea that "we" are superior to "them" and the chasms that result. It is possible to form a child whose outlook is informed by the knowledge of a certain cultural, familial past, by pride in a Canadian present, and by hope in a Canadian future. There is no need to abandon that which has been, to devalue that which is, or to fear that which can be – no need for divided loyalties.

Let me cite the words of the accomplished journalist and feminist Laura Sabia from an address to the Empire Club of Canada in October 1978: "I was born and bred in this amazing land. I've always considered myself a Canadian, nothing more, nothing less, even though my parents were immigrants from Italy. How come ... we have all acquired a hyphen? We have allowed ourselves to become divided along the lines of ethnic origins, under the pretext of the 'Great Mosaic.' A dastardly deed has been perpetrated upon Canadians by politicians whose motto is 'divide and rule.' I, for one, refuse to be hyphenated. I am a Canadian, first and foremost. Don't hyphenate me."[9]

With this as a guiding vision, whatever may come after multiculturalism will aim not at preserving differences but at melding them into a new vision of Canadianness, pursuing a Canada where inherent differences and inherent similarities blend easily and where no one is alienated with hyphenation. A nation of cultural hybrids – where every individual is unique, every individual distinct. And every individual is Canadian, undiluted and undivided.

NOTES

1 Canadian Multiculturalism Act, RS 1985, c. 24 (4th Supp.).
2 Richard Gwyn, *The Northern Magus* (Toronto: McClelland and Stewart, 1989).
3 René Lévesque, quoted in John Robert Colombo, ed., *The Dictionary of Canadian Quotations* (Toronto: Stoddart, 1991).
4 "MPP Won't Apologize," *Globe and Mail*, 7 Dec. 1991.
5 Sherri Davis Barron, "Doctors Draw up Policy on Female Circumcision," *Toronto Star*, 6 Jan. 1992.
6 Oath of Affirmation, Citizenship Act, 1974–75–76, c. 108, s. 1.
7 Dr. Suwanda Sugunasiri, "Keep the Great Experiment Going," commentary in the *Globe and Mail*, 18 July 1991.
8 Peter Gzowski, "Whistling down the Northern Lights," in *The Fourth Morningside Papers* (Toronto: McClelland and Stewart, 1991).
9 Laura Sabia, quoted in Colombo, ed., *Dictionary*.